the
CIVIL WAR
C·H·R·O·N·I·C·L·E

the CIVIL WAR

C·H·R·O·N·I·C·L·E

The Only Day-by-Day Portrait of America's Tragic Conflict
As Told by Soldiers, Journalists, Politicians, Farmers,
Nurses, Slaves, and Other Eyewitnesses

GENERAL EDITOR

J. Matthew Gallman

INTRODUCTION BY

Eric Foner

EDITED BY

David Rubel and Russell Shorto

GRAMERCY BOOKS
New York

This 2003 edition published by Gramercy Books, an imprint of Random House Value Publishing, a division of Random House, Inc., New York by arrangements with Crown Publishers, New York.

Gramercy is a registered trademark and the colophon is a trademark of Random House, Inc.

Crown is a registered trademark and the colophon is a trademark of Random House, Inc.

Printed in the United States of America

Random House
New York • Toronto • London • Sydney • Auckland
www.randomhouse.com

Library of Congress Cataloging-in-Publication Data

The Civil War chronicle : the only day-by-day portrait of America's tragic conflict as told
   by soldiers, journalists, politicians, farmers, nurses, slaves, and other eyewitnesses /
   general editor, J. Matthew Gallman ; introduction by Eric Foner ; edited by David Rubel
   and Russell Shorto.
      p. cm.
   Includes index.
   Originally published: New York : Crown Publishers, 2000.
   ISBN 0-517-22181-0
      1. United States—History—Civil War, 1861-1865—Personal narratives. 2. United
   States—History—Civil War, 1861-1865—Sources. 3. United States—History—Civil War,
   1861-1865—Social aspects. I. Gallman, J. Matthew (James Matthew) II. Rubel, David.
   III. Shorto, Russell.

E655.C49 2003
973.7'8—dc21

2002192891

9 8 7 6 5 4 3 2 1

Contents

Preface

J. MATTHEW GALLMAN

THE CIVIL WAR CHRONICLE provides an unusual window not only into life during the Civil War but also into the world of the Civil War historian. On the most obvious level, the documents and annotation assembled here tell one of this nation's most powerful stories. Even those readers familiar with the broad outline of the war will find in these pages a stimulating and diverse array of voices revealing unknown facts and presenting unconsidered perspectives. On another level, however, taken together, these primary sources demonstrate that the Civil War was more than simply a military conflict—that many different sorts of experiences contributed to the substance of the Civil War years. You will find here the stories of soldiers, of course, but also those of noncombatants at all levels of Union and Confederate life—including widows, slaves, farmers, businessmen, artists, and foreign observers. Covering every theater of the war as well as all the political and home fronts, *The Civil War Chronicle* manages the significant feat of producing a fresh and unique perspective on the much-examined Civil War period.

I take a special personal pleasure in working with these documents because they remind me why—and how—I came to study this period in American history. I actually began my professional career as a historian of colonial America. Early on, however, I discovered that the historical record prior to 1776 was scant: Most of this country's anonymous early settlers entered the historical record only when they were born, married, and died, or perhaps when they appeared in court. Thus, my desire to illuminate the lives of everyday people led me into demographic analysis, interesting and valuable in its own right but lacking narrative depth. In the meantime, I developed a profound admiration for those of my colleagues who were able to bring the colonial world to life through close examination of the tiniest evidentiary details—and before long, I must confess, I found myself drawn instead into the more abundant world of nineteenth-century research, with its diaries, letters, newspapers, pamphlets, song sheets, and all other manner of manuscript documents and printed materials.

Those sources relating to the Civil War I found to be particularly rich. The war's leading participants, aware of the historical importance of their actions, left behind plentiful reports, correspondence, and personal memoirs. Meanwhile, men and women of the rank and file—both at home and on the battlefields—also recognized the great significance of those terrible years and felt compelled to record their thoughts. Young men who might otherwise have remained close to home suddenly found themselves forced to produce letters in order to communicate with friends and family, and other observations were recorded in private journals and diaries. The impulse to remember was felt strongly at the time and hardly dissipated as descendants and archivists carefully preserved these myriad documents. In general, the nation's enduring fascination with all things related to the Civil War has ensured that even apparently insignificant scraps of paper are likely to have survived for inspection by historians. For a social historian such as myself, the Civil War years are thus a marvelous source for many obscure aspects of nineteenth-century life.

For my first extended work on the Civil War period, I chose wartime Philadelphia as its focus and proceeded to read four years' worth of the *Philadelphia Public Ledger* (as well as large chunks of the years immediately before and after the war). I still recall reading an extended description of Philadelphia's 1861 Washington's Birthday celebrations and then spending half an hour looking for similar references to celebrations honoring Lincoln's Birthday— only to realize, finally, that the president-elect's birthday had not yet become a national holiday! From this inauspicious beginning, I proceeded to cast my net wider, visiting archives throughout the Philadelphia area in search of diaries, letters, annual reports, government documents, and anything else that might illuminate daily life in wartime Philadelphia. The search yielded many exciting discoveries, including a tiny diary with no attribution and no clear origin that I found at the Historical Society of Pennsylvania. I noticed, however, that the young author described joining a voluntary society whose records had survived, thus allowing me to identify her. On another occasion, during a visit to Columbia

University, I stumbled across the revealing journal of a Philadelphia woman whose papers had been deposited with the
university because she had married a New Yorker. And at
Harvard's Baker Library, I spent many hours reading the ledger
books of R. G. Dun and Company, searching for references to
Philadelphia businesses. Every historian has dozens of such stories in which chance discoveries have caused troublesome
narrative pieces to fall unexpectedly into place. This book is, in
many ways, the fruit of similar labor.

★

BY COLLECTING FOR YOUR EXAMINATION these unexpected and
unusual pieces of evidence, *The Civil War Chronicle* offers a perspective on the period (and history in general) usually reserved
for professional historians. As I read through these documents
myself, I am perhaps most struck by the disparity of the voices
that emerges. Side-by-side accounts of the same event, for example, illuminate dramatically the biases inherent in human
observation; in other cases, accounts contained in official reports
written soon after the fact contrast tellingly with those produced
for postwar memoirs, which are more reflective but also often
thick with self-interested special pleading. Meanwhile, private
writings present the depth of felt emotion and suggest the
cadence of nineteenth-century speech (as well as the widely vary-
ing levels of formal education). Newspaper columns, which
typically catered to competing political factions, recall not only
the scathing partisanship of the time but also the biting humor of
the mid-nineteenth century press.

Similarly, by virtue of its arrangement, this collection also dra-
matizes the serendipity of chronology—reminding us that events
separated by hundreds of miles, such as the battle of Gettysburg
and the fall of Vicksburg, happened just twenty-four hours apart.
Of course, it can sometimes be difficult to read history this way,
which is why the scholars involved in this project have provided
helpful contextualizing notes to aid the reader—but not to the
extent of camouflaging the essential truth that history is messy.
Although one of the historian's chief tasks is teasing larger themes
from the jumble of events, immediacy matters as well. That is why
I often suggest to my students that they look to period newspapers
for the immediate response to a particular event. One goal of such
an assignment is to encourage students to think about the ways

in which notions of what is important have changed over time, but another is to remind them that many different things are always taking place at the same time and competing for public attention. Reading this book re-creates that experience and provides some insight into how people managed to live through such disturbing and consequential times.

★ ★ ★ ★

Introduction

ERIC FONER

ALL HISTORIANS STAND ON THE SHOULDERS of their predecessors. They build, that is, on the insights of previous scholars, even while developing interpretations of their own. Yet no matter how indebted we are to other historians, it is usually engagement with primary sources that enables us to think in new ways about the past. Records produced by contemporaries as they experienced historical events offer a drama and immediacy that no work of scholarship can duplicate. "Go to the sources" is a maxim that has been passed down from generation to generation of historians. Indeed, some of the most influential works of recent scholarship—for example, the multivolume *Freedmen and Southern Society* series, which makes available long-forgotten documents relating to the black experience during the Civil War era—are collections of primary sources that have forced historians to rethink this critical period in our past.

My own experience has demonstrated to me over and over again the indispensability of primary sources. A quarter of a century ago, I was asked by Richard Morris to write the volume on Reconstruction (the era that followed the Civil War) for the *New American Nation* series. At first, I assumed that like other volumes in this series, mine would synthesize existing scholarship. But in 1978, while teaching for a semester at the University of South Carolina in Columbia, I encountered in the state archives 121 thickly packed boxes of correspondence received by the state's Reconstruction governors. These letters contained an incredibly rich record, almost entirely untapped by scholars, of local social and political life. Before my eyes unfolded tales of utopian hopes and shattered dreams, of struggles for human dignity and ignoble violence by the Ku Klux Klan, of racism and black-white cooperation, of everyday life that had become politicized in ways barely hinted at in the existing literature. I realized that in order to tell the story of Reconstruction I would have to look beyond the available scholarship, impressive as much of it was, and instead recover this lost texture of life.

My research introduced me to an amazing range of historical personages—former slaves seeking to breathe substantive meaning into the freedom they had acquired, upcountry farmers struggling to throw off the heritage of racism, planters attempting to retain control of their now-emancipated labor force, and Klansmen seeking to subvert the far-reaching changes of the era. It was my encounters with the documents left behind by these people, and not any preconceived interpretation, that convinced me that the central actors in the drama of Reconstruction had been the freed people, whose demand for individual and community autonomy helped set the agenda for Reconstruction-era politics and whose struggle for freedom (as they understood it) was the most potent force for change during that turbulent period.

★

AN EVEN MORE TURBULENT PERIOD than Reconstruction, the Civil War remains, a century and a half later, the most decisive turning point in American history. The war's continued relevance lies not only in its great accomplishments—the preservation of the Union and the destruction of slavery—but also in the fact that it raised so many questions central to our understanding of ourselves as a nation: What should be the balance of power between local authority and the national government? Who is entitled to citizenship? What are the concrete meanings of freedom and equality in the United States? These questions, at the core of the Civil War's meaning, remain subjects of controversy today. In that sense, the Civil War is not yet over.

In the physical destruction and social and economic changes it wrought, the war transformed the lives and consciousness of several generations of Americans. It also changed the nature of warfare, gave rise to the modern American nation-state, and ended the greatest slave society the modern world has known. It was one of the first wars to bring the contrivances of the Industrial Revolution—including railroads, ironclad ships, and rifled muskets—to bear on the battlefield, resulting in appalling casualties.

At Gettysburg, for example, nearly fifty thousand soldiers were listed as killed, wounded, or missing, a figure dwarfed during World War I but enormous for the nineteenth century. Total casualties for the entire war numbered well over one million people from an American population of just thirty-two million.

Beginning as a conventional contest of army versus army, the war, by its end, became one of society against society—with slavery, the foundation of the Southern social order, a principal Union target. In such a contest, civilian morale was as crucial to sustaining and winning the war as events on the battlefield; therefore, crushing the other side's will to fight became as much of a military objective as subjugating its armies in the field. Meanwhile, the Civil War substantially consolidated the American Union. It is easy to forget how decentralized the United States was in 1861, and how limited were the powers of its federal government. There was no national banking system, no standard railroad gauge, no reliable statistics of manufacturing— and not even accurate maps of the areas where the war's most important battles would be fought. How different was the prospect in 1865. "It is war," declared nineteenth-century German historian Heinrich von Treitschke, "which turns a people into a nation." Begun to preserve the old Union, the Civil War brought into being, as Treitschke suggested, a new nation-state. To mobilize the North's economic resources, the Lincoln administration instituted the first national currency, the first federal income tax, the first highly protective tariffs, and it laid the foundation for the first transcontinental railroad. (These economic policies and others would later form the basis of the long-lasting alliance between the Republican party and the emerging class of industrial capitalists.)

Yet as historian Hans Kohn has written, a nation is "first and foremost a state of mind, an act of consciousness." Above all, the Civil War forged a new American self-consciousness. Before the war, Northerners and Southerners spoke with little irony of their slaveholding republic as an empire of liberty. But as Frederick Douglass recognized as early as 1862, the Civil War merged "the cause of the slaves and the cause of the country." The scale of the Union's triumph and the sheer drama of emancipation fused nationalism and morality into an entirely new combination that provided to many Americans what seemed like incontrovertible proof of the progressive nature and global significance of their country's historical development.

The United States that emerged from the Civil War had been transformed, not only in the power of its national state but also in the newly expanded boundaries of its "imagined community." Before the Civil War, the members of that imagined community, those entitled to enjoy the "blessings of liberty" protected by the Constitution, had been defined by race. Out of the Civil War, however, there emerged the understanding that all Americans, by virtue of their birthright and regardless of race, belonged to a national citizenship and were entitled to equal protection under the law. Resulting not simply from the logic of liberty but also from the enlistment of some two hundred thousand African Americans in the armed forces of the Union, these principles of birthright citizenship and equal protection are today central elements of the American understanding of freedom.

★

MORE WORKS HAVE BEEN WRITTEN about the American Civil War than about any other event in history. Yet *The Civil War Chronicle* is unique in tracing the war's progress, day by day, through primary sources produced during the period itself. All the issues mentioned above, and many more, are presented here in the words of those who personally experienced the momentous events of 1860–65. These documents cover the entire range of the war experience: Battles and political debates are, of course, well represented, but so are the Northern and Southern home fronts, and the cast of characters is indeed expansive—from Lincoln and Davis, Grant and Lee, to less well known soldiers, women, slaves, and laborers. Taken as a whole, the book offers a remarkable kaleidoscope of thoughts about and reaction to the greatest crisis in American history.

Like all great historical events, the Civil War settled some fundamental questions—notably the fates of the Union and slavery—while leaving to future generations the implementation of many of the basic principles for which the war was fought. *The Civil War Chronicle* enables us to understand these principles as they were experienced by the people who lived through the war—and how, in the process, they helped create a new America.

★ ★ ★ ★

THE CHRONICLE
1860–1865

NOVEMBER
1860

TUE 6 NOV. LINCOLN ELECTED PRESIDENT

The election of 1860, probably the most momentous in the nation's history, laid bare the bitter division between North and South that had been festering for more than a decade. In a four-way contest, Abraham Lincoln, the Republican candidate, who opposed the expansion of slavery into new territories, won less than a majority of the popular vote but 59 percent of the electoral college, thus becoming the nation's sixteenth president. The North-South split was so decisive that Lincoln did not receive a single electoral vote from the South, which lined up solidly behind proslavery candidate John C. Breckinridge of Kentucky, James Buchanan's vice president and a leader of the Southern wing of the Democratic party. (Illinois senator Stephen A. Douglas ran as the candidate of the Northern Democrats, following a sectional split at the party's national convention.) Lincoln's election pleased most Northerners, but not radical abolitionists, who criticized him for being a fence-sitter on the issue of slavery, and not Democrats, who thought him too radical. Meanwhile, in the South, whites vilified Lincoln and saw his election as nothing less than the Republic's death knell. These accounts—from abolitionst Wendell Phillips; from Horace Greeley, the Republican editor of the New York Tribune; *and from the* Atlanta Confederacy—*give an indication of the enormous breadth of opinion.*

This muslin banner was printed by Philadelphia lithographer H. C. Howard.

IF THE TELEGRAPH SPEAKS TRUTH, for the first time in our history the *slave* has chosen a president of the United States....Not an abolitionist, hardly an antislavery man, Mr. Lincoln consents to represent an antislavery idea. A pawn on the political chessboard, his value is his position; with fair effort, we may soon charge him for knight, bishop, or queen.

ABRAHAM LINCOLN ILLUSTRATES [the Republican party's] position and enforces our argument. His career proves our doctrine sound. He is Republicanism embodied and exemplified. Born in the very humblest Whig stratum of society, reared in poverty, earning his own livelihood from a tender age by the rudest and least recompensed labor...picking up his education as he might by the evening firelight of rude log cabins...and so gradually working his way upward to knowledge, capacity, esteem, influence, competence...his life is an invincible attestation of the superiority of Free Society, as his election will be its crowning triumph.

LET THE CONSEQUENCES BE what they may—whether the Potomac is crimsoned in human gore, and Pennsylvania Avenue is paved ten fathoms deep with mangled bodies, or whether the last vestige of liberty is swept from the face of the American continent, the South will never submit to such humiliation and degradation as the inauguration of Abraham Lincoln.

In this speech to the Georgia legislature delivered immediately after Lincoln's

election, Robert Toombs, a future Confederate cabinet member and general at Antietam, encapsulated the South's perception of Lincoln and the Republican party.

THE INSTANT THE GOVERNMENT was organized, at the very first Congress, the Northern States evinced a general desire and purpose to use it for their own benefit, and to pervert its powers for sectional advantage, and they have steadily pursued that policy to this day....

Our property has been stolen, our people murdered; felons and assassins have found sanctuary in the arms of the party which elected Mr. Lincoln. The Executive power, the last bulwark of the Constitution to defend us against these enemies of the Constitution, has been swept away, and we now stand without a shield, with bare bosoms presented to our enemies, and we demand at your hands the sword for our defence, and if you will not give it to us, we will take it—take it by the divine right of self-defence, which governments neither give nor can take away. Therefore, redress for past and present wrongs demands resistance to the rule of Lincoln and his Abolition horde over us; he comes at their head to shield and protect them in the perpetration of these outrages upon us, and, what is more, he comes at their head to aid them in consummating their avowed purposes by the power of the Federal Government. Their main purpose, as indicated by all their acts of hostility to slavery, is its final and total abolition. His party declare it; their acts prove it.

★ ★ ★ ★

DECEMBER
1860

**MON
17
DEC.**

"LET THEM GO!"

*On the day that South Carolina began
formal consideration of its secession
from the Union, Horace Greeley, editor
of the* New York Tribune *and a powerful
Republican opinion shaper, published
this editorial, which echoed the feelings
of many Northerners. Although Greeley
had supported Lincoln during the election, he argued now that if the Northern
states did not allow the South to secede,
they would be violating the Jeffersonian
principle that governments derive their
just powers from the consent of the governed. Greeley would later change his
mind on this issue, but his editorial,
published as the situation approached
its most critical stage, demonstrates the
wide range of views in the North as to
what should be done.*

Horace Greeley

IF SEVEN OR EIGHT CONTIGUOUS States shall present themselves authentically at Washington, saying, "We hate the Federal Union; we have withdrawn from it; we give you the choice between acquiescing in our secession and arranging amicably all incidental questions on the one hand, and attempting to subdue us on the other,"—we could not stand up for coercion, for subjugation, for we do not think it would be just. We hold the right of Self-Government sacred, even when invoked in behalf of those who deny it to others. So much for the question of Principle.

Now as to the matter of Policy:

South Carolina will certainly secede. Several other cotton States will probably follow her example. The Border States are evidently reluctant to do likewise. South Carolina has grossly insulted them by her dictatorial, reckless course. What she expects and desires is a clash of arms with the Federal government, which will at once commend her to the sympathy and cooperation of every Slave State, and to the sympathy (at least) of the Pro-Slavery minority in the Free States. It is not difficult to see that this would speedily work a political revolution, which would restore to slavery all, and more than all, it has lost by the canvass of 1860. We want to obviate this. We would expose the seceders to odium as disunionists, not commend them to pity as the gallant though mistaken upholders of the rights of their section in an unequal military conflict.

We fully realize that the dilemma of the incoming administration will be a critical one. It must endeavor to uphold and enforce the laws, as well against rebellious slaveholders as fugitive slaves. The new President must fulfill the obligations assumed in his inauguration oath, no matter how shamefully his predecessor may have defied them. We fear the Southern madness may precipitate a bloody collision that all must deplore. But if ever "seven or eight States" send agents to Washington to say, "We want to get out of the Union," we shall feel constrained by our devotion to Human Liberty to say, "Let them go!" And we do not see how we could take the other side without coming in direct conflict with those Rights of Man which we hold paramount to all political arrangements, however convenient and advantageous.

THE CRITTENDEN COMPROMISE

TUE 18 DEC.

In one of the last legislative attempts to avert war, Kentucky senator John Crittenden introduced a compromise measure that would draw a line between North and South; slavery would be outlawed to the north of this line and permitted to the south. In addition, under Crittenden's proposed constitutional amendment, excerpted below, newly admitted states would be free to decide the contentious slavery question for themselves.

A JOINT RESOLUTION PROPOSING CERTAIN AMENDMENTS TO THE CONSTITUTION OF THE UNITED STATES.

Whereas serious and alarming dissensions have arisen between the northern and southern states, concerning the rights and security of the rights of the slaveholding

John Crittenden

ARTICLE 1: In all the territory of the United States now held, or hereafter acquired, situate north of 36 degrees 30 minutes, slavery or involuntary servitude, except as a punishment for crime, is prohibited while such territory shall remain under territorial government. In all the territory south of said line of latitude, slavery of the African race is hereby recognized as existing, and shall not be interfered with by Congress, but shall be protected as property by all the departments of the territorial government during its continuance. And when any territory, north or south of said line, within such boundaries as Congress may prescribe, shall contain the population requisite for a member of Congress according to the then Federal ratio of representation of the people of the United States, it shall, if its form of government be republican, be admitted into the Union, on an equal footing with the original States, with or

States, and especially their rights in the common territory of the United States; and whereas it is eminently desirable and proper that these dissensions, which now threaten the very existence of this Union, should be permanently quieted and settled by constitutional provisions, which shall do equal justice to all sections, and thereby restore to all the people that peace and goodwill which ought to prevail between all the citizens of the United States: Therefore, Resolved by the Senate and House of Representatives of the United States of America in Congress assembled (two-thirds of both Houses concurring), That the following articles be, and are hereby, proposed and submitted as amendments to the Constitution of the United States, which shall be valid to all intents and purposes, as part of said Constitution, when ratified by conventions of three-fourths of the several States:

Senator Andrew Johnson of Tennessee was a cosponsor of the Crittenden Resolutions.

without slavery, as the constitution of such new State may provide.

ARTICLE 2: Congress shall have no power to abolish slavery in places under its exclusive jurisdiction, and situate within the limits of States that permit the holding of slaves.

ARTICLE 3: Congress shall have no power to abolish slavery within the District of Columbia, so long as it exists in the adjoining States of Virginia and Maryland, or either, nor without the consent of the inhabitants, nor without just compensation first made to such owners of slaves as do not consent to such abolishment. Nor shall Congress at any time prohibit officers of the Federal Government, or members of Congress, whose duties require them to be in said District, from bringing with them their slaves, and holding them as such during the time their duties may require them to remain there, and afterwards taking them from the District.

ARTICLE 4: Congress shall have no power to prohibit or hinder the transportation of slaves from one State to another, or to a Territory, in which slaves are by law permitted to be held, whether that transportation be by land, navigable river, or by the sea.

ARTICLE 5: That in addition to the provisions of the third paragraph of the second section of the fourth article of the Constitution of the United States, Congress shall have power to provide by law, and it shall be its duty so to provide, that the United States shall pay to the owner who shall apply for it, the full value of his fugi-

tive slave in all cases where the marshall or other officer whose duty it was to arrest said fugitive was prevented from so doing by violence or intimidation, or when, after arrest, said fugitive was rescued by force, and the owner thereby prevented and obstructed in the pursuit of his remedy for the recovery of his fugitive slave under the said clause of the Constitution and the laws made in pursuance thereof. And in all such cases, when the United States shall pay for such fugitive, they shall have the right, in their own name, to sue the county in which said violence, intimidation, or rescue was committed, and to recover from it, with interest and damages, the amount paid by them for said fugitive slave. And the said county, after it has paid said amount to the United States, may, for its indemnity, sue and recover from the wrong-doers or rescuers by whom the owner was prevented from the recovery of his fugitive slave, in like manner as the owner himself might have sued and recovered.

ARTICLE 6: No future amendment of the Constitution shall affect the five preceding articles; nor the third paragraph of the second section of the first article of the Constitution; nor the third paragraph of the second section of the fourth article of said Constitution; and no amendment will be made to the Constitution which shall authorize or give to Congress any power to abolish or interfere with slavery in any of the States by whose laws it is, or may be, allowed or permitted.

Before the Crittenden Compromise was defeated in Congress (on January 16), the state of Tennessee passed a resolution supporting the effort. This editorial in the Nashville Republican Banner *argued that while the sympathies of Tennessee were "emphatically Southern," the state's overall goal should be to perpetuate the Union if at all possible.*

THIS SETTLEMENT CAN BE agreed upon by the people of both sections without the sacrifice of a principle or of any material interest. It would be acceptable, we believe, to a majority of the people in the seceding States, and the State of Tennessee could take no course better calculated to befriend and conserve the interests of those States than by maintaining such a position as will enable her, in conjunction with other Southern States, to negotiate the adoption of this compromise with the North. That the sympathies of Tennessee are emphatically Southern, no one will deny. She will take no course, in any event, calculated to militate against the interests of her Southern sisters. But the question for her to decide—and it is a question upon which hangs her own and the destiny of the South and the Union—is what course is most judicious, most patriotic, and best calculated to conserve the interests of her Southern sisters, and if possible preserve the Union? Upon this question there is a difference of opinion....We should rejoice to see this difference of opinion reconciled or compromised, so that we might all move in solid phalanx, and as a unit. It would add immensely to our influence in the crisis, and might, indeed, be the means of securing what, under existing circumstances, may not be attained—a perpetuation of the Government.

WED 19 DEC. *During the confusing winter of 1860, opinions varied as to the outcome of the national crisis. Some prominent thinkers still believed that war was avoidable. Others took a dimmer view. In this excerpt, written as Christmas 1860 approached, a Methodist newspaper in Ohio predicted that civil war loomed as a near certainty.*

THE DISSOLUTION OF THIS Union can not be a peaceable affair. Civil war is as certain to follow secession as darkness to follow the going down of the sun. There are a thousand things to precipitate it....We regret to say that, in our humble opinion, the dangers which threaten the Union of these states are greater now than at any former period in our history.

THU 20 DEC. SOUTH CAROLINA SECEDES

Always a hotbed of secessionist sentiment, South Carolina was the first of the Southern states to respond to Lincoln's election by formally withdrawing from the Union. After three days of discussion, the members of its secession convention found that they had little to debate. The vote on the following ordinance was 169–0. "The revolution of 1860 has been initiated," rejoiced the Charleston Mercury.

AN ORDINANCE
To dissolve the union between the state of South Carolina and other states

CHARLESTON MERCURY

EXTRA:

Passed unanimously at 1.15 o'clock, P. M., December 20th, 1860.

AN ORDINANCE

To dissolve the Union between the State of South Carolina and other States united with her under the compact entitled "The Constitution of the United States of America."

We, the People of the State of South Carolina, in Convention assembled, do declare and ordain, and it is hereby declared and ordained,

That the Ordinance adopted by us in Convention, on the twenty-third day of May, in the year of our Lord one thousand seven hundred and eighty-eight, whereby the Constitution of the United States of America was ratified, and also, all Acts and parts of Acts of the General Assembly of this State, ratifying amendments of the said Constitution, are hereby repealed; and that the union now subsisting between South Carolina and other States, under the name of "The United States of America," is hereby dissolved.

THE

UNION IS DISSOLVED!

of this State, ratifying amendments of the said Constitution, are hereby repealed; and that the union now subsisting between South Carolina and other States, under the name of "The United Sates of America," is hereby dissolved.

THU 27 DEC. *In the North, in addition to the "let them go" faction, there was another group that wanted to negotiate with those Southern states moving closer to secession. Its argument in favor of conciliation, as reflected in this Philadelphia Press editorial, was based on economics: Because of the heavy trade between Northern and Southern states, the reasoning went, both sides had a strong economic incentive to maintain the Union. Therefore, the North should press for a diplomatic solution.*

BUT THE NORTH HAS A VITAL interest in the preservation of the Union on its own account. The well-being of our millions of men and women is not to be endangered or thrown away upon a sentiment of doubtful philanthropy, to result in a state of things which can do no good in any way to the objects for which the sacrifice is made. Our trade with the slaveholding states is much greater than is commonly thought. Every man in business, and every laborer depending upon full employment for his daily bread, now feels the mischief which a temporary suspension of trade and credit between the sections has the power to inflict upon him....In 1859 we exported to foreign countries thirty-four millions worth of manufactured commodities, which would

united with her under the compact entitled "The Constitution of the United States of America."

We, the People of the State of South Carolina, in Convention assembled, do declare and ordain, and it is hereby declared and ordained,

That the Ordinance adopted by us in Convention, on the twenty-third day of May, in the year of our Lord one thousand seven hundred and eighty-eight, whereby the Constitution of the United States of America was ratified, and also, all Acts and parts of Acts of the General Assembly leave nineteen hundred and sixty-six millions worth that must find a home market and home consumption. If the South supplies herself with only one-tenth this amount, and consumes only one-fourth of them, she gives the Northern States a market for two hundred and ninety-six millions of her manufactures. We do not stop to inquire now how the balance of agricultural exchanges stands between the sections. The Northern farmer has his share of this trade in manufactures of which we are now speaking, and participates largely in its profits, and as largely in its losses and suspensions. It is enough that, without pretending to statistical accuracy, we show a market for our surplus manufactures in the South nine times larger than all the world besides affords us. The foreign exports of all the free States of every kind do not average more than one hundred and twenty millions a year; their sales to the Southern States are more than twice that amount. The slave States trade is of as great value annually to the free States as that of the Union is to all Europe, Asia, and South America.

Is it any wonder that our prosperity and our labor decline twenty-five per cent, in present value, when so large a commerce as this is interrupted, and the commercial confidence of the parties is shaken?

Cotton bales awaiting shipment in Charleston, South Carolina.

JANUARY
1861

SUN
6
JAN.

New York City, with its polyglot immigrant population, tended to go its own way both before and during the war. In an address to the city council, excerpted here, Mayor Fernando Wood proposed that the city should maintain economic ties with South Carolina and any other states that followed South Carolina out of the Union. Not only did Wood support the right of Southern states to secede, but he also predicted that other parts of the country—such as California and even his own city—would set themselves up as independent republics.

WITH OUR AGGRIEVED BRETHREN of the slave States, we have friendly relations and a common sympathy. We have not participated in the

New York City mayor Fernando Wood in a portrait taken by Mathew Brady.

warfare upon their constitutional rights or their domestic institutions. While other portions of our State have unfortunately been imbued with the fanatical spirit which actuates a portion of the people of New England, the City of New York has unfalteringly preserved the integrity of its principles in adherence to the compromises of the Constitution and the equal rights of the people of all the States. We have respected the local interests of every section, at no time oppressing, but all the while aiding in the development of the resources of the whole country. Our ships have penetrated to every clime, and so have New York capital, energy and enterprise found their way to every State and, indeed, to almost every county and town of the American Union. If we have derived sustenance from the Union, so have we in return disseminated blessings for the common benefit of all. Therefore, New York has a right to expect, and should endeavor to preserve, a continuance of uninterrupted intercourse with every section....

Much, no doubt, can be said in favor of the justice and policy of a separation. It may be said that secession or revolution in any of the United States would be a subversion of all Federal authority and, so far as the Central Government is concerned, the resolving of the community into its original elements—that, if part of the States form new combinations and Governments, other States may do the same. California and her sisters of the Pacific will no doubt set up an independent republic and husband their own rich mineral resources. The Western States, equally rich in cereals and other agricultural products, will probably do the same.

Then it may be said, why should not New York City, instead of supporting by her contributions in revenue two-thirds of the expenses of the United States, become also equally independent? As a free city, with but nominal duty on imports, her local government could be supported without taxation upon her people. Thus we could live free from taxes and have cheap goods nearly duty free. In this she would have the whole and united support of the Southern States, as well as of all other States, to whose interests and rights under the Constitution she has always been true.

The streets of New York City as they appeared shortly before the Civil War.

STAR OF THE WEST FIRED UPON

WED 9 JAN.

In one of the first acts of hostility between North and South, cadets of the Citadel, stationed on Morris Island outside Charleston Harbor, opened fire on the civilian ship Star of the West, *which was bringing supplies to Federal troops at Fort Sumter. Only one shot hit the ship; it caused no damage but considerable outrage among the officers at Fort Sumter, as the following letter from the fort's commander to South Carolina governor F. W. Pickens makes clear.*

SIR: TWO OF YOUR BATTERIES fired this morning upon an unarmed vessel bearing the flag of my Government. As I have not been notified that war has been declared by South Carolina against the Government of the United States, I can not but think that this hostile act was committed without your sanction or authority. Under that hope, and that alone, did I refrain from opening fire on your batteries.

I have the honor, therefore, respectfully to ask whether the above-mentioned act—one that I believe without a parallel in the history of our country, or of any other civilized Government—was committed in obedience to your instructions, and to notify you, if it be not disclaimed, that I must regard it as an act of war, and that I shall not, after a reasonable time for the return of my messenger, permit any vessels to pass within range of my fort.

In order to save as far as is in my power the shedding of blood, I beg that you will have due notification of this my decision given to all concerned.

Hoping, however, that your answer may be such as will justify a further continuance of forbearance on my part, I have the honor to be,

Very respectfully, your obedient servant,

Robert Anderson,
Major, First Artillery, U.S.A.,
commanding Fort Sumter,
South Carolina

Maj. Robert Anderson

In his reply, Governor Pickens reveals the great distance that many Southerners had already placed between

themselves and the United States government.

SIR: YOUR LETTER HAS BEEN received. In it you make certain statements which very plainly show that you have not been fully informed by your Government of the precise relations which now exist between it and the State of South Carolina. Official information has been communicated to the Government of the United States that the political connection heretofore existing between the State of South Carolina and the States which were known as the United States had ceased, and that the State of South Carolina had resumed all the power it had delegated to the United States under the compact known as the Constitution of the United States. The right which the State of South Carolina possessed to change the political relations which it held with other States, under the Constitution of the United States, has been solemnly asserted by the people of this State in convention, and now does not admit of discussion....

...The attempt to re-enforce the troops now at Fort Sumter, or to retake and resume possession of the forts within the waters of this State which you abandoned after spiking the guns placed there and doing otherwise much damage, cannot be regarded by the authorities of this State as indicative of any other purpose than the coercion of the State by the armed force of the Government. To repel such an attempt is too plainly its duty to allow it to be discussed. But, while defending its waters, the authorities of the State have been careful so to conduct the affairs of the State that no act, how-ever necessary for its defense, should lead to a useless waste of life....

Under these circumstances, the *Star of the West,* it is understood, this morning attempted to enter the harbor, with troops on board; and having been notified that she could not enter, was fired into. The act is perfectly justified by me. In regard

A view of the Citadel.

to your threat in regard to the vessels in the harbor, it is only necessary to say that you must judge of your own responsibilities. Your position in this harbor has been tolerated by the authorities of the State, and while the act of which you complain is in perfect consistency with the rights and duties of the State, it is not perceived how far the conduct which you propose to adopt can find a parallel in the history of any country, or be reconciled with any other purpose of your Government than that of imposing upon this State the condition of a conquered province.

F. W. Pickens, Governor

FRI 18 JAN. DEATH THREATS AGAINST LINCOLN

Assassination threats dogged Abraham Lincoln from the moment he was elected president on November 6 until his inauguration on March 4. Emotions ran higher with every passing day; by the date this Lincoln supporter sent a letter of warning to the president-elect, four Southern states had already voted to secede, with Georgia to follow on the next day.

DEAR SIR: I HAVE HEARD several persons in this place say that if you ever did take the President Chair that they would go to washington City expressly to kill you. for your wife and Children sake dont take the Chair if you do you will be murdered by some cowardly scoundrel have you had any application for this post if not I wish you would let me have it—if you take the Chair as the president of the United States but dont you take it. resign. if you dont you will be murdered I write you this as a friend I am a friend of yours please answer this letter so I can know whether I must go to washington City and raise a body of men to guard you.

Yours truly &c

R. A. Hunt

Allan Pinkerton headed Lincoln's security.

SUN 20 JAN.

Jefferson Davis, once Franklin Pierce's secretary of war and lately a U.S. senator from Mississippi, was in many ways a moderate, counseling caution in the face of what he and most white Southerners considered unwarranted Yankee interference in their "domestic institution" of slavery. When the break finally came, however, Davis resigned his Senate seat and stood firmly with the secessionists. Here, he writes to Pierce of his regret (and of Caleb Cushing, a friend from their shared days in Pierce's cabinet).

DEAR FRIEND: I HAVE OFTEN and sadly turned my thoughts to you during the troublous times through which we have been passing and now I come to the hard task of announcing to you that the hour is at hand which closes my connection with the United States, for the independence and Union for which my Father bled and in the service of which I have sought to emulate the example he set for my guidance. Mississippi, not as a matter of choice but of necessity, has resolved to enter on the trial of secession. Those who have driven her to this alternative threaten to deprive her of the right to require that her government shall rest on the consent of the governed, to

This cartoon ridiculed the precautions (specifically a secret night train) taken to protect the president-elect.

substitute foreign force for domestic support, to reduce a state to the condition from which the colony rose.

When Lincoln comes in he will have but to continue in the path of his predecessor to inaugurate a civil war, and leave a *soi-disant* democratic administration responsible for the rest.

Genl. Cushing was here last week and when we parted it seemed like taking leave of a Brother.

I leave immediately for Missi. and know not what may devolve upon me after my return. Civil war has only horror for me, but whatever circumstances demand shall be met as a duty and I trust be so discharged that you will not be ashamed of our former connection or cease to be my friend.

Do me the favor to write to me often, address Hurricane P.O. Warren County, Missi.

May God bless you is ever the prayer of your friend
Jefferson Davis

THU 31 JAN. *Some of the most forceful arguments for conciliation came from west of the Appalachian Mountains. Many Northern cities in this region, such as Cincinnati, shared extensive commercial and kinship ties with the South and would be particularly affected by armed hostilities. The following editorial—published in the Columbus, Ohio, journal* The Crisis— *outlined Cincinnati's historical dependence on Southern trade and predicted a sad fate for the city should the present difficulties lead to war.*

No GREAT CITY IN THE WEST, and certainly no commercial point in Ohio, is so deeply and so fearfully affected by our sectional difficulties as Cincinnati. She has been termed the "Queen City," but if her river and Southern trade is cut off, she can be the "Queen City" no longer. Her every interest is identified with the Southern trade, and such has been the fact since the first house was built within her corporate limits.

When we first saw the city, it contained a population of about 25,000, all told. She now numbers near 200,000, with 500,000 more outside her city government, identified with her trade and dependent upon her thrift and commercial prosperity. The disturbing elements now afflicting the country come home to her in a fearful volume. If these troubles are prosecuted to a bloody issue, Cincinnati will be converted into a camp of soldiers instead of a busy mart of peace and prosperous commerce. With the Ohio River only dividing her from a hostile foe, she will be exposed to the shell and the ball from the overlooking hills beyond. Fear and absolute safety would compel thousands to remove to a more distant point, and give the city up to camp life and all the ills that follow. And for what are we to be driven to this desolate condition? Can any one answer?

As long as peace is preserved we have everything to hope; when that is discarded, all hope of restoration of order and a return to duty as good citizens is lost, in all reasonable calculation, for ever.

★ ★ ★ ★

FEBRUARY
1861

MON 11 FEB. LINCOLN'S SPRINGFIELD FAREWELL

Nearly one thousand people gathered at the Springfield, Illinois, railroad depot on this rainy morning to say good-bye to their neighbor, whose election to the presidency seemed certain to bring the national crisis to a head. As Lincoln boarded the train that would carry him to Washington, he offered these remarks.

MY FRIENDS, NO ONE, NOT IN my situation, can appreciate my feeling of sadness at this parting. To this place, and the kindness of these people, I owe everything. Here I have lived a quarter of a century, and have passed from a young to an old man. Here my children have been born, and one is buried. I now leave, not knowing when, or whether ever, I may return, with a task before me greater than that which rested upon Washington. Without the assistance of the Divine Being who ever attended him, I cannot succeed. With that assistance I cannot fail. Trusting in Him who can go with me, and remain with you, and be everywhere for good, let us confidently hope that all will yet be well. To His care commending you, as I hope in your prayers you will commend me, I bid you an affectionate farewell.

MON 18 FEB. JEFFERSON DAVIS INAUGURATED

On a mild, sunny afternoon, Jefferson Davis acknowledged the smiles and cheers of hundreds of well-wishers as he stood in front of the state capitol in Montgomery, Alabama. Fireworks exploded in the blue sky, the band played "Dixie," and Davis, who had been elected provisional president by the delegates to the provisional Confederate Congress, gave an address, excerpted here, in which he stated the South's grievances.

GENTLEMEN OF THE CONGRESS of the Confederate States of America, Friends and Fellow-Citizens: Called to the difficult and responsible station of Chief Executive of the Provisional Government which you have instituted, I approach the discharge of the duties assigned to me with an humble distrust of my abilities, but with a sus-

taining confidence in the wisdom of those who are to guide and to aid me in the administration of public affairs, and an abiding faith in the virtue and patriotism of the people.

Looking forward to the speedy establishment of a permanent government to take the place of this, and which by its greater moral and physical power will be better able to combat with the many difficulties which arise from the conflicting interests of separate nations, I enter upon the duties of the office to which I have been chosen with the hope that the beginning of our career as a Confederacy may not be obstructed by hostile opposition to our enjoyment of the separate existence and independence which we have asserted, and, with the blessing of Providence, intend to maintain. Our pres-

Theodore Davis created this view of Montgomery to honor the February 1861 inauguration of Jefferson Davis.

ent condition, achieved in a manner unprecedented in the history of nations, illustrates the American idea that governments rest upon the consent of the governed, and that it is the right of the people to alter or abolish governments whenever they become destructive of the ends for which they were established.

The declared purpose of the compact of Union from which we have withdrawn was "to establish justice, insure domestic tranquillity, provide for the common defense, promote the general welfare, and secure the blessing of liberty to ourselves and our posterity;" and when, in the judgment of the sovereign States now composing this Confederacy, it had been perverted from the purposes for which it was ordained, and had ceased to answer the ends for which it was established, a peaceful appeal to the ballot-box declared that so far as they were concerned, the government created by that compact should cease to exist. In this they merely asserted a right which the Declaration of Independence of 1776 had defined to be inalienable....The right solemnly proclaimed at the birth of the States, and which has been affirmed and reaffirmed in the bills of rights of States subsequently admitted into the Union of 1789, undeniably recognizes in the people the power to resume the authority delegated for the purposes of government. Thus the sovereign States here represented proceeded to form this Confederacy, and it is by abuse of language that their act has been denominated a revolution....

An agricultural people, whose chief interest is the export of a commodity required in every manufacturing country, our true policy is peace, and the freest trade which our necessities will permit. It is alike our interest, and that of all those to whom we would sell and from whom we would buy, that there should be the fewest practicable restrictions upon the interchange of commodities. There can be but little rivalry between ours and any manufacturing or navigating community, such as the Northeastern States of the American Union. It must follow, therefore, that a mutual interest would invite good will and kind offices. If, however, passion or the lust of dominion should cloud the judgment or inflame the ambition of those States, we must prepare to meet the emergency and to maintain, by the final arbitrament of the sword, the position which we have assumed among the nations of the earth.

FRI 22 FEB. LINCOLN SPEAKS AT INDEPENDENCE HALL

Lincoln's rail journey from Springfield, Illinois, to Washington, D.C., was a mixture of euphoria—with exuberant crowds gathering at many stops to cheer the president-elect—and foreboding, brought on by rumors of planned assassination attempts. Several of Lincoln's advisers urged him to cancel his scheduled public appearances, including a Washington's Birthday ceremony at Independence Hall, but Lincoln went ahead with the ceremony and delivered a powerful impromptu speech expressing his hope for peace but also invoking the Declaration of Independence as the basis for actions he might soon be forced to take.

Abraham Lincoln in a photograph taken in Springfield on June 3, 1860.

I AM FILLED WITH DEEP EMOTION at finding myself standing here, in this place, where were collected together the wisdom, the patriotism, the devotion to principle, from which sprang the institutions under which we live. You have kindly suggested to me that in my hands is the task of restoring peace to the present distracted condition of the country. I can say in return, Sir, that all the political sentiments I entertain have been drawn, so far as I have been able to draw them, from the sentiments which originated and were given to the world from this hall. I have never had a feeling politically that did not spring from the sentiments embodied in the Declaration of Independence. I have often pondered over the dangers which were incurred by the men who assembled here, and framed and adopted that Declaration of Independence. I have pondered over the toils that were endured by the officers and soldiers of the army who achieved that Independence. I have often inquired of myself what great principle of idea it was that kept this Confederacy so long together. It was not the mere matter of the separation of the Colonies from the motherland; but that sentiment in the Declaration of Independence which gave liberty, not alone to the people of this country, but, I hope, to the world, for all future time. It was that which gave promise that in due time the weight would be lifted from the shoulders of all men. This is a sentiment embodied in the Declaration of Independence. Now, my friends, can this country be saved upon that basis? If it can, I will consider myself one of the happiest men in the world, if I can help to save it. If it cannot be saved upon that principle, it will be truly awful. But if this country cannot be saved without giving up that principle, I was about to say I would rather be assassinated on this spot than surrender it. Now, in my view of the present aspect of affairs, there need be no bloodshed or war. There is no necessity for it. I am not in favor of such a course, and I may say, in advance, that there will be no bloodshed unless it be forced upon the Government, and then it will be compelled to act in self-defence.

★ ★ ★ ★

MARCH 1861

MON 4 MAR. LINCOLN'S FIRST INAUGURATION

Sharpshooters peered down on the crowd that flowed from the steps of the U.S. Capitol as Abraham Lincoln delivered his first inaugural address. Cannon were deployed at key points to deter pro-Southern violence. In this atmosphere of overwhelming tension, Lincoln attempted to strike a note of compromise. While he wanted Southerners to understand that he intended to stand by the Republican party's commitment to contain slavery's growth, he also wanted to make clear his position that slavery could not be abolished in the states where it already existed. Reaction to his address was predictably mixed: Some observers thought it too conciliatory, others too warlike.

APPREHENSION SEEMS TO EXIST among the people of the Southern States that by the accession of a Republican Administration their property and their peace and personal security are to be endangered. There has never been any reasonable cause for such apprehension. Indeed, the most ample evidence to the contrary has all the while existed and been open to their inspection. It is found in nearly all the published speeches of him who now addresses you. I do but quote from one of those speeches when I declare that—"I have no purpose, directly or indirectly, to interfere with the institution of slavery in the States where it exists. I believe I have no lawful right to do so, and I have no inclination to do so."

Those who nominated and elected me did so with full knowledge that I had made this and many similar declarations and had never recanted them....

I now reiterate these sentiments, and in doing so I only press upon the public attention the most conclusive evidence of which the case is susceptible: that the property, peace, and security of no section are to be in any wise endangered by the now incoming Administration....

It is seventy-two years since the first inauguration of a President under our National Constitution. During that period fifteen different and greatly distinguished citizens have in succession administered the executive branch of the Government. They have conducted it through many per-

ils, and generally with great success. Yet, with all this scope of precedent, I now enter upon the same task for the brief constitutional term of four years under great and peculiar difficulty. A disruption of the Federal Union, heretofore only menaced, is now formidably attempted.

I hold that in contemplation of universal law and of the Constitution the Union of these States is perpetual. Perpetuity is implied, if not expressed, in the fundamental law of all national governments. It is safe to assert that no government proper ever had a provision in its organic law for its own termination. Continue to execute all the express provisions of our National Constitution, and the Union will endure forever, it being

The scene of Lincoln's first inauguration on the steps of the U.S. Capitol.

impossible to destroy it except by some action not provided for in the instrument itself.

Again: If the United States be not a government proper, but an association of States in the nature of contract merely, can it, as a contract, be peaceably unmade by less than all the parties who made it? One party to a contract may violate it— break it, so to speak—but does it not require all to lawfully rescind it?...

It follows from these views that no State upon its own mere motion can lawfully get out of the Union; that resolves and ordinances to that effect are legally void, and that acts of violence within any State or States against the authority of the United States are insurrectionary or revolutionary, according to circumstances.

I therefore consider that in view of the Constitution and the laws, the Union is unbroken, and to the extent of my ability, I shall take care, as the Constitution itself expressly enjoins upon me, that the laws of the Union be faithfully executed in all the States. Doing this I deem to be only a simple duty on my part, and I shall perform it so far as practicable unless my rightful masters, the American people, shall withhold the requisite means or in some authoritative manner direct the contrary. I trust this will not be regarded as a menace, but only as the declared purpose of the Union that it will constitutionally defend and maintain itself.

In doing this there needs to be no bloodshed or violence, and there shall be none unless it be forced upon the national authority. The power confided to me will be used to hold, occupy, and possess the property and places belonging to the Government and to collect the duties and imposts; but beyond what may be necessary for these objects, there will be no invasion, no using of force against or among the people anywhere....

Plainly the central idea of secession is the essence of anarchy. A majority held in restraint by constitutional checks and limitations, and always changing easily with deliberate changes of popular opinions and sentiments, is the only true sovereign of a free people. Whoever rejects it does of necessity fly to anarchy or to despotism....

Physically speaking, we can not separate. We can not remove our respective sections from each other nor build an impassable wall between them. A husband and wife may be divorced and go out of the presence and beyond the reach of each other, but the different parts of our country can not do this. They can not but remain face to face, and intercourse, either amicable or hostile, must continue between them. Is it possible, then, to make that intercourse more advantageous or more satisfactory after separation than before? Can aliens make treaties easier than friends can make laws? Can treaties be more faithfully enforced between aliens than laws can among friends? Suppose you go to war, you can not fight always; and when, after much loss on both sides and no gain on either, you cease fighting, the identical old questions, as to terms of intercourse, are again upon you....

My countrymen, one and all, think calmly and well upon this whole subject. Nothing valuable can be lost by taking time. If there be an object to hurry any of you in hot haste to a step which you would never take deliberately, that object will be frustrated by taking time; but no good object can be frustrated by it....

In your hands, my dissatisfied fellow-countrymen, and not in mine, is the momentous issue of civil war. The Government will not assail you. You can have no conflict without being yourselves the aggressors. You have no oath registered in heaven to destroy the Government, while I shall have the most solemn one to "preserve, protect, and defend it."

I am loath to close. We are not enemies, but friends. We must not be enemies. Though passion may have strained it must not break our bonds of affection. The mystic chords of memory, stretching from every battlefield and patriot grave to every living heart and hearthstone all over this broad land, will yet swell the chorus of the Union, when again touched, as surely they will be, by the better angels of our nature.

MON 11 MAR. CONFEDERATE CONSTITUTION RATIFIED

Meeting in Montgomery, Alabama, in February 1861, the Confederacy's founding fathers drafted a provisional constitution in just four days. A month later, they ratified a permanent document, which is excerpted below. Much of this document's language was taken directly from the U.S. Constitution—except, of course, its references to decentralized national government, the supremacy of states' rights, and the continued existence of slavery.

WE, THE PEOPLE OF THE Confederate States, each State acting in its sovereign and independent character, in order to form a permanent federal government, establish justice, insure domestic tranquillity, and secure the blessings of liberty to ourselves and our posterity—invoking the favor and guidance of Almighty God—do ordain and establish this Constitution for the Confederate States of America....

The President may approve any appropriation and disapprove any other appropriation in the same bill. In such case he shall, in signing the bill, designate the appropriations disapproved; and shall return a copy of such appropriations, with his objections, to the House in which the bill shall have originated....

[Congress shall have the power] to lay and collect taxes, duties, imposts, and excises for revenue, necessary to pay the debts, provide for the common defense, and carry on the Government of the Confederate States; but no bounties shall be granted from the Treasury; nor shall any duties or taxes on importations from foreign nations be laid to promote or foster any branch of industry; and all duties, imposts, and excises shall be uniform throughout the Confederate States....

Congress shall also have power to prohibit the introduction of slaves from any State not a member of, or Territory not belonging to, this Confederacy....

No bill of attainder, ex post facto law, or law denying or impairing the right of property in negro slaves shall be passed....

The citizens of each State shall be entitled to all the privileges and immunities of citizens in the several States; and shall have the right of transit and sojourn in any State of this Confederacy, with their slaves and other property; and the right of property in said slaves shall not be thereby impaired....

No slave or other person held to service or labor in any State or Territory of the Confederate States, under the laws thereof, escaping or lawfully carried into another, shall, in consequence of any law or regulation therein, be discharged from such service or labor; but shall be delivered up on claim of the party to whom such slave belongs, or to whom such service or labor may be due.

MON 18 MAR. *Mary Chesnut, wife of a wealthy South Carolina planter, personified the contradiction under which many Southerners lived: She benefited materially from the slaveholding society of which she was a member while also believing slavery to be an evil institution. In this journal entry, however, she shows that her condemnation of slavery had more to do with its moral and spiritual effects on slaveholders than any harm done to the enslaved. She also gives a glimpse of the chillingly routine sexual predation that male slaveholders practiced on their female slaves. The reference in the second sentence is to Senator Charles Sumner of Massachusetts, who was caned on the floor of the Senate five years earlier because of his vehemently antislavery views.*

I WONDER IF IT BE A SIN TO think slavery a curse to any land. Sumner said not one word of this hated institution which is not true. Men and women are punished when their masters and mistresses are brutes and not when they do wrong—and then we live surrounded by prostitutes. An abandoned woman is sent out of any decent house elsewhere. Who thinks any worse of a Negro or mulatto woman for being a thing we can't name? God forgive us, but ours is a *monstrous* system and wrong and iniquity. Perhaps the rest of the world is as bad—this *only* I see. Like the patriarchs of old our men live all in one house with their wives and their concubines, and the mulattoes one sees in every family exactly resemble the white children—and every lady tells you who is the father of all the mulatto children in everybody's household, but those in her own she seems to think drop from the clouds, or pretends so to think. Good women we have, *but* they talk of all *nastiness*.... [M]y disgust sometimes is boiling over—but they are, I belive, in conduct the purest women God ever made. Thank God for my countrywomen—alas for the men! No worse than men everywhere, but the lower their mistresses, the more degraded they must be.

THU 21 MAR. # THE "CORNER-STONE" OF SLAVERY

Historians have long debated the fundamental reason for the creation of the Confederacy. Was the new nation founded to protect states' rights, a unique Southern plantation culture, or the institution of slavery? Those who believe that the Confederacy was primarily a bulwark for human bondage point to this acidic, unapologetic speech

This compound was typical of the conditions under which slaves lived in the Deep South.

delivered in Savannah, Georgia, by Confederate vice president Alexander H. Stephens.

THE NEW CONSTITUTION HAS put at rest, *forever,* all the agitating questions relating to our peculiar institution—African slavery as it exists among us—the proper *status* of the negro in our form of civilization. This was the immediate cause of the late rupture and present revolution. Jefferson in his forecast, had anticipated this, as the "rock upon which the old Union would split." He was right. What was conjecture with him, is now a realized fact. But whether he fully comprehended the great truth upon which the rock *stood* and *stands,* may be doubted. The prevailing ideas entertained by him

and most of the leading statesmen at the time of the formation of the old constitution, were that the enslavement of the African was in violation of the laws of nature; that it was wrong in *principle,* socially, morally, and politically. It was an evil they knew not well how to deal with, but the general opinion of the men of that day was that, somehow or other in the order of Providence, the institution would be evanescent and pass away. This idea, though not incorporated in the constitution, was the prevailing idea at that time. The constitution, it is true, secured every essential guarantee to the institution while it should last, and hence no argument can be justly urged against the constitutional guarantees thus secured, because of the common sentiment of the day. Those ideas, however, were fundamentally wrong. They rested upon the assumption of the equality of races. This was an error. It was a sandy foundation, and the government built upon it fell when the "storm came and the wind blew."

Our new government is founded upon exactly the opposite idea; its foundations are laid, its corner-stone rests upon the great truth, that the negro is not equal to the white man; that slavery—subordination to the superior race—is his natural and normal condition.

This, our new government, is the first, in the history of the world, based upon this great physical, philosophical, and moral truth. This truth has been slow in the process of its development, like all other truths in the various departments of science. It has been so even amongst us. Many who hear me, perhaps, can recollect well, that this truth was not generally admitted, even within their day. The errors of the past generation still clung to many as late as twenty years ago. Those at the North, who still cling to these errors, with a zeal above knowledge, we justly denominate fanatics....They assume that the negro is equal, and hence conclude that he is entitled to equal privileges and rights with the white man. If their premises were correct, their conclusions would be logical and just—but their premise being wrong, their whole argument fails....

Many governments have been founded upon the principle of the subordination and serfdom of certain classes of the same race; such were and are in violation of the laws of nature. Our system commits no such violation of nature's laws. With us, all of the white race, however high or low, rich or poor, are equal in the eye of the law. Not so with the negro. Subordination is his place. He, by nature, or by the curse against Canaan, is fitted for that condition which he occupies in our system. The architect in the construction of buildings, lays the foundation with the proper material—the granite; then comes the brick or the marble. The substratum of our society is made of the material fitted by nature for it, and by experience we know, that it is best, not only for the superior, but for the inferior race, that it should be so. It is, indeed, in conformity with the ordinance of the Creator. It is not for us to inquire into the wisdom of his ordinances, or to question them. For his own purposes, he has made one race to differ from another, as he has made "one star to differ from another star in glory."...

I have been asked, what of the future? It has been apprehended by some that we would have arrayed against us the civilized world. I care not who or how many they may be against us; when we stand upon the eternal principles of truth, *if we are true to ourselves and the principles for which we contend,* we are obliged to, and must triumph.

★ ★ ★ ★

APRIL 1861

CONFEDERATES FIRE ON FORT SUMTER

The Civil War began at half past four in the morning, when Confederate forces under Gen. P. G. T. Beauregard fired on Fort Sumter. Over the course of the previous month, Charleston Harbor had become the focal point for military tensions between North and South, as the new Confederate government came to see the Federal garrisons there as a threat. When Maj. Robert Anderson refused to surrender the fort to Confederate troops, the bombardment began. The following excerpts—the first from the New York Herald, *the second from the* Charleston Mercury—*show that newspapers north and south treated the event as both thrilling and ominous.*

BOMBARDMENT OF FORT SUMTER. Civil War has begun! General Beauregard, in accordance with instructions received on Wednesday from the Secretary of War of the Southern confederacy, opened fire upon Fort Sumter yesterday morning at twenty-seven minutes after four o'clock. Forts Johnson and Moultrie, the iron battery at Cummings' Point, and the Stevens Floating Battery kept up an active cannonade during the entire day, and probably during the past night. The damage done to Fort Sumter had been, up to the last accounts, considerable. Guns had been dismounted, and a part of the parapet swept away.

Major Anderson had replied vigorously to the fire which had been opened upon him, but our despatches represent the injury inflicted by him to have been but small. The utmost bravery had been exhibited on both sides, and a large portion of the Charleston population, including five thousand ladies, were assembled upon the Battery to witness the conflict.

Down to our latest advices the battle had been carried on solely by the batteries of the revolutionists and Fort Sumter. The *Harriet Lane, Captain Faunce,* the *Pawnee,* and another United States vessel were off the harbor, but had taken no part in the conflict. The *Harriet Lane* is said to have received a shot through her wheelhouse.

The opinion prevailed in Charleston that an attempt would be made during the night to reinforce Fort Sumter by means of small boats from the three vessels in the offing.

No one had been killed by the fire of Major Anderson and the casualties among the Confederate troops in the batteries were inconsiderable. There is, of course, no account of the loss, if any, among the garrison of Fort Sumter.

BOMBARDMENT OF FORT SUMTER!
SPLENDID PYROTECHNIC EXHIBITION.

As may have been anticipated from our notice of the military movements in our city yesterday, the bombardment of Fort Sumter, so long and anxiously expected, has at length become a fact accomplished. The restless activity of the night before was gradually worn down, the citizens who had thronged the battery through the night, anxious and weary, had sought their homes, the Mounted Guard, which had kept watch and ward over the city, with the first grey streak of morning were preparing to retire, when two guns in quick succession from Fort Johnson announced the opening of the drama.

Currier & Ives's Bombardment of Fort Sumter, Charleston Harbor.

This photograph, taken on April 14, shows the Confederate flag recently hoisted over Fort Sumter.

Upon that signal, the circle of batteries with which the grim fortress of Fort Sumter is beleaguered opened fire. The outline of this great volcanic crater was illuminated with a line of twinkling lights; the clustering shells illuminated the sky above it; the balls clattered thick as hail upon its sides; our citizens, aroused to a forgetfulness of their fatigue through many weary hours, rushed again to the points of observation; and so, at the break of day, amidst the bursting of bombs, and the roaring of ordnance, and before thousands of spectators, whose homes, and liberties, and lives were at stake, was enacted this first great scene in the opening drama of what, it is presumed, will be a most momentous military act. It may be a drama of but a single act. The madness which inspires it may depart with this single paroxysm. It is certain that the people of the North had rankling at their hearts no sense of wrong to be avenged; and exhibiting to those who expect power to reconstruct the shattered Union, its utter inadequacy to accomplish a single step in that direction, the Administration of the old Government may abandon at once and forever its vain and visionary hope of forcible control over the Confederate States. But it may not be so; they may persist still longer in assertions of their power, and if so, they will arouse an independent spirit in the South, which will exact a merciless and fearful retribution.

Despite hopes that the day might see both the beginning and the end of armed conflict, as Southern batteries fired on Fort Sumter, Southern women braced for war. Writing in her journal,

Meta Morris Grimball of South Carolina revealed both the South's frenzied preparations and her own concerns for her sons, four of whom had already joined military outfits established in defense of their state.

THE 17TH REGIMENT HAS BEEN ordered down to Morris's Island, and the Northern Government have sent to inform the Southern that they intend to reinforce the Forts, and collect the revenue. A fleet is expected off the Harbour, and every thing is in a state of preparation.—4 of the boys are on duty, Berkley in the Sumpter Guards, and Arthur and William in the Cadet Riflemen. Lewis wants to volunteer in the Sumpters, I think he ought not. John is now on constant duty, and seems actively engaged; he wrote to us yesterday....He said he was

These enthusiastic Charleston Zouave cadets pose in full uniform at the outset of the war. Behind them can be seen two well-outfitted black orderlies.

alive but he could not say kicking, for he could hardly move one leg before the other, he was so tired....All yesterday I was in a most terrible state of anxiety and misery, about my boys—but I know my case is not different from others. Mrs. Elliott, the Mother of William's Captain, has her only child down there, Mrs. Lowndes her only son, & many others, but mine are very fine boys, and very dear to me, still they must do their duty to their State; and I put my trust in my God, & their God, my Savior & their Savior,— and I Pray for them & for myself.—The Government at Washington seem full of duplicity, and in looking back to the conduct of the seceding States, there seems to have been a truthful and noble faith actuating them.

MON 15 APR. LINCOLN CALLS FOR TROOPS

Two days after the fall of Fort Sumter, President Lincoln issued the following proclamation, in which he called for seventy-five thousand state militia troops to fight what he, and most of the rest of the country, believed would be a short war.

A PROCLAMATION

Whereas the laws of the United States have been for some time past, and now are opposed, and the execution thereof obstructed, in the States of South Carolina, Georgia, Alabama, Florida, Mississippi, Louisiana and Texas, by combinations too powerful to be suppressed by the ordinary means of judicial

THE WAR.

Highly Important News from Washington.

Offensive War Measures of the Administration.

The President's Exposition of His Policy Towards the Confederate States.

A WAR PROCLAMATION.

Seventy-five Thousand Men Ordered Out.

Thirteen Thousand Required from New York.

Call for an Extra Session of Congress.

Preparations for the Defence of the National Capital.

The Great Free States Arming for the Conflict.

Thirty Thousand Troops to be Tendered from New York.

Strong Union Demonstrations in Baltimore.

THE BATTLE AT CHARLESTON.

EVACUATION OF FORT SUMTER.

From the New York Herald.

proceedings, or by the powers vested in the Marshals by law,

Now therefore, I, Abraham Lincoln, President of the United States, in virtue of the power in me vested by the Constitution, and the laws, have thought fit to call forth, and hereby do call forth, the militia of the several states of the Union, to the aggregate number of seventy-five thousand, in order to suppress said combinations, and to cause the laws to be duly executed. The details, for this object, will be immediately communicated to the state authorities through the War Department.

I appeal to all loyal citizens to favor, facilitate and aid this effort to maintain the honor, the integrity, and the existence of our national union, and the perpetuity of popular government; and to redress wrongs already long enough endured.

I deem it proper to say that the first service assigned to the forces hereby called forth will probably be to re-possess the forts, places, and property which have been seized from the Union; and in every event, the utmost care will be observed, consistently with the objects aforesaid, to avoid any devastation, any destruction of, or interference with, property, or any disturbance of peaceful citizens in any part of the country.

And I hereby command the persons composing the combinations aforesaid to disperse, and retire peaceably to their respective abodes within twenty days from this date.

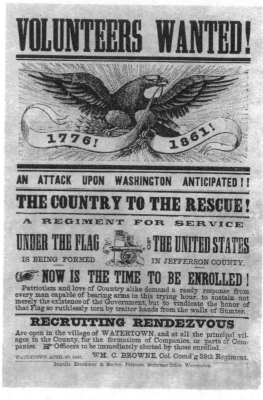

Recruiting posters such as this one contributed to the rush of patriotic youth into the ranks of both armies.

brating the surge of patriotism in the North. Although dissent did not altogether disappear—the editorial exaggerates when it claims "party bonds flashed into nothingness"—the firing on Fort Sumter did bring Northerners together with a common goal: preservation of the Union.

THE INCIDENTS OF THE LAST two days will live in History. Not for fifty years has such a spectacle been seen, as that glorious uprising of American loyalty which greeted the news that open war had been commenced upon the Constitution and Government

TUE 16 APR. *Four days after the firing on Fort Sumter, the following editorial ran in the* New York Times, *cele-*

The First Michigan Volunteer Infantry receives its regimental colors in Detroit on May 1, 1861.

of the United States. The great heart of the American people beat with one high pulsation of courage, and of fervid love and devotion to the great Republic. Party dissensions were instantly hushed; political differences disappeared, and were as thoroughly forgotten as if they had never existed; party bonds flashed into nothingness in the glowing flame of patriotism—men ceased to think of themselves or their parties—they thought only of their country and the dangers which menace its existence. Nothing for years has brought the hearts of all the people so close together—or so inspired them all with common hopes, and common fears, and a common aim, as the bombardment and surrender of an American fortress.

...The best among us began to despair of a country which seemed incompetent to understand its dangers, and indifferent to its own destruction.

But all this is changed. The cannon which bombarded Sumter awoke strange echoes, and touched forgotten chords in the American heart....

It is a mistake to suppose that War—even Civil War—is the greatest evil that can afflict a nation. The proudest and noblest nations of the earth have the oftenest felt its fury, and have risen the stronger, because the braver, from its overwhelming wrath. War is a far less evil than degradation—than the national and social paralysis which can neither feel a wound nor redress a wrong. When War becomes the only means of sustaining a nation's honor, and of vindicating its just and rightful supremacy, it ceases to be an evil and becomes the source of actual and positive good.

Brig. Gen. Joseph E. Johnston

THU 18 APR. SOUTHERN OFFICERS RESIGN

A total of 286 U.S. Army officers (out of approximately 1,000 on active duty) resigned their comissions to join the Confederate cause. For some—notably Joseph E. Johnston, who resigned as quartermaster general on this date and eventually took command of the Confederate Army of Tennessee—the decision came swiftly and was based upon what the officers believed to be inviolable principles of individual and states' rights. A brigadier general, Johnston was the highest-ranking officer to defect. He explained his reasoning in a postwar memoir.

I BELIEVED, LIKE MOST OTHERS, that the division of the country would be permanent; and that, apart from any right of secession, the revolution begun was justified by the maxims so often repeated by Americans, that free government is founded on the consent of the governed, and that every community strong enough to establish and maintain its independence has a right to assert it. Having been educated in such opinions, I naturally determined to return to the

State of which I was a native, join the people among whom I was born, and live with my kindred, and, if necessary, fight in their defense.

Two days later (and three days after his home state of Virginia had voted preliminarily for secession), Col. Robert E. Lee also left the U.S. Army. Yet, in contrast to Johnston's decision to resign, Lee's was agonizing, akin to abandoning one's family. His feelings of regret Lee expressed in this letter to his mentor, Gen.-in-Chief Winfield Scott.

GENERAL: SINCE MY INTERVIEW with you on the 18th inst. I have felt that I ought no longer to retain my commission in the Army. I therefore tender my resignation, which I request you will recommend for acceptance. It would have been presented at once but for the struggle it has cost me to separate myself from a service to which I have devoted the best years of my life, and all the ability I possessed.

During the whole of that time—more than a quarter of a century—I have experienced nothing but kindness from my superiors and a most cordial friendship with my comrades. To no one, General, have I been as much indebted as to yourself for uniform kindness and consideration, and it has always been my ardent desire to merit your approbation. I shall carry to the grave the most grateful recollections of your kind consideration, and your name and fame shall always be dear to me.

Save in the defense of my native State, I never again desire to draw my sword.

Be pleased to accept my most earnest wishes for the continuance of your happiness and prosperity, and believe me most truly yours,
    R. E. Lee

FRI 19 APR. LINCOLN DECLARES A BLOCKADE

With the following proclamation, President Lincoln declared an official Union blockade of the entire Confederate coast. Yet the prospect of carrying out such an extensive mission was daunting. The South possessed over a thousand miles of coastline, with myriad harbors, inlets, and other natural hideouts from which blockade runners could periodically sally forth. There were difficult diplomatic issues as well. International law suggested that blockades could be declared only against sovereign nations. Therefore, some in government argued, declaring a blockade against the South granted de facto recognition to the Confederacy. Such legalistic considerations aside, Lincoln's policy made excellent military sense, and the blockade eventually proved instrumental in starving the Confederate economy.

A PROCLAMATION

Whereas an insurrection against the Government of the United States has broken out in the States of South Carolina, Georgia, Alabama, Florida, Mississippi, Louisiana, and Texas, and the laws of the United States for the collection of the revenue cannot be effectually executed therein comfortably to

The Rebel blockade runner Robert E. Lee *was later captured and renamed the USS* Fort Donelson.

that provision of the Constitution which requires duties to be uniform throughout the United States:

And whereas a combination of persons engaged in such insurrection, have threatened to grant pretended letters of marque to authorize the bearers thereof to commit assaults on the lives, vessels, and property of good citizens of the country lawfully engaged in commerce on the high seas, and in waters of the United States....

Now, therefore, I, Abraham Lincoln, President of the United States, with a view to the same purposes before mentioned, and to the protection of the public peace, and the lives and property of quiet and orderly citizens pursuing their lawful occupations, until Congress shall have assembled and deliberated on the said unlawful proceedings, or until the same shall have ceased, have further deemed it advisable to set on foot a blockade of the ports within the States aforesaid, in pursuance of the laws of the United States, and of the law of Nations, in such case

provided. For this purpose a competent force will be posted so as to prevent entrance and exit of vessels from the ports aforesaid. If, therefore, with a view to violate such blockade, a vessel shall approach, or shall attempt to leave either of the said ports, she will be duly warned by the Commander of one of the blockading vessels, who will endorse on her register the fact and date of such warning, and if the same vessel shall again attempt to enter or leave the blockaded port, she will be captured and sent to the nearest convenient port, for such proceedings against her and her cargo as prize, as may be deemed advisable.

THE BALTIMORE RIOTS

As a result of President Lincoln's call for troops following the bombardment of Fort Sumter, a steady flow of volunteer militia units from New England streamed toward Washington, D.C. When the Sixth Massachusetts Volunteer Infantry Regiment arrived in Baltimore en route to the capital, it was met by angry pro-Southern crowds. First, the Marylanders taunted the soldiers; then, Confederate flags appeared. After stones began to pelt the troops, shots were fired on both sides. At least four soldiers and nine civilians were killed. In this report on the riots, prepared for the city council, Baltimore mayor George William Brown describes the volatile and uncertain climate in the border states, where most elected officials were trying to read the leanings of their constituents before openly supporting either side. As Brown notes, after the riots, Lincoln instructed other New England units to avoid Baltimore entirely; instead, they moved by sea from New York to Annapolis, thence overland to Washington.

ON APPROACHING PRATT-STREET bridge I saw several companies of Massachusetts troops…moving in column rapidly towards me. An attack on them had begun, and the noise and excitement were great. I ran at once to the head of the column, some persons in the crowd shouting, as I approached, "Here comes the mayor." I shook hands with the officer in command, saying, as I did so, "I am the mayor of Baltimore." I then placed myself by his side and marched with him as far as the head of Light-street wharf, doing what I could by my presence and personal efforts to allay the tumult. The mob grew bolder and the attack became more violent. Various persons were killed and wounded on both sides. The troops had some time previously begun to fire in self-defense, and the firing, as the attack increased in violence, became more general….

The facts which I witnessed myself, and all that I have since heard, satisfy me that the attack was the result of a sudden impulse, and not of a premeditated scheme. But the effect on our citizens was for a time uncontrollable. In the intense excitement which ensued, which lasted for many days, and which was shared by men of all parties, and by our volunteer soldiers as well as citizens, it would have been impossible to convey more troops from the North through the city without a severe fight and bloodshed. Such an occurrence would have been fatal to the city, and accordingly to prevent it the bridges on the Northern Central Railroad and on the Philadelphia, Wilmington and Baltimore Railroad were, with the consent of the governor and by my order, with the co-operation of the board of police (except Mr. Charles D. Hinks, who was absent from the city), partially disabled and burned, so as to prevent the immediate approach of troops to the city, but with no purpose of hostility to the Federal Government. This act, with the motive which prompted it, has been reported by the board of police to the legislature of the State and approved by that body, and was also immediately communicated by me in person to the President of the United States and his Cabinet.

This account of the riots in Baltimore appeared in the New York Herald *the following day. As was the case with many hastily written breaking news stories, it included many inaccuracies (such as the number reported killed and wounded), but it gives a vivid picture of the passions and confusion during the first days of the war.*

IMPORTANT FROM MARYLAND. FIGHT IN BALTIMORE BETWEEN THE TROOPS AND THE MOB—TWO SOLDIERS AND SEVEN CITIZENS KILLED. A terrible scene is now going on in Pratt street. The track has been torn up. The troops attempted to march through, when they were attacked by a mob with stones and bricks, and then fired upon. The troops returned the fire. Two of the Seventh regiment of the Massachusetts were killed. The fight is still going on.

There is intense excitement here. The soldiers are now forcing their way through. They fired on the mob, killing ten.

It is impossible to say what portion of the troops have been attacked. They bore a white flag as they marched up Pratt street, and were greeted with showers of paving stones. The Mayor of the city went ahead of them, with the police. An immense crowd blocked up the streets. The soldiers finally turned and fired on the mob. Several of the wounded have just gone up the street in carts.

At the Washington depot an immense crowd assembled. The rioters attacked the soldiers, who fired on the mob. Several were wounded, and some fatally. It is said that four of the military and four rioters are killed. The city is in great excitement. Martial law has been proclaimed. The military are rushing to the armories.

Civil war has commenced. The railroad track is said to be torn up outside the city. Parties threaten to destroy the Baltimore street bridge. As the troops passed along Pratt street a perfect

Because early photographs had to be exposed for long periods of time, action shots were impossible. Instead, images of newsworthy events such as the Baltimore riots were distributed as lithographs and printed woodcuts.

shower of paving stones rained on their heads. The cars have left for Washington, and were stoned as they left.

It was the Seventh regiment of Massachusetts which broke through the mob. Three of the mob are known to be dead, and three soldiers. Many were wounded. Stores are closing, and the military rapidly forming. The Minute Men are turning out.

SAT 20 APR. *Emancipation did not become an official war aim of the Union until 1863. Nevertheless, many Northerners believed from the start that ending slavery was the goal of the sectional conflict. This thoughtful editorial from an Indiana newspaper points out the North's previous complicity in maintaining the institution of slavery and speculates on the possibility that the present war may be a form of divine retribution for this national sin.*

[PERHAPS] GOD HAS INSTITUTED the present troubles to rid the country of the predominance of slavery in its public affairs. The whole country, North as well as South, has been instrumental in the endeavor to spread it over the continent, and to force it on unwilling people. While the South has been actively propagating and perpetuating the institution, the North has winked at the wrongful business and encouraged it. Therefore, in the coming troubles, the North must not expect to escape the penalty of her lack of principle. She must suffer, like the South.

It may even be possible that Providence designs by means of these troubles to put a summary end to slavery. The institution has gone on to spread until it interferes materially with the progress of the Nation. Our country can never reach its full stature and importance so long as this baleful influence extends over it. It is a paradoxical state of things to see a country, which boasts of its freedom, nursing and sustaining the most odious system of slavery known on earth....There is truly an "irrepressible conflict" between free and slave labor, and eventually the country must be all slave or all free, or the two parts must separate; which, we shall soon know....

The people of the North as a body have been willing to let slavery alone—to have nothing to do with it one way or the other. They have no other desire now. But if the war goes on...the contest sound[s] the death-knell of slavery. Thomas Jefferson said that, in such a contest as the present, God has no attribute that could cause him to take sides with the slave-owners....And, if the peculiar institution is doomed to come to an end by the acts of its friends, who will mourn its loss? It has kept the country in a ferment since its organization and hindered its progress and it would be truly a God's blessing to be rid of it. So every patriot feels in his heart of hearts.

THU 25 APR. *This account of an impromptu Wisconsin town meeting, reported in the* Prairie du Chien Courier, *indicates that during the early days of the war, patriotic fervor was no less strong in the West than in the East.*

Last Friday evening, after only an hour's notice, Union Hall was crowded with the most enthusiastic audience ever assembled in Prairie du Chien. It was composed of the most substantial citizens of this vicinity, representing every class and every interest, every opinion and every party. They all seemed to be fully aroused to the importance of the events now transpiring, and had met together with one will to counsel and hear the suggestions of patriotic and practical men. Several speakers, including the venerable Chairman, spoke to the people calmly, deliberately, and determinedly, but without rashness. The fact of a general civil war being already commenced, was freely discussed and fearlessly confronted. The only sentiment of all was a common cause in support of the Government, the Constitution, and the Flag of the Union. Resolutions loyal to the Government were unanimously adopted; volunteers enlisted, and a subscription of over three hundred dollars subscribed to begin the work of organization. The feeling here is all on the side of sustaining the Government in the enforcement of all constitutional law.

SAT
27
APR. *Although Abraham Lincoln would find himself the subject of numerous photographs, engravings, and written profiles as the war progressed, Jefferson Davis was not nearly so well publicized. Southerners typically paid more attention to their military leaders than to their political ones. The following is a rare description* of Davis at work. The author, J. B. Jones, was a Maryland native who applied to Davis for work in the new Confederate government.*

Was introduced to the President today. He was overwhelmed with papers and retained a number in his left hand, probably of more importance than the rest. He received me with urbanity; and while he read the papers I had given him, as I had never seen him before I endeavored to scruti-

Jefferson Davis

nize his features, as one would naturally do....His stature is tall, nearly six feet; his frame is very slight and seemingly frail; but when he throws back his shoulders he is as straight as an Indian chief. The features of his face are distinctly marked with character; and no one gazing at his profile would doubt for a moment that he beheld more than an ordinary man. His face is handsome, and [on] his thin lip often basks a pleasant smile. There is nothing sinister or repulsive in his manners or appearance; and if there are no special indications of great grasp of intellectual power on his forehead and on his sharply defined nose and chin, neither is there any evidence of weakness or that he could be easily moved from any settled purpose. I think he has a clear conception of matters demanding his cognizance and a nice discrimination of details. As a politician he attaches the utmost importance to consistency—and here I differ with him. I think that to be consistent as a politician is to change with the circumstances of the case....

When the President had completed the reading of my papers, and during the perusal I observed him make several emphatic nods, he asked me what I wanted. I told him I wanted employment with my pen, perhaps only temporary employment. I thought the correspondence of the Secretary of War would increase in volume, and another assistant besides Major [John] Tyler would be required in his office. He smiled and shook his head, saying that such work would be only temporary indeed; which I construed to mean that even he did not then suppose the war to assume colossal proportions.

TUE 30 APR. *Women no less than men sought to defend their homes and families. The mocking tone of this article from the New York Herald, regarding a company of Mississippi women allegedly training to be home guards, may reflect both contemporary attitudes about proper women's behavior and Yankee disdain for the Confederacy's chances on the battlefield.*

A SOUTHERN PAPER SAYS THAT a county of Chicasaw, Miss., has a regularly officered and drilled company of young ladies, who have pledged themselves, in the event that the men are called into service, to protect their homes and families during their absence, and see that the farms are properly cultivated, and full crops raised not only for the support of the country, but of the army of Mississippi. The Day Book suggests that these Chicasaw beauties should be sent against the Seventh Regiment of New York, since the well-known gallantry of this favorite corps would naturally induce them to present arms to it. Another paper—which even these troubled times cannot tutor into seriousness—inclines to the belief that they would be better employed in raising and drilling Infantry. At all events, this regiment of the Misses of Mississippi would be invaluable in a Nursery of soldiers. These episodes resemble the silver lining of that terrible cloud now passing over us, but still they are hardly subjects for humor.

★ ★ ★ ★

MAY 1861

SAT
4
MAY *Although Northern morale was running high, there was great concern over the fate of Washington, D.C. With Virginia having joined the Confederacy and Maryland's status uncertain, the Union capital appeared surrounded by Southern, or Southern-leaning, territory and thus vulnerable to capture, as this report in* Harper's Weekly *makes clear.*

THE WAR HAS NOW BEGUN IN earnest. The secession of Virginia, and the attempts of rebels to seize the Arsenal at Harpers Ferry and the Navy-yard at Norfolk; the bombardment of Fort Sumter; the investment of Fort Pickens; the seizure of the *Star of the West* by a Southern privateer; the threatened seizure of the Federal Capital by the rebels; the murder of Massachusetts men in Baltimore, and the refusal of Maryland to permit Northern troops to pass through that city to defend the capital—these facts explain the situation without further comment....

Guards at the ferry landing on Mason's Island (in the Potomac River) inspect a pass.

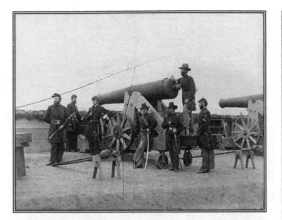

One of the larger guns defending the capital.

At this moment—it may be passed when the writing becomes print—the fear is the capture of Washington. By the treason of Virginia, which is the meanest treason of the whole, and the defection of Maryland, our chief point is far within the lines of the enemy and communication well-nigh cut off. The great hope of the rebellion is a sudden blow. If it can fall upon Washington successfully, it will move triumphantly across Maryland, and give battle to the patriots along the Pennsylvania line.

In contrast to the martial enthusiasm prevailing in both North and South, the tone of this letter from a Monroe County, Alabama, man to Confederate president Jefferson Davis expressed certain misgivings some Southerners had about the efficacy of the Confederate war effort. William H. Lee was particularly concerned about the possibility of a slave revolt.

DEAR SIR: I HAVS TO IN FORM you that thire is a good meny pore men with large famely to susport An if they have to go in to the Army there famelys will sufer   thire is a Nother question to rise with us   the Negroes is very Hiley Hope up that they will soon Be free so I think that you Had Better order out All the Negroe felers from 17 years oald up   Ether fort them up or put them in the army and Make them fite like good fells for wee ar in danger of our lives hear among them   So I Will close with my Best love to you
Wm H Lee

MON 6 MAY *British journalist William Howard Russell, who had already served as a correspondent during the recent Crimean War, traveled to North America in the spring of 1861 to report on the newly divided continent. He arrived in Montgomery, Alabama, in May, while the city was still the Confederate capital, and quickly filed this vivid, if rather disparaging, account of the new nation's fledgling Congress.*

AT THE END OF THIS LONG street, on a moderate eminence, stands a whitewashed or painted edifice, with a gaunt lean portico, supported on lofty lanky pillars, and surmounted by a subdued and dejected-looking little cupola. Passing an unkempt lawn, through a very shabby little gateway in a brick frame, we ascend a flight of steps into a hall, from which a double staircase conducts us to the vestibule of the chamber. Any thing much more offensive to the eye cannot well be imagined than the floor and stairs. They are stained deeply by tobacco juice, which has left its marks

Cartoonists enjoyed caricaturing the portly William Howard Russell, shown here covering the first battle of Bull Run in July 1861.

on the white stone steps and on the base of the pillars outside. In the hall which we have entered there are two tables, covered with hams, oranges, bread and fruits, for the refreshment of members and visitors, over which two sable goddesses, in portentous crinoline, preside. The door of the chamber is open and we are introduced into a lofty, well-lighted and commodious apartment, in which the Congress of the Confederate States holds its deliberations. A gallery runs half round the room, and is half filled with visitors—country cousins, and farmers of cotton and maize, and, haply, seekers of places great or small. A light and low semicircular screen separates the body of the house, where the members sit, from the space under the gallery, which is appropriated to ladies and visitors. The clerk sits at a desk above this table, and on a platform behind him are the desk and chair of the presiding officer or Speaker of the Congress. Over his head hangs the unfailing portrait of Washington, and a small engraving, in a black frame, of a gentleman unknown to me. Seated in the midst of them, at a senator's desk, I was permitted to "assist," in the French sense, at the deliberations of the Congress. Mr. Howell Cobb took the chair, and a white-headed clergyman was called upon to say prayers, which he did, upstanding, with outstretched hands and closed eyes, by the side of the speaker. The prayer was long and sulphureous. One more pregnant with gunpowder I never heard, nor could aught like it have been heard since....

The reverend gentleman prayed that the Almighty might be pleased to inflict on the arms of the United States such a defeat that it might be the example of signal punishment....

...The prayer was over at last, and the house proceeded to business. Although each state has several delegates in Congress, it is only entitled to one vote on a strict division. In this way some curious decisions may be arrived at, as the smallest state is equal to the largest, and a majority of the Florida representatives may neutralize a vote of all the Georgia representatives. For example, Georgia has ten delegates; Florida has only three. The vote of Florida, however, is determined by the action of any two of its three representatives, and these two may, on a division, throw the one state vote into the scale against that of Georgia, for which ten members are agreed. The Congress transacts all its business in secret session, and finds it a very agreeable and commendable way of doing it. Thus, today, for example, after the presentation of a few unimportant motions and papers, the speaker rapped his desk, and announced that the house would go into secret session, and that all who were not members should leave.

FRI
10
MAY

For many in the North and South, life during the first months of the war was an odd mixture of the strange and the familiar. Judith McGuire was a middle-aged wife and mother living in comfortable wealth near Alexandria, Virginia. Like many of her neighbors, she became caught up in the surge of war fever that swept over men and women alike. Her journal entry for this day contains a surreal jumble of military and gardening notes. In it, she laments the fragmentation of Alexandria society caused by more and more families moving farther and farther south to escape the possibility of a Northern invasion—which became a reality just two weeks later.

WE ARE NOW HOPING THAT Alexandria will not be a landing-place for the enemy, but that the forts will be attacked. In that case, they would certainly be repulsed, and we could stay quietly at home. To view the progress of events from any point will be sad enough, but it would be more bearable at our own home, and surrounded by our family and friends. With the supposition that we may remain, and that the ladies of the family

The Marshall House in Alexandria, Virginia, to which McGuire refers, was two weeks later the setting for the famous death of Col. Elmer Ellsworth.

at least may return to us, I am having the grounds put in order, and they are now so beautiful! Lilacs, crocuses, the lily of the valley, and other spring flowers, are in luxuriant bloom, and the roses in full bud. The greenhouse plants have been removed and grouped on the lawn, verbenas in bright bloom have been transplanted from the pit to the borders, and the grass seems unusually green after the late rains; the trees are in full leaf; every thing is so fresh and lovely. "All, save the spirit of man, is divine."

War seems inevitable, and while I am trying to employ the passing hour, a cloud still hangs over us and all that surrounds us. For a long time before our society was so completely broken up, the ladies of Alexandria and all the surrounding country were busily employed sewing for our soldiers. Shirts, pants, jackets, and beds, of the heaviest material, have been made by the most delicate fingers. All ages, all conditions, meet now on one common platform. We must all work for our country. Our soldiers must be equipped. Our parlor was the rendezvous for our neighborhood, and our sewing-machine was in requisition for weeks. Scissors and needles were plied by all. The daily scene was most animated. The fires of our enthusiasm and patriotism were burning all the while to a degree which might have been consuming, but that our tongues served as safety-valves. Oh, how we worked and talked, and excited each other! One common sentiment animated us all; no doubts, no fears were felt. We all have such entire reliance in the justice of our cause and the valor of our men, and above all, on the blessing of Heaven! These meetings have necessarily ceased with us, as so few of any age or degree remain at home; but in Alexandria they are still kept up with great interest. We who are left here are trying to give the soldiers who are quartered in town comfort, by carrying them milk, butter, pies, cakes, etc....

The Confederate flag waves from several points in Alexandria: from the Marshall House, the Market-house, and the several barracks. The peaceful, quiet old town looks quite warlike. I feel sometimes, when walking on King's street, meeting men in uniform, passing companies of cavalry, hearing martial music, etc., that I must be in a dream. Oh that it were a dream, and that the last ten years of our country's history were blotted out!

THE "BATTLE" OF ST. LOUIS

Meanwhile, secessionists in St. Louis, Missouri, demanded the removal of Federal troops from all public buildings and arsenals. When Capt. Nathaniel Lyon, commander of the St. Louis Arsenal, refused, some seven hundred local militiamen began gathering outside the city at Camp Jackson. In response, Lyon, leading nearly seven thousand men, surrounded the pro-Confederate militiamen, who surrendered without a fight. During the march back to St. Louis, however, a crowd shouting pro-Southern slogans and throwing rocks and bottles formed around the Union troops. Soon a firefight began in the streets, during which twenty-eight people died. Several days of rioting followed, but the Union held St. Louis and with it, Missouri. In the dispatch excerpted below, the brigadier

This painting depicts the fighting between Lyon's men and rock-throwing Confederate sympathizers in the streets of St. Louis.

commanding the Missouri militia attempts to persuade Captain Lyon that his troops mean no harm to the Federal forces in St. Louis. Lyon's reply follows.

SIR: I AM CONSTANTLY IN receipt of information that you contemplate an attack upon my camp, whilst I understand that you are impressed with the idea that an attack upon the arsenal and United States troops is intended on the part of the militia of Missouri. I am greatly at a loss to know what could justify you in attacking citizens of the United States who are in the lawful performance of duties devolving upon them under the Constitution in organizing and instructing the militia of the State in obedience to her laws, and therefore have been disposed to doubt the correctness of the information I have received.

I would be glad to know from you personally whether there is any truth in the statements that are constantly poured into my ears. So far as regards any hostility being intended toward the United States or its property or representatives, by any portion of my command, or, as far as I can learn (and I think I am fully informed), of any other part of the State forces, I can say positively that the idea has never been entertained. On the contrary, prior to your taking command of the arsenal, I proffered to Major Bell, then in command of the very few troops constituting its guard, the services of myself and all my command, and, if necessary, the whole power of the State, to protect the United States in the full possession of all her property....

I trust after this explicit statement, we may be able, by fully understanding each other, to keep far from our borders the misfortunes which so unhappily afflict our common country.

I am, sir, very respectfully, your obedient servant,

D. M. Frost,
Brig. Gen.,
Comdg. Camp Jackson

SIR: YOUR COMMAND IS REGARDED as evidently hostile towards the Government of the United States. It is, for the most part, made up of those secessionists who have openly avowed their hostility to the General Government, and have been plotting at the seizure of its property and the overthrow of its authority.

You are openly in communication with the so-called Southern Confederacy, which is now at war with the United States; and you are receiving at your camp, from the said Confederacy, and under its flag, large supplies of the material of war, most of which is known to be the property of the United States.

These extraordinary preparations plainly indicate none other than the well-known purpose of the governor of this State, under whose orders you are acting, and whose purposes, recently communicated to the legislature, have just been responded to by that body in the most unparalleled legislation, having in direct view hostilities to the General Government and co-operation with its enemies.

In view of these considerations, and of your failure to disperse in obedience to the proclamation of the President, and of the eminent necessities of State policy and welfare, and the obligations imposed upon me by instructions from Washington, it is my duty to demand, and I do hereby demand, of you an immediate surrender of your command, with no other conditions than that all persons surrendering under this demand shall be humanely and kindly treated. Believing myself prepared to enforce this demand, one-half hour's time, before doing so, will be allowed for your compliance therewith.

Very respectfully, your obedient servant,

N. Lyon,
Captain, Second Infantry

FRI 24 MAY THE DEATH OF ELLSWORTH

In an effort to secure the Federal capital, elements of three Union regiments crossed the Potomac River on this day and seized the city of Alexandria, Virginia. Scattered state militia units promptly abandoned the town after firing just a few shots. Quite apart from these minor skirmishes, one notorious bullet (fired by an innkeeper) struck and killed twenty-four-year-old Elmer Ellsworth, the dashing and politically connected colonel commanding the

Currier and Ives used the numerous published accounts of Ellsworth's death to create this lithograph.

New York Fire Zouaves (the Eleventh New York, so nicknamed because most of the volunteers had been city firemen). Ellsworth's death, the first of a socially prominent Union officer, sent much of the North into grief. His body lay in state in the White House, and not long after this, songs, poems, and patriotic artwork memorializing him became commonplace. No one yet imagined that six hundred thousand more would die. The New York Times *carried this account of his death the next day on its front page.*

THE ZOUAVES LANDED IN GOOD order in double quick time, each company forming in company order on the street facing the river....Col. Ellsworth and his detachment proceeded in double quick time up the street. They had proceeded three blocks, when the attention of Colonel Ellsworth was attracted by a large secession flag flying from the Marshall House, kept by J. W. Jackson. Col. Ellsworth entered the hotel, and seeing a man in the hall asked, "Who put that flag up?" The man answered, "I don't know; I am a boarder here." Col. Ellsworth, Lieut. Winser, the chaplain of the regiment, Mr. House, a volunteer aide, and the four privates, went up to the roof and Col. Ellsworth cut down the flag.

The party were returning down the stairs, preceded by Private Francis E. Brownell, of Company A. As they left the attic, the man who had said he was a boarder, but proved to be the landlord, Jackson, was met in the hall, having a double-barrel gun, which he leveled at Brownell. Brownell struck up the gun with his musket, when Jackson pulled both triggers of the gun. The contents lodged in the body of Col. Ellsworth, entering between the third and fifth ribs. Col. Ellsworth at the time was rolling up the flag. He fell forward on the floor of the hall and expired instantly, only exclaiming "My God."

Private Brownell, with the quickness of lightning, leveled his musket at Jackson and fired. The ball struck Jackson on the bridge of the nose, and crashed through his skull, killing him instantly. As he fell Brownell followed his shot by a thrust of his bayonet which went through Jackson's body.

SUN
26
MAY

Even Nathaniel Hawthorne was caught up in the patriotic excitement. In the letter excerpted here, Hawthorne admits to feeling unusually flushed with national pride while also confused as to what the Union's war aims will be.

THE WAR, STRANGE TO SAY, HAS had a beneficial effect upon my spirits, which were flagging woefully before it broke out. But it was delightful to share in the heroic sentiment of the time, and to feel that I had a country—a consciousness which seemed to make me young again. One thing, as regards this matter, I regret, and one thing I am glad of;—the regrettable thing is, that I am too old to shoulder a musket myself; and the joyful thing is, that Julian is too young. He drills constantly with a company of lads, and means to enlist as soon as he reaches the minimum age; but I trust we shall either be victorious or vanquished before that time. Meantime (though I approve the war as much as any man) I don't quite

This young slave escaped from his master to become a drummer boy in the Union army.

understand what we are fighting for, or what definite result can be expected. If we pummel the South ever so hard, they will love us none the better for it; and even if we subjugate them, our next step should be to cut them adrift. If we are fighting for the annihilation of slavery, to be sure, it may be a wise object, and offers a tangible result, and the only one which is consistent with a future Union between North and South. A continuance of the war would soon make this plain to us; and we should see the expediency of preparing our black brethren for future citizenship by allowing them to fight for their own liberties, and educating them through heroic influences.

What ever happens next, I must say that I rejoice that the old Union is smashed. We never were one people, and never really had a country since the Constitution was formed.

MON 27 MAY *Gen. Benjamin F. Butler— commanding Fort Monroe, the Union's most vital installation on Virginia soil—found himself faced with an unusual military problem: Escaped slaves seeking refuge kept appearing in large numbers at his fort overlooking the Hampton Roads estuary. In this letter to Gen.-in-Chief Winfield Scott, Butler explained the situation and defended his* *decision to admit the slaves—a decision subsequently endorsed by Scott.*

SINCE I WROTE MY LAST DISPATCH the question in regard to slave property is becoming one of very serious magnitude. The inhabitants of Virginia are using their Negroes in the batteries, and are preparing to send the women and children south. The escapes from them are very numerous, and a squad has come in this morning to my pickets bringing their women and children. Of course these cannot be dealt with upon the theory on which I designed to treat the services of able-bodied men and women who might come within my lines and of which I gave you a detailed account in my last dispatch. I am in the utmost doubt what to do with this species of property. Up to this time I have had come within my lines men and women with their children— entire families—each family belonging to the same owner. I have therefore determined to employ, as I can do very profitably, the able-bodied persons in the party, issuing proper food for the support of all, and charging against their services the expense of care and sustenance of nonlaborers, keeping a strict and accurate account as well of the services as of the expenditure, having the worth of the services and the cost of the expenditure determined by a board of survey hereafter to be detailed. I know of no other manner in which to dispose of this subject and the questions connected therewith. As a matter of property to the insurgents it will be of very great moment, the number that I now have amounting as I am informed to what in good times would be of the value of sixty thousand dollars. Twelve of these

negroes I am informed have escaped from the erection of the batteries on Sewall's Point which this morning fired upon my expedition as it passed by out of range.... Without them the batteries could not have been erected at least for many weeks. As a military question it would seem to be a measure of necessity to deprive their masters of their services. How can this be done? As a political question and a question of humanity can I receive the services of a father and a mother and not take the children? Of the humanitarian aspect I have no doubt. Of the political one I have no right to judge. I therefore submit all this to your better judgment, and as these questions have a political aspect, I have ventured— and I trust I am not wrong in so doing—to duplicate the parts of my dispatch relating to this subject and forward them to the Secretary of War.

EX PARTE MERRYMAN

When the Civil War began, the chief justice of the Supreme Court was eighty-four-year-old Roger B. Taney, the Maryland slaveholder and Southern sympathizer who had delivered the majority opinion in Dred Scott v. Sanford *(1857), quite possibly the most racist decision in American legal history. Taney disliked Republicans and despised abolitionists even more, so it came as no surprise when he and Lincoln tangled over the new president's decisive—and, even to some Northerners, excessive— policy regarding Confederate sympathizers in Maryland and the other Union-controlled border states. Essentially,*

Roger B. Taney

Lincoln had these people—who were suspected of, but not charged with, treason—arrested and held. At the same time, to prevent their release, he suspended their right to a writ of habeas corpus (the common-law rule requiring the government to show cause for an arrest). What was to Lincoln a necessary exercise of wartime authority outraged Taney, who considered the suspension a gross violation of the suspects' civil liberties and constitutional rights. Acting this day in the case of John Merryman, the chief justice declared (in the following ruling) Lincoln's suspension of the writ illegal. The president responded that, as commander-in-chief during wartime, he was empowered by the

Constitution to suspend the writ when, according to Article I, Section 9, "the public safety may require it." Lincoln's interpretation prevailed, and Ex Parte Merryman *went down in history as the only significant legal challenge to Lincoln's policies during his lifetime.*

ON THE 25TH MAY 1861, THE petitioner, a citizen of Baltimore County, in the state of Maryland, was arrested by a military force, acting under orders of a major general of the United States army, commanding in the state of Pennsylvania, and committed to the custody of the general commanding Fort McHenry, within the district of Maryland; on the 26th May 1861, a writ of habeas corpus was issued by the chief justice of the United States, sitting at chambers, directed to the commandant of the fort, commanding him to produce the body of the petitioner before the chief justice, in Baltimore city, on the 27th day of May 1861; on the last mentioned day, the writ was returned served, and the officer to whom it was directed declined to produce the petitioner, giving as his excuse the following reasons: 1. That the petitioner was arrested by the orders of the major general commanding in Pennsylvania, upon the charge of treason, in being "publicly associated with and holding a commission as lieutenant in a company having in their possession arms belonging to the United States, and avowing his purpose of armed hostility against the government." 2. That he (the officer having the petitioner in custody) was duly authorized by the president of the United States, in such cases, to suspend the writ of habeas corpus for the public safety.

Held, that the petitioner was entitled to be set at liberty and discharged immediately from confinement, upon the grounds following: 1. That the president, under the constitution of the United States, cannot suspend the privilege of the writ of habeas corpus, nor authorize a military officer to do it. 2. That a military officer has no right to arrest and detain a person not subject to the rules and articles of war, for an offence against the law of the United States, except in aid of the judicial authority, and subject to its control; and if the party be arrested by the military, it is the duty of the officer to deliver him over immediately to the civil authority, to be dealt with according to law....Under the Constitution of the United States, Congress is the only power which can authorize the suspension of the privilege of the writ....

The case, then, is simply this: a military officer, residing in Pennsylvania, issues an order to arrest a citizen of Maryland, upon vague and indefinite charges, without any proof, so far as appears; under this order, his house is entered in the night, he is seized as a prisoner, and conveyed to Fort McHenry, and there kept in close confinement; and when a habeas corpus is served on the commanding officer, requiring him to produce the prisoner before a justice of the Supreme Court, in order that he may examine into the legality of the imprisonment, the answer of the officer, is that he is authorized by the president to suspend the writ of habeas corpus at his discretion, and in the exercise of that discretion, suspends it in this case, and on that ground refuses obedience to the writ.

As the case comes before me, therefore, I understand that the president not only claims the right to suspend the writ of habeas corpus himself, at his discretion, but to delegate that discretionary power to a military officer, and to leave it to him to determine whether he will or will not obey judicial process that may be served upon him. No official notice has been given to the courts of justice, or to the public, by proclamation or otherwise, that the president claimed this power, and had exercised it in the manner stated in the return. And I certainly listened to it with some surprise, for I had supposed it to be one of those points of constitutional law upon which there was no difference of opinion, and that it was admitted on all hands, that the privilege of the writ could not be suspended, except by act of Congress....

[T]he documents before me show, that the military authority in this case has gone far beyond the mere suspension of the privilege of the writ of habeas corpus. It has, by force of arms, thrust aside the judicial authorities and officers to whom the Constitution has confided the power and duty of interpreting and administering the laws, and substituted a military government in its place, to be administered and executed by military officers....I can only say that if the authority which the Constitution has confided to the judiciary department and judicial officers, may thus, upon any pretext or under any circumstances, be usurped by the military power, at its discretion, the people of the United States are no longer living under a government of laws, but every citizen holds life, liberty and property at the will and pleasure of the army officer in whose military district he may happen to be found.

★ ★ ★ ★

JUNE 1861

MON 10 JUN. BIG BETHEL (BETHEL CHURCH)

In one of the first significant Eastern Theater engagements, seven Federal regiments, marching from Fort Monroe, attempted to strike Confederate positions near Big Bethel (also known as Bethel Church), Virginia. However, inexperience, confusion, and poor planning produced little more than a Federal retreat. Of twenty-five hundred Union soldiers engaged (the Confederate commander, Col. John Bankhead Magruder, incorrectly estimated thirty-five hundred Union troops), seventy-six were casualties. Colonel Magruder, in comparison, lost just eight of his twelve hundred men. As is evident from the exuberant tone of Magruder's dispatch, excerpted below, the victory boosted Southern morale. In fact, trophies of the fight were later displayed in Richmond. The work, or earthwork, to which Magruder refers would have been a simple field forti-

View of Bethel Church.

fication. During the Civil War, these were usually berms or trenches dug in a straight line. Normally, they were temporary, but they could become permanent if given time.

SIR: THE ENEMY, THIRTY-FIVE hundred strong, attacked us at our post, and after a very animated conflict of two hours and a half was repulsed at all points and totally muted. Four companies of cavalry are now in hot pursuit toward Newport News. I cannot speak too highly of the devotion of our troops, all of whom did their duty nobly, and whilst it might appear invidious to speak particularly of any regiment or corps where all behaved so well, I am compelled to express my great appreciation of the skill and gallantry of Major Randolph and his howitzer batteries, and Colonel Hill, the officers and men of the North Carolina regiment. As an instance of the latter I will merely mention that a gun under the gallant Captain Brown, of the howitzer battery, having been rendered unfit for service by the breaking of a priming wire in the vent, and not being defended by infantry from the small number we had at our command, Captain Brown threw it over a precipice, and the work was occupied for a moment by the enemy. Captain Bridgers, of the North Carolina regiment, in the most gallant manner retook it and held it until Captain Brown had replaced and put in position another piece, and then defended it with his infantry in the most gallant manner....

There were many acts of personal gallantry, some under my own observation, and others which were reported to me, that I will take occasion to mention in a subsequent communication. At present I expect another attack, and have no time....

I have the honor to be, very respectfully, your obedient servant,
J. Bankhead Magruder,
Colonel, Commanding

TUE
11
JUN.

Uncle Tom's Cabin *author Harriet Beecher Stowe had a son who enlisted early on in one of the Massachusetts volunteer regiments. In the following letter, she recounts to her husband a brief visit she had with their son as his regiment stopped off in Jersey City, New Jersey, en route south. (Stowe*

Harriet Beecher Stowe

was living in Brooklyn at the time.) Her letter makes plain that, at this early stage of the war, such meetings were characterized more by enthusisasm than by heartache.

YESTERDAY NOON HENRY CAME in, saying that the *Commonwealth*, with the First Regiment on board, had just sailed by. Immediately I was of course eager to get to Jersey City to see Fred. Sister Eunice said she would go with me, and in a few minutes she and I were in a carriage, driving towards the Fulton Ferry. Upon reaching Jersey City we found that the boys were dining in the depot, an immense building with many tracks and platforms. It has a great cast-iron gallery just under the roof, apparently placed there with prophetic instinct of these times. There was a crowd of people pressing against the grated doors, which were locked, but through which we could see the soldiers. It was with great difficulty that we were at last permitted to go inside....

When we were in, a vast area of gray caps and blue overcoats were presented. The boys were eating, drinking, smoking, talking, singing, and laughing. Company A was reported to be here, there, and everywhere. At last S. spied Fred in the distance, and went leaping across the tracks towards him. Immediately afterwards a blue-overcoated figure bristling with knapsack and haversack, and looking like an assortment of packages, came rushing towards us.

Fred was overjoyed, you may be sure, and my first impulse was to wipe his face with my handkerchief before I kissed him. He was in high spirits, in spite of the weight of the blue overcoat, knapsack, etc., etc., that he would formerly have declared intolerable for half an hour. I gave him my handkerchief and Eunice gave him hers, with a sheer motherly instinct that is so strong within her, and then we filled his haversack with oranges.

We stayed with Fred about two hours, during which time the gallery was filled with people, cheering and waving their handkerchiefs. Every now and then the band played inspiriting airs, in which the soldiers joined with hearty voices. While some of the companies sang, others were drilled, and all seemed to be having a general jollification. The meal that had been provided was plentiful, and consisted of coffee, lemonade, sandwiches, etc.

MON 17 JUN. BOONVILLE

After turning out Camp Jackson on May 10, Capt. Nathaniel Lyon completed his rout of pro-Southern forces in Missouri with a victory this day at Boonville on the Missouri River. Having already captured Jefferson City, the state capital, on June 15, Lyon followed Missouri's pro-Confederate governor, Claiborne Jackson, to Boonville, where Lyon's seventeen hundred men scattered Jackson's still largely disorganized followers, again forcing the governor to take flight. Lyon's boldness secured the state and kept the Missouri River under Union control. It also resulted in his promotion to brigadier general of volunteers. In his official report, excerpted below, Lyon described the actions at both Jefferson City and Boonville.

Capt. Nathaniel Lyon

THE PROCLAMATION OF Governor Jackson, of this State, on the 12th instant, calling for 50,000 men to war upon the United States, made it necessary for me to move up the river, in order to anticipate the collection of his forces where it appeared likely such collection would be made. I accordingly proceeded on the 13th instant from Saint Louis…and advanced by boats to Jefferson City, where I arrived on the 15th about 2 o'clock P.M., and found the governor had fled and taken his forces to Boonville, where, so far as I could then learn, a large force was gathering. Leaving Colonel

Boernstein at Jefferson City, with three companies of his regiment, I proceeded on the following day (16th) towards this place….

After proceeding about one mile, the enemy was discovered in force. Company B, Second Infantry, on the left, was now supported by Company B, First Missouri Volunteers, Captain Maurice. The enemy, having shelter of a house (owned by Win. M. Adams) and a thicket of wood behind it, held their position for a while, during which time our approach brought us on to high and open ground, and here most of our casualties occurred. Captain Totten's battery here did effective service, and our troops on both flanks steadily advanced. Captain Burke's company, K, First Regiment Missouri Volunteers, now came forward on the left, and engaged the enemy. In falling back the enemy took advantage of sundry points to deliver a fire and continue retreating. This continued till we arrived above their camp, which was situated to our right, near the river, and which about this time was taken possession of by Captain Cole….Considerable camp equipage and about 500 stand of arms of all sorts were taken. About 60 prisoners taken were released upon oath to obey the laws of the General Government and not oppose it during the present civil troubles.

On approaching this city I was met by a deputation of citizens, asking security from plunder from my troops, to which I gave an affirmative response, on condition of no opposition to my entrance and occupying of it. This was promised, so far as in their power, and on reaching the town I required the mayor and city council to accompany my entrance. A part of my command was now quartered in the city, and the remainder returned to the boats, now located opposite the fair grounds, at the lower side of the town. This fair ground had been taken by the State for an arsenal, and a considerable number of old rusty arms and cartridges were found. Our loss consisted of 2 killed, 1 missing, and 9 wounded, two of whom have since died. The loss of the rebel force is not known. The troops of Governor Jackson dispersed, but for the purpose of assembling at Lexington. This assembly, however, did not continue, and was broken up soon after, many persons, I am informed, returning to their homes, and a considerable portion going south, in expectation of meeting re-enforcements from Arkansas. It is certain that Governor Jackson, with an escort, has gone from here in that direction, and most of his military leaders with him: I had intended pursuit soon after the breaking up of the Lexington camp, but have been unavoidably delayed by the trouble of getting up a train here and by continued and heavy rains. I hope to start soon with about 2,400 troops and some artillery, and proceed to Springfield, and there conform to emergencies—as they shall be found to exist.

Including this regiment, 109,000 Missourians fought for the Union cause (40,000 served the Confederacy).

JULY 1861

THU
4
JUL.

Because both sides claimed the proud heritage of the patriots of 1776, the Independence Day holiday was observed with unusual vigor in both North and South. Presiding over a nation that was rapidly turning itself into an armed camp, Abraham Lincoln felt compelled to send a special message to Congress on the causes and nature of the Civil War as he understood them.

HAVING BEEN CONVENED ON AN extraordinary occasion, as authorized by the Constitution, your attention is not called to any ordinary subject of legislation. At the beginning of the present Presidential term, four months ago, the functions of the Federal Government were found to be generally suspended within the several States of South Carolina, Georgia, Alabama, Mississippi, Louisiana, and Florida, excepting only those of the Post Office Department....Finding this condition of things, and believing it to be an imperative duty upon the incoming Executive, to prevent, if possible, the consummation of such an attempt to destroy the Federal Union, a choice of means to that end became indispensable. This choice was made...the policy chosen looked to the exhaustion of all peaceful measures, before a resort to stronger ones....And the issue embraces more than the fate of these United States. It presents to the whole family of man, the question, whether a constitutional republic, or a democracy—a government of the people, by the same people—can, or cannot, maintain its territorial integrity, against its own domestic foes....So viewing the issue, no choice was left but to call out the war power of the Government;

and so to resist force, employed for its destruction, by force, for its preservation.

This report from the Lafayette, Indiana, Daily Courier suggests the fanfare and great eruptions of patriotic sentiment that accompanied many local festivities. According to that newspaper, the first Fourth of July of the war was the most animated anyone in Lafayette could remember. The Ellsworth referred to midway through the article is Col. Elmer Ellsworth, killed during the Union invasion of Alexandria on May 24. Ellsworth also happened to be an officer of Zouaves, which were specially trained (ostensibly elite) regiments distinguished by their colorful uniforms.

THE EIGHTY-FIFTH ANNIVERSARY of American Independence was celebrated in this city yesterday with a degree of enthusiasm unparalleled in the memory of the oldest inhabitant. Before the hour indicated in the published programme for the commencement of the patriotic exercises, the public square and all its approaches presented a dense mass of human beings.

The most careless observer could not fail to be struck with the undue proportion of females in the throng,—a fact no wise remarkable when we reflect that the Battle Ground county has nearly one thousand fighting men in the field. But as the eye surveyed the vast multitude, the towering forms of stalwart men gave ample assurance that the reserve guard of the Grand Army would be equal to any emergency which may yet arise, and that sooner or later this wicked rebellion must

yield to the irresistible power of numbers....A more enthusiastic, and at the same time more orderly demonstration was never witnessed in this city. The published programme was carried out spiritedly and to the letter. Col. Brown, at the head of his gallant command, joined in the parade, and his regiment was everywhere hailed with the waving of handkerchiefs and the plaudits of the multitude. Capt. Cassell, with the Zouaves, won encomiums of which the lamented Ellsworth might have been proud, and the Star City Cavalry, under Dr. Worrall, and the Chauncey Home Guard completed a military pageant worthy of the day and of the occasion. The firemen, although but few in number made a handsome appearance. Dr. A. M. Moore, Chief Marshal of the day, and his efficient aides, deserve honorable mention for the admirable manner in which they conducted the exercises. There was no confusion—everything on the programme, from the rope walking to the oration, passed off decently and in order. Altogether it was a day to be remembered; and whatever may be the future of our unhappy country, the 4th of July, 1861, will be golden with memories to those who participated in the varied enjoyments of the Star City celebration.

However, not everyone was caught up in the martial spirit. In this letter to a Northern friend, historical novelist William Gilmore Simms of South Carolina lamented the current state of affairs and blamed "mob rule" in the North, which he believed precipitated the conflict.

WAR IS HERE THE ONLY IDEA. Every body is drilling and arming. Even I practise with the Colt. I am a dead shot with rifle & double barrel, & can now kill rabbit or squirrel with the pistol. Our women practise, & they will fight, too, like she wolves. Your Yankees are converting our whole people to Unionism. If you ask me about myself, I have only to say that I am sad & sick & suffering....Crops are good—mine never better. We shall make abundance of corn, & the Cotton crop will probably exceed that of last year by 300,000 bales. The seasons have been very favorable. We have been eating at Woodlands, for months, strawberries, green peas, green corn, okra, irish potatoes, snap beans, squashes, radishes, blackberries, June berries, artichokes, &c. &c. My wife sells $2 of butter weekly. Her pocket money. We have milk, butter milk, curds, clabber, spring chickens & eggs in abundance. But we want peace! We are invaded! Every hour widens & deepens the breach between the two sections; and passion is succeeded by Hate, & Hate by Vindictiveness, and if the war continues, there will be no remedy. Your city will be utterly ruined by the Black Republicans who dare not think of peace, and who, if the people once come to their senses, will be torn to pieces. You, perhaps, do not think all this. But you had warning of every syllable a year ago & last summer. The cowardice of your conservatives is the secret of your evil. You have no moral at the North. The mob rules you. If the war is persevered in, it must be a war of extermination. Our people will fight to the last!

THU 11 JUL. *What role should women play in the war? Most people believed that women should sew, cook, nurse, and otherwise care for the exclusively male soldiers. Yet some women found ways to do more. In this letter to Col. Henry Lockwood of the First Delaware Volunteers, Capt. James Green and Lt. E. J. Smithers praise the bravery of one Jane Bowman, a bridge keeper's daughter living near Camp Dare, Maryland, who single-handedly resisted a Confederate attempt (albeit a successful one) to burn her father's bridge.*

SIR: AS PART OF THE COMMAND stationed on the line of the Philadelphia, Wilmington and Baltimore Railroad, we deem it but right and proper to make known to you the heroic conduct of the daughter of Mr. Bowman, the keeper of the bridge at this place, on the night of the burning of the bridge by Trimble and his men. From Mr. Smith, the master carpenter of the road,...we have learned the following particulars:

When the train bearing the bridge-burners had crossed the bridge, and Trimble had drawn his men in line immediately in front of Mr. Bowman's house, the object of their coming was announced in the hearing of Miss Jane by Trimble himself. She pronounced him a coward, and in a loud voice called upon the men, who had been armed by the road and placed there to protect the bridge, to defend it, and when she saw these men throw away their arms, some of them taking to the woods and others hiding within her father's house, she called upon them again not to run, but to stand fast and

In conclusion, permit us to say that such heroism in a young lady as shown in the conduct of Miss Bowman on this occasion has rarely been met with anywhere, and, in our opinion, should not be suffered to go unrewarded.

RICH MOUNTAIN

Soon after taking command of the newly formed Department of the Ohio in early May, Maj. Gen. George B. McClellan ordered three columns of Federal troops into western Virginia to protect the Baltimore & Ohio Railroad and also safeguard the many Union sympathizers living there. In early July, McClellan arrayed his army against the Confederate positions near Rich Mountain, which were under the command of Lt. Col. John Pegram. On July 11, McClellan sent two thousand of his men, led by Brig. Gen. William S. Rosecrans, along animal trails and mountain paths to the Confederate rear. It was assumed that, when Rosecrans attacked from the rear, the remainder of McClellan's forces would join in from the front. However, when Rosecrans attacked, McClellan held back—and when Rosecrans defeated the Confederates (forcing 555 of Pegram's 1,300 men to surrender), McClellan claimed the credit. Below is McClellan's self-promoting telegram to the War Department.

A group of patriotic women in Philadelphia sew a regimental flag.

show themselves to be men. At this time, seeing one of the pistols lying upon the floor of the porch, which had been thrown away by one of the bridge-guards, she picked it up and ran with it. Meeting Mr. Smith she gave it to him, saying at the same time, "Use it; if you will not, I will."

Another evidence of the wonderful courage and presence of mind of Miss Jane was shown in her anxiety for the safety of one of the men employed by her father to assist him in taking care of the bridge. This man was on the draw at the time the firing of the bridge commenced. Miss Jane…promptly called upon her father, or some one, to go for him in a boat, saying, "If no one else will go, I will."

HAVE MET WITH COMPLETE success; captured the enemy's entire camp, guns, tents, wagons, etc. Many prisoners, among whom several officers. Enemy's loss severe, ours very small. No officers lost on our side. I turned the position. All well.

A railroad bridge crosses the Potomac River at Harpers Ferry in western Virginia.

In this diary excerpt, Lt. Col. John Beatty of the Third Ohio Volunteers described the hesitancy to attack that would later infuriate President Lincoln and define McClellan's career.

BETWEEN TWO AND THREE o'clock we heard shots in the rear of the fortifications; then volleys of musketry and the roar of artillery. Every man sprang to his feet, assured that the moment for making the attack had arrived. General McClellan and staff came galloping up, and a thousand faces turned to hear the order to advance; but no order was given. The General halted a few paces from our line, and sat on his horse listening to the guns, apparently in doubt as to what to do; and as he sat there with indecision stamped on every line of his countenance, the battle grew fiercer in the enemy's rear. Every volley could be heard distinctly. There would occasionally be a lull for a moment, and the uproar would break out again with increased violence. If the enemy is too strong for us to attack, what must be the fate of Rosecrans' four regiments, cut off from us, and struggling against such odds?

FRI 12 JUL. *Ulysses S. Grant did not begin the war in a position of authority—or even with a position in the army. In fact, prior to the Civil War, Grant failed at nearly every enterprise he attempted. After graduating from West Point in 1843 and serving with distinction in the Mexican War, he left the military in 1854, largely because of his dissatisfaction with life in the peacetime army. He then failed at farming and later at real estate before finally ending up a clerk in his father's leather goods store in Galena, Illinois. To make ends meet, he chopped firewood. When the Civil War began, he drilled troops in Galena until Illinois governor Richard Yates made him colonel of the Twenty-first Illinois Volunteer Infantry Regiment. This was a generous, face-saving gesture on Yates's part, because the War Department never responded to Grant's request for a recommission. Grant's regiment first saw action in Florida, Missouri, where it was detailed to relieve Union troops besieged by Confederates under Col. Thomas Harris. As Grant recounted in his memoirs, despite his previous combat experience, he felt unsure and unready, a far cry from the grimly determined military leader who would win the Civil War.*

My sensations as we approached what I supposed might be "a field of battle" were anything but agreeable. I had been in all the engagements in Mexico that it was possible for one person to be in; but not in command. If some one else had been colonel and I had been lieutenant-colonel I do not think I would have felt any trepidation....

As we approached the brow of the hill from which it was expected we could see Harris' camp, and possibly find his men ready formed to meet us, my heart kept getting higher and higher until it felt to me as though it was in my throat. I would have given anything then to have been back in Illinois, but I had not the moral courage to halt and consider what to do; I kept right on. When we reached a point from which the valley below was in full view I halted. The place where Harris had been encamped a few days before was still there and the marks of a recent encampment were plainly visible, but the troops were gone. My heart resumed its place. It occurred to me at once that Harris had been as much afraid of me as I had been of him. This was a view of the question I had never taken before; but it was one I never forgot afterwards. From that event until the close of the war, I never experienced trepidation upon confronting an enemy, though I always felt more or less anxiety. I never forgot that he had as much reason to fear my forces as I had his. The lesson was valuable.

SAT 13 JUL. CORRICK'S FORD

After scattering Pegram's men (those that Rosecrans didn't capture) on July 11, McClellan turned his attention to the main Rebel force in the area: the four thousand troops under Brig. Gen. Robert S. Garnett at Laurel Hill (to the north of Rich Mountain). On this date, McClellan's troops engaged the rear guard of Garnett's retreating army at Corrick's Ford. In the skirmish, fifty Confederate soldiers were wounded and twenty killed—most notably Garnett, who became the first general of either side to die in battle. McClellan's victory secured the east-west rail lines of the B&O as well as most of western

Brig. Gen. Ulysses S. Grant

Virginia, but his failure to pursue the bulk of Garnett's forces allowed the vulnerable Rebels to escape. Two days after the engagement, in a letter to Gen.-in-Chief Winfield Scott, McClellan grandly updated his initial telegraphed record of the battle.

AFTER CLOSING MY LETTER LAST night a courier arrived with the news that the troops I had sent in pursuit of Garnett had caught him, routed his army, captured his baggage, one gun, taken several prisoners, and that Garnett himself lay dead on the field of battle! Such is the fate of traitors: one of their leaders a prisoner, the other killed; their armies annihilated, their cause crushed in this region.

WED
17
JUL.

Some women were so moved by their patriotism that they masqueraded as men in order to enlist as soldiers. Because she left such a long and detailed paper trail for historians to follow, Sarah Emma Edmonds of New Brunswick, Canada, has become the most famous of these transgendered soldiers. Under the alias Franklin Thompson, Edmonds served for two years as a private in the Second Michigan Infantry. In this extract from her 1864 memoir, she reflects just as any male soldier might on her regiment's preparations for the coming battle at Bull Run.

THE 17TH OF JULY DAWNED bright and clear, and everything being in readiness, the Army of the Potomac took up its line of march for Manassas. In gay spirits the army moved forward, the air resounding with the music of the regimental bands, and patriotic songs of the soldiers. No gloomy forebodings seemed to damp the spirits of the men, for a moment, but "On to Richmond" was echoed and re-echoed, as that vast army moved rapidly over the country. I felt strangely out of harmony with the wild, joyous spirit which pervaded the troops. As I rode slowly along, watching those long lines of bayonets as they gleamed and flashed in the sunlight, I thought that many, very many, of those enthusiastic men who appeared so eager to meet the enemy, would never return to relate the success or defeat of that splendid army. Even if victory should perch upon their banners, and I had no doubt it would, yet many noble lives must be sacrificed ere it could be obtained.

THU
18
JUL.

BLACKBURN'S FORD

From the moment the war began, people on both sides expected the principal fighting to be for control of one or both of the national capitals. With Washington, D.C., and Richmond, Virginia, a scant hundred miles apart, the territory between them was destined to be the scene of intense conflict. After Union forces secured a buffer zone around Washington by taking Alexandria (and with Northern newspapers urging an attack), Federal military planners began considering various routes to Richmond. Meanwhile, the Confederates took up defensive positions in northern Virginia near the critical railroad junc-

This photograph of Blackburn's Ford was taken shortly after Second Bull Run in August 1862.

support of P. G. T. Beauregard's army at Manassas equalized the strength of the combatants and imperiled the entire Union plan. Even so, as the recollections of Edward P. Alexander (later Lee's chief of artillery) suggest, the Confederates had problems of their own that nearly kept Johnston out of the battle. It is worth noting that the phrase "if practicable," to which Alexander makes special reference, is the same phrase used by Robert E. Lee at Gettysburg, when he instructed Richard Ewell to capture the high ground outside town on the first day of the battle. Much as Johnston did, Ewell took the words to mean "at your discretion" rather than as a direct order. In this earlier instance, the Confederates nearly lost First Bull Run because Johnston's forces arrived late. Two years later, they did lose at Gettysburg, in part because of Ewell's failure to take Cemetery Ridge.

tion at Manassas. The campaign that led to the first battle of Bull Run (known to the South as Manassas) began on July 16, when Union commander Irvin McDowell began moving his Army of Virginia toward Centerville. On this day, advance units engaged at Blackburn's Ford, resulting in 68 Confederate and 101 Federal casualties amid fighting marked by ineptitude, inexperience, and indecision on both sides. The Confederates proclaimed the skirmish a victory, although McDowell's forces continued moving toward Manassas. More importantly, Union Brig. Gen. Robert Patterson had meanwhile failed to hold the forces of Confederate Brig. Gen. Joseph E. Johnston at Winchester in the Shenandoah Valley. The subsequent arrival of Johnston's men in

ABOUT NOON, JULY 16, McDowell put his army in motion. There were ten brigades in four divisions, comprising about 30,000 men, with 49 guns....The four divisions moved by different roads, converging toward our advanced positions about Fairfax. They made on the first day only short marches of six or eight miles, going into camp far outside of our picket lines, so as not to divulge the movement. This was so well managed that, although rumors reached the Confederates, yet nothing was known until next morning. Then our advanced posts were driven in and a few of our pickets were captured. At this moment Johnston's army should have been ready to march to Beauregard over roads previ-

Brig. Gen. Irvin McDowell

ously selected and reconnoitered. The men should have been kept for days encamped where they could stretch out on the proper roads. For many contingencies beset all marches, and preparation can save hours big with fate.

The whole day of the 17th was lost to the Confederates by the news having to go to the President. Beauregard, sometime during the day, telegraphed [Jefferson Davis] as follows—

Manassas, July 17, 1861
The enemy has assailed my outposts in heavy force, I have fallen back on the line of Bull Run, and will make a stand at Mitchell's Ford. If his force is overwhelming, I shall retire to the Rappahannock railroad bridge, saving my command for defense there, and for future operations. Please inform Johnston of this, via Staunton [Virginia], and also Holmes. Send forward any

reinforcements at the earliest possible moment, and by every possible means. —P. G. T. Beauregard

Apparently after some deliberation, the Executive acted, for about 1 A.M. on July 18, Johnston in Winchester received a telegram. It is a worth study as a model not to be followed in such cases. It was as follows—

Richmond, July 17, 1861
Gen. Beauregard is attacked. To strike the enemy a decisive blow all of your effective force will be needed. If practicable, make the movement, by sending your sick and baggage to Culpepper C. H. [Court House] either by railroad or by Warrenton. In all arrangements exercise your discretion.—S. Cooper, Adj't. and Ins. General.

The words "if practicable" are always of such doubtful interpretation that they should be excluded from all important orders. They leave matters in doubt. Every order should be distinctly either the one thing or the other.

FRI 19 JUL. *Soon after Fort Sumter, people north and south began wondering how their relationships with friends, relatives, and business associates in the opposite section would be affected by the hostilities. On this date, the* **Charleston Daily Courier** *published a lengthy column entitled "Intercourse in War—The Duties of Citizens," which advised a complete break with all persons in the North, regardless of ties of blood or affection.*

Brig. Gen. P. G. T. Beauregard

IT IS VERY DIFFICULT FOR THOSE who have grown up in a state of peace, interrupted in this generation by only two short wars, with foreign nations, to realize the momentous and extensive consequences which follow from a state of war. And it is especially difficult, and seemingly almost impossible, for our people, hitherto bound to the citizens of the United States by such close social and business ties, to realize the absolute sundering of those ties, which necessarily follows a war between the two countries.

War, however, is not a matter between Governments in their political character merely; it affects every citizen of both countries. As soon as the Government, which is the acknowledged agent of the public will, has declared war, it is a war between all the individuals of the one and all the individuals of which the other nation is composed, irrespective of the ties of blood, and of social, political or business affinities.

It follows from this universal hostility, which is the necessary incident of war, not only that the Government has a right to deal with the persons and property of the enemy which shall fall into its power, in such a manner as it shall deem best for the interest of the whole…but also that all relations, other than those of hostility, between the subjects of the belligerent countries, must entirely cease.

Judith McGuire, whose May 10 diary entry lamented the breaking up of her beloved Alexandria society, abandoned her home when Union troops occupied the city on May 24. Seeking refuge, she traveled south to the home of a friend; fatefully, that friend lived in Manassas. The onset of First Bull Run is almost palpable in the lines of McGuire's diary entry for this day.

THIS DAY IS PERHAPS THE MOST anxious of my life. It is believed that a battle is going on at or near Manassas. Our large household is in a state of feverish anxiety; but we cannot talk of it. Some sit still, and are more quiet than usual; others are trying to employ themselves. N. is reading aloud, trying to interest herself and others; but we are all alike anxious, which is betrayed by the restless eye and sad countenance. Yesterday evening we were startled by the sound of myriads of horses, wheels, and men on the turnpike.

We soon found the whole of General Johnston's army was passing by, on its way to join Beauregard, below the mountain. They were passing here from about four in the afternoon until a late hour in the night. After midnight the heavy army wagons were lumbering by, and we ever and anon heard the tap of the drum. We did not retire until all was still, and then none of us slept.

McDowell's headquarters outside Manassas.

SUN 21 JUL. FIRST BULL RUN (FIRST MANASSAS)

In the early morning, after several days of maneuvering, thirty-seven thousand Union troops engaged thirty-five thousand Confederates in the first large-scale battle of the war. At nine o'clock, Maj. Gen. Irvin McDowell led thirteen thousand Federals across Bull Run creek. This force scored several quick tactical victories, driving Rebel defenders across the fields and low hills north of the town of Manassas, but the Confederates eventually managed to turn the Union line—and what began as an orderly Union retreat soon turned into a full-scale rout, with terrified, inexperienced troops running headlong into bewildered civilians (including many congressmen) who had ridden out for the day from Washington. A panicked swarm of wagons, artillery pieces, horses, and men quickly choked the few fords and bridges leading back to the Union camp at Centerville, but the Confederates were simply too exhausted and inexperienced to mount much of a pursuit. While losses were modest in comparison to what would follow, they were nevertheless at the time considered extremely heavy: 2,896 Federal and 1,982 Confederate casualties. Although the victory boosted Southern morale, the major outcome was the realization, on both sides, that the war would not be shortly concluded. Union artillery chief Maj. William F. Barry described some of the action in his report, excerpted below.

THE RHODE ISLAND BATTERY came first upon the ground, and took up, at a gallop, the position assigned it. It was immediately exposed to a sharp fire from the enemy's skirmishers and infantry posted on the declivity of the hill and in the valley in its immediate front, and to a well-sustained fire of shot and shell from the enemy's batteries posted behind the crest of the range of hills about one thousand yards distant. This battery sustained in a very gallant manner the whole force of this fire for nearly half an hour, when the howitzers of the Seventy-first New York Militia came up, and went into battery on its left....

...I received an order from General McDowell to advance two batteries to an eminence specially designated by him, about eight hundred yards in front of the line previously occupied by our artillery, and very near the position first occupied by the enemy's batteries....We were soon upon the ground designated, and the two batteries at once opened a very effective fire upon the enemy's left.

The new position had scarcely been occupied when a troop of the enemy's cavalry, debouching from a piece of woods close upon our right flank, charged down upon the New York Eleventh. The Zouaves, catching sight of the cavalry a few moments before

Federal cavalry at Sudley Ford on Bull Run.

they were upon them, broke ranks to such a degree that the cavalry dashed through without doing them much harm. The Zouaves gave them a scattering fire as they passed, which emptied five saddles and killed three horses. A few minutes afterwards a regiment of the enemy's infantry, covered by a high fence, presented itself in line on the left and front of the two batteries at not more than sixty or seventy yards' distance, and delivered a volley full upon the batteries and their supports. Lieutenant Ramsay, First Artillery, was killed, and Captain

A destroyed bridge on the Manassas battlefield.

Mathew Brady took this photograph of Bull Run not long after the first battle there.

Ricketts, First Artillery, was wounded, and a number of men and horses were killed or disabled by this close and well-directed volley. The Eleventh and Fourteenth Regiments instantly broke and fled in confusion to the rear, and in spite of the repeated and earnest efforts of Colonel Heintzelman with the latter, and myself with the former, refused to rally and return to the support of the batteries. The enemy, seeing the guns thus abandoned by their supports, rushed upon them, and driving off the cannoneers, who, with their officers, stood bravely at their posts

until the last moment, captured them, ten in number.

Many of the civilian spectators at Bull Run had considered the impending battle something of an entertainment and therefore brought along picnic baskets to appease their appetites as the fighting unfolded. The flight of the Union troops, however, unpleasantly interrupted their lunches. Here, Ohio congressman Albert Riddle describes the the wild-eyed terror of the routed Federals.

WE CALLED TO THEM... implored them to stand. We called them cowards, denounced them in the most offensive terms, put out our heavy revolvers and threatened to shoot them, but all in vain; a cruel, crazy, mad, hopeless panic possessed them, and communicated to everybody about in front and rear. The heat was awful, although it was now about six; the men were exhausted—their mouths gaped, their lips cracked and blackened with the powder of the cartridges they had bitten off in the battle, their eyes staring in frenzy; no mortal ever saw such a mass of ghastly wretches.

A crucial event in the battle was the determined stand of Confederate Brig. Gen. Thomas J. Jackson atop Henry House Hill. In fact, it was the sight of Jackson holding this line that prompted Brig. Gen. Bernard Bee to cry out famously, "Look, there is Jackson with his Virginians, standing like a stone wall!" The excerpt below from Jackson's battle report suggests that the general's inspiration may have come in part from his devout belief that the Almighty was on the side of the Confederates.

GENERAL BEE, WITH HIS RALLIED troops, soon marched to my support and as re-enforcements continued to arrive General Beauregard posted them so as to strengthen the flanks of my brigade. The enemy not being able to force our lines by a direct fire of artillery, inclined part of his batteries to the right, so as to obtain an oblique fire; but in doing so exposed his pieces to a more destructive

Brig. Gen. Thomas J. "Stonewall" Jackson

fire from our artillery, and one of his batteries was thrown so near to Colonel Cummings that it fell into his hands in consequence of his having made a gallant charge on it with his regiment; but owing to a destructive small-arm fire from the enemy he was forced to abandon it. At 3.30 P.M. the advance of the enemy having reached a position which called for the use of the bayonet, I gave the command for the charge of the more than brave Fourth and Twenty-seventh, and, under commanders worthy of such regiments, they, in the order in which they were posted, rushed forward obliquely to the left of our batteries, and through the blessing of God, who gave us the victory, pierced the enemy's center, and by co-operating with the victorious Fifth and other forces soon placed the field essentially in our possession.

Maj. Gen. George B. McClellan

SAT 27 JUL. McCLELLAN TAKES CHARGE

On this date, President Lincoln made George B. McClellan, promoted to major general just two months earlier, the new commander of the Division of the Potomac, replacing Major General McDowell. In this letter to his wife, written the same day, McClellan states the belief, which he maintained throughout his command, that he was destined to save the Republic.

I HAVE BEEN ASSIGNED TO THE command of a Division—composed of Depts of N.E. Va (that under McDowell) & that of Washington (now under Mansfield)—neither of them like it much—especially Mansfield, but I think they must ere long become accustomed to it, as there is no help for it....

I find myself in a strange & new position here—Presdt, Cabinet, Genl Scott & all deferring to me—by some strange operation of magic I seem to have become *the* power of the land. I almost think that were I to win some small success now I could become Dictator or anything else that might please me— *therefore* I *won't* be Dictator. Admirable self denial! I see already the main causes of our recent failure [at Bull Run]—I am sure that I can remedy these & am confident that I can lead these armies of men to victory once more.

WED 31 JUL.

This article from the Richmond Enquirer *complained of the Unionist sympathies being exhibited by Elizabeth Van Lew and her mother. However, even the* Enquirer *didn't suspect that Van Lew was in fact a Union spy who would later become famous for her role in leading Richmond's Unionist resistance.*

TWO LADIES, MOTHER AND daughter, living on Church Hill, have lately attracted public notice by their assiduous attentions to the Yankee prisoners confined in this City. Whilst every true woman in this community has been busy making articles of comfort or necessity for our troops, or administering to the wants of the many hundreds of sick, who, far from their homes, which they left to defend our soil, are fit subjects for our sympathy, these two women have been expending their opulent means in aiding and giving comfort to the miscreants who have invaded our sacred soil, bent on raping and murder, the desolation of our homes and sacred places, and the ruin and dishonour of our families.

Out upon all pretexts of humanity! The largest human charity can find ample scope in kindness and attention to our own poor fellows, who have been stricken down while battling for our country and our rights. The Yankee wounded have been put under charge of competent surgeons and provided with good nurses. This is more than they deserve and have any right to expect, and the course of these two females in providing them with delicacies, buying them books, stationery and paper, cannot but be regarded as an evidence of sympathy amounting to an endorsement of the cause and conduct of these Northern Vandals.

AUGUST 1861

THU 1 AUG. BAYLOR CLAIMS NEW MEXICO

On July 26, an invasion force of 250 Texans led by Lt. Col. John R. Baylor attacked Fort Fillmore in the New Mexico Territory. Despite the fact that his Federals outnumbered the attackers by two to one, Maj. Isaac Lynde decided to abandon his post. The next day, he surrendered his force to the pursuing Baylor without firing a shot. Following this success, Baylor claimed the entire New Mexico Territory (including Arizona) for the Confederacy. In the following report, sent from his headquarters at Fort Bliss on August 14, Baylor described his recent efforts to round up the remaining Union soldiers and establish a Confederate administration in the territory.

SIR: I REGRET TO REPORT THAT the United States troops, consisting of four companies—two of cavalry and two infantry—that were en route from Fort Buchanan to Fort Fillmore, succeeded by ignominious flight in making their escape. On the night of the 7th instant an express reached them from Fort Craig, when they immediately burned all their transportation and supplies, and fled in great disorder and haste, saving nothing but their arms and animals.

By express from Fort Stanton I learned that upon the receipt of the news that Major Lynde had surrendered, Colonel Roberts, in command of that post, fled in haste, leaving the post on fire, which was extinguished by a storm of rain. Most of the commissary and quartermaster's supplies were saved and a battery. On the receipt of this intelligence I sent Captain Walker's company to occupy Stanton, and will send a train for the commissary and quartermaster's stores, leaving only two months' supply for the troops now there. The families there were at the mercy of Indians and Mexicans, and I thought it proper to garrison the post, at least until I could learn the wishes of the Government. I have also established a Provisional Government for the Territory of Arizona, and made the appointments to fill the offices necessary to enforce the laws. I have proclaimed myself the governor, have authorized the raising of four companies to hold the Territory and afford protection to the citizens, and extended the limits of the Territory to the parallel of 36° 30' thence due west to the Colorado, and down that stream to its mouth.

The vast mineral resources of Arizona, in addition to its affording an outlet to the Pacific, make its acquisition a matter of some importance to our Government, and now that I have taken possession of the Territory, I trust a force sufficient to occupy and hold it will be sent by the Government, under some competent man.

SUN
4
AUG. *The great intellectuals of the age were far from immune to the national preoccupation with the Civil War. In this letter to James Eliot Cabot, Ralph Waldo Emerson discussed his sense of the conflict's deeper meanings. Emerson's belief that the war offered America a chance to redeem itself for the sin of slavery would later be* *echoed in Lincoln's second inaugural address.*

THE WAR, THOUGH FROM SUCH despicable beginnings, has assumed such huge proportions that it threatens to engulf us all—no preoccupation can exclude, & no hermitage hide us. And yet, gulf as it is, the war with its defeats & uncertainties is immensely better than what we lately called the integrity of the Republic, as amputation is better than cancer. I think we are all agreed in this, and find it out by wondering why we are so pleased, though so beaten & so poor. No matter how low down, if not in false position. If the abundance of heaven only sends us a fair share of light & conscience, we shall redeem America for all its sinful years since the century began. At first sight, it looked only like a war of manners, showing that the southerner

Ralph Waldo Emerson

who owes to climate & slavery his suave, cool, & picturesque manners, is so impatient of ours, that he must fight us off.

MON 5 AUG. *The rout of the Federal army at First Bull Run was front-page news in England, where Henry Brooks Adams (the grandson and great-grandson of U.S. presidents) was living at the time. In this letter from London to his brother, a Union officer, Adams detailed the humiliation that such news occasioned for Northerners living abroad.*

AFTER STUDYING OVER THE accounts of the battle and reading Russell's letter to the *Times,* I hardly know whether to laugh or cry. Of all the ridiculous battles there ever were fought, this seems to me the most so. To a foreigner or to any one not interested in it, the account must be laughable in the extreme. But the disgrace is frightful. The exposé of the condition of our army is not calculated to do us anything but the most unmixed harm here, though it might have the good effect at home of causing these evils to be corrected. If this happens again, farewell to our country for many a day. Bull's Run will be a byword of ridicule for all time. Our honor will be utterly gone. But yesterday we might have stood against the world. Now none so base to do us reverence. Let us stop our bragging now and henceforward. Throw Bull's Run in the teeth of any man who dares to talk large. In spite of my mortification, I could not help howling with laughter over a part of Russell's letter. Such a battle of heels. Such a bloodless, ridiculous race for dis-

Henry Adams's brother, Charles Francis Adams Jr. (center), flanked by two fellow Union officers.

grace, history does not record. Unpursued, untouched, without once having even crossed bayonets with the enemy, we have run and saved our precious carcasses from a danger that does not exist. Our flag, what has become of it? Who will respect it? What can we ever say for it after this?

My determination to come home is only increased by this disgrace. I cannot stay here now to stand the taunts of everyone without being able to say a word in defence. Unless I hear from you at once, I shall write myself to Gov. Andrew and to Mr. Dana and to everyone else I can think of, and raise Heaven and earth to get a commission. If we must be beaten, and it looks now as though that must ultimately be the case, I want to do all I can not to be included among those who ran away.

TUE 6 AUG. THE FIRST CONFISCATION ACT

This day President Lincoln reluctantly signed a bill legalizing the confiscation of Confederate property used to further the rebellion. The difficulty that Lincoln had in signing the new law was similar to that he faced April 19 in declaring a blockade of the Confederate coast: Under international law, nations could confiscate the property only of a belligerent foreign powers. Therefore, in signing this bill, Lincoln was again, one could argue, granting de facto recognition to the Confederacy. The Confiscation Act also aroused controversy among abolitionists on the one

hand and, on the other, those in the North who did not want to make slavery the principal issue of the war. Because the Confederacy considered slaves property, under the new law Rebel-owned slaves employed in the war effort could be confiscated and freed. The act can thus be seen as a precursor of the Emancipation Proclamation.

AN ACT TO CONFISCATE PROPERTY USED FOR INSURRECTIONARY PURPOSES.

Be it enacted by the Senate and House of Representatives of the United States of America in Congress assembled, That if, during the present or any future insurrection against the Government of the United States, after the President of the United States shall have declared, by proclamation, that the laws of the United States are opposed, and the execution thereof obstructed, by combinations too powerful to be suppressed by the ordinary course of judicial proceedings, or by the power vested in the marshals by law, any person or persons, his, her, or their agent, attorney, or employé, shall purchase or acquire, sell or give, any property of whatsoever kind or description, with intent to use or employ the same, or suffer the same to be used or employed, in aiding, abetting, or promoting such insurrection or resistance to the laws, or any person or persons engaged therein; or if any person or persons, being the owner or owners of any such property, shall knowingly use or employ, or consent to the use or employment of the same as aforesaid, all such property is hereby declared to be lawful subject of prize and capture wherever found; and it shall be the duty of the

President of the United States to cause the same to be seized, confiscated, and condemned....And be it further enacted, That whenever hereafter, during the present insurrection against the Government of the United States, any person claimed to be held to labor or service under the law of any State shall be required or permitted by the person to whom such labor or service is claimed to be due, or by the lawful agent of such person, to take up arms against the United States, or shall be required or permitted by the person to whom such labor or service is claimed to be due, or his lawful agent, to work or to be employed in or upon any fort, navy yard, dock, armory, ship, entrenchment, or in any military or naval service whatsoever, against the Government and lawful authority of the United States, then, and in every such case, the person to whom such labor or service is claimed to be due shall forfeit his claim to such labor, any law of the State or of the United States to the contrary notwithstanding. And whenever thereafter the person claiming such labor or service shall seek to enforce his claim, it shall be a full and sufficient answer to such claim that the person whose service or labor is claimed had been employed in hostile service against the Government of the United States, contrary to the provisions of this act.

SAT 10 AUG. WILSON'S CREEK

Nathaniel Lyon, promoted to brigadier general following his successes at St. Louis on May 10 and Boonville on June 17, committed his fifty-four hundred Federals to the first major battle of the Trans-Mississippi West when he decided to meet the attack of eleven thousand Confederates at Wilson's Creek, outside Springfield. His decision was fateful. During the second assault of the Rebel forces under Benjamin McCulloch and Sterling Price, Lyon was killed while trying to rally his troops. Thus ended a career that had promised much for the Union cause. Lyon's death also resulted in a Federal retreat that left vulnerable to the Confederates the southwestern corner of Missouri. The Union lost 1,317 men, nearly one-quarter of its force, while the Rebels took 1,230 casualties. Never again would a battle in Missouri be so hard fought; yet the Confederate victory ensured that the Rebels, though unable to hold the state, would maintain a presence there for the duration (mostly through a guerrilla campaign). In his official report, Capt. Frederick Steele (who would later, as a major general, lead the Union's 1863 conquest of Arkansas) described the early stages of the action. The grape to which Steele refers is grapeshot, or small iron balls fired by cannon for antipersonnel purposes. Similarly, canister (which generally replaced grapeshot after 1863) refers to cylindrical tin cases containing cast-iron balls (similar to grape) that were used by artillery in close-range firing.

 AFTER A HEAVY FIRING ON BOTH sides...without any apparent advantage on either side, the contest ceased for a short time, as if by mutual consent.

An unknown artist painted this 1861 oil-on-canvas recreation of the death of Lyon at Wilson's Creek.

We were opposed to vastly superior numbers, and many of our men were killed and wounded, so that I did not deem it discreet to charge upon the enemy without support, although Captain Gilbert suggested it.

During this suspension of hostilities, I received orders from Major Sturgis to send a company of skirmishers on the brow of the hill to our left and front. Lieutenant Lothrop went in command of this company, but was met with such a galling fire from the enemy that he was obliged to retire—all of which service he performed with coolness and intrepidity. Lieutenant Lothrop's retreat was followed up by a vigorous attack from the enemy upon us, as well as upon Totten's battery on our left and rear. The enemy had a field piece established under the crest of the hill to our left and front, which threw grape with spitefulness, and occasionally a shell, with more moral effect than damage to us. This piece was now re-enforced by one or two pieces of the same character, all of which threw an incessant shower of missiles at us; but my men were ordered to stoop, and very few took effect upon us. It was now evident that the enemy intended to take Totten's battery, as a strong column of infantry was advancing upon it. Totten mowed them down with canister in front, and our infantry poured a murderous fire into their flanks, which compelled them to a hasty retreat. The enemy had failed in all his endeavors to dislodge us from our position, which I conceived to be the strategic point of the battlefield, and was determined to hold it at all hazards.

MON 12 AUG. *Raids by hostile Native Americans presented a problem for Confederate troops in Texas throughout the war—much as they had for the Union troops the Southerners displaced. In this dispatch written after another bloody skirmish with Mescalero Apaches, Lt. Col. John Baylor, commanding Fort Bliss, begged Richmond for some—any—reinforcements. Because of this ongoing problem, many Texans who would otherwise have been sent east were left behind to garrison the frontier.*

SIR: I REGRET TO INFORM YOU that Lieutenant Mays, with a party of 14 men from Fort Davis, went in pursuit of Indians and attacked a village of Apaches, and after a desperate fight were all killed except a Mexican, who came in, bringing the intelligence. Lieutenant White, in command of that post, sent out a detachment to ascertain if any were left, but found nothing but the hats, boots, and a number of horses that had been killed, besides several bodies of men, who were recognized as men of Lieutenant Mays' party.

I would urge the importance of more men being sent to me, as I can't hold the United States troops in check and operate against the Indians with the limited number of men under my command.

Very respectfully,
John R. Baylor, Lieut. Col.,
Comdg. Second Mounted Rifles,
C.S. Army

FRI 23 AUG. *One of the most famous spies for the Confederacy was Rose O'Neal Greenhow. For many years a*

Rose O'Neal Greenhow with her daughter.

socialite in Washington, she knew most of the powerful men in the capital, and, after the war began, she turned many of those acquaintanceships into useful sources of information. For example, historians in her own time and since have given Greenhow credit for providing Gen. P. G. T. Beauregard with the data on Union troop movements that gave the Confederates an important advantage at First Bull Run. In this excerpt from her 1863 memoir, Greenhow describes her capture by Federal authorities.

ON FRIDAY, AUGUST 23RD, IN Washington City...I was made a prisoner in my own house....My blood boils when I think of it....For several weeks I had been followed, and my house watched, by...the detective police....[That day,] on returning from a promenade, I was arrested by two men, one in citizen's dress, and the other in the fatigue dress of an officer of the United States Army. This latter was called Major Allen, and was the chief of the detective police of the city… and before I could open the door, the two men…rapidly ascended also, and asked, with some confusion of manner, "Is this Mrs. Greenhow?" I answered, "Yes."… [T]hen both stationed themselves upon either side of me, and followed into the house.…I knew that the fate of some of the best and bravest belonging to our cause hung upon my own coolness and courage.

By this [time] the house had become filled with men; who also surrounded it outside, like bees from a hive.…An indiscriminate search now commenced throughout my house. Men rushed with frantic haste into my chamber, into every sanctuary. My beds, drawers, and wardrobes were all upturned; soiled clothes were pounced upon with avidity, and mercilessly exposed; papers that had not seen the light for years were dragged forth. My library was taken possession of, and every scrap of paper, every idle line was seized; even the torn fragments in the grates or other receptacles were carefully gathered together by these latter-day Lincoln resurrectionists.…

I was a keen observer of their clumsy activity, and resolved to test the truth of the old saying that *"the devil is no match for a clever woman!"*…so, feigning the pretext of a change of dress…I was allowed to go to my chamber, and then resolved to accomplish the destruction of some important papers which I had in my pocket, even at the expense of life. (The papers were my cipher, with which I had corresponded with my friends at Manassas, and others of equal importance.) Happily I succeeded without such a fearful sacrifice.

TUE 27 AUG. OPERATIONS BEGIN AGAINST HATTERAS

On August 26, a flotilla of warships and transports left Hampton Roads bound for the Outer Banks of North Carolina. The object of this joint army-navy expedition, totaling eight ships and nine hundred men, was the seizure of two exposed Confederate forts, Clark and Hatteras, from which the efforts of the blockading Union fleet could be supported. Pvt. Erhard Futterer, a German immigrant serving with Company B of the Twentieth New York Infantry (known as the United Turner Rifles), described his experiences in an autobiography entitled Der Turner Soldat. *Here he writes vividly of the harrowing landing operation. The hulks to which Futterer makes reference were ships that could not sail under their own power (we might call them barges today); the surf boats were rowboats launched from larger ships, able to carry a fair number of men.*

DURING THE NIGHT, THE SEA became quite rough, rough enough to make many troops seasick but not rough enough to do damage to the hulks or small ships. At 9:30 A.M., on August 27, we sighted the Hatteras lighthouse. By afternoon, we anchored off the inlet, lowered our surf boats into the water, and tied them to the hulks....At daybreak, on August 28, the sailors made ready for the bombardment and we boarded our landing craft. At 10:30 A.M., the warships opened fire following Stringham's plan. The shore batteries returned the fire; but, even with elevation for maximum distance, they could not reach our ships...at one point in the attack, the smoke was so dense that the gunners were unable to see the forts. The Rebels were shocked as timber and sand were sucked into the air and splashed down again to the ground....

We were halfway to the beach, when the wind shifted to the East, and our situation became more dangerous. Waves broke over the sides of the hulks and drenched us. The cannons, lashed to the sides, almost broke loose. If the ropes had split, we would have been crushed! As it was, several of our men suffered cuts and bruises....

Once we were ashore our real troubles began. We were wet to our shoulders, we had wet ammunition, we had no provisions, and we were informed that there would be no reinforcements. Fortunately, the *Harriet Lane* and the *Monticello* were nearby at sea and Colonel Weber assured us that their guns had the range to protect us until our ammunition dried and the artillery unit could become operational.

WED 28 AUG. SURRENDER OF FORT HATTERAS

The two Outer Banks forts were well protected from invasion by land, but their position, jutting out into the Atlantic, made them vulnerable to Union naval assault. Facing a steady shelling from the Union's shipboard guns, the Confederate commander sent this message of surrender to Maj. Gen. Benjamin Butler, whose firm, uncompromising response follows.

This sketch depicts the landing at Hatteras Inlet on August 28, the first amphibious operation of the war.

FLAG-OFFICER SAMUEL BARRON, C.S. Navy, offers to surrender Fort Hatteras, with all the arms and munitions of war. The officers allowed to go out with side-arms and the men without arms to retire.

> S. Barron,
> Commanding Naval Defenses,
> Virginia and North Carolina

BENJ. F. BUTLER, MAJOR-general, U.S. Army, commanding, in reply to the communication of Samuel Barron, commanding forces at Fort Hatteras, cannot admit the terms proposed. The terms offered are these: Full capitulation; the officers and men to be treated as prisoners of war. No other terms admissible. Commanding officers to meet on board flag-ship *Minnesota* to arrange details.

FRI 30 AUG. *The defeat of the Union army at First Bull Run produced a variety of responses from different groups within Northern society. In the letter excerpted below, abolitionist leader Frederick Douglass lamented to Samuel J. May, a Unitarian minister active in many reform causes, that the government now seemed even less willing to embrace emancipation as a war aim. The General Banks mentioned by Douglass is Nathaniel P. Banks, who had assumed command of the Department of the Shenandoah in late July.*

IT NOW SEEMS TO ME THAT OUR Government has resolved that no good shall come to the Negro from this war, and that it means by every means in its power to convince the slaveholders that slavery is safer in than out of the union—that the slaveholding rebel is an object of higher regard than is his humble slave. The hope that the war would finally become an abolition war has been dissipated and men are now preparing for another attempt to preserve the liberty of the white man at the expense of that of the black. I have tried to be hopeful and do still try to be so—but I confess that it seems much like hoping against hope. What I feared would result from sudden success has come from defeat. The Government defeated seems as little disposed to carry the war to the abolition point as before. Who would have supposed that General Banks would have signalized the first week of his campaign on the Potomac by capturing slaves and returning them to their masters? He has done less to punish the rebels than to punish their victims.

Maj. Gen. John C. Frémont, the Republican party's first presidential candidate (he ran in 1856) and a passionate opponent of slavery, had assumed command of the Union's Department of the West in late July. Most importantly, this department contained the troublesome border state of Missouri, where a particularly bloody guerrilla campaign was being waged against the Union garrison. On August 30, a determined Frémont declared martial law and made guerrilla activity punishable by summary execution. However, an equally controversial aspect of Frémont's new policy was his order that the slaves of Confederate loyalists be confiscated and freed. With this last point, as well as the summary nature of the executions, Lincoln believed that Frémont had gone too far. In the following letter of September 2, the president asked Frémont to rescind his proclamation. When Frémont refused to do so without a direct order from Lincoln, the president complied; two months later, he relieved the general of his command.

MY DEAR SIR: TWO POINTS IN your proclamation of August 30th give me some anxiety. First, should you shoot a man, according to the proclamation, the confederates would very certainly shoot our best man in their hands in retaliation; and so, man for man, indefinitely. It is therefore my order that you allow no man to be shot, under the proclamation, without first having my approbation or consent.

Secondly, I think there is great danger that the closing paragraph, in relation to the confiscation of property, and the liberating slaves of traitorous owners, will alarm our Southern Union friends, and turn them against us—perhaps ruin our rather fair prospect for Kentucky. Allow me therefore to ask, that you will as of your own motion, modify that paragraph so as to conform to the *first* and *fourth* sections of the act of Congress, entitled, "An act to confiscate property used for insurrectionary purposes," approved August 6th, 1861, and a copy of which act I herewith send you. This letter is written in a spirit of caution and not of censure.

I send it by a special messenger, in order that it may certainly and speedily reach you.

Yours very truly
A. Lincoln

SEPTEMBER
1861

TUE 3 SEP. PILLOW INVADES KENTUCKY

On orders from Maj. Gen. Leonidas Polk, Confederate forces under Brig. Gen. Gideon Pillow entered Kentucky on this date, seizing the towns of Hickman and Columbus on the Mississippi River. (Just three days later, U. S. Grant, now a brigadier general, crossed the Ohio River to capture Paducah, but—significantly—the Rebels had already violated Kentucky's neutrality.) In this exchange of letters, Polk wrote from his new headquarters at Columbus to Kentucky governor Beriah Magoffin in justification of the invasion. Responding on behalf of the state government, Kentucky legislator John M. Johnston had none of it—and when the Confederates refused to withdraw, the slave state of Kentucky joined the Union. More than seventy-five thousand Kentuckians would wear Union blue, while approximately twenty-five thousand joined the Confederate ranks.

GOVERNOR MAGOFFIN, FRANKfort, Ky.: I should have dispatched to you immediately, as the troops under my command took possession of this position, the very few words I addressed to the people here; but my duties since that time so preoccupied me, that I have but now the first leisure moment to communicate with you.

It will be sufficient for me to inform you (as my short address herewith will do) that I had information on which I could rely that the Federal forces intended and were preparing to seize Columbus. I need not describe to you the danger resulting to Western Tennessee from such occupation. My responsibility could not permit me quietly to lose to the command intrusted to me so important a position. In evidence of the accuracy of the information I possessed, I will state that as the Confederate forces approached this place the Federal troops were found in formidable numbers in position upon the opposite bank, with their cannons turned upon Columbus. The citizens of the town had fled with terror, and not a word of assurance of safety or protection had been addressed to them. Since I have taken possession of this place I have been informed by highly respectable citizens of your State that certain representatives of the Federal Government are seeking to

Maj. Gen. Leonidas Polk

take advantage of its own wrongs and setting up complaints against my act of occupation, and are making it a pretext for seizing other points.

Upon this proceeding I have no comment to make. But I am prepared to say that I will agree to withdraw the Confederate troops from Kentucky, provided that she will agree that the troops of the Federal Government be withdrawn simultaneously, with a guarantee (which I will give reciprocally for the Confederate Government) that the Federal troops shall not be allowed to enter or occupy any part of Kentucky in the future.

I have the honor to be, respectfully, your obedient servant,

L. Polk,
Major-General, Commanding

SIR: I HAVE THE HONOR TO INCLOSE herewith a resolution of the Senate of Kentucky, adopted by that body upon the reception of intelligence of military occupation of Hickman, Chalk Bank, and Columbus by the Confederate troops under your command. I need not say that the people of Kentucky are profoundly astonished that such an act should have been committed by the Confederate States, and especially that they should have been the first to do so with an equipped and regularly organized army.

The people of Kentucky having with great unanimity determined upon a position of neutrality in the unhappy war now being waged, and which they had tried in vain to prevent, had hoped that one place at least in this great nation might remain uninvaded by passion, and through whose good offices something might be done to end the war or at least to mitigate its horrors, or, if this were not possible, that she might be left to choose her destiny without disturbance from any quarter.

In obedience to the thrice repeated will of the people, as expressed at the polls and in their name, I ask you to withdraw your forces from the soil of Kentucky.

I will say in conclusion that all the people of the State await in deep suspense your action in the premises.

I have the honor to be, your obedient servant,

John M. Johnston,
Chairman of Committee

WED 11 SEP. CHEAT MOUNTAIN

On August 1, Robert E. Lee, then military adviser to Confederate president Jefferson Davis, had assumed command of the crumbling Confederate forces in western Virginia. During August and early September, he consolidated his men while continuing to engage the Federals. Beginning on this date a campaign against the Union position at Cheat Mountain, Lee divided his forces into multiple columns in an attempt to encircle the Federal force under Brig. Gen. Joseph J. Reynolds (McClellan having already left western Virginia for the Divsion of the Potomac). Greatly hampering Lee's plan were heavy rains and poor communications. In fact, by September 15 Lee was forced to admit failure and withdraw his men entirely from western Virginia—a major blow to

Confederate morale in the area and, it was then believed, to Lee's future in the Confederate army. In this letter to his wife, Lee summarized the significant events of the campaign.

I HAVE RECEIVED, DEAR MARY, your letter of the 5th by Beverly Turner, who is a nice young soldier. I am pained to see fine young men like him, of education and standing, from all the old and respectable families in the State, serving in the ranks. I hope in time they will receive their reward. I met him as I was returning from an expedition to the enemy's works, which I had hoped to have surprised on the morning of the 12th, both at Cheat Mountain and on Valley River. All the attacking parties with great labour had reached their destination, over mountains considered impassable to bodies of troops, notwithstanding a heavy storm that set in the day before and raged all night, in which they had to stand up until daylight. Their arms were then unserviceable, and they in poor condition for a fierce assault against artillery and superior numbers. After waiting until 10 o'clock for the assault on Cheat Mountain, which did not take place, and which was to have been the signal for the rest, they were withdrawn, and after waiting three days in front of the enemy, hoping he would come out of his trenches, we returned to our position at this place [Valley Mount]. I can not tell you my regret and mortification at the untoward events that caused the failure of the plan. I had taken every precaution to ensure success and counted on it. But the Ruler of the Universe willed otherwise and sent a storm to disconcert a well-laid plan, and to destroy my hopes.

Gen. Robert E. Lee

FRI 20 SEP. THE SIEGE OF LEXINGTON

After defeating the Federals at Wilson's Creek on August 10, Confederate Maj. Gen. Sterling Price devoted his efforts to securing Springfield and building up his forces. Finally, on September 12, nearly eighteen thousand Confederates under Price encircled thirty-six hundred Union soldiers at Lexington, besieging them for nine days. Although the Federals ultimately surrendered (on September 20), their hard-fought stand gave the Union command the time it needed to shift troops to more strategi-

cally important locations and to isolate Price's command. While ostensibly a Confederate victory, Lexington actually cost Price the rest of Missouri. Nevertheless, in his report to the governor, Price ignored the length of the siege and instead focused on the battle itself, which he considered a decisive win.

ON THE 10TH INSTANT, JUST AS we were about to encamp for the day a mile or two west of Rose Hill, I learned that a detachment of Federal troops and Home Guards were marching from Lexington to Warrensburg, to rob the bank in that place and plunder and arrest the citizens of Johnson County, in accordance with General Frémont's proclamation and instructions....

About daybreak the next morning [September 13] a sharp skirmish took place between our pickets and the enemy's outposts. This threatened to become general. Being unwilling, however, to risk a doubtful engagement, when a short delay would make success certain, I fell back 2 or 3 miles and awaited the arrival of my infantry and artillery. These having come up, we advanced upon the town, driving the enemy's pickets until we came within a short distance of the city [Lexington] itself. Here the enemy attempted to make a stand, but they were speedily driven from every position and forced to take shelter within their intrenchments....

After 2 o'clock in the afternoon of the 20th, and after fifty-two hours of continuous firing, a white flag was displayed by the enemy on that part of the works nearest to Colonel Green's position, and shortly afterwards another was displayed opposite to Colonel Rives'. I immediately ordered a cessation of all firing on our part, and sent forward one of my staff officers to ascertain the object of the flag and to open negotiations with the enemy if such should be their desire. It was finally, after some delay, agreed by Colonel Marshall and the officers associated with him for that purpose by Colonel Mulligan that the United States forces should lay down their arms and surrender themselves as prisoners of war to this army. These terms having been made known, were ratified by me and immediately carried into effect.

This victory has demonstrated the fitness of our citizen soldiers for the tedious operations of a siege as well as for a dashing charge. They lay for fifty-two hours in the open air without tents or covering, regardless of the sun and rain and in the very presence of a watchful and desperate foe, manfully repelling every assault and patiently awaiting any orders to storm the fortifications. No general ever commanded a braver or a better army. It is composed of the best blood and the bravest men of Missouri.

★ ★ ★ ★

OCTOBER
1861

CSS MANASSAS

The first Confederate ironclad, the river ram CSS Manassas, *steamed down the Mississippi River on this date to engage the Union squadron blockading New Orleans. Taking the Federal navy completely by surprise, the* Manassas *quickly forced aground two ships, the* Richmond *and the* Vincennes. *At first, U.S. naval commanders refused to believe that the era of wooden sailing ships was ending, preferring to see the debacle as an isolated incident caused by poor naval leadership (which a subsequent investigation of all officers involved attempted to confirm). The efforts of the* Manassas *indeed lifted the blockade at the Head of the Passes, as the following report to Navy Secretary Gideon Welles notes—but only for a short time. Meanwhile, on the same day at Carondelet, Missouri, the Union launched its own riverine ironclad, the USS* St. Louis. *Thus began an important, though largely unnoticed, revolution in naval warfare.*

SIR: THE STEAMER *McCLELLAN* has just arrived with disasterous news from the Mississippi. Our ships have been driven from the Head of the Passes.

The *Richmond* had several of her planks stove in by the steam ram *[Manassas],* and all the guns of the *Vincennes* except four have been thrown overboard.

Nothing but the arrival in the *McClellan* of the rifled guns loaned from

A contemporary engraving of the Mississippi River ram CSS Manassas.

Fort Pickens saved the vessels from another and, probably, more destructive attack.

The South, meanwhile, reveled in the swift success brought about by technological prowess, as this news report in the New Orleans Daily True Delta *indicates.*

AT MIDNIGHT LAST NIGHT THE steamer *Calhoun* arrived at the wharf, foot of Bienville street, having on board Commodore Hollins.

A dispatch to announce her arrival had been received from the fort, but few persons saw it, as it was not published.

Nevertheless, a considerable crowd collected on the wharf about 9 o'clock and waited a couple of hours, but when the *Calhoun* finally arrived there were not more than two dozen present. These, however, sent up a hearty shout for the hero of the naval victory....

...Commodore Hollins [had] proceeded down the river with the gunboats for the purpose of making a legitimate attack upon [the Union ships]. The vessels of the enemy found lying at the Head of the Passes were the steam frigate *Richmond*, the sailing sloop of war *Vincennes*, the sailing sloop of war *Preble*, and the steam gunboat *Water Witch*. They were taken completely by surprise, and had not the steamers had steam up at the time, perhaps none of them would have escaped. As it was, their firing, maneuvers, and general conduct showed that they were thunderstruck and frightened.

THU 17 OCT. *As the armies of the Union marched southward, they increasingly attracted large numbers of runaway slaves, known as contrabands. During the first few months of the war, this trend posed a serious political problem for the officers of the North, who—prior to emancipation—were uncertain as to the exact legal status of these runaways. Meanwhile, many Southern and border-state slaveholders boldly crossed Union lines in order to reclaim their lost "property." In the following unpublished account, George E. Stephens, a correspondent for an African-American newspaper in Philadelphia, vividly described one such scene.*

A MAN WHO IS DIGNIFIED WITH the title of sheriff, rode into camp with a posse of five persons, and seized a little boy about 15 years of age, a fugitive from *slavery.* He dared not attempt to take the boy with his posse, but secured a sergeant and a guard to escort them over the lines and to prevent his rescue. So you see it required 13 men to take one boy of 15 years. Great Heavens, how many men would it require to re-enslave ten thousand full-grown men? We did all in our power to aid him, but the vigilance of the guards outwitted us. Poor Frank was surrendered up, and now swells the list of the thousands sacrificed upon the altar of the "jealous God of Slavery." We resort to another method now; we hurry the panting fugitive to the Virginia side, and urge him to enter the Federal lines from that direction. But, my dear sir, it is hard to elude the vigilance of Federal man catchers.

MON 21 OCT. BALL'S BLUFF (HARRISON'S ISLAND)

Following McClellan's orders to advance on Leesburg, Brig. Gen. Charles P. Stone began shuttling his men across the Potomac River at Ball's Bluff and farther downstream at Edward's Ferry. When a Confederate force of roughly equal size attempted to push back the Federals at Ball's Bluff, the result was the first major Eastern Theater battle since Bull Run. In direct command at Ball's Bluff (Stone was at Edward's Ferry) was Col. Edward D. Baker, a U.S. senator from Oregon and friend of the president. When Confederate resistance stiffened, the Union problem became clear: Baker's boats were inadequate, and he had no other retreat strategy. Of 1,700 effectives, the Union lost 917 men, the majority drowned in the Potomac, while the Confederates lost only 155. The foray into Virginia was a military and—because Baker died in the action—political disaster. Although the error was largely Baker's, for advancing too rashly, he was made a martyr, while the press charged the generally blameless Stone with treason and incompetence. In fact, without objection from Lincoln, the general was held under arrest, without being charged, until the furor had passed. In his official report, one officer on the scene, Col. Edward Hinks, detailed some of the reasons for the Union failure at Ball's Bluff. The island to which Hinks refers is Harrison's Island, and it was at this point in the Potomac that the crossing was made.

Brig. Gen. Charles P. Stone

I CANNOT CLOSE THIS REPORT with justice to our troops, who fought valiantly, without commenting upon the causes which led to their defeat and complete rout. The means of transportation for advance in support or retreat were criminally deficient, especially when we consider the facility for creating proper means for such purposes at our disposal. The place for landing upon the Virginia shore was most unfortunately selected, being at a point where the shore rose with great abruptness for a distance of some 150 yards, at an angle, in many places of at least 25 degrees, and was studded with trees, being entirely impassable to artillery or infantry in line. At the summit the surface is undulating, where the enemy were placed in force, out of view, and cut down our troops with a murderous fire, which we could not return with any effect. The entire island was also commanded by the enemy's artillery and rifles. In fact, no more unfortunate position could have been forced upon us by the enemy for making an attack, much less selected by ourselves.

As this letter to his wife shows, Major General McClellan was quick to blame others for the Ball's Bluff fiasco and to absolve himself of responsibility. His insistence that the attack took place without his orders seems directly contradicted by a telegram that he sent to Brigadier General Stone prior to the engagement, containing the explicit order: "Take Leesburg."

THAT AFFAIR OF LEESBURG ON Monday last was a terrible butchery—the men fought nobly, but were penned up by a vastly superior force in a place where they had no retreat. The whole thing took place some 40 miles from here without my orders or knowledge—it was entirely unauthorized by me & I am in no manner responsible for it.

The man directly to blame for the affair was Col Baker who was killed—he was in command, disregarded entirely the instructions he had received from Stone, & violated all military rules & precautions....During the night I withdrew everything & everybody to this side of the river which in truth they should have never left.

★ ★ ★ ★

NOVEMBER
1861

FRI 1 NOV. McCLELLAN REPLACES SCOTT

Under pressure from President Lincoln, the cabinet, and the press, Lt. Gen. Winfield Scott, the ancient and ailing commander of all Union forces, retired this day to West Point. An able leader who had served the nation since the War of 1812, Scott was simply unfit for the massive undertaking that the Civil War had become. Replacing him, Lincoln named George Brinton McClellan general-in-chief of the army. These excerpts from letters written by McClellan to his wife show the ambitious younger man maneuvering to supersede his former mentor.

[AUGUST 15, 1861]
Gen. Scott is the most dangerous antagonist I have. Our ideas are so widely different that it is impossible for us to work together much longer.

[SEPTEMBER 27, 1861]
[The president] sent a carriage for me to meet him and the cabinet at Gen. Scott's office. Before we got through the general "raised a row with me." I kept cool. In the course of the conversation he very strongly intimated that we were no longer friends. I said nothing, merely looked at him and bowed. He tried to avoid me when we left, but I walked square up to him, looked him fully in the eye, extended my hand and said "Good morning, Gen. Scott." He had to take my hand and so we parted. As he threw down the glove and I took it up, I presume war is declared. So be it.

Gen.-in-Chief Winfield Scott posing with his staff.

The new Union general-in-chief, George B. McClellan, with his wife, Mary Ellen.

[OCTOBER 26, 1861]

For the last three hours I have been at Montgomery Blair's, talking with Senators Wade, Trumbull and Chandler about war matters. They will make a desperate effort tomorrow to have Gen. Scott retired at once; until that is accomplished I can effect but little good. He is ever in my way, and I am sure does not desire effective action.

[NOVEMBER 3, 1861]

I have already been up once this morning—that was at four o'clock to escort Gen. Scott to the depot. It was pitch-dark and a pouring rain; but with most of my staff and a squadron of cavalry I saw the old man off. He was very polite to me; sent various kind messages to you and the baby; so we parted. The old man said that his sensations were very peculiar in leaving Washington and active life. I can easily understand them; and it may be that at some distant day I, too, shall totter away from Washington, a worn-out soldier, with naught to do but make my peace with God. The sight of this morning was a lesson to me which I hope not soon to forget. I saw there the end of a long, active, and ambitious life, the end of the career of the first soldier of his nation; and it was a feeble old man scarce able to walk; hardly any one there to see him off but his successor. Should I ever become vainglorious and ambitious, remind me of that spectacle. I pray every night and every morning that I may become neither vain nor ambitious, that I may be neither depressed by disaster or elated by success, and that I may keep one single object in view—the good of my country. At last I am the "major-general commanding the army."

THU
7 PORT ROYAL SOUND
NOV.

A crucial, though unheralded, component of Northern military strategy involved blockading Southern ports in order to choke off the Confederacy's supply routes. For the blockade to be successful, however, the Union navy needed its supply stations on the Southern coast. Flag Officer Samuel F. Du Pont provided an important new base on this date when he led the Union navy to its greatest victory yet at Port Royal Sound, South Carolina. Du Pont's seventy-five ships—carrying twelve thousand men under Brig. Gen. Thomas W. Sherman—were opposed by a pair of Confederate forts, isolated by swamps and water from the mainland, guarding the entrance to the sound. The inexperienced Rebel artillerymen blasted away at the fleet, but they were no match for the professional gunners of the U.S. Navy, whose superior accuracy and firepower forced a Confederate surrender late in the afternoon. This circular, sent by General Sherman three days before the battle, impressed upon the men his reliance on their bravery in action.

THE GENERAL COMMANDING HAS the unparalleled gratification to congratulate the officers and men of his command upon their safe arrival at this point, after a most perilous and tempestuous passage from Hampton Roads.

Some vessels probably have been lost, but it is believed that the hand of Providence has saved the lives of all. For

Brig. Gen. Thomas W. Sherman

this let us be thankful to the Ruler of our destinies, in whom we must ever trust for protection.

Soldiers! Let the dangers you have encountered and the anxieties you have experienced be an incentive to a greater exertion on your part in the holy cause in which you are engaged. The eyes of your country are upon you. She expects you to conquer. Deceive not her expectations. Be cool and determined. Act only at the command of your officers, and be prompt to do so. Be not led away by a vain and spontaneous enthusiasm, nor restrained by a want of willingness or alacrity. Let your officers judge when you are to act; to do otherwise would lead to confusion and disgrace. Some of you have not had proper opportunities for instruction; let coolness, firmness, and the cold steel take the place of better instruction.

Soldiers! You are contending against an enemy who depreciates your manhood,
who denies that your prowess is equal to his. Belie this sentiment, or you will disgrace yourselves and your nativity.

On the same day, Brig. Gen. Ulysses S. Grant received his Civil War baptism of fire near Belmont, Missouri (the seizure of Paducah on September 6 had been bloodless). In this excerpt from his memoirs, Grant described the action at Belmont, during which his three thousand men took the town only to lose it again. The fighting was inconclusive but, for Grant, instructive.

ABOUT TWO O'CLOCK ON THE morning of the 7th, I learned that the enemy was crossing troops from Columbus [Kentucky] to the west bank [of the Mississippi River] to be dispatched, presumably, after Oglesby. I knew there was a small camp of Confederates at Belmont, immediately opposite Columbus, and I speedily resolved to push down the river, land on the Missouri side, capture Belmont, break up the camp and return....

The officers and men engaged at Belmont were then under fire for the first time. Veterans could not have behaved better than they did up to the moment of reaching the rebel camp. At this point they became demoralized from their victory and failed to reap its full reward.... The moment the camp was reached our men laid down their arms and commenced rummaging the tents to pick up trophies. Some of the higher officers were little better than the privates. They galloped about from one cluster of men to another and at every halt delivered a short eulogy upon the Union cause and the achievements of the command.

All this time the troops we had been engaged with for four hours lay crouched under cover of the river bank, ready to come up and surrender if summoned to do so; but finding that they were not pursued, they worked their way up the river and came up on the bank between us and our transports....Some of my men were engaged in firing from captured guns at empty steamers down the river, out of range, cheering at every shot. I tried to get them to turn their guns upon the loaded steamers above and not so far away. My efforts were in vain. At last I directed my staff officers to set fire to the camps. This drew the fire of the enemy's guns located on the heights of Columbus....The alarm "surrounded" was given. The guns of the enemy and the report of being surrounded, brought officers and men completely under control. At first some of the officers seemed to think that to be surrounded was to be placed in a hopeless position, where there was nothing to do but surrender. But when I announced that we had cut our way in and could cut our way out just as well, it seemed a new revelation to officers and soldiers.

FRI
8
NOV.
THE TRENT AFFAIR

The most serious diplomatic crisis of the war began on this date, when Capt. Charles Wilkes, commanding the Union warship San Jacinto, *boarded a British steamer, the* Trent, *and arrested two Confederate diplomats, James Mason and John Slidell, both en route to*

England. From Wilkes's point of view, Mason and Slidell were outlaw insurgents; the British, however, legitimately cried Yankee piracy. Ill disposed by this affront to its national sovereignty, the British government reinforced the Royal Navy's Atlantic squadrons and readied its army for war. Shortly after Christmas, however, the Lincoln administration quietly freed the two men, and the British allowed the matter to drop. This article from the The Times *of London, written at the height of the affair, suggests the depth of British concern.*

LAST WEEK IT SEEMED DIFFICULT TO obtain attention for any subject save that of the American crisis....

From a meaningless declaration that the President [Lincoln] does not desire hostilities with England, some sanguine writers have hastened to assume that the

Capt. Charles Wilkes

act of Captain Wilkes will be disavowed, and the Southern Commissioners handed over to us….We should be too happy to believe that so wise a course was that designed for adoption by the American Government, but we are afraid to resign ourselves to so agreeable a hope. It contradicts the general expression of that part of the American public which makes itself heard, and which exercises a fatal control over the so-called government of the American press (with one or two honourable exceptions), and of the American Secretary of State. The House of Representatives has deliberately offered a vote of thanks to the pirate Wilkes; and though it is technically true that this is not precisely the same thing as a vote of our House of Commons, it is equally true, and more to the purpose, that the House of Representatives expresses the senti-ments of those who, to the disgrace of the higher classes in the States, are permitted to engross political power.

MON 11 NOV. *The male-dominated United States Sanitary Commission, created in June 1861 to aid and comfort Union soldiers, immediately took up the work of coordinating and directing the many relief efforts already under way. Some states, including Iowa, established state sanitary commissions, which were essentially satellites of the national organization. However—as this article from the Keokuk, Iowa,* Daily Gate City *makes plain—the many Northern women already deeply entrenched in aiding the soldiers did not appreciate these male efforts to control their work.*

A U.S. Sanitary Commission office near Petersburg, photographed in 1864.

DURING THREE OR FOUR MONTHS past many kind-hearted women, zealous in good works, have devoted their time, influence and energies to organizing Soldiers' Aid Societies and collecting and preparing articles for our sick and wounded soldiers in the hospitals. Through their efforts societies were gradually organized all over the State and a very general interest aroused in behalf of the object of their efforts....

The Aid Associations are in very fair working order, and, in the hands of the benevolent women who had initiated them and rendered them effective, gave promise and assurance of being equal to the work they had taken in hand....

All at once...an idea seems to have struck our State authorities....There is a chance for salaries and fees in carrying out this benevolent measure which may be parcelled out to the wealthy men of the State....

A Sanitary Commission has been constituted....

This Commission have issued a circular to the women of Iowa, in which they ignore the existence of any Soldiers' Aid Society, and *scold* because nothing has been done in the State by the ladies to relieve the sick and wounded soldiers. And we presume that the gentlemen constituting that Commission have taken so little interest in the subject that they were substantially in entire ignorance of what has been done.

We trust that the Honorables and their graces, and the Reverends and the Bankers who constitute the Sanitary Commission, will "post up," roll up their sleeves and "pitch in," and show the women how matters ought to be done. We should be right glad to see them take a personal interest in the matter and make a personal effort, or else get out of the way and not stand as an obstruction in the way of the women of Iowa, who would do this thing up much better without them.

WED 13 NOV. *During the Civil War, tens of thousands of women left their homes for the battlefront to serve as badly needed nurses and hospital staff. Only one woman, however, on either side is known to have sought a formal commission as an army surgeon. Dr. Mary Edwards Walker, an 1855 graduate of the Syracuse Medical College, traveled to Washington in September 1861 and immediately began caring for the sick and wounded as a volunteer while pressing her case with the Union's Medical Department. In this letter home, she wrote about conditions at the makeshift hospital (housed in the Patent Office) where she was serving unofficially.*

I AM ASSISTANT PHYSICIAN & Surgeon in this Hospital. We have about 80 patients now. We have 5 very nice lady nurses, and a number of gentlemen nurses. We have several cooks; and a dispenser to put up and prepare the medicine, after our orders.

Every soul in the Hospital has to abide by my orders as much as though Dr. Green gave them. & not a soldier can go out of the building after stated hours, without a pass from him or myself.

This building is a fine one built of white marble, and has marble floors....It is warmed with hot air and well lighted with gas that burns all night.

Abraham Lincoln

SUN 17 NOV. MCCLELLAN ON LINCOLN

George McClellan and Abraham Lincoln were as different as two men could be. McClellan was the scion of a prosperous Philadelphia physician; Lincoln, the son of a poor Kentucky farmer. McClellan, a Democrat with Southern sympathies who once declared that he couldn't "stand the odor of billy goats or niggers"; Lincoln, an antislavery Republican who respected the humanity of slaves. McClellan possessed a keen sense of decorum and detested what he considered inadequate social behavior; Lincoln was famous for a wit that flouted social conventions. By the fall of 1861, McClellan's contempt for his

commander-in-chief, not to mention most of the Republican party leadership, was palpable. He often confided his feelings to his wife, Mary Ellen, in their voluminous correspondence. Here he disparages both Lincoln—whom he refers to as a gorilla—and Secretary of State William H. Seward.

IT IS SICKENING IN THE EXTREME & makes me feel heavy at heart when I see the weakness & unfitness of the poor beings who control the destinies of this great country. How I wish that God had permitted me to live quietly & unknown with you—but His will be done!

I will do my best—try to preserve an honest mind—to do my duty as best I may—& will ever, I hope, continue to pray that He will give me that wisdom, courage & truth that are so necessary to me now, & so little of which I possess. The outside

William H. Seward

world may envy me—no doubt they do not know the weight of care that presses on me....

I went to the White House shortly after tea where I found "the *original gorilla*," about as intelligent as ever. What a specimen to be at the head of our affairs now!

After I left the Prince's I went to Seward's where I found the "Gorilla" again, & was of course much edified by his anecdotes—ever apropos, & ever unworthy of one holding his high position. I spent some time there & *almost* organized a little quarrel with that poor little varlet Seward....It is a terrible dispensation of Providence that so weak & cowardly a thing as that should now control our foreign relations—unhappily the Presdt is not much better, except that he is honest & means well. I suppose our country has richly merited some great punishment, else we should not now have such wretched triflers at the head of affairs....

As I parted from the Presdt on Seward's steps he said that it had been suggested to him that it was no more safe for me than for him to walk out at night without some attendants; I told him that I felt no fear, that no one would take the trouble to interfere with me, on which he deigned to remark that they would probably give more for my scalp at Richmond than for his.

Maj. Gen. Henry W. Halleck

TUE **19** NOV. *On this date, Maj. Gen. Henry W. Halleck, nicknamed Old Brains for his intellectual leanings, assumed command in St. Louis of the newly created Department of the Missouri, which oversaw the war in* Missouri, Arkansas, Illinois, and Kentucky west of the Cumberland River. For Halleck, it marked the beginning of his rise to the highest levels of Union leadership. Among his first acts were the imposition of martial law and the suspension of the writ of habeas corpus. By providing a legal basis for their subsequent actions, these orders ultimately gave Federal forces in Missouri the power to wage a brutal counterguerrilla campaign against Rebel bushwhackers and partisan rangers (locally organized militia units). Union commanders henceforth ran the state as they wished—with summary execution, forced deportations, and seizures of private property common, all with no more legal process than the consent of a Federal officer. This left Southern irregulars with little hope but fighting and* *winning. In the message of December 2 reprinted below, President Lincoln stated his unequivocal support for Halleck's actions.*

GENERAL: AS AN INSURRECTION exists in the United States and is in arms in the State of Missouri, you are hereby authorized and empowered to suspend the Writ of Habeas Corpus within the limits of the military division under your command and to exercise martial law as you find it necessary in your discretion to secure the public safety and the authority of the United States.

In witness whereof, I have hereunto set my hand and caused the seal of the United States to be affixed at Washington, this second day of December, A.D. 1861.

Abraham Lincoln

WED
27
NOV.

In the following letter addressed to U.S. Secretary of War Simon Cameron, William Jones of Oberlin, Ohio, echoed the desire of many Northern blacks to join the Union army (and also the navy). Nearly a year would pass, however, before Congress repealed on July 17, 1862, the long-standing ban on blacks in the U.S. Army.

SIR: VERY MANY OF THE COLORED citizens of Ohio and other states have had a great desire to assist the government in putting down this injurious rebellion.

Since they have heard that the rebels are forming regiments of the free blacks and compelling them to fight against the Union as well as their slaves, they have urged me to write and beg that you will receive one or more regiments (or companies) of the colored of the free States to counterbalance those employed against the Union by Rebels.

We are partly drilled and would wish to enter active service immediately.

We behold your sick list each day and Sympathize with the Soldiers and the government. We are confident of our ability to stand the hardships of the field and the climate So unhealthy to the Soldiers of the *North.*

To prove our attachment and our will to defend the government we only ask a trial. I have the honor to remain your humble Servant

Wm. A. Jones

SAT
30
NOV.

Not every segment of Northern society was entirely behind the Union war effort. Some religious groups, most prominently the Quakers, were opposed to war, no matter the reason. However, as the following excerpt from the Friends' Intelligencer *suggests, some young Quakers found it difficult to escape the "whirlpool of popular enthusiasm" for the war.*

WE HAVE HERETOFORE ABSTAINED from much remark on the civil war, which is now sorrowfully distracting our country, but it is in vain to ignore the fact that this subject is uppermost in the minds of the mass of the people, and that Friends are not only deeply interested in it, but in too many instances are carried away by the prevailing spirit of the communities around them....

That many of the young and ardent in our own religious Society should have

THE FLAG OF OUR UNION.

STRIKE— till the last armed foe expires. | STRIKE— for the green graves of your sires.
STRIKE— for your altars and your fires! | GOD— and your native land!

This is one of many flag-motif prints that took commercial advantage of the patriotic fervor that swept through the North in 1861.

its very nature, incapable of settling differences on principles of justice and equity....

...It is the peculiar mission of the Society of Friends to hold up the principles of peace, setting the example of returning good for evil, and owning, before all men, the brotherhood of the human race, their common obligations to the Author of their being, and to each other. These principles never shine so brightly as when contrasted with the spirit of strife and contention; and those who are favored with strength to maintain them, in such times as these, will be a blessing to the nation at large, by cultivating the arts of peace, exercising the ministrations of humanity and Christian kindness to all alike, and preserving much that is good from the destruction that follows in the train of war.

been drawn into the whirlpool of popular enthusiasm, is not to be wondered at. The apparent connection of this contest with the anti-slavery movement, in which Friends have taken such a lively interest, has induced the desire, on the part of some, to have a war prosecuted with vigor, which seems to them to promise, as one of its results, the long-desired enfranchisement of the colored race. But happy as such a consummation would be, if accomplished by wise and moderate means, we must not forget that the ground of our Christian profession is equally at variance with war as with oppression, and that they are twin offspring of the uncontrolled and corrupted passions of the human heart....War is, in

Of course, there were those in the North who merely wanted life to continue as usual, despite the war. Boston music critic John Sullivan Dwight, for example, interrupted a review (somewhat ironically) to argue that cultural and intellectual pursuits should continue as before.

IT IS HARD TO REALIZE THAT WE are in the midst of civil war—that we are fighting the fight, perhaps the final one, of Civilization against a treacherous and arrogant pro-Slavery rebellion, with all its backward and Barbarian proclivities, when we can come together in peace and comfort, just as in the unsuspecting days, to meet the familiar music-loving faces, and listen to a concert of the

Mendelssohn Quintette Club. Nothing perhaps in Boston could show so little change to one who went away not dreaming of what the year was to bring forth for us politically, as that quiet scene in Chickering's Hall, on Wednesday evening....

...Whatever stern work is required of us, whatever rough necessities of war are forced upon us peaceful and peace-loving people, we cannot forget that peaceful things are all the while the real end of life, and we must carry on a settled *life* of some sort, in times of war as well as of peace. Our fight is for Civilization; and we do well therefore to keep up all the civilizing elements and influences, and let all the sweet flowers blow, and wholesome fruits ripen, that we can, amid the storm. We must shelter all the seeds and nurseries of Civilization, of true culture and humanity, all the more jealously while the storm rages....

...We have not loved music from sheer idleness; it has been earnest breath of life to us. And so we contrive to make room for it even now and allow the hot chambers of our straightened anxious life a little of its wholesome ventilation even in these dark days of the nation's trial.

★ ★ ★ ★

DECEMBER
1861

MON 9 DEC. *The Civil War forced many Native Americans living on the periphery of the Confederacy to choose sides. The Cherokees, Creeks, Chickasaws, and Choctaws largely allied themselves with the Southerners, with whom they had much in common, including ownership of slaves and an intense dislike of the United States government. Others, including many Seminoles, sided with the North, setting up a much smaller (though at times just as fierce) civil war. The first battle of this microcosmic war took place in the Indian Territory (now Oklahoma), where a pro-Federal faction of a thousand Creeks and Seminoles, along with several hundred African Americans—all under the leadership of Chief Hopoeithleyohola—engaged a combined Confederate-Indian column. After its defeat, Hopoeithleyohola's force subsequently fled into Union-controlled Kansas and Missouri. In his official report addressed to Confederate Secretary of War Judah P. Benjamin, Col. Douglas H. Cooper described the victorious action.*

SIR: HAVING EXHAUSTED EVERY means in my power to procure an interview with Hopoeithleyohola, for the purpose of effecting a peaceful settlement of the difficulties existing between his party and the constituted authorities of the Creek Nation, finding that my written overtures, made through several of the leading captains, were treated with silence, if not contempt, by him, and having received positive evidence that he had been for a considerable length of time in correspondence, if not alliance, with the Federal authorities in Kansas, I resolved to advance upon him with the forces under my command, and either compel submission to the authorities of the nation or drive him and his party from the country....

At Tulsey Town information was received from a prisoner escaped from Hopoeithleyohola's camp that an immediate attack was intended by the enemy, 2,000 strong....After proceeding down Bird Creek about 5 miles two runners from Captain Foster reached me at the head of the column, stating he had found the enemy in large force below. Parks had exchanged a few shots with them, taken 6 prisoners, and was retreating, hotly pursued. Scarcely had this intelligence reached me before shots were heard in the rear. Hastily directing the Cherokee train to be parked on the prairie and a sufficient guard placed over it, the forces were formed in three columns, the Choctaws and Chickasaws on the right, the Texans and Cherokees in the center, and the Creeks on the left, and the whole advanced at quick gallop upon the enemy, who had by this time shown himself in large force above us, along the timber skirting the main creek for over 2 miles, as well as a ravine extending far out into the prairie. A party of about 200 having attacked our rear guard, Captain Young, in command of a squadron of the Choctaw and Chickasaw regiment, being in rear of the main column, perceiving the encounter, wheeled his squadron and advanced rapidly towards the enemy. Upon his approach the party retreated towards the timber on Bird Creek.

The Creeks, commanded by Col. D. N. McIntosh, on the left came soon into action, and, charging the enemy with great impetuosity, met them in hand-to-hand encounter, drove them from the timber, and dispersed them in every direction. On the right the Choctaws and Chickasaws boldly charged on horse to the bank of a ravine near the creek under a heavy fire, and, dismounting, drove back the enemy, who disputed every step of their advance with the greatest obstinacy and bravery....The enemy were driven from their stronghold and pursued far into the bend, where, receiving on the flank an unexpected fire, the squadron took position at the house. Being then re-enforced by some men from Captains Reynolds', McCurtain's, and Hall's companies, of the Choctaw and Chickasaw regiment, the conflict with the persistent foe was renewed with increased vigor, and after a fierce struggle the enemy was forced, with heavy loss, through the bend and across the creek.

The Republicans who controlled Congress, though still confident of President Lincoln's leadership, were not about to let him run the country by himself without any oversight. Therefore, on this date, they created the Joint Committee on the Conduct of the War, which subsequently engaged in a broad range of activities, ranging from investigating the conduct of several Union generals to assessing the administration's wartime Reconstruction policies. Most Northerners, however, considered the committee a meddlesome body, more interested in political grandstanding than substantive policy making. The following poem, which originally appeared in the July 1862 issue of Vanity Fair,

Zachariah Chandler (pictured above in a Mathew Brady portrait) later served as secretary of the interior during the second Grant administration.

castigated Zachariah Chandler, a leading member of the committee, for his rampant pomposity.

WHO IS THIS CHANDLER—
inquisitive wretch! —
Who clamors so loud and so long
For papers and letters,
And bothers his betters—
Insisting that somebody's wrong?

Who made him Senator—
dignified name!—

And sent him to Washington,
Bawling and brawling,
Disgracing his calling
In the light of the midday sun?

Why should our country—best and
        beloved—
Suffer her secrets of State
To open so easy
To Chandler the greasy—
While the Wheels of Government wait?

WED 18 DEC. *The first Christmas season of the war was a particularly lonely time for the majority of men in uniform, most of whom were unable to get a furlough home for the holidays. The following letter, written from Manassas by Georgia volunteer Josiah Patterson to his children, conveys the anguish of a father unable to embrace his sons and daughter on Christmas morning.*

I DO NOT KNOW WHAT MY LITTLE boys and my angel Anna will do for a Santa Claus this Christmas. It would be fine if the little fellows could get up in the morning and find their little stockings full of goodies and cry out, "Sure, it was Pa! Pa is old Santa Claus!" But I don't think we will have such a happy Christmas morning. But it will be hard if the old fellow did not come just because Pa is not at home. Ma would neither kiss nor whip him if she found him in the house filling your little socks with delicacies. I must try and get the old fellow to call and see you, if I am so fortunate as to see him before that time. But he may be afraid of soldiers and keep out of my way.

A newly uniformed Union volunteer bids farewell to his family in Currier & Ives's Off for the War.

SUN 22 DEC. *Maj. Gen. Henry W. Halleck, commanding (since November 19) the Department of the Missouri, issued the following general order on this date, escalating the already harsh guerrilla warfare in Missouri and elsewhere in the Trans-Mississippi West. Federal troops would later burn entire towns along the Mississippi River (such as Austin, Mississippi, and Hopefield, Arkansas) in retribution for Confederate guerrilla attacks, even if the local residents weren't necessarily to blame. In 1863, on the Kansas-Missouri border, several counties were entirely denuded of their populations because of guerrilla activities (and with no other legal basis). Those residents remaining behind were simply labeled insurgents and shot.*

GENERAL ORDERS, No. 32

I. Insurgent rebels scattered through the northern counties of this State, which are occupied by our troops, under the guise of peaceful citizens, have resumed their occupation of burning bridges and destroying railroads and telegraph wires. These men are guilty of the highest crime known to the code of war and the punishment is death. Any one caught in the act will be immediately shot, and any one accused of this crime will be arrested and placed in close confinement until his case can be examined by a military commission, and, if found guilty, he also will suffer death.

II. Where injuries are done to railroads or telegraph lines the commanding officer of the nearest post will immediately impress into service, for repairing damages, the slaves of all secessionists in the vicinity, and, if necessary, the secessionists themselves and their property. Any pretended Union man having information of intended attempts to destroy such roads and lines or of the guilty parties, who does not communicate such intention to the proper authorities, and give aid and assistance in arresting and punishing them, will be regarded as *particeps criminis,* and treated accordingly.

III. Hereafter the towns and counties in which such destruction of public property takes place will be made to pay the expenses of all repairs, unless it be shown that the people of such towns or counties could not have prevented it on account of the superior force of the enemy.

SUN 29 DEC. *By the winter of 1861, hopes for a short and painless war seemed bygone folly. As general-in-chief of the Union army, George McClellan, a naturally cautious man, adapted to this new, long-term view of the war by instituting a rigorous training program and establishing boards of review to weed out incompetent and cowardly junior officers (captains and lieutenants). In this diary entry, Col. Charles S. Wainwright of the First New York Artillery, who served on one of the many screening panels, reflected on the changes taking place in the Army of the Potomac (created on August 17 when the Departments of Northeastern Virginia, Washington, and the Shenandoah were merged to form a single Department of the Potomac under McClellan's command). Although the general conducted no offensive actions during the fall of 1861, the investment he was instead making in training and organizing his men seemed by this time to be paying off, as the new Army of the Potomac evolved from an untrained rabble into the elite force of the Union army.*

THE EXAMINING BOARD HAVE met three times....Colonel Bailey has sent up the names of Captains Tamblin, Cothran, and Slocum....We have made some way with the three captains. Cothran knew but very little of the tactics, but had so many excuses for not being better posted, and is so evidently a man of sufficient intellect and education to make a good officer, that the board would not throw him, but recommended he should have another chance. Tamblin and Slocum have not been finished yet. The latter made wretched work of it and

This oil-on-canvas painting (created by an unknown artist in late 1861) shows the Army of the Potomac carrying out Maj. Gen. George B. McClellan's extensive new drilling and training program.

will doubtless have to go. I am almost sorry, for the poor man has worked very hard to learn his drill, but cannot get over his lack of early education; he makes the most fearful blunders with the mounted drill and although I have some days spent two hours with him in my tent trying to explain the orders and movement so as to get it through his head, he makes the very same blunders the next day. There is no saying what his written statement will be, as he can hardly write at all, and cannot spell....As for old Tamblin, he has proved a much harder subject to deal with than I expected. He not only answered pretty much every question out of the tactics, but when corrected as to some reply about the use of artillery in action, shewed fight, and quoted from authors which none of the rest of us had ever heard of. We had finally to summon witnesses in his case. Colonel Bailey shewed that he was not able to impart his knowledge to others, however much he might know himself; and that he was greatly wanting in efficiency as an officer, not having the respect of his men.

★ ★ ★ ★

JANUARY
1862

**FRI
10
JAN.**

Before the Emancipation Proclamation settled the matter, the issue of slavery was handled inconsistently by the North. Runaway slaves were a particular worry for Union officers, who didn't know what to do with the thousands routinely seeking Federal protection. Meanwhile, some white Southerners brazenly chased runaways right into Union camps, expecting to leave with their "property." The front lines of battle thus doubled as front lines in the moral and political struggle over emancipation, as suggested by this newspaper correspondent's account of an incident that took place while the Army of the Potomac was camped in Maryland.

ONE OF THE MOST CRUEL AND atrocious deeds of the barbarous slavemaster was perpetrated by one Samuel Cox, living five miles below Port Tobacco, who is said to be an ex–state representative, a returned rebel, the Captain of a Cavalry company organized for the rebel army, but disbanded by the Federal troops, and a contraband trader. When Col. Dwight, of the Excelsior Brigade, scoured that portion of the country with his regiment, Jack Scroggins, a slave, reported to the Colonel that Cox and his confederates had secreted quite a large amount of ammunition and arms, and true enough, these arms and ammunition were found in Cox's house and in an adjoining marsh. The regiment moved down to its present encampment above Hilltop. Jack joined them, and this was about eleven miles from his home. Cox dared to lay claim to his slave, and under the promise that he would not harm the slave he was surrendered up to him, but not without difficulty, for the men protested and forcibly rescued him when an officer rode up and declared he would shoot the first man that again interfered with the master, and thus was this man returned to bondage by an officer of the United States army. Such was the reward of disinterested loyalty. Cox, the cursed fiend, tied the man to his horse and rode at a rapid rate, the poor slave running to keep up behind him. When he left the regiment he had on a pair of good shoes, but when he reached his master's house his shoes were gone, and his bleeding feet were found to be bursting open from coming in contact with pebbles and stones. He had been dragged eleven miles behind his master's horse! They arrived

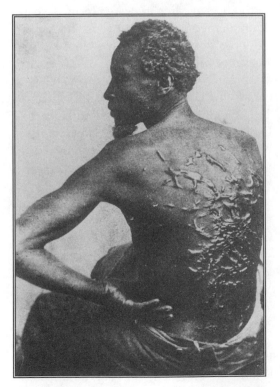

A slave shows the scars he received from whipping.

home in the evening about 11 o'clock on a Friday. He tied him to a tree and called his overseer, Franklin Roby, and a man by the name of John Robinson. They commenced whipping him about twelve o'clock and whipped him until three o'clock, three hours taking turns with the whip, when one was tired and breathless another would apply the lash. The only words he uttered up to two o'clock were, "I shall not live after this." "Oh, no you rascal I intend to kill you!" said Cox. "Mr. Cox," said Robinson, "he is dying." "No he is not. He is stout-hearted and able-bodied. He can stand as much more. However, give me the whip, let his blood be upon my head," replied Cox. The lash was then applied until about two hours before day. Say the narrators about 3 o'clock he was cut down and sank to the earth insensible. He had on a new cotton shirt when they began to whip him, and when they were done there was nothing left of it but the collar-band and the wrist-bands. Then commenced the rubbing down to bring back sensibility, but all of no avail. Their unfortunate victim breathed his last before sun-down on Saturday evening. Thus perished a loyal negro at the hands of a traitor. Oh, what a terrible reward for patriotism; death in its worst and hideous form, by torture! Yet the villain who did this is at liberty! This is the way United States officers treat traitors. They would plunge all of the country's wealth, learning and prosperity in a vortex of ruin; yes even hurl it from amongst the family of nations. But my dear sir, when I dwell on the diabolism of the deed my hand trembles, my nerves lose their steadiness, my mind its self-possession.

SUN 12 JAN. *While fugitive slaves increasingly sought protection in Union camps, U.S. law still required that army officers return them to their masters unless the runaways could prove they had been employed in the war effort against the Union. Some soldiers, however, disregarded the law and offered asylum to the fugitives. Among them were soldiers of the Fourteenth New York Militia Regiment, stationed at Upton Hill, Virginia. These Brooklyn natives harbored one John Boston, a runaway slave from Maryland. In the following letter to his wife, Boston rejoiced in his freedom yet bemoaned the necessary separation from his family.*

Contrabands in Culpeper, Virginia.

MY DEAR WIFE   IT IS WITH grate joy i take this time to let you know Whare i am   i am now in Safety in the 14th Regiment of Brooklyn   this Day i can Adress you thank god as a free man i had a little truble in giting away But as the lord led the Children of Isrel to the land of Canon So he led me to a land Whare freedom Will rain in spite Of earth and hell   Dear you must make your Self content i am free from al the Slavers Lash and as you have chose the Wise plan Of Serving the lord i hope you Will pray Much and i Will try by the help of god To Serv him With all my hart   i am With a very nice man and have All that hart Can Wish But My Dear I Cant express my grate desire that i Have to See you   i trust the time Will Come When We Shal meet again   And if We don't met on earth We Will Meet in heven Whare Jesas ranes Dear Elizabeth tell Mrs Owens That i trust that She Will Continue Her kind-ness to you and that god Will Bless her on earth and Save her In grate eternity   My Acomplements To Mrs Owens and her Children   may They Prosper through life I never Shall forgit her kindness to me Dear Wife i must Close   rest yourself Contented i am free   i Want you to rite To me Soon as you Can Without Delay Direct your letter to the 14th Regiment New york State malitia Uptons Hill Virginea In Care of Mr Cranford Comary Write my Dear Soon As you C   Your Affectionate Husban   Kiss Daniel For me
     John Boston
Give my love to Father and Mother

TUE 14 JAN. # FREDERICK DOUGLASS SPEAKS IN PHILADELPHIA

While other Americans continued to debate the causes of the war, committed abolitionists such as Frederick Douglass

Frederick Douglass

proclaimed slavery its obvious primary cause and, therefore, emancipation its ultimate goal. During the first year of the war, and thereafter, Douglass criss-crossed the North on speaking tours, urging his audience to accept emancipation as a principal war aim. The following is taken from a speech that Douglass delivered in Philadelphia on this date.

TODAY, ALL IS CHANGED. THE face of every loyal citizen is sicklied over with the pale cast of thought. Every pillar in the national temple is shaken. The nation itself has fallen asunder in the center. A million of armed men confront each other....

To what cause may we trace our present sad and deplorable condition? A man of flighty brain and flippant tongue will tell you that the cause of all our national troubles lies solely in the election of Abraham Lincoln to the President of the Republic. To the superficial this is final....Beyond all question, the facts show that this rebellion was planned and prepared long before the name of Abraham Lincoln was mentioned in connection with the office he now holds, and that though the catastrophe might have been postponed, it could not have been prevented, nor long delayed. The worst of our condition is not to be sought in our disaster on flood or field. It is to be found rather in the character which contact with slavery has developed in every part of the country, so that at last there seems to be no truth, no candor left within us....

...Jefferson Davis is reticent. He seems ashamed to tell the world just what he is fighting for. Abraham Lincoln seems equally so, and is ashamed to tell the world what he is fighting against....

Just here lies a true explanation of our troubles....We have attempted to maintain our Union in utter defiance of the moral chemistry of the universe. We have endeavored to join together things which in their nature stand eternally asunder. We have sought to bind the chains of slavery on the limbs of the black man, without thinking that at last we should find the other end of that hateful chain about our own necks....

We are fighting the rebels with only one hand, when we ought to be fighting them with both. We are recruiting our troops in the towns and villages of the North, when we ought to be recruiting them on the plantations of the South. We are striking the guilty rebels with our soft, white hand, when we should be striking with the iron hand of the black man, which we keep chained behind us. We have been catching slaves, instead of arming them....

I say here and now, that if this nation is destroyed—if the Government shall, after all, be broken to pieces, and degraded in the eyes of the world—if the Union shall be shattered into fragments, it will neither be for the want of men, nor of money, not even physical courage, for we have all these in abundance; but it will be solely owing to the want of moral courage and wise statesmanship in dealing with slavery, the cause and motive of the rebellion.

THU
16
JAN.
Hundreds of notices like this one from the Richmond Daily Dispatch *appeared in papers north and south throughout the war.*

FOURTH STREET HOSPITAL

The Ladies of the First Baptist Church have procured a house on Fourth street, beyond Leigh, and propose opening it as a hospital for sick and wounded soldiers, on Monday next. They will be grateful for any supplies either of provisions or clothing, from the city or country, that may be adapted to the wants of the patients. Contributions for this purpose may be left at the hospital, or at the store of Mr. Wm G. Dandridge, 106 Broad street.

FRI 31 JAN. EMERSON ON LINCOLN

During a visit to Washington, Ralph Waldo Emerson recorded in his journal his impressions this day of Abraham Lincoln as well as life in the capital.

THE PRESIDENT IMPRESSED ME more favorably than I had hoped. A frank, sincere, well-meaning man, with a lawyer's habit of mind, good clear statement of his fact, correct enough, not vulgar, as described; but with a sort of boyish cheerfulness, or that kind of sincerity & jolly good meaning that our class meetings on Commencement Days show, in telling our old stories over. When he has made his remark, he looks up at you with great satisfaction, & shows all his white teeth, & laughs....When I was introduced to him, he said, "O Mr. Emerson, I once heard you say in lecture, that a Kentuckian seems to say by his air & manners, 'Here I am; if you don't like me, the worse for you.'"...

With the South the war is primary; with the North it is secondary; secondary of course to their trade, then also to their pleasure. The theatres & concerts are filled as usual.

Abraham Lincoln as he appeared in late 1861, from a collodion glass-plate negative made by Mathew Brady.

FEBRUARY
1862

SAT 8 FEB. ROANOKE ISLAND

After the capture of the forts guarding Hatteras Inlet in late August 1861, Roanoke Island to the north became the next logical target of the Union effort to control the North Carolina coastline. The fortifications on Roanoke Island, however, could not be reduced by naval gunfire alone, so a beach landing and infantry assault were planned. Delays followed delays, but the navy finally accomplished the arduous task of moving several warships over the shallow bar into Pamlico Sound in preparation for the attack. Because the idea of a flat-bottomed boat designed specifically for landing soldiers was still nearly a century away, the Union forces had to make do with rowboats. The February 7 landing, detailed in Brig. Gen. Ambrose Burnside's official report of the February 8 battle, was both innovative and appropriate for the available resources. Burnside had sailed from Hampton Roads with the fleet on January 11, arriving off Cape Hatteras on January

Brig. Gen. Ambrose E. Burnside

This illustration appeared on the cover of sheet music celebrating Burnside's early North Carolina successes.

13, at which time he had assumed command of the newly created Department of North Carolina.

IN LESS THAN TWENTY MINUTES from the time the boats reached the shore 4,000 of our men were passing over the marshes at a double-quick and forming in most perfect order on the dry land near the house; and I beg leave to say that I never witnessed a more beautiful sight than that presented by the approach of these vessels to the shore and the landing and forming of the troops. Each brigadier-general had a light-draught steamer, to which were attached some 20 surf-boats in a long line in the rear. Both steamers and boats were densely filled with soldiers, and each boat bearing the national flag....As the steamers approached the shore at a rapid speed each surf-boat was "let go," and with their acquired velocity and by direction of the steersman reached the shore in line.

SUN 16 FEB. GRANT TAKES FORT DONELSON

U. S. Grant, by now recognized as one of the more aggressive and successful commanders in the Western Theater, was soon put in command of a large river campaign aimed deep into the heart of Tennessee. Its success, however, required that Grant first subdue two troublesome forts, Henry amd Donelson, guarding the Tennessee and Cumberland Rivers. On February 6, Grant's

This Currier & Ives lithograph depicts the storming of Fort Donelson.

Federals fairly easily overwhelmed Fort Henry, but Donelson was much more heavily defended. At first, on February 14, Grant sent the four ironclads that had whipped the garrison at Fort Henry against Donelson, but nearly fifteen thousand Confederates under John B. Floyd, Gideon Pillow, and Simon Bolivar Buckner drove off the attack. The next day, the Confederates punched a hole in Grant's encircling army, opening an escape route to Nashville, but Grant counterattacked, filling the gap before the indecisive Confederates could seize their hard-won advantage. That night, abandoning their commands, Floyd and Pillow fled somewhat ignominiously the doomed garrison (neither would command troops again), while

the next morning Buckner—hoping for leniency from his West Point classmate Grant—offered a truce. Below are both Grant's famous reply, which begat his nickname, and Buckner's prickly rejoinder. Nearly 16,500 Confederates were lost defending the two forts, compared to about 3,000 Federal casualties. More importantly, with their capture, Tennessee and passage to the Deep South lay open to Grant's army.

General S. B. Buckner, Confederate Army.

Sir: Yours of this date, proposing armistice and appointment of Commissioners to settle terms of capitulation, is just received. No terms except an unconditional and immediate surrender can be accepted. I propose to move immediately upon your works.

> I am, sir, very respectfully,
> Your ob't se'v't,
> U. S. Grant
> Brig. Gen.

Brig. Gen'l U.S. Grant,
U.S. Army.

Sir: The distribution of the forces under my command, incident to an unexpected change of commanders, and the overwhelming force under your command, compel me, notwithstanding the brilliant success of Confederate arms yesterday, to accept the ungenerous and unchivalrous terms you propose.

> I am, sir,
> Your very ob't se'v't,
> S. B. Buckner
> Brig. Gen. C.S.A.

Brig. Gen. Henry Hopkins Sibley

FRI 21 FEB. VALVERDE

Carrying out his daring plan to build a "Confederate Southwest," Brig. Gen. Henry Hopkins Sibley led a force of four thousand Texans into New Mexico, where he attacked an equal force of Federals on this date at Valverde. The Union troops under Col. E. R. S. Canby withdrew, permitting Sibley to capture both Albuquerque (on March 2) and Santa Fe (on March 4). In the following report, Sibley subordinate Maj. C. L. Pyron described his unit's actions at Valverde. Note his concern regarding the availability of water: This logistical problem would eventually doom Sibley's

Col. E. R. S. Canby

campaign and force his withdrawal back to Texas.

MAJOR: ON THE MORNING OF the 21st instant I left our camp, opposite Fort Craig, with 180 men of my command…to reconnoiter the road leading to the river near Valverde. Upon reaching the river I could see the water, with none of the enemy intervening. I immediately dispatched a note to the general commanding, stating the road was clear and the water in sight, and proceeded leisurely to the river to water our horses, they having been over twenty-four hours without water.

When I reached the woods I discovered a body of cavalry, which I supposed to be about four companies, and immediately gave chase, they withdrawing to my left. I followed until reaching the bank of a slough in the bottom, when I found myself in front of a large force of all arms. Immediately my men were formed along the bank, when the action commenced, and for over one hour, by the courage and determination of the men, I was enabled to maintain the position in the unequal struggle, when I was relieved by the Fourth Regiment Texas Mounted Volunteers, under the command of Lieut. Col. W. R. Scurry.

For nearly two hours our joint commands held our position against odds of three to one, checking every attempt to outflank us and checking every effort to drive us back. The arrival of Teel's battery of artillery was the first re-enforcement we received, but it was soon followed by Major Lockridge's battalion, of the Fifth Regiment Texas Mounted Volunteers, and about 1 o'clock Colonel Green reached the field and took command. Late in the afternoon a general charge was made along our line, by which a battery of artillery, consisting of six guns, was taken and their left driven back. Following rapidly up our successes, the enemy were driven back at all points, and the field of Valverde was won.

SAT 22 FEB. JEFFERSON DAVIS INAUGURATED (AGAIN)

On a stormy Washington's Birthday, a year after his first inauguration as provisional president of the Confederacy, Jefferson Davis was finally sworn in as permanent president of the Confederate States of America for a six-year term. The swearing-in ceremony followed a November 6, 1861, popular election in which Davis had run unopposed. He took the prescribed oath of office at the Virginia state capitol in Richmond, to the strains of "Dixie" and "La Marseillaise," while a hardy crowd braved mud and torrential rain to hear him speak. In that address, excerpted below, Davis invoked the Founding Fathers in an attempt to lend some historical luster to the Confederacy.

IT IS WITH MINGLED FEELINGS of humility and pride that I appear to take, in the presence of the people and before high Heaven, the oath prescribed as a qualification for the exalted station to which the unanimous voice of the people has called me.…The experiment instituted by our revolutionary fathers, of a voluntary Union of sovereign States for the purposes specified in a solemn compact, [was] perverted by those who, feeling power and forgetting right, were determined to respect no law but their own will. The Government had ceased to answer the ends for which it was ordained and established....

The first year in our history has been the most eventful in the annals of this continent. A new Government has been established, and its machinery put in operation over an area exceeding seven hundred thousand square miles. The great principles upon which we have been willing to hazard everything that is dear to man have made conquests for us which could never have been achieved by the sword....Our people have rallied with unexampled unanimity to the support of the great principles of constitutional government, with firm resolve to perpetuate by arms the right which they could not peacefully secure. A million of men, it is estimated, are now standing in hostile array, and waging war along a frontier of thousands of miles....

The Virginia state capitol in Richmond, which also served as the Confederate capitol.

This great strife has awakened in the people the highest emotions and qualities of the human soul. It is cultivating feelings of patriotism, virtue, and courage. Instances of self-sacrifice and of generous devotion to the noble cause for which we are contending are rife throughout the land. Never has a people evinced a more determined spirit than that now animating men, women, and children in every part of our country....

With humble gratitude and adoration, acknowledging the Providence which has so visibly protected the Confederacy during its brief but eventful career, to thee, O God, I trustingly commit myself, and prayerfully invoke thy blessing on my country and its cause.

Meanwhile, the driving rains prevented Judith McGuire, late of Alexandria (and Manassas), from attending the inaugural. McGuire, who had since relocated to a boardinghouse in Richmond, confessed her disappointment in this diary entry.

TODAY I HAD HOPED TO SEE OUR President inaugurated, but the rain falls in torrents, and I cannot go. So many persons are disappointed, but we are comforted by knowing that the inauguration will take place, and that the reins of our government will continue to be in strong hands. His term of six years must be eventful, and to him, and all others, so full of anxiety! What may we not experience during those six years? Oh, that all hearts may this day be raised to Almighty God for his guidance! Has there been a day since the Fourth of July, 1776, so full of interest, so fraught with danger, so

encompassed by anxiety, so sorrowful, and yet so hopeful, as this 22d of February, 1862? Our wrongs then were great, and our enemy powerful, but neither can the one nor the other compare with all that we have endured from the oppression, and must meet in the gigantic efforts of the Federal Government. Our people are depressed by our recent disasters, but our soldiers are encouraged by the bravery and endurance of the troops at Donelson. It fell, but not until human nature yielded from exhaustion.

WED 26 FEB. THE LEGAL TENDER ACT

By 1862, the mounting cost of the war had drawn down the federal treasury to critically low levels. Bonds were offered and taxes levied, particularly in the later years, but the need for cash in early 1862 was desperate and pressing. The Legal Tender Act, signed this day, embodied one of the more controversial solutions to this problem: It permitted the government to issue paper money, or greenbacks, not supported by specie— that is, not backed by gold or silver. In designating these paper dollars legal tender, the U.S. government was forcing merchants and others to accept them in satisfaction of current and previously existing debt. Without this status, as Rep. George Dawson correctly notes in the following February 6 letter, their value would have been insignificant because no one would have accepted them as long as other forms of payment, such as gold coins and gold-backed state

The House floor as it appeared during the Civil War.

currency. If made a legal tender, these notes could never sink below the best bank paper. If not so made, they would very soon cease to be available as a circulating medium....

It was not strange that members of the same political family, differed on a question of really doubtful expediency. And but for the necessities of Government, I doubt whether the "legal tender" principle would have received a dozen votes in the House. It is a new financial principle, and its workings may result in some, if not all the evils predicted from it. Nevertheless, as Treasury notes *had* to be resorted to, the common sense of the House, as well as the common sense of the people, determined that they should be made as near the practical value of gold as possible....

The country breathes freer! The legal tender bill has passed the House, and national bankruptcy is averted. The grateful thanks of all loyal men are due to Mr. Spaulding and the representatives who supported the measure, for this timely effort in behalf of the public credit. The relief comes not a moment too soon. Now let the Senate do its duty promptly, and we shall be clear "of the breakers."

notes, were available. The value of these greenbacks, whose worth depended on the government's ability to meet its obligations, fluctuated with the ups and downs of the war, reaching its lowest point (thirty-nine cents on the dollar) in early 1864. Retiring the greenbacks after the war, of course, would be a political problem all its own.

THIS HAS BEEN AN EXCITING DAY in the House. A fierce battle has been waged against the "legal tender" Treasury notes. But, as I think, the right has prevailed, and by a vote of 95 to 59—a much stronger force than was counted upon. The real argument was reduced to a very small compass. All admitted the necessity of a resort to paper currency; and the question was whether that paper should be made as nearly par value as possible, or subjected to fluctuations and depreciations of an ordinary irredeemable

★ ★ ★ ★

MARCH 1862

FRI 7 MAR. PEA RIDGE (ELKHORN TAVERN)

After forcing the withdrawal of Maj. Gen. Sterling Price's Confederate regulars from Missouri, the superior Federal force of Brig. Gen. Samuel Curtis followed the Rebels into Arkansas. Curtis's plan was to destroy Price's army and then advance on Little Rock. Price's soldiers, however, were soon reinforced by a second Rebel army under Maj. Gen. Earl Van Dorn, so that Curtis's twelve thousand Federals now faced some sixteen thousand Confederates. Deciding to attack while he had the advantage, Van Dorn engaged Curtis on this day about thirty miles northeast of Fayetteville, near Elkhorn Tavern. With the Federals dug in along Pea Ridge, Van Dorn moved his men to the north so that they could attack from the Union rear. The battle, which concluded the next day, was an odd one, with fierce frontal assaults and heavy artillery cannonades. The mix of soldiers was also unusual: On the Rebel side, pro-Confederate tribesmen from the Indian Territory fought next to Texas Rangers; while German immigrants and Kansas Jayhawkers fought under Old Glory. A terrific artillery barrage finally forced Van Dorn's retreat. Brig. Gen. Franz Sigel, the most famous of the "immigrant generals" and an influential Republican, congratulated his divisions with this message, issued soon after the battle.

YOU MAY LOOK WITH PRIDE ON the few days just passed, during which you have so gloriously defended the flag of the Union. From two o'clock on the morning of the sixth, when you left McKissick's farm, until four o'clock in the afternoon of the ninth, when you arrived from Keitsville in the common encampment, you marched fifty miles, fought three battles, took not only a battery and a flag from the enemy, but more than one hundred and fifty prisoners....

You have done your duty, and justly claim your share in the common glory of this victory. But let us not be partial, unjust or haughty. Let us not forget that alone we were too weak to perform the great work before us. Let us acknowledge the great services done by all the brave soldiers of the Third and Fourth divisions, and always keep in mind that "united we stand, divided we fall." Let us hold out and push the work through—not by mere words and great clamor, but by good marches, by hardships and fatigues, by strict discipline and effective battles.

Brig. Gen. Franz Sigel

Columbus has fallen—Memphis will soon follow—and if you do in future as you have done in these past days of trial, the time will soon come when you will pitch your tents on the beautiful shores of the Arkansas River, and there meet our ironclad propellers at Little Rock and Fort Smith. Therefore, keep alert, my friends, and look forward with confidence.

To the Confederate presence in Arkansas and Missouri, the loss at Pea Ridge was devastating. As the armies of Van Dorn and Price retreated, they also disintegrated. In this letter home, an English expatriate described the Confederate withdrawal.

OUR SUFFERINGS DURING THE campaign had been extreme, but setting the inconveniences aside, had tended to harden us and make our limbs tough as steel. Continually marching through noninhabited districts, we had to depend upon Providence for supplies. Over mountains, through "gaps," across rivers and creeks, our progress was toilsome and weary; but few doctors meddled with anyone, and not more than a hundred names could be found upon the sick-list at any time during our frequent and rapid journeyings. Our cavalry led a hard life, and must have been made of brass to support the trials incident to their daily duty. Among the mountains a party of these "irregular" horse would watch all the roads, conceal their fires, and hang around the enemy with a pernicious determination that no man should stir without their knowledge, and at the least opportunity making a dash at the foe, cap-

This print of Pea Ridge, published as part of the 1889 Kurz & Allison Civil War series, shows how romanticized the war had become in just two decades.

turing and destroying as they went, living as best they might, and doing whatever they pleased generally....

This is a terribly wild, barren country for a campaign. The boys enjoy good health, however; but it would be of much greater advantage to the cause did proper disciplinarians come among us, for although brave and hard enough for any enterprise, we lack educated officers; and without them, little of importance can be effected against a numerous, well-appointed, and highly disciplined enemy. The late battle proved all this; and although we whipped the Yankees by sheer audacity, "rough and ready" fighting, with any weapons that may be at hand, we can not maintain a contest success-

fully with an army ever increasing in number, and supplied with the most costly arms in the world, and with every comfort and improvement provided which science or money can procure.

SUN 9 MAR. THE MONITOR AND THE MERRIMACK

Much of naval history is the history of technological advancement, and the battle that took place in the Hampton Roads channel off Norfolk, Virginia, this day was a technological milestone. The two contending ships, the USS Monitor and CSS Virginia (more commonly

known by its original name, the
Merrimack), *were the first fully ironclad steam-propelled ships to fight one
another. The Monitor, designed by the
mercurial Swedish-born inventor John
Ericsson, was a shallow-draft vessel with
a small rotating turret located amidship.
The ironclad looked, according to contemporary descriptions, like a "tin set
upon a shingle." The Virginia was a
converted U.S. Navy frigate. Unable to
sail from the soon-to-be-overrun Norfolk
Navy Yard, the powerful ship had been
burned to the waterline by retreating
Federal sailors in late April 1861. A
month later, however, the Merrimack
was raised and rechristened by the
Confederates, who proceeded to refit
the ship with armor plating set upon its
slanting sides. The Virginia's objective
was simple: to break the Union blockade. The Monitor's mission was to stop
the Virginia. The Confederate ironclad
struck first, savaging four warships in a
little more than four hours on March 8.
That night, the Monitor arrived. Its
chief engineer described the action on
March 9 in this letter to Ericsson.*

John Ericsson

MY DEAR SIR: AFTER A STORMY
passage, which proved us to be the
finest seaboat I was ever in, we fought the
Merrimack for more than three hours this
forenoon and sent her back to Norfolk in
a sinking condition. Ironclad against ironclad. We maneuvered about the bay here
and went at each other with mutual
fierceness. I consider that both ships were
well fought. We were struck 22 times—
pilot house twice, turret 9 times, side
armor 8 times, deck 3 times. The only
vulnerable point was the pilot house.

Crewmen aboard the USS Monitor.

One of your great logs (9 by 12 inches thick) is broken in two. The shot struck just outside of where the Captain had his eye, and it has disabled him by destroying his left and temporarily blinding the other. The log is not quite in two, but is broken and pressed inward 1½ inches. She tried to run us down and sink us, as she did the *Cumberland* yesterday, but she got the worst of it. Her bow passed over our deck and our sharp upper edged side cut through the light iron shoe upon her stem and well into her oak. She will not try that again. She gave us a tremendous thump, but did not injure us in the least. We are just able to find the point of contact.

The turret is a splendid structure. I do not think much of the shield, but the pendulums are fine things, though I can-not tell you how they would stand the shot, as they were not hit.

You are very correct in your estimate of the effect of shot upon the man on the inside of the turret when it was struck near him. Three men were knocked down, of whom I was one; the other two had to be carried below, but I was not disabled at all and the others recovered before the battle was over. Captain Worden stationed himself at the pilot house, Greene fired the guns, and I turned the turret until the captain was disabled and was relieved by Greene, when I managed the turret myself, Master Stodder having been one of the two stunned men.

Captain Ericsson, I congratulate you upon your great success. Thousands have this day blessed you. Every man feels that

Currier & Ives's lithograph Terrific Engagement Between the "Monitor" and "Merrimac" in Hampton Roads.

you have saved this place to the nation by furnishing us with the means to whip an ironclad frigate that was, until our arrival, having it all her own way with our most powerful vessels.

I am, with much esteem, very truly, yours,

Alban C. Stimers
Chief Engineer

FRI 14 MAR. NEW BERN

Having taken control of the Outer Banks with victories at Hatteras Inlet and Roanoke Island, the Union forces in North Carolina turned their attention inland, conducting a raid on this date up the Neuse River to the town of New Bern. Opposing the raiders were several state militia regiments and one regiment of citizen soldiers. Raised from the local population and armed with a mishmash of personal weapons, these men were simply not prepared, physically or mentally, for the sights and sounds of the battlefield. In his report, North Carolina militia colonel H. J. B. Clark described their performance.

 AS SOON AS THE FIRING COMmenced the ground in front of me was so obscured by smoke that I could see but a short distance, and as firing had commenced on my left with guns of longer range, as soon as I thought the enemy within reach of my guns commenced the fire by file, which order was promptly obeyed with coolness and determination. After firing three rounds I commanded the fire to cease. Soon after,

the smoke cleared away and the enemy were plainly seen drawn up in force on our right, and a company of sharpshooters commenced pouring a fire into our rear, doing considerable execution and causing confusion in my ranks, but an order to rally and take position was promptly obeyed, and calmness restored by the assurance that you would soon send reenforcements; but the fire was continued on us and with redoubled energy, while they (the enemy) crossed the railroad, took possession of the rifle pits on our right and rear, and planted the Stars and Stripes.

Previous to this, however, they had fired upon a reconnoitering party I sent in that direction and upon the quartermaster and teamsters I had sent to recover the ammunition.

I at one time intended to leave the breastworks and charge upon the enemy, and for this purpose caused bayonets to be fixed; but when I saw the sharpshooters were supported by so large a force of the enemy, concluded that such attempt

A lieutenant colonel from North Carolina.

would result in great loss of life to my command without being able to effect corresponding good to our cause, and that a failure might have an evil effect on others. At this moment, and just as Colonel Vance poured his first fire into the enemy, a panic seized my command and part of them broke ranks.

Believing it impossible to reform under the fire of these sharpshooters at this moment of confusion I commanded a retreat in order, which was succeeded by a stampede of most of the command. As soon as they had reached a small brushwood, perhaps 60 yards distant, I ordered a rally and reformation of the line, in which I was promptly aided by every officer present to my view and for the moment thought I should succeed, but the cry was made that the regulars had retreated; the panic was renewed and increased and my influence as a commander gone.

These Confederate fortifications outside Yorktown, Virginia, were reinforced with bales of cotton.

MON 17 MAR. THE PENINSULAR CAMPAIGN BEGINS

Though much savaged in later years for his lack of aggressiveness, Maj. Gen. George McClellan was no doubt a superb manager of men. His grand plan for the capture of Richmond, and thereby the destruction of the Confederacy, was innovative and sophisticated, and it made clever use of two potentially decisive Union advantages: its control of the seas and its existing foothold at Fort Monroe on the peninsula formed by the James and York Rivers. (Richmond itself lay just upstream on the James.) The long-awaited Peninsular Campaign finally commenced this day as soldiers of the Army of the Potomac began boarding troop carriers at Alexandria. Contemporaries would soon complain repeatedly about McClellan's ultraslow movement up the peninsula—as military historians have ever since, some even going so far as to blame McClellan for not ending the war in 1862—but to the soldier on the ground, the rights and wrongs were much less clear. What follows is Pvt. Warren Lee Goss's opinion of his army's march toward Richmond.

AFTER LEAVING BIG BETHEL WE began to feel the weight of our knapsacks. Castaway overcoats, blankets, parade-coats, and shoes were scattered along the route in reckless profusion, being dropped by the overloaded soldiers, as if after ploughing the roads with heavy teams they were sowing them for a harvest.

The march up the Peninsula seemed very slow, yet it was impossible to increase our speed, owing to the bad condition of the roads. I learned in time that marching on paper and the actual march made two very different impressions. I can easily understand and excuse our fireside heroes, who fought their or our battles at home over comfortable breakfast-tables, without impediments of any kind to circumscribe their fancied operations; it is so much easier to manoeuvre and fight large armies around the corner grocery, where the destinies of the human race have been so often discussed and settled, than to fight, march and manoeuvre in mud and rain, in the face of a brave and vigilant enemy.

★ ★ ★ ★

Marshy ground made travel so difficult during the Peninsular Campaign that McClellan's army was often forced to construct its own roads, such as the one pictured above.

APRIL
1862

SUN 6 APR. SHILOH (PITTSBURG LANDING)

Ulysses S. Grant knew that the Confederates in Tennessee would have to engage his invading army at some point, but he expected their attack to come nearer the strategic road and rail center of Corinth in northeastern Mississippi—not at the little hamlet of Pittsburg Landing on the west bank of the Tennessee River. (The battle takes its more common name from the Shiloh Church around which Grant's army was camped at the time of the attack.) The all-out assault this day, led by Confederate generals Albert Sidney Johnston and P. G. T. Beauregard, caught Grant completely off guard and resulted in the war's bloodiest battle yet, with the Union forces gradually recovering from their surprise and fighting the Rebels to a standstill. Although Grant was later faulted for his egregious lack of preparedness, he nevertheless managed to deprive the South of what Johnston (who received a fatal wound in the battle) and Beauregard expected would be a decisive victory. More than thirteen thousand of the sixty-two thousand Union soldiers involved were reported killed, wounded, or missing. The Confederates suffered even worse casualties, amounting to a full quarter of the forty thousand men on hand. Pvt. Lucius Barber of the Fifteenth Illinois Volunteer Infantry recalled the alarm that shot through the Union camp as the attack began.

Maj. Gen. Ulysses S. Grant

THE ENEMY WAS IN CAMP BEFORE it [the camp] had time to arouse and form a line. Some were shot in their sleep, never knowing what hurt them. Terrible and complete was the surprise. Our boys fought as only those can fight who are fighting for the right. Rally[ing] amidst a perfect storm of bullets, shot and shell, they tried to form a new line, and as the infuriated enemy, made mad with whisky and gunpowder, hurled themselves against the line, it gradually fell back, step by step, forming new and stronger lines and leaving their track strewn with the dead and dying. The onset of the foe was terrific, but instead of the easy victory that had been promised them, they were met with a valor superior to their own, as the cool aim of our boys which strewed the ground with dead amply testified.

MON 7 APR. *Pvt. John Jackman, a Confederate soldier serving in a nearby hospital tent, received a taste of the Union onslaught on the second day of the battle.*

The tents of a Virginia field hospital.

ONCE THAT MORNING A BODY OF Federal cavalry came close enough to fire on us, tearing up the tents but fortunately hurting no one. Dr. P. and I were standing close together talking when a ball passed between our noses which instantly stopped our conversation. We soon hung up [crossed] strips of red flannel to prevent further accidents of the kind. A little after the middle of the day, the battle raged terribly—it was the last struggle of the Confederates, ending in defeat. Soon after I saw Genl. Beauregard, accompanied by one or two of his staff, ride leisurely back to the rear as cool and unperturbed as if nothing had happened.

As Shiloh raged in its second day, Kate Cumming and a small group of likeminded civilians from Mobile, Alabama, including a clergyman and several ladies, boarded a train with the intention of traveling to Corinth to nurse the sick and wounded from the battle. Cumming's contemporary journal entry expressed her anxiety regarding the fate of loved ones engaged in the fighting.

I LEFT MOBILE BY THE MOBILE and Ohio Railroad for Corinth, with Rev. Mr. Miller and a number of Mobile ladies. We are going for the purpose of taking care of the sick and wounded of the army.

As news has come that a battle is now raging, there are not a few anxious hearts in the party—my own among the number, as I have a young brother, belonging to Ketchum's Battery, who I know will be in the midst of the fight, and I have also many dear friends there.

Winslow Homer's 1862 wood engraving
News from the War: Wounded.

A gentleman, Mr. Skates, has heard that his son is among the killed, and is with us on his way to the front to bring back the remains of him who a short time since formed one of his family circle. May God give strength to the mother and sisters now mourning the loss of their loved one! May they find consolation in the thought that he died a martyr's death; was offered up a sacrifice upon the altar of his country; and that, when we have gained our independence, he, with the brave comrades who fought and fell with him, will ever live in the hearts and memories of a grateful people! I can not look at Mr. Skates without asking myself how many of us may ere long be likewise mourners! It is impossible to suppress these gloomy forebodings.

About midnight, at one of the stations, a dispatch was received prohibiting any one from going to Corinth without a special permit from headquarters. Our disappointment can be better imagined than described. As military orders are peremptory, there is nothing for us to do but to submit. Mr. Miller has concluded to stop at one of the small towns, as near Corinth as he can get, and there wait until he receives permission for us to go on.

THE FALL OF ISLAND NO. 10

Located forty miles south of Cairo, Illinois, at New Madrid Bend, Island Number 10 was a strategically important choke point in the Mississippi River. The Confederates had it heavily fortified, and if the big guns weren't enough to deter a Union assault, the swampy topography of the island and its environs further stymied Union plans to capture the Confederate stronghold. In order to overcome both the geography and the Confederate batteries, Maj. Gen. John Pope ran past the guns two riverine ironclads, the USS Carondelet (on April 4) and the USS Pittsburg (on April 7). Pope then began bombarding nearby Rebel positions. The next day, on April 8, Confederate Brig. Gen. W. W. Mackall surrendered his thirty-five hundred men, twenty-five field guns, and a large store of supplies. Pope became an overnight hero, and soon afterward, with this telegram, several prominent Illinois politicians petitioned the president to have the major general of volunteers promoted.

Currier & Ives's lithograph The Bombardment and Capture of Island Number 10.

WE APPEAL TO YOU TO TRANSFER Maj Genl John Pope to the regular army with his present rank as a token of gratitude to Illinois. Give one of her sons a position in the U.S. army who has so gloriously achieved the just reward we ask for him.

Lincoln, perhaps knowing the limitations of his fellow Illinoisan (which would become apparent enough at Second Bull Run), sent back one of his famously witty replies.

I FULLY APPRECIATE GEN. POPE'S splendid achievements with their invaluable results; but you must know that Major Generalships in the Regular Army, are not as plenty as blackberries.

A. Lincoln

Maj. Gen. John Pope

WED 9 APR. *As this message to George McClellan makes plain, President Lincoln was by now becoming quite exasperated with his general-in-chief's slow pace and apparent refusal to engage the enemy—as well as with McClellan's tendency to overestimate the strength of his oppponent and to insist that Lincoln send him more troops. The Army of the Potomac possessed at this point an enormous advantage in numbers yet crept cautiously up the peninsula as though it had none.*

MY DEAR SIR: YOUR DESPATCHES complaining that you are not properly sustained, while they do not offend me, do pain me very much....

I do not forget that I was satisfied with your arrangement to leave Banks at Manassas Junction; but when that arrangement was broken up, and *nothing* was substituted for it, of course I was not satisfied. I was constrained to substitute something for it myself. And now allow me to ask "Do you really think I should permit the line from Richmond, *via* Manassas Junction, to this city to be entirely open, except what resistance could be presented by less than twenty thousand unorganized troops?" This is a question which the country will not allow me to evade.

There is a curious mystery about the *number* of the troops now with you. When I telegraphed you on the 6th saying you had over a hundred thousand with you, I had just obtained from the Secretary of War, a statement, taken as he said, from your own returns, making 108,000 then with you, and en route to you. You now say you will have but 85,000, when all en route to you shall have reached you. How can the discrepancy of 23,000 be accounted for?...

I suppose the whole force which has gone forward to you, is with you by this time; and if so, I think it is the precise time for you to strike a blow. By delay the enemy will relatively gain upon you— that is, he will gain faster, by *fortifications* and *re-inforcements,* than you can by re-inforcements alone.

And, once more let me tell you, it is indispensable to *you* that you strike a blow. I am powerless to help this. You will do me the justice to remember I always insisted, that going down the Bay in search of a field, instead of fighting at or near Manassas, was only shifting, and not surmounting, a difficulty—that we would find the same enemy, and the same, or equal, intrenchments, at either place. The country will not fail to note—is now noting—that the present hesitation to move upon an intrenched enemy, is but the story of Manassas repeated.

I beg to assure you that I have never written you, or spoken to you, in greater kindness of feeling than now, nor with a fuller purpose to sustain you, so far as in my most anxious judgment, I consistently can. *But you must act.*

Yours very truly

A. Lincoln

SAT
12
APR.

THE GREAT LOCOMOTIVE CHASE

The Chattanooga-to-Atlanta railroad line, of vital strategic importance to the Confederacy, was the scene this day of one of the war's most thrilling adventures. In Marietta, Georgia, twenty-two Union volunteers wearing civilian disguises boarded a passenger train of the Western & Atlantic line. When the train's crew stopped for breakfast at Big Shanty, the Union infiltrators, led by James J. Andrews, took off with the engine and three freight cars (having already uncoupled the passenger carriages). Aided by local Confederate troops, the crew soon gave chase in another engine. The Great Locomotive Chase lasted all day, ending when Andrews's train ran out of fuel outside Ringgold, Georgia, the raiders having done little more than cut a few telegraph wires. They took to the woods but were all captured by the pursuing Confederates. Andrews and seven others were executed, another eight escaped from prison, and the remaining six were eventually paroled. The mission was a failure, but its audacity and daring caught the attention of both North and South. In the letter below, John S. Rowland, superintendent of the Western & Atlantic Railroad, reported (not very accurately) the details of the incident to Georgia governor Joseph E. Brown, who also happened to be the railroad's chief executive.

ONE OF OUR ENGINES AND two cars were cut loose yesterday morning while our hands were at breakfast at Big Shanty. Sixteen bridge burners took charge, and ran at a rapid rate, tearing up track and breaking down the telegraph wires before they got to Etowah. Our railroad men pursued with a hand car, had the rails put back, took Cooper's engine and procured another engine. Freight was started in pursuit, from Big Shanty with Col. Philips and a body of armed men. They all ran rapidly and were not able to overtake them until they got a mile above Ringgold. They were getting out of water and wood, and seeing they would be taken, jumped off the car and took to the woods, but were pursued and 3 of them taken last night and are now in custody here. The up train has just arrived, and on examination another is arrested and identified as one of the gang that was along yesterday. He will be secured well with the others. One of them took 150 lashes at Ringgold before he would acknowledge and then said there were sixteen of them sent as spies to burn our railroad bridges. 5 made their escape from the cars last night that have not yet been caught. But Col. C. Philips and others were after them when I left Ringgold.

I learn that two have been arrested at Big Shanty yesterday. The prisoners acknowledged that they left four of the gang in Atlanta. They have been passing up and down our railroad for many days looking into the condition of things, got our schedules, etc. As they came on with our engine and cars they said they had pressed our engine to take powder to the battlefield. They got the switch keys from some of our railroad agents, passed on without being suspected until overtaken. It was a very daring act and I hope we will get them all.

SUN
13
APR.
Most of the escaped slaves who sought refuge with the Union army were men. Yet in this extract

from her memoirs Susie King Taylor describes her own childhood flight from slavery to freedom. The Fort Pulaski to which she refers guarded Savannah Harbor. It fell to the Union on April 11.

ON APRIL 1, 1862, ABOUT THE time the Union soldiers were firing on Fort Pulaski, I was sent out into the country with my mother. I remember what a roar and din the guns made. They jarred the earth for miles. The fort was at last taken by them. Two days after the taking of Fort Pulaski, my uncle took his family of seven and myself to St. Catherine Island. We landed under the protection of the Union fleet...and at last, to my unbounded joy, I saw the "Yankee."

After we were all settled aboard and started on our journey, Captain Whitmore, commanding the boat, asked me where I was from. I told him Savannah, Ga. He asked if I could read; I said, "Yes!" "Can you write?" he next asked. "Yes, I can do that also," I replied, and as if he had some doubts of my answers he handed me a book and a pencil and told me to write my name and where I was from. I did this; then he wanted to know if I could sew. On hearing I could, he asked me to hem some napkins for him. He was surprised at my accomplishments...for he said he did not know there were any negroes in the South able to read or write. He said, "You seem to be so different from the other colored people who came from the same place you did." "No!" I replied, "the only difference is, they were reared in the country and I in the city..." That seemed to satisfy him, and we had no further conversation that day on the subject.

TUE
15
APR.

PERALTA

The Confederate loss at La Glorieta Pass on March 28 marked the farthest extent of H. H. Sibley's foray into New Mexico. The loss of Albuquerque and Santa Fe in early March had persuaded the Union high command to reinforce Col. E. R. S. Canby's army in the territory. Sibley, meanwhile, had supply problems that eventually forced him to abandon his gains and fall back to Texas. During this retreat—at Peralta, twenty miles south of Albuquerque—Canby attacked, turning Sibley's orderly withdrawal into a rout. The remnants of the Rebel force, completely disorganized, didn't reach El Paso until late May, and Sibley never received another significant command. Canby, however, rose to the rank of major general and directed the successful siege of Mobile, Alabama. Below is an excerpt from Confederate Maj. T. T. Teel's postwar analysis of Sibley's New Mexico campaign.

 THE DIRECT CAUSE OF OUR discomfiture and the failure of our campaign was the want of supplies of all kinds for the use of our army. The territory which we occupied was no storehouse. Colonel Canby's order to destroy everything that would be of use to the Confederates had been fully enforced. Thus we were situated in the very heart of the enemy's country, with well-equipped forces in our front and rear.

General Sibley was not a good administrative officer. He did not husband his resources, and was too prone to let the morrow take care of itself. But for this the expedition never would have been undertaken, nor would he have left the enemy between him and his base of supplies, a mistake which he made at Fort Craig. The other reasons for the failure of the campaign were want of supplies, ammunition, discipline, and confidence. Under such circumstances failure was inevitable.

WED
16
APR.

THE CONFEDERATE CONSCRIPTION ACT

If it wasn't clear already, the lengthy casualty lists from places like Bull Run, Wilson's Creek, and Shiloh persuaded all that the Civil War would not be a short, grand adventure. Equally clear, the days of enthusiastic volunteers lining up to enlist were over. Both governments made preparations for compulsory service, but the Confederacy moved first. The Confederate Congress passed, and on this day President Davis signed, an unprecedented military conscription act, creating the first general draft in American history. (Five days later, however, the first of many, many exceptions were added to the law, exempting not only government officials but also postal workers, ferrymen, ironworkers, academics, and pharmacists, among others.)

SECTION 1. The Congress of the Confederate States of America do enact, That the President be, and he is hereby authorized to call out and place in the military service of the Confederate

States, for three years, unless the war shall have been sooner ended, all white men who are residents of the Confederate States, between the ages of eighteen and thirty-five years at the time the call or calls may be made, who are not legally exempted from military service. All of the persons aforesaid who are now in the armies of the Confederacy, and whose term of service will expire before the end of the war, shall be continued in the service for three years from the date of their original enlistment, unless the war shall have sooner ended.

To no one's surprise, the new Conscription Act was enormously unpopular in areas of the South where loyalty to the new nation was lukewarm at best. The North Carolina hill country, for example, was a hotbed of Unionist sentiment, and this letter from an angry conscripted Tarheel to the Confederate president illustrates the bitterness engendered by the draft.

EXCELLENCY DAVIS: IT IS WITH feelings of undeveloped pleasure that an affectionate conscript intrusts this sheet of confiscated paper to the tender mercies of a Confederate States mail-carrier, addressed as it shall be to yourself, O Jeff, Red Jacket of the Gulf and Chief of the Six Nations—more or less. He writes on the stump of a shivered monarch of the forest, with the pine trees wailing round him, and "Endymion's planet rising on the air." To you, O Czar of all Chivalry and Khan of Cotton Tartery! he appeals for the privilege of seeking, on his own hook, a land less free—a home among the hyenas

of the North. Will you not halt your "brave columns" and stay your gorgeous career for a thin space? and while the admiring world takes a brief gaze at your glorious and God forsaken cause, pen for the happy conscript a furlough without end?...

...Your happy conscript would go to the far-away North whence the wind comes and leave you to reap the whirlwind with no one but your father the devil to rake and bind after you....

And now, bastard President of a political abortion, farewell.

"Scalp-hunters," relic, pole, and chivalrous Confederates in crime, goodbye. Except it be in the army of the Union, you will not again see the conscript.

Norm. Harrold,
of Ashe County, N.C.

CONGRESS ABOLISHES SLAVERY IN THE DISTRICT OF COLUMBIA

The buying and selling of human beings within sight of the U.S. Capitol had long offended Northerners in Washington. Before the war, abolitionists had regularly demanded that the district's slave pens be outlawed, but Southern legislators routinely blocked these efforts. By April 1862, however, with the Southerners long gone, Congress finally passed a law abolishing slavery in the district, signed by President Lincoln this day. Emancipation created a new problem, however: how to compensate the loyal slaveholders. The solution was found in a complex system

Confederate soldiers from an unidentified regiment.

of federal reimbursement for the human "property" taken.

BE IT ENACTED BY THE SENATE and House of Representatives of the United States of America in Congress assembled, That all persons held to service or labor within the District of Columbia by reason of African descent are hereby discharged and freed of and from all claim to such service or labor; and from and after the passage of this act neither slavery nor involuntary servitude, except for crime, whereof the party shall be duly convicted, shall hereafter exist in said District.

...And be it further enacted, That all persons loyal to the United States, holding claims to service or labor against persons discharged therefrom by this act, may, within ninety days from the passage thereof, but not thereafter, present to the commissioners hereinafter mentioned their respective statements or petitions in writing, verified by oath or affirmation, setting forth the names, ages, and personal description of such persons, the manner in which said petitioners acquired such claim, and any facts touching the value thereof....The President of the United States, with the advice and consent of the Senate, shall appoint three commissioners, residents of the District of Columbia, any two of whom shall have power to act, who shall receive the petitions above mentioned, and who shall investigate and determine the validity and value of the claims therein presented, as aforesaid, and appraise and apportion, under the proviso hereto annexed, the value in money of the several claims by them found to be valid,...the parties found by said report to be entitled thereto as aforesaid, and the same shall be received in full and complete compensation....And be it further enacted, That the sum of one hundred thousand dollars, out of any money in the Treasury not otherwise appropriated, is hereby appropriated, to be expended under the direction of the President of the United States, to aid in the colonization and settlement of such free persons of African descent now residing in said District, including those to be liberated by this act, as may desire to emigrate to the Republics of Hayti or Liberia, or such other country beyond the limits of the United States as the President may determine: Provided, The expenditure for this purpose shall not exceed one hundred dollars for each emigrant.

SUN
20
APR.

Improvements in the technology of killing were a major cause of the terrific Civil War carnage. Having changed only slightly during the previous two centuries, military technology experienced something of a revolution during the years immediately preceding Fort Sumter, when the lethality of weapons took a sudden leap. Before this time, muskets, the American soldier's principal weapon, had an effective range of 150 yards. However, in 1849, a French munitions officer named Claude-Étienne Minié developed the first conical-shaped bullet, known as the Minié ball. Fired from one of the new rifled muskets, with spiraled grooves running through their barrels, these bullets could reach targets 1,000 and more yards away. Taking advantage of this new technology, the Union army created elite units of men recruited for their marksmanship and equipped them with special breech-loading Sharps rifles (hence, "Sharps shooters," or sharpshooters). The members of the Second U.S. Sharpshooters (also known as Berdan's Brigade after their commander) were certainly of a different breed than ordinary soldiers. One of the latter offered this account of sharpshooter activity during the lengthy Peninsular Campaign.

OUR GUNS KEEP UP A CONSTANT shelling both day and night, which is seldom responded to by the rebels, because of the terrible Berdan sharpshooters, who cover the guns to such an extent that they cannot work them. I never before saw such a set of men as these same Berdan sharpshooters. They are armed with the telescope sighted rifles peculiar to their calling, some of which weigh the extraordinary heft of 57 to 60 pounds. These men speak confidently of killing, without the slightest difficulty, at a mile distant. The impression left upon the minds of the soldiers by these people is not at all a pleasant one, and as they come out each morning after breakfast strutting leisurely along, the men look askance and rather shrink from them. As far as I am able to judge, although receiving a general order to occupy certain portions of the line, it is left discretionary with them to select their own position. So that good service is done, the method is with the individual. It has frequently occurred that one or more of them have occupied my post, and I have watched their proceedings very closely. They remind one of the spider who, hour after hour, so patiently waits for the unhappy fly. These men will, after cutting crotches and resting their rifles on them, coolly take a camp stool, and adjusting the telescopic sight, wait for some poor devil to show himself, when, quick as a flash, bang goes the rifle, and the soldier has solved the Trinity. I have often looked through their sight pieces, and been amazed at their power and the distinctness with which objects of at least a mile distant are brought under the eye of the observer.

Yesterday four of these demons occupied the post with me, and after busying themselves with suitably and satisfactorally adjusting their rifles, sat down to await a victim. They had not long to wait, however, as soon were seen four men leaving the enemy's works, who proceeded towards the works on our left, apparently with no thought of danger at least so early in this day. At their distance they would have been perfectly secure from our muskets, but were in easy range of the murderous Berdan rifle. The sharpshooters consulted for a moment, and three of them removing the rearmost support from their rifles, brought them to bear upon the men, and at the word from the fourth, fired. Three of them dropped instantly, while the fourth, after standing in apparent bewilderment suddenly [fell] beside his dead comrades, adjusting their bodies as a protection, and stayed there all day long....

Shortly after the firing having ceased, four other men bearing stretchers were seen to suddenly leave the works and approach the dead men. I can scarcely bring my pencil to write it, but these inhuman fiends, these vaunted brave Berdan sharpshooters, murdered these poor fellows also. I will add that there was a good deal of feeling displayed by my men, and [the sharpshooters were] requested to go somewhere else, as their presence was distasteful.

FARRAGUT CAPTURES NEW ORLEANS

THU
24
APR.

As early as the fall of 1861, Union leaders approved a plan calling for the amphibious invasion of New Orleans, the main seaport of the South. To command this expedition, the navy selected Flag Officer David Glasgow Farragut. The sixty-year-old Farragut had begun his naval career at the age of ten and since fought the British, French, Berber Pirates, and now the Confederates, becoming a living legend as well as the most experienced naval officer on either side. His army counterpart, Maj. Gen. Benjamin Butler, led a force of fifteen thousand. For an entire week, Farragut bombarded the two forts guarding the city—St. Philip and Jackson—to little effect. Losing patience, he next ordered his fleet to "run the guns"—that is, bypass the forts. The attempt was made shortly after midnight on April 24, precipitating a sharp fight involving all the Rebel ships and Farragut's fleet as well as the forts. In the end, the feisty Federal admiral won, and the next day (April 25) a detachment of Union troops raised the Stars and Stripes over the captured city. In the passage below, John H.

Bartlett, an officer of the USS Brooklyn, *recalled the dramatic nighttime battle.*

AT 2 O'CLOCK ON THE MORNING of the 24th two red lights were hoisted at the peak of the flag-ship as a signal to get under way. All hands had been on deck since midnight to see that everything about the deck and guns was ready for action, and when the decks were wet down and sanded, it really began to look as if we were going to have some pretty hot business on our hands. The anchor was hove up with as little noise as possible, and at half-past 2 we steamed off, following the *Hartford* toward the entrance to the opening we had made in the obstructions [a chain and series of hulks]. The Confederates opened fire about 3 o'clock, when the advance division came in sight and range of the forts, and as we passed ahead of the mortar-vessels we also came in range; but the forts were so far ahead that we could not bring our broadside guns to bear. For twenty minutes we stood silent beside the guns, with the shot and shell from Forts St. Philip and Jackson passing over us and bursting everywhere in the air. As we came to the obstruction the water-battery on the Fort Jackson side opened a most destructive fire, and here the *Brooklyn* received her first shot. We gave the water-battery a broadside of grape. With our own smoke and the smoke from the vessels immediately ahead, it was impossible to direct the ship, so that we missed the opening between the hulks and brought up the chain. We dropped back and tried again; this time the chain broke, but we swung alongside of one of the hulks, and the

Flag Officer David G. Farragut

seemed imminent, a thrill of alarm ran through the ship. The alarm was groundless, however, as no injury was done, and presently, the engines started again, and the ship moved on.

There were many fire-rafts, and these and the flashing of the guns and bursting shells made it almost as light as day, but the smoke from the passing fleet was so thick at times one could see nothing ten feet from the ship. While entangled with the rafts, the *Brooklyn* was hulled a number of times; one shot from Fort Jackson struck the rail just at the break of the poop and went nearly across, ploughing out the deck in its course. Another struck Barney Shields, the signal quartermaster, and cut his body almost in two. The first lieutenant, Lowry, coming along at the time, inquired who it was, and understanding the response to be "Bartlett" instead of "Barney," he passed the word that he had sent down "all that was left of poor Bartlett." As he came on deck and was about in all parts of the ship during the fight, he gave the men news of the progress of the fight and of the casualties, and for once I was completely out of existence.

★ ★ ★ ★

stream-anchor, hanging on the starboard quarter, caught, tore along the hulk, and then parted its lashings. The cable secured us just where the Confederates had the range of their guns, but somebody ran up with an axe and cut the hawser, and we began to steam up the river. A few moments later there was a sudden jar, and the engines stopped. The propeller had no doubt struck some hard object, but no one knew the cause of the stoppage; and as Craven called out, "Stand by the starboard anchor," and a fatal pause under the enemy's fire

MAY
1862

THU 1 MAY *Winchester, Virginia, at the northern end of the Shenandoah Valley, was a strategic objective for both Union and Confederate armies. By war's end, the city had changed hands nearly one hundred times. Twenty-five-year-old Laura Lee, who lived in Winchester with her aunt, recorded her experience of Federal occupation and Confederate liberation in a wartime diary. Her entry for this date is excerpted below.*

WE ARE ALSO IN A STATE OF starvation here. No fresh meat for a fortnight and almost impossible to get eggs and butter, and what we do get [is] at fabulous prices. We can scarcely get wood enough to cook with and the country people as well as the merchants are charging an immense discount on Virginia money.

FRI 2 MAY *On occasion, fugitive slaves unable to reach Union lines sought refuge within the Confederate ranks, gambling that Southern soldiers would accept the comforts of a servant (even if that servant belonged to someone else). In many cases, this gamble paid off, and runaways were indeed sheltered within the Rebel ranks. In the following letter, a Virginia slaveholder entreats Secretary of War George W. Randolph (Judah P. Benjamin's replacement) to end the practice.*

DEAR SIR: MANY FARMERS IN Virginia are injured by a practice which has become habitual and extensive among the soldiers of our own army. The soldiers employ runaway negroes to cook for the mess, clean their horses, and so forth. The consequence is that negroes are encouraged to run away, finding a safe harbour in the army. Two of my neighbors have each recovered runaway negroes within the last few weeks; who were actually found in the employment of the soldiers on the Peninsula and these negroes had been runaway many months. I therefore write to ask you to issue a general order forbidding this practice and annexing a penalty sufficiently severe to break it up.

All that is necessary is to forbid the employment of any coloured person unless he can show free papers or a pass from his master; and hold the soldier responsible, for the genuineness of the free papers or pass.

In this section of country a heavy draught has been made upon the farmers (half of our available working force) to work on fortifications. I, for one, rendered this tribute cheerfully to a cause which is

An African-American army cook at work.

dear to my heart, though that, together with the excessive rains, will materially shorten my crop. I think however, we ought to be protected by the army authorities from the abuses above mentioned.

Yours &c

L. H. Minor

[P.S.] I can scarcely see to sign my name. One of my negro men has been runaway for many months and I have reason to believe that he is in the service of the soldiers.

SAT 3 MAY LOWE'S BALLOON CORPS

Eight days after Beauregard opened fire on Fort Sumter, Prof. Thaddeus S. C. Lowe landed his hot-air balloon in an open field outside Unionville, South Carolina. He had just completed a nine-hour, five-hundred-mile flight from Cincinnati, but his timing was terrible: The local militiamen promptly arrested him as a Northern spy. Fortunately, Lowe (who was somewhat famous) managed to persuade state officials in Columbia that his mission was scientific, and they permitted him to return to Ohio. There, Lowe asked an influential friend to write to Treasury Secretary Salmon P. Chase, proposing that the government establish a balloon corps under Lowe's command. Chase invited Lowe to meet with President Lincoln on June 11, 1863. Intrigued by the possibility of using balloons to make reconnaissance flights, Lincoln made Lowe chief of army aeronautics.

Between 1861 and 1863, Lowe and his crew made more than three thousand flights over or near enemy territory. During the Peninsular Campaign, in particular, Lowe made nearly daily flights to observe Confederate deployments. He describes one such flight in the report below. Lowe finally resigned in May 1863 after Joseph Hooker, then commanding the Army of the Potomac, dramatically reduced the role and funding of his Balloon Corps.

ON THE 3D OF MAY I MADE A reconnaissance near Warwick Court-House....General McClellan and staff being on the spot; General Porter and myself ascended. No sooner had the balloon risen above the tops of the trees than the enemy opened all of their batteries commanding it, and the whole atmosphere was literally filled with bursting shell and shot, one, passing through the cordage that connects the car with

Prof. Thaddeus Lowe aboard the balloon Intrepid.

the balloon, struck near to the place where General McClellan stood. Another 64-pounder struck between two soldiers lying in a tent, but without injury. Fearing that by keeping the balloon up the enemy's shots would do injury to the troops that were thickly camped there, General Porter ordered the balloon down. At about midnight...I was aroused by Captain Moses...who informed me that the general was apprehensive that the enemy were evacuating....I immediately ascended and saw that the fire was confined to one building...and therefore I did not consider it a sufficient indication that they were evacuating....I did not sleep any more, however, that night, and got the balloon ready for another ascension, which I made before daylight....As soon as it became a little lighter I discovered that the enemy had gone.

THU 8 MAY JACKSON'S VALLEY CAMPAIGN

During May (and early June) 1862, while Union forces under Maj. Gen. George B. McClellan conducted the laborious Peninsular Campaign, Maj. Gen. Thomas "Stonewall" Jackson completed one of the most impressive months in military history. Assigned by Robert E. Lee to delay and harass the invading Federals under the overall command of John C. Frémont, Jackson demonstrated the initiative and decisiveness that made him feared by his enemies and worshiped by his men. On this date, his army successfully engaged Federals under Robert Schenck at the

Brig. Gen. Robert C. Schenck

battle of McDowell, Virginia. Then Jackson turned and attacked a second Federal army under Nathaniel P. Banks, who had been moving to join McClellan's forces outside Richmond. On May 23, Jackson again defeated some of Banks's men at Front Royal, Virginia. This led, on May 25, to the battle of Winchester, in which Jackson routed Banks's retreating Federals, who were forced to abandon their wounded as well as their artillery and tons of their supplies. Lincoln dispatched two additional armies, one under Irvin McDowell and the other under Frémont, to cut off Jackson's line of retreat, but Stonewall unexpectedly turned south again, defeating Frémont at Cross Keys on June 8. Then, dizzyingly, he pivoted to fight McDowell to a standstill at nearby Port Republic on June 9. During this one-month period, Jackson's Confederates held nearly sixty thousand Federals in the Shenandoah

Valley, thus preventing them from joining McClellan outside Richmond. His men marched more than 350 miles, fought four major battles (as well as scores of smaller skirmishes), seized badly needed supplies, and forced the Union high command onto the defensive. In the following excerpts from their postwar autobiographies, two Confederate participants recall the legendary Valley Campaign. In the first, Edward Moore of the Rockbridge Artillery writes of the misery and confusion that accompanied one night's agonizing march to Port Republic. In the second, infantryman John Worsham describes Jackson personally leading his army into battle at Front Royal.

AFTER SPENDING ABOUT TEN days in this wretched camp we marched again, following the Shenandoah River along the base of the mountains toward Port Republic. After such weather, the dirt roads were, of course, almost bottomless. The wagons monopolized them during the day, so we had to wait until they were out of the way. When they halted at night, we took the mud. The depth of it was nearly up to my knees and frequently over them. The bushes on both sides of the road, and the darkness, compelled us to wade right in. Here was swearing and growling....An infantryman was cursing Stonewall most eloquently, when the old Christian rode by, and hearing him, said, in his short way, "It's for your own good, sir!" The wagons could make only six miles during the day, and, by travelling this distance after night, we reached them about nine o'clock. We would then build fires, get

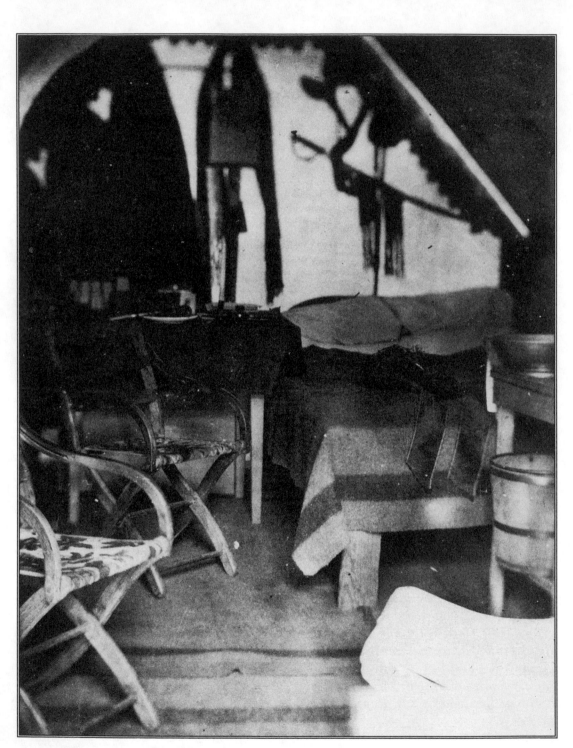

The field tent of Maj. Gen. Thomas J. "Stonewall" Jackson.

our cooking utensils, and cook our suppers, and by the light of the fires, see our muddy condition and try to dry off before retiring to the ground. We engaged in this sort of warfare for three days, when we reached Port Republic, eighteen miles from our starting-point and about the same distance from Staunton. Our movements, or rather Jackson's, had entirely bewildered us as to his intentions.

THE ENEMY IN OUR FRONT WERE behind a stone wall that ran entirely across the open field, and a little way behind them were two batteries of artillery. A piece of the Rockbridge battery was run out on a knoll to our left, where they were met by grape and minié balls. Every man at the piece was killed or wounded. Nothing daunted, the battery ran forward another piece, but were careful not to expose it, as in the case of the other gun. The men were soon picked off by the infantry behind the wall, and they were forced to abandon both pieces. The pieces were safe, however, as they were in our line, and if the enemy wanted them they must fight for them. About this time, Gen. Jackson made his appearance, and rode to one of the hillocks in our front. Col. Campbell, commanding our brigade, accompanied him on horseback; Col. Patton of the 21st Va. Regt. and Col. Grigsby of the Stonewall Brigade on foot. They were met by a hail of grape and musket balls. Campbell was wounded, Grigsby had a hole shot through his sleeve, and said some ugly words to the Yankees for doing it. Gen. Jackson sat there, the enemy continuing to fire grape and musketry at him. It is right here he

issued his celebrated order to the commander of the Stonewall Brigade: "I expect the enemy to occupy the hill in your front with artillery; keep your brigade well in hand and a vigilant watch, and if such an attempt is made—it must not be done, sir! Clamp them on the spot." After satisfying himself as to the location of the enemy, he quietly turned his horse and rode back in a walk. Arriving at the road in our rear he called for Taylor's brigade, led them in person to their position, and gave Gen. Taylor his orders. Taylor says he replied, and added, "You had better go to the rear; if you go along the front this way, some damned Yankee will shoot you!" He says that Gen. Jackson rode back to him at once, and said, "General, I am afraid you are a wicked fellow, but I know you will do your duty."

TUE 13 MAY THE THEFT OF THE PLANTER

The Confederate transport ship Planter *had a white captain and a crew of thirteen slaves. On this date, while the captain was ashore, the crew, led by Robert Smalls, sailed the ship out of Charleston Harbor, steered it through the Confederate lines, and finally surrendered the steamer to the Union forces blockading the port. Afterward, the daring Smalls served as a pilot aboard the* Planter, *now in the service of the Union navy, and after the war he became active in politics, spending nine years as a U.S. congressman. Flag Officer Samuel F. Du Pont, commander of the South Atlantic Blockading*

The Planter *in use as a Union medical supply boat.*

Squadron, described the incident in his official report. The Ripley to whom Du Pont refers was Roswell S. Ripley, commander of the Confederate Department of South Carolina.

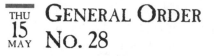 AT 4 IN THE MORNING SHE LEFT her wharf close to the Government office and headquarters, with palmetto and Confederate flag flying, passed the successive forts, saluting as usual by blowing her steam whistle. After getting beyond the range of the last gun she quickly hauled down the rebel flags and hoisted a white one....The steamer is quite a valuable acquisition to the squadron....You should have heard [Smalls's] modest reply when I asked him what was said of the carry away of General Ripley's barge some time ago. He said they made a great fuss but perhaps they would make more "to do" when they heard of the steamer being brought out.

THU 15 MAY GENERAL ORDER NO. 28

The Federal occupation of New Orleans that began on April 25 was not progressing as smoothly as Maj. Gen. Benjamin Butler would have liked. Particularly troublesome to the commander of the Union forces was the behavior of the women of the city, who left no doubt as to their disdain for the Federals, insulting them openly in both words and actions. Women of the Crescent City were spitting on Butler's troops and even emptying chamber pots onto the heads of the Yankee invaders. Concerned about his troops' declining morale, Butler issued General Order No. 28, under which any woman insulting a Union soldier became liable to prosecution as a prostitute.

Maj. Gen. Benjamin F. Butler

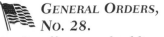 **GENERAL ORDERS, NO. 28.**

As the officers and soldiers of the United States have been subject to repeated insults from the women (calling themselves ladies) of New Orleans in return for the most scrupulous non-interference and courtesy on our part, it is ordered that hereafter when any female shall by word, gesture, or movement insult or show contempt for any officer or soldier of the United States she shall be regarded and held liable to be treated as a woman of the town plying her avocation.

In the following diary entry, New Orleans resident Sarah Morgan offers her own perspective on Butler's order.

A NEW PROCLAMATION FROM Butler has just come. It seems that the ladies have an ugly way of gathering their skirts when the Federals pass, to prevent contact, and some even turn up their noses—unladylike to say the least, but which may be owing to the odor they have, which is said to be unbearable even at this early season of year. Butler says, whereas the so-called *ladies* of New Orleans insult his men and officers, he gives one and all, permission to insult *any* or all who so treat them, then and there, with the assurance that the women will not receive the slightest protection from the government, and the men will all be justified. I did not have time to read it, but repeat it as it was told me by my mother who is in perfect despair at the brutality of the thing.

Although General Order No. 28 indeed quieted the streets of New Orleans, it meanwhile subjected Butler to a great deal of criticism, even from friends in the North, some of whom believed the policy overly harsh. In this letter of June 10 to one of those friends, Butler attempted to justify himself.

I AM GRIEVED THAT YOU SHOULD have misunderstood my order No. 28 concerning the women of New Orleans....I will take a moment from the time when I ought to be asleep if the heat and mosquitoes would let me, to say to you that if the order had not been issued I would issue it tomorrow in *ipsissimis verbis*. See where we were. We had come into a city where the dirt and pistol had ruled for ten years at least....The women, more bitter in their secession

General Orders, No. 28.

Head-Quarters, Department of the Gulf,
New Orleans, May 15, 1862.

General Orders, No. 28.

As the Officers and Soldiers of the United States have been subject to repeated insults from the women calling themselves ladies of New Orleans, in return for the most scrupulous non-interference and courtesy on our part, it is ordered that hereafter when any Female shall, by word, gesture, or movement, insult or show contempt for any officer or soldier of the United States, she shall be regarded and held liable to be treated as a woman of the town plying her avocation.

By command of Maj.-Gen. BUTLER,
GEORGE C. STRONG,
A. A. G. Chief of Staff.

than the men, were everywhere insulting my soldiers; deliberately spitting in their faces and upon their uniforms, making insulting gestures and remarks, tending to provoke retort, recrimination, and return of insult, which would have ended in disgraceful and murderous riot. What was there to be done? Oh, my friend, sitting in your easy chair at home! Is a she-adder to be preferred to a he-adder when they void their venom in your face? You say "arrest the women and put them in the Guard House." But that is the place where we shut up thieves and assassins and drunken soldiers, not a bower for lovely ladies....How many riots do you think I should have had dragging screeching women through the streets to the Guard House? If there had been any manhood in a New Orleans mob it would have felt itself called upon to have fought then or never.

What was done? An order characterising the acts of these women in plain English was made which at once executed itself....What has been the result? Since that order, no man or woman has insulted a soldier of mine in New Orleans, and from the *first hour* of our landing *no woman* has *complained of the conduct of my soldiers* toward her, nor has there been a single cause of complaint.

MON
19
MAY
Abraham Lincoln, being a seasoned politician, knew that timing in politics is everything, particularly when controversial matters are concerned. So when Maj. Gen. David Hunter—commander of the Union forces scattered along the coast of the Carolinas and, more importantly, an

Maj. Gen. David Hunter

antislavery Republican—issued a proclamation on May 9 freeing the slaves under his jurisdiction, Lincoln summarily revoked the emancipation order with a proclamation of his own, excerpted below.

WHEREAS THERE APPEARS IN THE public prints, what purports to be a proclamation of Major General Hunter....

And whereas the same is producing some excitement, and misunderstanding: therefore:

I, Abraham Lincoln, president of the United States, proclaim and declare, that the government of the United States, had no knowledge, information, or belief, of an intention on the part of General Hunter to issue such a proclamation; nor has it yet, any authentic information that the document is genuine. And further, that neither General Hunter, nor any other commander, or person, has been authorized by the Government of the United States, to make proclamations declaring the slaves of any State free; and that the supposed proclamation, now in question, whether genuine or false, is altogether void, so far as respects such declaration.

I further make known that whether it be competent for me, as Commander-in-Chief of the Army and Navy, to declare the Slaves of any state or states, free, and whether at any time, in any case, it shall have become a necessity indispensable to the maintainence of the government, to exercise such supposed power, are questions which, under my responsibility, I reserve to myself, and which I can not feel justified in leaving to the decision of commanders in the field. These are totally different questions from those of police regulations in armies and camps.

TUE 20 MAY THE HOMESTEAD ACT

The Civil War didn't stop, or even much slow, the nation's relentless march across the continent. In fact, the war actually accelerated the process of western settlement by removing Southern opposition to a pet Northern project: the free distribution of western land to those willing to farm it. Slaveholding whites had long resisted the plan because they believed it would preclude the westward expansion of slavery. With Southerners now out of the government, Northern legislators were able to proceed with a policy they believed vital to the nation's economic future. Under the Homestead Act, signed this day, any settler who laid claim to a quarter-section (160-acre) plot and farmed it for five years would

be given title to the land. (According to the previous policy of preemption, settlers were given only the right to buy the land.) By 1865, twenty thousand settlers had claimed Homestead Act farms.

AN ACT TO SECURE HOMESTEADS TO ACTUAL SETTLERS ON THE PUBLIC DOMAIN.

SEC. 1. Be it enacted by the Senate and House of Representatives of the United States of America in Congress assembled, That any person who is the head of a family, or who has arrived at the age of twenty-one years, and is a citizen of the United States, or who shall have filed his declaration of intention to become such, as required by the naturalization laws of the United States, and who has never borne arms against the United States Government or given aid and comfort to its enemies, shall, from and after the first of January, eighteen hundred and sixty-three, be entitled to enter one quarter-section or a less quantity of unappropriated public lands, upon which said person may have filed a preemption claim, or which may, at the time the application is made, be subject to preemption at one dollar and twenty-five cents, or less, per acre; or eighty acres or less of such unappropriated lands, at two dollars and fifty cents per acre, to be located in a body, in conformity to the legal subdivisions of the public lands, and after the same shall have been surveyed: Provided, That any person owning and residing on land may, under the provisions of this act, enter other land lying contiguous to his or her said land, which shall not, with the land so already owned and occupied, exceed in the aggregate one hundred and sixty acres.

Because not much wood was available on the Great Plains, many of the first homesteaders built sod houses.

Sec. 2. And be it further enacted, That the person applying for the benefit of this act shall, upon application to the register of the land office in which he or she is about to make such entry, make affidavit before the said register or receiver that he or she is the head of a family, or is twenty-one years or more of age, or shall have performed service in the army or navy of the United States, and that he has never borne arms against the Government of the United States or given aid and comfort to its enemies, and that such application is made for his or her exclusive use and benefit, and that said entry is made for the purpose of actual settlement and cultivation, and not either directly or indirectly for the use or benefit of any other person or persons whomsoever; and upon filing the said affidavit with the register or receiver, and on payment of ten dollars, he or she shall thereupon be permitted to enter the quantity of land specified: Provided, however, That no certificate shall be given or patent issued therefor until the expiration of five years from the date of such entry; and if, at the expiration of such time, or at any time within two years thereafter, the person making such entry; or, if he be dead, his widow; or in case of her death, his heirs or devisee; or in case of a widow making such entry, her heirs or devisee, in case of her death; shall prove by two credible witnesses that he, she, or they have resided upon or cultivated the same for the term of five years immediately succeeding the time of filing the affidavit aforesaid, and shall make affidavit that no part of said land has been alienated, and that he has borne true allegiance to the Government of the United States; then, in such case, he, she, or they, if at that time a citizen of the United States, shall be entitled to a patent, as in other cases provided for by law.

SUN 25 MAY *Stonewall Jackson's victory at Winchester this day occasioned celebrations throughout the Confederacy. Laura Lee, writing in her diary two days after the battle, rejoiced in the liberation of her town by the Confederates.*

THANKS BE TO THE LORD WE are free!!!!!!!!!!!!
A great many of the colored fugitives have been brought back. The slaves to be returned to their owners, and the free people to be held as prisoners of war. Numbers of the free people fled in terror on Sunday and have lost everything. Many children have died from exposure and from being accidentally killed in the terror and confusion of the flight.

FRI 30 MAY HALLECK'S MARCH ON CORINTH

After the bloody engagement at Shiloh on April 6–7, Grant came under fire from Washington politicians and the press, shocked at both the number of casualties and Grant's conduct of the battle. Rumors were spread that drunk-enness had been the cause of Grant's surprise before the battle, and groundless though these rumors were, they resulted in the assignment of Maj. Gen. Henry W. Halleck to direct command of Grant's army in the field. After relieving Grant on April 11, Halleck began a remarkably slow march in the direction of Corinth, the Rebel transportation hub in northern Mississippi, to which Maj. Gen. P. G. T. Beauregard's army had withdrawn. Halleck moved so slowly that it took his army nearly two months to travel thirty miles, and when his troops finally did move into Corinth on May 30, they found that the Confederates had left the night before. In the report excerpted below, Capt. J. H. Hammond, adjutant general to Maj. Gen. William T. Sherman's Fifth Division, described his experiences during the capture of Corinth, a victory tarnished somewhat by the Rebels' escape.

A CITIZEN INFORMED US THAT the main body of rebel troops had left about two o'clock in the night, and the rear-guard at daybreak. We pushed on into the square, where we arrived about half-past seven o'clock. General Smith caused guards to be placed over such property as was found, including a quantity of ammunition, and a large iron safe in the hotel; and I sent back to you [Sherman] various orderlies to report the condition of things, and to ask that one or two sections of artillery might be sent to our support, to make an attempt on the rear-guard of the enemy....

The cavalry not arriving, I pushed on across town with some Iowa cavalry, and finding near College Hill a house with a number of females in it, I placed my only remaining orderly in charge, directing him to prevent stragglers from annoying them....I had learned from an old man, captured by the Iowans, that many of the enemy's pickets were but a little way on, and from a negro that a piece of cannon was not far ahead....

A quarter of a mile of causeway brought us to a bridge, which was on fire in three places. I dismounted, and with the assistance of Private Hass, of the body-guard, threw off the first pile of fire, when Capt. Kendrick arrived, and immediately went to work with his men. As soon as we recovered from the effects of the smoke and heat, we pushed through the creek below the bridge and continued the pursuit. In a few moments we overtook a small party, one of whom stated that the gun he was carrying was private property, and belonged to Major-Gen. Price, who had given it to him not more than fifteen minutes before. As fast as we collected a batch of eight or ten prisoners, they were sent back to General Pope, leaving us free, and we pushed on still more rapidly....We came to one bridge just set on fire, and the half-dozen incendiaries fled into the swamp. Our horses' feet knocked the brands off, and a few minutes later we reached another... large bridge, where we rode upon four officers and nineteen men, hard at work piling wood, and with a fire alongside all ready. As the road made a sudden bend at this point, we were on them before they could make use of their arms. With pistols pointed at their heads, they piled their guns and accoutrements on the road. At this moment, as I turned to place them

under guard, I found that I had only three men, and the prisoners, seeing the same, and no sign of any more, made for their guns. We opened fire on them, and they speedily ran into the swamp, where pursuit was impossible....

In making this report I beg to say that while a pursuit by so small a number may seem rash, the circumstances justify it. The enemy were scattered in small parties of ten to fifty, and ran at the sight of horsemen.

The one procedure inextricably linked to the practice of medicine on the battlefields of the Civil War is amputation. With antispetic surgery still years away, the amputation of appendages, though gruesome, was usually the only way to save an injured man's life. A soft lead .58-caliber bullet generally made a rather large hole and, more often than not, shattered a bone. Even worse, it carried dirt and bits of soiled clothing into the wound, practically guaranteeing that gangrene would set in before the wound could heal. The only recourse available to military surgeons in most cases was to abandon the limb, creating a clean cut with a saw and then sealing it quickly in surgery. With huge numbers of casualties continuously pouring into makeshift field hospitals, doctors were often required to perform hundreds of these operations a day. (An experienced surgeon could relieve a soldier of a limb in as little as two minutes.) In this recollection, Capt. Francis Donaldson of the Army of the Potomac described how he lost his arm during the Peninsular Campaign.

IT WAS A SICKENING SCENE THAT presented itself upon arriving at the little two story and attic frame house now being used for surgical operations on the desperately wounded that needed immediate attention. The ground around was strewn with mangled fellows while away off, towards the front, streams more were either walking or being carried to this spot. The house had a one story extension back, used as a kitchen, a window on either side, and a door in the rear with steps leading down to the yard. The principal operations were being carried on in this small room, as I could judge from the pile of arms and legs that, on the ground outside the window, reached nearly up to it as they had been thrown out after amputation. As I came towards the front of the house I noticed that we were still within reach of artillery, as a round shot came howling along and struck a gray horse standing tied to a tree near the front door, completely carrying away his muzzle. The poor creature presented a most horrible appearance as he stood trembling while the blood streamed from his torn and bleeding head.

Seeing that I was an officer, an attendant took me inside, and as the lower rooms were loaded with wounded, I went back to the rear and found four tables being used as operating tables, each of which was occupied, while the surgeons with sleeves rolled up were literally working up to their elbows in blood, so busy

Wounded Union soldiers at a Savage Station, Virginia, field hospital after the June 27 battle there.

were they with knife and saw. One of the subjects then undergoing amputation seemed to be partially under the influence of chloroform, he struggled so. One of the surgeons, upon examining my arm, said that it would have to come off.

SEVEN PINES (FAIR OAKS)

SAT 31 MAY

By this time, McClellan had pushed the Confederates out of Yorktown and moved northeast, splitting his huge army into two wings along the Chickahominy River; the Army of the Potomac still posed a serious threat to Richmond, but it was little closer. Realizing that the two Union corps on the south bank of the Chickahominy were relatively isolated, Confederate Gen. Joseph E. Johnston attacked them east of Richmond at Seven Pines (also known as Fair Oaks). But poor communications hampered the Confederate offensive, and in the action Johnston himself was severely wounded. In this excerpt from his memoirs, Johnston describes the overall military situation and explains how the Seven Pines engagement (in which very little was decided) functioned as a precursor to the subsequent Seven Days' Campaign.

I HAD REPEATEDLY SUGGESTED to the Administration the formation of a great army to repel McClellan's invasion, by assembling all the Confederate forces, available for the object, near Richmond. As soon as I had lost command of the Army of Virginia by wounds in battle,

A Federal battery near Fair Oaks.

my suggestion was adopted. In that way, the largest Confederate army that ever fought, was formed in the month of June, by strengthening the forces near Richmond with troops from North and South Carolina and Georgia. But, while the Confederate government was forming this great army, the Federal general was, with equal industry, employed in making defensive arrangements; so that in the "seven days' fighting" his intrenchments so covered the operation of "change of base," that it was attended with little loss, considering the close proximity and repeated engagements of two such armies. Had ours been so strengthened in time to attack that of the United States when it reached the Chickahominy, and before being intrenched, results might and ought to have been decisive; still, that army, as led by its distinguished commander, compelled the Federal general to abandon his plan of operations, and reduced him to the defensive, and carried the war back to Northern Virginia.

★ ★ ★ ★

JUNE 1862

SUN
1
JUN.

LEE ASSUMES COMMAND OF THE ARMY OF NORTHERN VIRGINIA

The day after Seven Pines, Robert E. Lee, who had been serving as a senior military adviser to Pres. Jefferson Davis, replaced the injured Johnston as supreme commander of the Confederate forces in Virginia. The same day, the soon-to-be-legendary Army of Northern Virginia was formed. Lee considered McClellan a substantial threat, much more so than has previously been believed. (After the war, Lee went so far as to call McClellan "the most dangerous" of his opponents.) The Federal commander's wide military experience, including service as an observer during the Crimean War, guaranteed that he would make few blunders due to incompetence. In this letter of June 5 to President Davis, Lee outlined his plans to engage the slowly but steadily approaching McClellan and thereafter invade the North. This counteroffensive ultimately led to the bloody battle of Antietam (Sharpsburg) on September 17. Right off, Lee makes reference to Stonewall Jackson, whose ongoing Valley Campaign in the Shenandoah had brought fear to the North and raised the morale of Southerners, whose armies had been suffering defeat after defeat.

TO JEFFERSON DAVIS: AFTER much reflection I think if it were possible to reinforce Jackson strongly, it would change the character of the war. This can only be done by the troops in

A postwar photograph of Robert E. Lee with Joseph E. Johnston, whom Lee replaced as commander of the Confederate Army of Northern Virginia.

Georgia, South Carolina & North Carolina. Jackson could in that event cross Maryland into Pennsylvania. It would call all the enemy from our Southern coast & liberate those states. If these states will give up their troops I think it can be done. McClellan will make this a battle of posts. He will take position from position, under cover of his heavy guns, & we cannot get at him without storming his works, which with our new troops is extremely hazardous. You witnessed the experiment [at the battle of Seven Pines] Saturday. It will require 100,000 men to resist the regular siege of Richmond, which perhaps would only prolong not save it. I am preparing a line that I can hold with part of our forces in front, while with the rest I will endeavor to make a diversion to bring McClellan out. He sticks under his batteries & is working day & night. He is obliged to adhere to the railroad unless he can reach James River to provision his army. I am endeavoring to block his progress on the railroad & have written up to see if I can get made an iron battery on trucks with a heavy gun [an armored rail car], to sweep the country in our front. The enemy cannot move his heavy guns except on the railroad. You have seen nothing like the roads on the Chickahominy bottom. Our people are opposed to work. Our troops, officers, community & press. All ridicule & resist it. It is the very means by which McClellan has & is advancing. Why should we leave to him the whole advantage of labour. Combined with valour, fortitude & boldness, of which we have fair proportion, it should lead us to success. What carried the Roman soldiers into all countries, but this happy combination. The evidences of their labour last to this day. There is nothing so military as labour, & nothing so important to an army as to save the lives of its soldiers....

Very respy & truly,

R. E. Lee

Not all Northerners favored emancipation; some, including Rep. Samuel Sullivan Cox, opposed it on economic grounds. In a speech prepared for delivery to the House, the Ohio Democrat expressed his concern about the economic effect freeing the slaves would have on employment opportunities for whites in the North. Cox predicted a grim future for American labor, grounding his argument in the widely accepted racial stereotype that blacks were shiftless and unreliable.

LABOR WILL THEN [AFTER EMANcipation] go down to a song. It will be degraded by such association. Our soldiers, when they return, one hundred thousand strong, to their Ohio homes, will find these negroes, or the best of them, filling their places, felling timber, plowing ground, gathering crops, &c. How their martial laurels will brighten when they discover the result of their services! Labor that now ranges from one to two dollars per day, will fall to one half. Already in this District [of Columbia] the Government is hiring out the fugitives at from two to eight dollars per month, while white men are begging for work. Nor is the labor of most of these negroes desirable. No system of labor is so unless it be steady. They will get their week's wages, and then idle the next week away. Many will become a charge and nuisance upon the public charity and county poor tax....If they are distributed into the country, they may work for a little time and for small wages, and work well for a time; but when work grows irksome, and they "become too lazy to play," they will steal.

WED 11 JUN. *Among Southern families, the burden of populating the Confederate army was not always distributed equally. As the following Atlanta newspaper column suggests, some families gave more members to the war effort than others. This type of propaganda had at least two effects: It honored a few extraordinary families with public recognition and, more importantly, assured thousands of others with numerous sons, husbands, and sweethearts in the service that they were not alone in their sacrifice.*

LARGE FAMILIES IN THE ARMY

A few days ago, we mentioned the case of a Mr. Snead, living near Stone Mountain, who had six sons in the army.

Since then we have learned that Mr. Thompson, of Henry county, formerly of Newton, has *eight* sons in the army, and has two more not quite old enough to do service, who are eager to be in ranks. The Confederacy can have the services of the old gentleman as it needs him.

We are also informed that Mrs. Sarah Mangham, of Walton county, has *eight* sons now in service, who volunteered for the war. She has only one son at home, who has been a cripple from his infancy. The father of these brave sons lived to the age of 85 years, and was for forty years a resident of Walton county.

THU 12 JUN. STUART'S FIRST RIDE AROUND MCCLELLAN

Confederate cavalry commander Brig. Gen. J. E. B. Stuart was beloved in the South (and notorious in the North) for his dash and daring. Under Stuart's leadership, the Rebel cavalry became renowned for its willingness to take risks that usually paid off. The most famous of its flamboyant deeds was the circuit entirely around McClellan's Army of the Potomac that Stuart made betwen June 12 and June 15, 1862. The reconnaissance, which acted as a force mulitiplier because the Confederates seemed to be everywhere at once, disrupted the Union supply and communications networks (causing even greater delays), provided valuable intelligence about the disposition of McClellan's forces on the peninsula, and seriously undermined Federal morale. The feat was properly hailed in the South as the very acme of martial skill, while in the North it provided further ammunition for McClellan's detractors. Here are Robert E. Lee's June 11 orders to Stuart, followed by an account from a Confederate newspaper of one small action during the raid involving John S. Mosby, later the audacious commander of partisan rangers in Virginia.

GENERAL: YOU ARE DESIRED TO make a secret movement to the rear of the enemy now posted on the

Brig. Gen. J. E. B. Stuart

Chickahominy with a view of gaining intelligence of his operations, communications, &c, of driving in his forage parties & securing such grain, cattle, &c for ourselves as you can make arrangements to have driven in. Another object is to destroy his wagon trains, said to be daily passing from the Piping Tree road to his camp on the Chickahominy.

The utmost vigilance on your part will be necessary to prevent any surprise to yourself & the greatest caution must be practiced in keeping well in your fronts and flanks reliable scouts to give you information....

I recommend that you take only such men & horses as can stand the expedition & that you take every means in your power to save & cherish those that you do take. You must leave sufficient cavalry here for the service of this army, & remember that one of the chief objects of your expedition is to gain intelligence for the guidance of future operations.

Information received last evening, the points of which I sent you, lead me to infer that there is a stronger force on the enemy's right than was previously reported. A large body of infantry as well as cavalry was reported near the Central Railroad. Should you find upon investigation that the enemy is moving to his right, or is so strongly posted as to render your expedition inopportune, as its success in my opinion depends upon its secrecy, you will, after gaining all the information you can, resume your former position.

I am with great respect, your obt serv't

R. E. Lee
General

Lt. John S. Mosby (left) with an unidentified friend.

AFTER DESTROYING THE ENEMY'S camp near the old church, Lieutenant John S. Mosby, aide to General Stuart and who had been most daring and successful as a scout, was sent on in advance, with a single guide, towards Tunstall Station, to reconnoitre and ascertain the position and force of the enemy. On his way he met two Yankees whom he took prisoners and sent to the rear in charge of his guide. Alone he pushed on and overtook a cavalryman and an artilleryman of the enemy's forces, having in charge a quartermaster's wagon and stores. Lieutenant Mosby dashed up, and, drawing his pistols, demanded their surrender. The New Yorker surrendered at once, but [of] the Pennsylvanian, beginning to fumble for his pistol, the lieutenant made a more emphatic demand for his surrender, and at the same moment compelled him to look quite closely into the muzzle of his pistol. All this time there was drawn up, not four hundred yards distant, a company of Yankee cavalry in line of battle. In a moment a bugle sounded as for a movement on him, when, anxious to secure his prisoners and stores, Lieutenant Mosby put spurs and galloped across the field, at the same time shouting to his imaginary men to follow him, when none of the Confederacy cavalry were in sight and the swiftest more than a mile in the rear. The Yankees, hearing the word of command and apprehending the descent of an avalanche of Confederate cavalry upon them, broke line, each man galloping off to take care of himself. The wagon, prisoners, and stores were then secured and among them were found forty splendid Colt's pistols with holsters, besides boots, shoes, blankets, etc., etc.

TUE 17 JUN. *After the defeat of the Confederates at Pea Ridge on March 7–8, the Rebel armies prepared to abandon Arkansas (having already pulled out of Missouri). In response, Arkansas governor Henry M. Rector threatened to pull his state out of the Confederacy and negotiate a separate peace with the Union unless the troops were restored. Confederate president Jefferson Davis, although angered by Rector's threat, dispatched Maj. Gen. Thomas C. Hindman to assume command of the Trans-Mississippi District (which he did on May 31). Hindman, a veteran of the Mexican War and a powerful Arkansas politician, feared that the Federal army would quickly traverse northeastern Arkansas and seize the state capital before he could muster Little Rock's defenders. To slow this anticipated Federal advance, he ordered*

widespread guerrilla warfare. Below are his official orders for the people of the Trans-Mississippi District to rise up against the Federal army. Their unintended result was to encourage an influx of marauding bushwhackers from Missouri and Texas. Later Confederate attempts to revoke Hindman's orders were ignored by the bandits, who included such men as William C. Quantrill, and William "Bloody Bill" Anderson. Instead, the Civil War in the West entered a brutal, lawless phase that would not end until well after the surrender at Appomattox.

This posthumous photograph of "Bloody Bill" Anderson was taken to prove that he was dead.

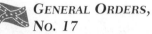

GENERAL ORDERS, No. 17

I. For the more effectual annoyance of the enemy upon our rivers and in our mountains and woods all citizens of this district who are not subject to conscription are called upon to organize themselves into independent companies of mounted men or infantry, as they prefer, arming and equipping themselves, and to serve in that part of the district to which they belong.

II. When as many as 10 men come together for this purpose they may organize by electing a captain, 1 sergeant, 1 corporal, and will at once commence operations against the enemy without waiting for special instructions. Their duty will be to cut off Federal pickets, scouts, foraging parties, and trains, and to kill pilots and others on gunboats and transports, attacking them day and night, and using the greatest vigor in their movements. As soon as the company attains the strength required by law it will proceed to elect the other officers to which it is entitled. All such organizations will be reported to these headquarters as soon as practicable. They will receive pay and allowances for subsistence and forage for the time actually in the field, as established by the affidavits of their captains.

III. These companies will be governed in all respects by the same regulations as other troops. Captains will be held responsible for the good conduct and efficiency of their men, and will report to these headquarters from time to time.

SUN 22 JUN. *By late June, it had become apparent that the presence of so many military-aged men in the Confederate army would substantially affect the South's ability to raise and harvest crops. In the following letter to Confederate Secretary of War George W. Randolph, a Virginia woman named Fannie Christian requested a discharge for her husband so that he could return to his duties as a plantation overseer. Because the army relied on agricultural production to feed its troops, she argued, her husband could better serve the cause as an excellent farmer than an ordinary soldier. As it happened, her request was not granted, and her husband, Pvt. James Christian, died in battle the following year.*

DEAR SIR: I TAKE MY SEAT TO arsk you to do me one favor and that is to give my husband a discharge from the Army. I think if you knew my situation you would. I will explain it to you now. my husband was doing business for Mr Jordan and also for his three sons which is in the Army and has been every since the war began leaveing both without any one on them white but myself and three Children the oldest not six years old and Mr Jordan confined to his bed and has been for some time. he is not able when he is well. he is sixty six years old and you know he is unable to attend to his bisness he has a large crop of wheat on hand now very near ripe and no one to attend to saveing it for him and a large crop of tobacco hanging in the house moulding no one to see to packing it down. im just surrounded with a gang of negroes i'am afraid abbout to get a breath....you know the farming must go on to keep up our Army. Mr Jordan told me he thought if I would write to you explain...his situation you would give my husband a discharge. he said he knew that his labor was worth more to the Confederacy than where he is. his health is very bad—not able for duty half of his time. he said if you can possible let him come home by the time his wheat get ripe if it is possible for you to discharge him....my husbands name is James B Christian belong to the 19 Regment Va Volinters Company G, W Boyd Captain. I am willing to spend half of my time in wating on the sick soldiers I feal it to be my duty to do all I can for our Confredracy as mutch so as any lady in the Confredracy and if please give him a discharge for the sake [of] one feeble woman. if you dont, write to me and let me know your reason for not dischargeing

him. my post office is at Dillards station Nelson Co Va let me hear as quick as posble if you please I [k]now it is in your power to say yes or no if you please dont say no. dont think because I write to you I think my husband better than any one else. no that is not my thought. it is the situation around me.

The son of Revolutionary War officer Henry "Light-Horse Harry" Lee, Confederate commander Robert E. Lee was an exemplary product of the Southern aristocracy's proud martial heritage. Born in 1807, he graduated second in his West Point class of 1829 and was subsequently commissioned as a second lieutenant in the elite engineering corps. A decade after distinguishing himself in the Mexican War, Lee led the force that suppressed John Brown's

Currier & Ives's idealized rendering of nineteenth-century farm life, The Farmer's Home.

The residence of W. H. Fitzhugh and Charlotte Lee at White House Landing, Virginia.

1859 raid on the arsenal at Harpers Ferry. Lee was bold yet also a master of timing, and a commander who was usually able to elicit the very last ounce of energy from his subordinates. His personal charisma was perfectly suited to the needs of the Army of Northern Virginia, which he would lead until war's end. At the same time, Lee was also a father and husband. In his many letters home, he has revealed to historians the private man beneath the general's clothing. Here, writing to daughter-in-law Charlotte (the wife of his son Fitzhugh), Lee painted a vivid word portrait of himself as he prepared for the Seven Days' Campaign.

I MUST TAKE A PART OF THIS holy day, my dear Chass, to thank you for your letter of the 14th....And now I must answer your inquiries about myself. My habiliments are not as comfortable as yours, not so suited to this hot weather, but they are the best I have. My coat is of gray, of the regulation style and pattern, and my pants of dark blue, as is also pre-

scribed, partly hid by my long boots. I have the same handsome hat which surmounts my gray head (the latter is not prescribed in the regulations) and shields my ugly face, which is masked by a white beard as stiff and wiry as the teeth of a card. In fact, an uglier person you have never seen, and so unattractive is it to our enemies that they shoot at it whenever visible to them, but though age with its snow has whitened my head, and its frosts have stiffened my limbs, my heart, you well know, is not frozen to you, and summer returns when I see you. Having now answered your questions, I have little more to say. Our enemy is quietly working within his lines, and collecting additional forces to drive us from our Capital. I hope we shall be able yet to disappoint him, and drive him back to his own country. I saw Fitzhugh the other day. He was looking very well in a new suit of gray....

And now I must bid you farewell. Kiss your sweet boy for me, and love always,

Your devoted papa
R. E. Lee

MON 23 JUN. *As Federal gunboats steamed up the White River in northeastern Arkansas, the flotilla fell under repeated attack not only from Confederate artillery but also from civilians operating under Maj. Gen. Thomas C. Hindman's orders of June 17 for a guerrilla campaign against Union troops. A frustrated Col. Graham Fitch, commander of the White River expedition, finally issued this notice to the residents of Monroe County. Hindman's June 25 rejoinder to Fitch follows.*

GUERRILLA BANDS RAISED IN your vicinity have fired from the woods upon the United States gunboats and transports in White River. This mode of warfare is that of savages. It is in your power to prevent it in your vicinity. You will therefore, if it is repeated, be held responsible in person and property. Upon a renewal of such attacks an expedition will be sent against you to seize and destroy your personal property. It is our wish that no occasion for such a course shall arise, but that every man shall remain at home in pursuit of his peaceful avocation, in which he will not be molested, unless a continuance of such barbarous guerrilla warfare renders rigorous measures on our part necessary.

COLONEL: A COPY OF YOUR proclamation of the 23d instant, addressed to the citizens of Monroe County, has come into my hands. I have the honor to inclose you a copy of an order recently issued by me, authorizing the formation of companies to operate at will, in the absence of specific instructions, against the forces of the United States Government, and accepting all such into the service and pay of the Confederate States. They are recognized by me, as the commander of this department, as Confederate troops, and I assert as indisputable the right to dispose and use those troops along the banks of White River, or wherever else I may deem proper, even should it prove annoying to you in your operations. I have thought it but just that I should furnish you with a copy of my order, that you may act advisedly, and I respectfully forewarn you that should your threat be executed against any citizens of this district I shall retaliate, man for man, upon the Federal officers and soldiers who now are, and hereafter may be, in my custody as prisoners of war.

The USS Cairo *was among the Federal ironclads operating along the Mississippi River and its tributaries.*

WED 25 JUN. THE SEVEN DAYS' CAMPAIGN

With McClellan's ninety-thousand-man Army of the Potomac still so close to Richmond, the mood among the Confederacy's political leadership became increasingly panicky. Secretary of War Randolph recommended that the government flee, but cooler heads prevailed—at least for the time being. Meanwhile, as Lee formulated a plan for the eviction of the Federals, McClellan, again overestimating his enemy's strength, requested more and more troops from Lincoln. The president's telegraphed responses to these requests, including the one of June 26 below, often assumed a tone of paternal exasperation. The Seven Days' Campaign—Lee's attempt to deflect the blow that McClellan seemed poised to strike at Richmond—began this day with a secondary engagement at Oak Grove. McClellan had ordered a preliminary advance on his left, but it was well met a few miles east of Richmond by Confederates under Benjamin Huger. The disposition of forces changed little, but McClellan's fear for the safety of his army increased dramatically.

[YOUR DISPATCH] SUGGESTING the probability of your being overwhelmed by 200,000, and talking of where the responsibility will belong, pains me very much. I give you all I can, and act on the presumption that you will do the best with what you have, while you continue, ungenerously I think, to assume that I could give you more if I would. I have omitted and shall omit no opportunity to send you reenforcements whenever I possibly can.

A. Lincoln

THU 26 JUN. MECHANICSVILLE (BEAVER DAM CREEK)

The first major battle of the Seven Days' Campaign took place near the town of Mechanicsville on the northern side of the Chickahominy River (most of the Federals were now posted south of the river). Lee planned a two-pronged assault on the thirty-thousand-man corps under Union Maj. Gen. Fitz John Porter, but there were communications problems. Maj. Gen. A. P. Hill indeed unleashed his infantry brigades against Porter, but a tardy Stonewall Jackson failed to join the attack, resulting in ample slaughter as Porter pulled back

Maj. Gen. Benjamin Huger

to well-prepared positions along Beaver Dam Creek. The Federal artillery raked the Confederate lines, then Union riflemen finished the work, halting the Rebel advance short of the creek. Evan M. Woodward of the Second Pennsylvania Reserves desribed the fight in his regimental history, excerpted below.

ABOUT THREE O'CLOCK THE enemy's lines were formed on the opposite side of the swamp and their skirmishers rapidly advanced, delivering their fire as they came forward. They were speedily driven back by the artillery and a rattling reply of musketry. In a short time, the main body, who were commanded by General Robert E. Lee, in person, boldly advanced in force under cover of a heavy artillery fire, and attacked the whole front. It soon became apparent that the main point of their attack was the extreme right, upon which they opened a heavy fire of round shot and shell, and precipitated column after column of Georgian and Louisiana troops, who waded to their middle through the water, and boldly advanced up through the woods. They were received by the 2nd on their knees, with a withering fire, which they maintained without a moment's cessation for over three hours. During this time, assault after assault was made on the position, and on three separate occasions the enemy succeeded in forcing themselves between us and the "bucktails" on our flank and gaining the clear ground, but they were each time driven back at the point of the bayonet and charges led in person by Colonel McCandless....General Reynolds, whose ever-watchful eye was upon the regiments of his brigade, several

Maj. Gen. Fitz John Porter with his staff (including a reclining Lt. George A. Custer).

times rode down to our position, at one time exclaiming, as he pointed with his sword, "Look at them boys, in the swamp there, they are as thick as flies on a ginger bread; fire low, fire low."

Pvt. Edgar Jackson belonged to the First North Carolina Infantry, one of the regiments that attacked John F. Reynolds's Pennsylvanians along Beaver Dam Creek. In this letter home to his parents, Jackson described the terror of the assault.

AS WE APPROACHED, THE bullets flew by us in torrents... Colonel [Mumford Stokes] orders us to fall down to escape the bullets then flying by; he soon orders us to rise up and charge, and at it we go with a yell; we proceed halfway down the hill, halt, and exchange shot for shot with the Yankees, who had the very best of covering...I have fired once and am now trying to ram down a ball which fits too tight—men are falling around me continually. I see one of our company rise up and try to get to the rear; he is wounded in the hip. For nearly half an hour our boys load and fire, firing by the light of the enemy's guns. We are ordered to retreat but it is not heeded; again our Colonel who lies wounded orders us to retreat, again it is not heeded.

FRI 27 JUN. GAINES' MILL

Because he had moved so many of his forces north of the Chickahominy, Lee had to strike again—there were simply too few troops guarding the capital to hold it if the Federals were not otherwise distracted. Hoping to recover the lost opportunity of the day before, he hit Porter's Federals with nearly sixty-five thousand men. The reinforcements that McClellan rushed across the Chickahominy to Porter enabled the general to retreat intact from Beaver Dam Creek to Gaines' Mill. Meanwhile, several generals tried to persuade McClellan that the Confederates under Maj. Gen. John Magruder interposed between the Union left and Richmond were in fact only a thin screen (as indeed they were). McClellan, however, refused to listen and instead ordered a general withdrawal to the James River. It would be two years before the Federals came this close to Richmond again. Again, as at Mechanicsville, Stonewall Jackson's failure to arrive on time left the Rebels vulnerable to considerable Federal firepower. The Confederates finally broke through Porter's lines at dusk, but too

late to stop his retreat across the Chickamoniny to rejoin McClellan's command. In the passage from his regimental history below, Capt. James Stevenson of the First New York Cavalry describes his experiences at Gaines' Mill—where he and his men, riding as escorts to McClellan, traversed the battlefield throughout the day.

[I]T BECAME NECESSARY TO FALL back upon the James River for a new base of supplies. To facilitate this movement Porter had to fight nearly the whole Confederate army on the 27th, and he was pretty roughly handled. Our regiment was with General McClellan nearly all that day, riding from point to point at a gallop. In the afternoon, Captain Harkins, with one squadron, was sent to report to General Slocum, and did good service in

This Michigan private fought at Gaines' Mill.

stopping the stragglers, which at one point in the battle were quite numerous. The enemy outnumbered Porter three to one, and at night he crossed the river, destroying all the bridges behind him. This was the battle of Gaines' Mill.

Everything was in confusion that night, and the men felt sullen because they were about to retreat. On the 28th the paymaster appeared among us, to pay the regiment, and while he was thus engaged the Confederates burst several shells in the camp, which caused him to pack up and drive off in his ambulance in a hurry. Our corps, under Franklin, was left to cover the retreat and we had to fight the enemy all day of the 28th. We slept on our arms that night, and at 3 A.M. on the 29th set out to follow the army.

SUN 29 JUN. *As McClellan fell back toward the James River, Lee pursued him, striking the Federals in a series of inconclusive battles on June 29 and June 30. McClellan left charge of these battles to his various corps commanders—Porter, William B. Franklin, Edwin V. Sumner, Erasmus D. Keyes, and Samuel P. Heintzelman—who won every engagement. Yet McClellan continued to fall back to the James River, ordering the destruction of huge supply depots and ammunition dumps painstakingly created during the opening months of the now-defunct Peninsular Campaign. He even denied the soldiers permission to use fire in destroying the supplies, because he was worried that the enemy would recognize that he was retreating. In a postwar narrative of his wartime experiences, Pvt. Warren Lee*

Goss recalled the scene of destruction, which at times became even humorous.

DETAILS WERE MADE TO DESTROY such stores as could not easily be removed in wagons, and some of our officers, high in rank, set an unselfish example by destroying their personal baggage. Fires were not allowed in the work of destruction. Tents were cut and slashed with knives; canteens punched with bayonets; clothing cut into shreds; sugar and whiskey overturned on the ground, which absorbed them. Some of our men stealthily imitated mother earth as regards the whiskey. Most of our officers appreciated the gravity of the situation, and were considerate enough to keep sober, in more senses than one. Early on the morning of the 29th the work of destruction was complete, our picket-line was relieved, and with faces that reflected the gloom of our hearts, we turned our backs on Richmond, and started upon the retreat. The gloom was rather that of surprise than of knowledge, as the movement was but slightly under-

McClellan's headquarters at Savage Station.

stood by the mass of the army, or for that matter by most of the officers.

The weather was suffocatingly hot; dust rose in clouds, completely enveloping the marching army; it filled our nostrils and throats, and covered every part of our clothing as if ashes had been sifted upon us. About nine o'clock line of battle was formed near Allen's farm. Occasionally the report of a sharpshooter's rifle was heard in the woods. Some of the men took advantage of such shade as was afforded by the scattering trees and went to sleep. All were suddenly brought to their feet by a tremendous explosion of artillery. The enemy had opened from the woods south of the railroad, with great vigor and precision. This attack was, after some sharp fighting, repelled, and, sling knapsacks, the march was again resumed over the dusty roads. It was scorching hot when we arrived at Savage's Station, and there again we formed line of battle.

Franklin's corps, which had fallen back from Golding's farm, joined us here, and a detail was made as at other places to destroy supplies; immense piles of flour, hard bread in boxes, clothing, arms, and ammunition were burned, smashed, and scattered. Two trains of railroad cars, loaded with ammunition and other supplies, were here fired, set in motion toward each other, and under a full head of steam came thundering down the track like flaming meteors. When they met in collision there was a terrible explosion. Other trains and locomotives were precipitated from the demolished Bottom's bridge. Clouds of smoke rose at various points north of us, showing that the work of destruction was going on in other places.

JULY 1862

TUE 1 JUL.

MALVERN HILL

Of all the battles that made up the Seven Days' Campaign, none was more bloody, or more futile, than Malvern Hill. The retreating Union forces made their stand at Malvern Hill, whose elevation provided the Federals with a strong defensive position. Unwisely, Lee, who still wanted a decisive victory, attacked. The result was nearly five thousand Confederate casualties in just two hours. (Overall casualties for the Seven Days' Campaign were more than twenty thousand for the Confederates, nearly sixteen thousand for the Union.) The Union victory ended Lee's pursuit and permitted the remainder of

McClellan's army to fall back to Harrison's Landing, where it dug in under the protection of the navy's powerful guns. In his official report, Maj. Albert J. Myer, the Army of the Potomac's chief signal officer, detailed the destructiveness of the Federal artillery.

ABOUT NOON THE ENEMY advanced on our left. Our batteries on land opened, and a signal order brought to their assistance the fire of the fleet, the shells of the great guns passing high over portions of our army and plunging into the woods through which the enemy were moving. The conflict at this point terminated, after a severe struggle, with the repulse of the enemy. One of the first messages sent from the signal station

The battle of Malvern Hill, as rendered for popular consumption by Nathaniel Currier and James Merritt Ives.

on the left was a call for more men. At that time our lines seemed hard pressed. A message from this station announced to General McClellan, upon his arrival on the field about 2 P.M., the repulse of the enemy, then just effected by General Couch's division....

The messages to open fire, to cease firing, to fire rapidly, to fire slowly, to fire to the right or left, to alter the elevation of the guns, the ranges, the length of fuses, &c., passed continuously. At one time the order went to fire only single guns, and to wait after each the signal report of the shot. About 6 P.M., while the last attack was raging, it was signaled, "Fire rapidly; this is the crisis of the day."

The fire of the Navy covered the left of our army. It was turned upon our enemy, more than 2 miles distant from the ships in the woods and invisible from the vessel, with precision. It was not the fault of naval officers or men that one or two of the shells struck in our own ranks. The guns had been trained in obedience

Union naval officers pose soon after Malvern Hill.

to signal messages closer and closer to our lines, until the variations usual in such long flights of the shell caused the accident.

It must be borne in mind that from early in the day until dark they threw an almost continuous fire, and sometimes by broadsides, along the flank of our army, and over a part of it up to its front....

The battle of Malvern Hill closed after dark with a terrific cannonade and the absolute repulse of the enemy. The plain was held by our troops, and the foe, beaten everywhere, were flying. The signal officers were ordered to bivouac at their stations, to be ready to join the expected movement of the troops at daylight.

THE PACIFIC RAILWAY ACT

For obvious reasons, the Civil War accelerated the development of railroads in the United States. Wartime freight and transportation needs promoted track construction by such private firms as the Baltimore & Ohio Railroad; however, the federal government also pursued its long-standing goal of constructing a transcontinental line. Funding for this project had long been delayed by Southerners who wanted its eastern terminus located in the South. With the Southerners gone, however, Congress was now able to pass the Pacific Railway Act, signed this day by President Lincoln, authorizing land grants, construction loans, and the eradication of Native American land claims as inducement to two railroads. The excerpt reprinted below pertains to the Union Pacific, which would lay track west from

Nebraska; similar terms applied to the Central Pacific laying track east from California.

AN ACT TO AID IN THE CONSTRUCTION OF A RAILROAD AND TELEGRAPH LINE FROM THE MISSOURI RIVER TO THE PACIFIC OCEAN....

Be it enacted, That…"The Union Pacific Railroad Company"…is hereby authorized and empowered to lay out, locate, construct, furnish, maintain and enjoy a continuous railroad and telegraph line… from a point on the one hundredth meridian of longitude west from Greenwich, between the south margin of the valley of the Republican River and the north margin of the valley of the Platte River, to the western boundary of Nevada Territory, upon the route and terms hereinafter provided…That the right of way through the public lands be…granted to said company for the construction of said railroad and telegraph line; and the right…is hereby given to said company to take from the public lands adjacent to the line of said road, earth, stone, timber, and other materials for the construction thereof; said right of way is granted to said railroad to the extent of two hundred feet in width on each side of said railroad when it may pass over the public lands, including all necessary grounds, for stations, buildings, workshops, and depots, machine shops, switches, side tracks, turn tables, and water stations. The United States shall extinguish as rapidly as may be the Indian titles to all lands falling under the operation of this act…That there be…granted to the said company, for the purpose of aiding in the construction of said railroad

and telegraph line, and to secure the safe and speedy transportation of mails, troops, munitions of war, and public stores thereon, every alternate section of public land, designated by odd numbers, to the amount of five alternate sections per mile on each side of said railroad, on the line thereof, and within the limits of ten miles on each side of said road…Provided That all mineral lands shall be excepted from the operation of this act; but where the same shall contain timber, the timber thereon is hereby granted to said company…That for the purposes herein mentioned the Secretary of the Treasury shall,…in accordance with the provisions of this act, issue to said company bonds of the United States of one thousand dollars each, payable in thirty years after date, paying six per centum per annum interest,…to the amount of sixteen of said bonds per mile for each section of forty miles; and to secure the repayment to the United States…of the amount of said bonds…the issue of said bonds… shall ipso facto constitute a first mortgage on the whole line of the railroad and telegraph line.

WED
2 THE MORRILL ACT
JUL.

In addition to promoting construction of a transcontinental railroad, the Civil War also opened the door to federal funding for institutions of higher learning. As Southern congressmen had blocked the railroad, so had they opposed federal aid to education. Now Congress passed the Land-Grant College Act, signed by President Lincoln this day. Commonly known as the Morrill Act after its sponsor, Sen. Justin Morrill of Vermont, the new law transferred to the states public lands. The states could then sell these lands and use the proceeds from such sales to establish state universities for the teaching of "agricultural and the mechanic arts."

BE IT ENACTED BY THE SENATE and House of Representatives of the United States of America in Congress assembled, That there be granted to the several States, for the purposes hereinafter mentioned, an amount of public land, to be apportioned to each State a quantity equal to thirty thousand acres for each Senator and Representative in Congress to which the States are respectively entitled by the apportionment under the census of eighteen hundred and sixty; Provided, That no mineral lands shall be selected or purchased under the provisions of this act. And be it further enacted, That the land aforesaid, after being surveyed, shall be apportioned to the several States in sections or subdivisions of sections, not less than one-quarter of a section; and whenever there are public lands in a State subject to sale at private entry at one dollar and twenty-five cents per acre, the quantity to which said State shall be entitled shall be selected from such lands within the limits of such State, and the Secretary of the Interior is hereby directed to issue to each of the States in which there is not the quantity of public lands subject to sale at private entry at one dollar and twenty-five cents per acre, to which said State may be entitled under the provisions of this act, land scrip to the amount in acres for the deficiency of its distributive share; said scrip to be sold by said States and the proceeds thereof applied to the uses and purposes prescribed in this act, and for no other use or purpose whatsoever; Provided, That in no case shall any State to which land scrip may thus be issued be allowed to locate the same within the limits of any other State, or of any Territory of the United States, but their assignees may thus locate said land scrip upon any of the unappropriated lands of the United States subject to sale at private entry at one dollar and twenty-five cents, or less, per acre; And provided, further, That not more than one million acres shall be located by such assignees in any one of the States; And provided, further, That no such location shall be made before one year from the passage of this act....And be it further enacted, That all moneys derived from the sale of the lands...shall be inviolably appropriated, by each State which may take and claim the benefit of this act, to the endowment, support, and maintenance of at least one college where the leading object shall be, without excluding other scientific and classical studies, and including military tactics, to teach such branches of learning as are related to agriculture and the mechanic arts, in such manner as the legislatures of the States may respectively prescribe, in order to promote the liberal and practical education of the industrial classes in the several pursuits and professions in life.

MON 7 JUL. *Now that the Army of the Potomac was safely back at Harrison's Landing, where it had begun the Peninsular Campaign four months ear-*

lier, George McClellan had plenty of time to correspond with the president. He disagreed with Lincoln not only regarding military matters but on the war's purpose as well. Lincoln was already leaning toward declaring emancipation a principal war aim when this letter from McClellan reached him. McClellan, at the time, was busy himself cultivating Democratic congressmen and newspaper editors for a potential (political) campaign against Lincoln in 1864.

MR. PRESIDENT: ...I EARNESTLY desire, in view of possible contingencies, to lay before your excellency, for your private consideration, my general views concerning the existing state of the rebellion, although they do not strictly relate to the situation of this army or strictly come within the scope of my official duties....

This rebellion has assumed the character of war; as such it should be regarded, and it should be conducted upon the highest principles known to Christian civilization. It should not be a war looking to the subjugation of the people of any State in any event. It should not be at all a war upon population, but against armed forces and political organization. Neither confiscation of property, political executions of persons, territorial organization of States, or forcible abolition of slavery should be contemplated for a moment. In prosecuting the war all private property and unarmed persons should be strictly protected, subject only to the necessity of military operations. All private property taken for military use

This anti-McClellan cartoon from the 1864 presidential campaign shows the general watching the battle of Malvern Hill from the safety of the USS Galena *off Harrison's Landing.*

should be paid or receipted for; pillage and waste should be treated as high crimes; all unnecessary trespass sternly prohibited, and offensive demeanor by the military towards citizens promptly rebuked. Military arrests should not be tolerated, except in places where active hostilities exist, and oaths not required by enactments constitutionally made should be neither demanded nor received. Military government should be confined to the preservation of public order and the protection of political rights. Military power should not be allowed to interfere with the relations of servitude, either by supporting or impairing the authority of the master, except for repressing disorder, as in other cases. Slave contraband under the act of Congress, seeking military protection, should receive it. The right of the Government to appropriate permanently to its own service claims to slave labor should be asserted, and the right of the owner to compensation therefor should be recognized.

This principle might be extended, upon grounds of military necessity and security, to all the slaves within a particular State, thus working manumission in such State; and in Missouri, perhaps in Western Virginia also, and possibly even in Maryland, the expediency of such a measure is only a question of time.

A system of policy thus constitutional and conservative, and pervaded by the influences of Christianity and freedom, would receive the support of almost all truly loyal men, would deeply impress the rebel masses and all foreign nations, and it might be humbly hoped that it would commend itself to the favor of the Almighty.

Unless the principles governing the future conduct of our struggle shall be made known and approved, the effort to obtain requisite forces will be almost hopeless. A declaration of radical views, especially upon slavery, will rapidly disintegrate our present armies....

I may be on the brink of eternity; and as I hope forgiveness from my Master, I have written this letter with sincerity towards you and from love of my country.

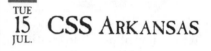

TUE
15
JUL.

CSS ARKANSAS

The March 9 duel between the USS Monitor and the CSS Virginia (or Merrimack) announced the onset of the ironclad revolution, and the performace of the newly completed Rebel ram Arkansas this day off Vicksburg delivered the message again. The most important Confederate stronghold on the Mississippi River was then being threatened by two Federal fleets, one under Flag Officer Charles H. Davis operating to the north of Vicksburg and another under Rear Adm. David G. Farragut to the south. As the Arkansas steamed down the Yazoo River toward Vicksburg, it met three Federal gunboats: the USS Carondelet, USS Tyler, and USS Queen of the West. In the ensuing battle, the Carondelet was crippled, while the Tyler and Queen of the West fled back to the protection of Davis's fleet. The thick armor of the Arkansas had stopped the fire of the Federal ships, whose wooden hulls were in turn easily splintered by the Rebel ram's guns. Later, when the Arkansas

reached the Mississippi, her comman-
der, Lt. Isaac Brown, found his single
ship opposed by thirty Union vessels.
In a feat unequaled in naval history,
Brown ran his ship through the Union
fleet, firing continual broadsides from
both his port and starboard batteries.
Again, little damage was done to the
Arkansas, *while the Union ships took*
serious hits. In the exchange below, the
aggressive Farragut attempted to per-
suade a chastened Davis to join him
in an all-out attack on the Arkansas.
Following Davis's refusal, Farragut
(now north of Vicksburg, having run
the city's guns) attacked again on his
own, and the damage he did to the
Arkansas *took the Rebels nearly a*
month to repair.

 Flagship *Hartford,*
Below Vicksburg, July 16, 1862

Dear Flag-Officer: I find that we are
peculiarly situated just now both in reference to the trust we have for the country
and the great responsibility to which we
would be held for any disastrous result
from the escape of this ram and the evils
attending such a misfortune. I can but
think, as you have the ironclad boats, the
country will expect to look to you for his
destruction, but I desire to do my part
and full share in this matter, and therefore have to propose that we make a
combined attack upon him in Vicksburg,
taking the fire of the batteries and looking
only to the destruction of the ram, regardless of consequences to ourselves.

Now, if you will come down in the
morning, pass the first battery on the
bend of the river before day, so as to arrive

off Vicksburg at daylight, I will meet you
with my forces, and we will fight the forts
and the ram, while your ironclads look to
the destruction of the ram particularly.
We know by experience, having twice
passed these forts, that we can keep them
well employed, so that you can have full
play at the ram, and we will be able to
help you occasionally. I propose, therefore, that you take this matter into
consideration and name your day and
hour. We will meet off Vicksburg....

D. G. Farragut

 U.S. Flagship *Benton*
Off Vicksburg, July 17, 1862

My Dear Admiral (or Rear-Admiral,
I believe it is): Finally I will write you in
reply to your letter of this morning this
afternoon, and meaning to do so I will not
detain your orderly any longer. But you
will not be surprised that having myself
learned a lesson of patience at Fort Pillow,
and witnessed its exercise at Columbus
and Island No. 10, I should be unwilling
to put in jeopardy all the great triumphs
and interests which are placed in my
keeping. I have watched eight rams for a
month, and now find it no hard task to
watch one. I think patience as great a
virtue as boldness, and feel anxious, above
all things, to save that portion of the
Republic which lies adjacent to and
dependent upon the Mississippi from an
alarm which would interrupt its business,
destroy its peace, and affect the public
credit at home and abroad....

C. H. Davis

★ ★ ★ ★

AUGUST
1862

FRI
1
AUG.
The Second Confiscation Act, signed by President Lincoln on July 17 after an acrimonious congressional debate and the threat of a presidential veto, was decidedly a victory for the abolitionists. Most controversial was its provision that slaves of all those supporting the rebellion would be freed once they reached Union territory. Consequently, a great number of runaways flocked to Washington, D.C. Among those who helped aid these refugees were two highly respected women (and former slaves themselves): Harriet Jacobs, author of the rediscovered slave narrative Incidents in the Life of a Slave Girl; *and Elizabeth Keckley, Mary Todd Lincoln's personal seamstress. In one of the earliest accounts of the plight of newly freed people, Jacobs reported in this letter to the editor of the* Liberator *(William Lloyd Garrison's abolitionist newspaper) the "most pitiable" condition of the "contrabands."*

A group of contrabands at Cumberland Landing, Virginia, during the Peninsular Campaign.

DEAR MR. GARRISON: I WENT to Duff Green's Row, Government headquarters for the contrabands here. I found men, women, and children all huddled together without any distinction or regard to age or sex. Some of them were in the most pitiable condition. Many were sick with measles, diphtheria, scarlet and typhoid fever. Some had a few filthy rags to lie on, others had nothing but the bare floor for a couch. They were coming in at all times, often through the night and the Superintendent had enough to occupy his time in taking the names of those who came in and those who were sent out. His office was thronged through the day by persons who came to hire the poor creatures. Single women hire at four dollars a month, a woman with one child two and a half or three dollars a month. Men's wages are ten dollars per month. Many of them, accustomed as they have been to field labor, and to living almost entirely out of doors, suffer much from the confinement in this crowded building. The little children pine like prison birds for their native element. It is almost impossible to keep the building in a healthy condition. Each day brings the fresh additions of the hungry, naked and sick.

Hoping to help a little in the good work I wrote to a lady in New York, a true and tried friend of the slave, to ask for such articles as would make comfortable the sick and dying in the hospital. On the Saturday following an immense box was received from New York. Before the sun went down, I had the satisfaction of seeing every man, woman, and child with clean garments, lying in a clean bed. What a contrast! They seemed different beings.

On July 22, Lincoln had surprised his cabinet by presenting it with a preliminary draft of the Emancipation Proclamation. (Following Secretary of State William H. Seward's advice, public announcement of the decision was withheld until military success could provide a suitable opportunity, an opportunity that finally came in September following the battle of Antietam.) However, even the North's eventual embrace of emancipation as a war aim did not mean that African Americans living in the North enjoyed equality with their white neighbors. Discriminatory laws and widespread racism made black Northerners the constant victims of bias and mistreatment. The following letter—written by John Rock, a Massachusetts justice of the peace—describes the conditions experienced even by well-educated African Americans in the wartime North.

THE PRESENT POSITION OF THE colored man is a trying one; trying because the whole nation seems to have entered into a conspiracy to crush him. But few seem to comprehend our position in the free States. The masses seem to think that we are oppressed only in the South. This is a mistake; we are oppressed everywhere in this slavery-cursed land. Massachusetts has a great name, and deserves much credit for what she has done, but the position of the colored people in Massachusetts is far from being an enviable one. While colored men have many rights, they have few privileges here. To be sure, we are seldom insulted by passersby, we have the right of suffrage, the free schools and colleges are opened to our children, and from them have come forth young men capable of filling any post of profit or honor. But there is no field for these young men. Their education aggravates their suffering....The educated colored man meets, on the one hand, the embittered prejudices of the whites, and on the other the jealousies of his own race....You can hardly imagine the humiliation and contempt a colored lad must feel by graduating the first in his class, and then being rejected everywhere else because of his color....

Nowhere in the United States is the colored man of talent appreciated. Even in Boston, which has a great reputation for being anti-slavery, he has no field for his talent.

Salmon P. Chase

SUN
3
AUG.

Salmon P. Chase, Lincoln's abolitionist secretary of the treasury, was considered the voice of radicalism in the cabinet. Vain, stubborn, and irascible, Chase had decided early on that the administration should pursue a policy of emancipation. In this diary entry, he related how, at a cabinet meeting this day, he had once again made his opinion clear to his colleagues.

THERE WAS A GOOD DEAL OF conversation on the connection of the Slavery question with the rebellion. I expressed my conviction for the tenth or twentieth time, that the time for the suppression of the rebellion without interference with slavery had passed; that it was possible, probably, at the outset, by striking the insurrectionists wherever found, strongly and decisively; but we had elected to act on the principles of a civil war, in which the whole population of every seceding state was engaged against the Federal Government, instead of treating the active secessionists as insurgents and exerting our utmost energies for their arrest and punishment; that the bitternesses of the conflict had now substantially united the white population of the rebel states against us; that the loyal whites remaining, if they would not prefer the Union without Slavery, certainly would not prefer Slavery to the Union; that the blacks were really the only loyal population worth counting; and that, in the Gulf States at least, their right to Freedom ought to be at once recognized, while, in the Border States, the President's plan of Emancipation might be made the basis of the necessary measures for their ultimate enfranchisement; that the practical mode of effecting this seemed to me quite simple; that the

President had already spoken of the importance of making of the freed blacks on the Mississippi, below Tennessee, a safeguard to the navigation of the river....

Mr. Seward expressed himself as in favor of any measures likely to accomplish the results I contemplated, which could be carried into effect without Proclamations; and the President said he was pretty well cured of objections to any measure except want of adaptedness to put down the rebellion; but did not seem satisfied that the time had come for the adoption of such a plan as I proposed.

Probably the most famous of the women engaged in espionage on behalf of the South was Belle Boyd, a native of Martinsburg in western Virginia. A teenager when the war broke out, Boyd was fiercely devoted to the Confederacy. Her exploits resulted in her being imprisoned twice and ultimately banished to England. Boyd received a good deal of attention from the Yankee press, including this short portrait published in the **New York Herald.**

Belle Boyd

THE NOTORIOUS FEMALE SPY, Belle Boyd, familiarly known as the betrayer of our forces at Front Royal,...was arrested at Winchester on Wednesday last, and is now confined in the Old Capitol prison. Romancers have given this female undue repute by describing her as beautiful and educated. She is merely a brusque, talkative woman, perhaps twenty-five years of age, red haired, with keen, courageous gray eyes. Her teeth are prominent and she is meagre in person. There is a certain dash and naivete in her manner and speech that might be called fascinating, but she is by no means possessed of brilliant qualities, either of mind or body. Being insanely devoted to the rebel cause she resolved to act as a spy within the Union lines, and managed in diverse ways to recommend herself to our officers....Our young officers, dazzled, perhaps, took her out riding often, and she was frequently a habitant of our camps in the Shenandoah. From facts gleaned in this way of our movements and projects, she kept up a pretty regular budget of intelligence, and the enemy was advised of our favorite designs. She admitted in prison today that she had informed Jackson of our situation at Front Royal; but this, she said, was done to prevent the effusion of blood....A leading secessionist of Washington visited her in jail today, where her quarters are comfortable, and gave her luxuries. Some gentlemen likewise waited upon her. She talked with them at random, and with much abandon, and said that she intended to be paroled. A soldier guards her room, and paces up and down continually before the door. Her own admissions will convict her of being a spy. She was dressed today in a plain frock, low in the neck, and her arms were bare....She takes her arrest as a matter of course, and is smart, plucky, and absurd as ever. A lunatic asylum might be recommended for her.

African-American teamsters near the signal tower at Bermuda Hundred along the James River.

TUE
5
AUG.

By this point in the war, the Union army employed black men and women in all manner of jobs—including laborer, cook, and laundress. Yet African Americans were still denied the opportunity to serve as soldiers in the Union army. (This was notably not the case with the Union navy, which had been accepting black enlistments to relieve severe manpower shortages since September 1861.) In the following racially charged letter to Gen.-in-Chief Henry W. Halleck, Iowa governor Samuel J. Kirkwood argued that more black men were indeed needed for the war effort—just not as soldiers. (Lincoln had named Halleck general-in-chief on July 11, having relieved McClellan of that specific responsibility on March 11, shortly before the onset of the Peninsular Campaign.) The congressional bill to which the colonel refers is the Second Confiscation Act, signed by Lincoln on July 17.

GENERAL: YOU WILL BEAR ME witness I have no trouble on the *"negro"* subject but there is as it seems to me so much good sense in the following extract from a letter to me from one of the best colonels this state has in the service that I have yielded to the temptation to send it to you—It is as follows. "I hope under the confiscation and emancipation bill just passed by Congress to supply my regiment with a sufficient number of 'contrabands' to do all the 'extra duty' labor of my camp. I have now *sixty men on extra duty* as teamsters &c. whose places could just as well be filled with *niggers*—We do not need a single negro in the army to fight but we could use to good advantage about one hundred & fifty with a regiment as teamsters & for making roads, chopping wood, policing camp &c. *There are enough soldiers on extra duty in the army to take Richmond or any other rebel city if they were in the ranks instead of doing negro work.*"

I have but one remark to add and that in regard to the negroes fighting—it is this—When this war is over & we have summed up the entire loss of life it has imposed on the country I shall not have any regrets if it is found that a part of the dead are *niggers* and that *all* are not white men.

BATON ROUGE

On this day, four thousand Confederates under Maj. Gen. John C. Breckinridge (the South's 1860 presidential candidate) moved against Baton Rouge, which was defended by a Union garrison of thirty-two hundred men backed by gunboats. Even before the battle began, things went badly for the Confederates. An unknown fever substantially weakened Breckinridge's force, and the ironclad ram Arkansas *failed to appear as expected (its engines had broken down on the way to Baton Rouge). Early in the morning, Breckinridge assaulted the Federal lines. In the thick morning fog, however, some Rebels lost their bearings and began shooting at their own positions. A strong push led by Brig. Gen. Charles Clark broke through the Union left, igniting a panic among the Northern soldiers. Confederate soldiers poured into the town, and Breckinridge thought he had won a great victory. But he had forgotten about the Federal gunboats, which raked his men with artillery fire. Unable to withstand this counteroffensive, Major General Breckinridge called off the pursuit and retreated from the city. In his official report, he attempted to explain why his mission had failed.*

ON THE AFTERNOON OF Monday, the 4th, the command having reached the Comite River, 10 miles from Baton Rouge, and learning by an express messenger that the *Arkansas* had passed Bayou Sara in time to arrive at the proper moment, preparations were made to advance that night. The sickness had been appalling. The morning report of the 4th showing but 3,000 effectives, and deducting those taken sick during the day and the number that fell out from weakness on the night march I did not carry into the action more than 2,600 men. This estimate does not include some 200 Partisan Rangers, who had performed efficient service in picketing the different roads, but who, from the nature of the ground, took no part in the action; nor about the same number of militia hastily collected by Col. D. C. Hardee in the neighborhood of Clinton, who, though making every effort, could not arrive in time to participate....

It was now 10 o'clock [on the 5th]. We had listened in vain for the guns of the *Arkansas*. I saw around me not more than 1,000 exhausted men, who had been unable to procure water since we left the Corette River. The enemy had several batteries commanding the approaches to the arsenal and barracks and the gunboats had already reopened upon us with a direct fire. Under these circumstances, although the troops showed the utmost indifference to danger and death, and were even reluctant to retire, I did not deem it prudent to pursue the victory further. Having scarcely any transportation, I ordered all the camps and stores of the enemy to be destroyed, and directing Captain Buckner to place one section

The battle of Baton Rouge as portrayed in an unusually imaginative lithograph by Currier & Ives.

of Semmes' battery, supported by the Seventh Kentucky, in a certain position on the field, withdrew the rest of the troops about 1 mile, to Ward's Creek, with the hope of obtaining water. But finding none there fit for man or beast, I moved the command back to the field of battle, and procured a very imperfect supply from some cisterns in the suburbs of the town. This position we occupied for the rest of the day....

I am unable to give the exact force of the enemy, but by comparing all my information with the number and size of their camps and the extent and weight of their fire I do not think they brought into action less than 4,500 men. We had eleven pieces of field artillery; they brought to bear on us not less than eighteen pieces, exclusive of the guns of the fleet. In one respect the contrast between the opposing forces was very striking. The enemy were well clothed, and their encampments showed the presence of every comfort and even luxury. Our men had little transportation, indifferent food, and no shelter. Half of them had no coats, and hundreds were without either shoes or socks; yet no troops ever behaved with greater gallantry and even reckless audacity. What can make this difference, unless it be the sublime courage inspired by a just cause?

...After the battle the enemy, who previously had been plundering, burning houses and other property, stealing negroes, and seizing citizens through a large region of the country, never ventured to send out another marauding force. Our pickets continued to extend to the immediate vicinity of Baton Rouge, and very soon the enemy abandoned the place and retired to New Orleans.

Two weeks later, the Federals evacuated Baton Rouge, allowing the Confederates to reoccupy the town with ease (only a weak screening force was left behind). In this August 21 report, the commander of a locally organized partisan ranger unit noted with disgust that the Union troops had been freeing and arming black inmates from the local penitentiary.

SIR: I HAVE TO REPORT THAT ON yesterday morning I drove in the Federal pickets and caused a general stampede of the forces in Baton Rouge, who, with the exception of those in the barracks, fled to the gunboats. They fired upon me with one company and afterward their gunboats shelled me for two hours. It is reported that they killed 1 woman and 5 children and 1 negro woman. This I do not know of my own knowledge. I captured 23 head of cattle from their slaughter-pen; I drove all the horses they had down to Bird's field and 33 down as far as Seth David's—a part of which I now have.

The Federals have released all the convicts from the penitentiary. All the negroes that were in the penitentiary have been uniformed and armed. This information regarding the penitentiary I have received from a convict who is now in my camp.

WED 20 AUG. THE SIOUX UPRISING

In Minnesota, the Civil War increased tensions between the Santee Sioux and the whites who lived around them. Specifically, the rising cost of the war had caused the government to postpone its guaranteed annual payments to the Sioux (granted them by treaty in exchange for land rights). The starving Santees had expected to use these funds to purchase food from the Indian agents. When the promised money failed to arrive, the Santees broke into the agents' well-stocked warehouses and simply took the food. Quickly, the violence escalated, and several settlers were killed. On this day, the Santees (believing that the Civil War had weakened the whites) attacked Fort Ridgely. The detachment of troops there was small, but its artillery was powerful enough to fend off this attack and another two days later. The official report below was written by Lt. T. J. Sheehan, commanding Company C, Fifth Minnesota Volunteers.

GENERAL: I HAVE THE HONOR TO report that this post was assaulted by a large force of Sioux Indians on the 20th instant. The small remnant of Company B, Fifth Regiment Minnesota Volunteers, together with a detachment of Company C, Fifth Regiment Minnesota Volunteers, and the Renville Rangers, a company just organized for one of the regiments of this State, were the only troops I had under my command for its defense, and nobly did they do their duty. The engagement lasted until dusk, when the Indians, finding that they could not effect a lodgment, which was prevented in a great measure by the superior fire of the artillery, under the immediate charge of Ordnance Sergt. J. Jones, U.S. Army, which compelled them to evacuate the ravines by which this post is surrounded, withdrew their forces, and the gallant little garrison rested on their arms, ready for any attack.

During the night several people, remnants of once thriving families, arrived at the post in a most miserable condition, some wounded—severely burned—having made their escape from their dwellings, which were fired by the Indians. The people in the immediate vicinity fled to the post for protection, and were organized and armed, as far as practicable, to aid in the defense.

On the 22d they returned with a much larger force and attacked us on all sides, but the most determined was on the east and west corners of the fort, which are in the immediate vicinity of ravines. The west corner was also covered by stables and log buildings, which afforded the Indians great protection, and, in order to protect the garrison, I ordered them to be destroyed. Some were fired by the artillery, and the balance by the Renville Rangers, under the command of First Lieut. J. Gorman, to whom, and the men under his command, great credit is due for their gallant conduct. The balls fell thick all over and through the wooden building erected for officers' quarters. Still the men maintained their ground. The Indians prepared to storm, but the gallant conduct of the men at the guns paralyzed them, and compelled them to withdraw, after one of the most determined attacks ever made by Indians on a military post.

THU
21
AUG.
This letter from Mariah Cotton to her husband, John W. Cotton, a cavalry private from Georgia, aches with all the emotions of war and separation. Reading it, one can sense

the struggle within her—the conflicting impulses to confess her pain and to comfort her husband with the impression that all is well.

MY DEAR HUSBAND I NOW SEAT my self to rite you a few to let you hear from me and the children…as for my self I am not atall sick but I trouble all most to death about you…it all most breaks my hart to think that you are gone so farr off from me and the children but I can ony hope that the time is coming when you will get home to us all again I hope thes few lines may find you well evreything is doing very well you stock is all doing vary well so far…I dont no what will become of us all crop is sarrow and worms is eaten up the grass and ther is some on the fodder I dont no whether tha will hurt the fodder or not…do you want me to sell any of you weet for seed or not you rite me about what to do about it you must rite me all the good advice you can for I need advice you no I received a letter from you a Monday it is now Thursday it was date the third of this I was glad to hear fom you.…you sed that you wood bee uneasy till you heard that the children was all well of the measels tha are all well of them now sweet and Jinny has no had than yet I dont think tha will have them now so you must not uneasy you self about the measels.…you dont no how bad I felt to hear of you beeing in a horsepitol sick Oh that I ony cood bee ther to wate on you I will bee so uneasy till I hear from you I cant rest but I hope you are better by this time and I hope by the time you get this letter you will bee well.…I nevery was as uneasy in my life…but remain you affecttion wife until death.

Brilliant, volatile, and energetic, New York Tribune editor Horace Greeley never lacked in passion for the cause of emancipation. In the Tribune of August 19, he published a fiery editorial entitled "The Prayer of Twenty Millions," urging Lincoln to free the slaves. A few days later, Lincoln replied to Greeley with this public letter explaining his views on the relationship between emancipation and the war.

FRI 22 AUG.

I HAVE JUST READ YOURS OF THE 19th, addressed to myself through the *New-York Tribune*....If there be perceptable in it an impatient and dictatorial tone, I waive it in deference to an old friend, whose heart I have always supposed to be right....

I would save the Union. I would save it the shortest way under the Constitution. The sooner the national authority can be restored, the nearer the Union will be "the Union as it was." If there be those who would not save the Union, unless they could at the same time save slavery, I do not agree with them. If there be those who would not save the Union unless they could at the same time destroy slavery, I do not agree with them. My paramount object in this struggle is to save the Union, and is not either to save or to destroy slavery. If I could save the Union without freeing any slave I would do it, and if I could save it by freeing all the slaves I would do it; and if I could save it by freeing some and leaving others alone I would also do that. What I do about slavery, and the colored race, I do because I believe it helps to save

Horace Greeley reads a newspaper in this famous portrait by Mathew Brady. The multiple page images indicate the lengthy exposure time.

the Union; and what I forbear, I forbear because I do not believe it would help to save the Union. I shall do less whenever I shall believe what I am doing hurts the cause, and I shall do more whenever I shall believe doing more will help the cause. I shall try to correct errors when shown to be errors; and I shall adopt new views so fast as they shall appear to be true views.

I have here stated my purpose according to my view of official duty; and I intend no modification of my oft-expressed personal wish that all men everywhere could be free.

FRI 29 AUG. SECOND BULL RUN (SECOND MANASSAS)

On August 16, after the Seven Days' Campaign had put the Union forces on the defensive, McClellan's 120,000 troops were ordered north to meet Maj. Gen. John Pope's 63,000-man corps near Alexandria. Still desiring a decisive victory, Confederate Gen. Robert E. Lee knew that any hope of such a victory would be lost once the forces of Pope and McClellan converged, thus giving the Federals a three-to-one advantage in manpower over Lee's Army of Northern Virginia. On August 25, following Lee's orders, Stonewall Jackson maneuvered his corps around Pope's army on the Rappahannock and on August 26 struck the huge Union supply depot at Manassas Junction, where First Bull Run had taken place thirteen months earlier. As Lee had expected, Pope moved (on August 29) to engage

Jackson; meanwhile, Lee sent Maj. Gen. James P. Longstreet through the Bull Run Mountains at Thoroughfare Gap with a second corps to attack Pope's left flank. Longstreet's surprise assault on August 30 forced the Federals to retreat once again in disarray across the creek. In his official report on the action, Union Brig. Gen. Carl Schurz hinted strongly at the disgust he felt regarding the incompetence of Pope (to whom, as commander of the Army of Virginia, the report is formally addressed). And although Pope was soon enough banished to the Department of the Northwest, much of the blame for the debacle also fell on Maj. Gen. Fitz John Porter, a pro-McClellan corps commander who would later be court-martialed for willfully disobeying Pope's direct order to attack.

Maj. Gen. Fitz John Porter

A LITTLE AFTER 4 O'CLOCK WE saw General Porter's troops, who had been engaged in our front, leave their position and retire in the direction of the place we occupied. You ordered Colonel McLean to occupy the bald-headed hill in our left front, and General Stahel's [brigade] forward to receive and support the retreating troops, who then passed through the intervals of my division and partly [turned] again behind me. About the same time General Reynolds' troops, who had occupied the heights in our front and left, fell back, and the enemy, after having obliged them to retire, planted a battery upon the high ground abandoned by them, directly opposite us, and opened a most disagreeable fire upon my three brigades. I ordered Captain Dilger to move his battery a little to the left and to open upon the enemy's battery above mentioned, which was done.

When Stahel's brigade had become engaged you ordered me to send Colonel Koltes forward to the support of its left, and a few minutes afterward, seeing Koltes hotly received and severely pressed, I ordered Colonel Krzyzanowski to ascend with his brigade the wooded hill-slopes on my left, in order to prevent Koltes from being turned on that side. This order was executed with great promptness and spirit.

But the heights on my left were soon abandoned by General Reynolds' troops, and my two brigades (Koltes' and Krzyzanowski's) found themselves severely pressed in front by overwhelming forces, exposed to a most destructive artillery fire, and turned by the enemy in their left and rear. The contest was sharp in the extreme. The gallant Koltes died a noble

Fugitive slaves in Virginia ford the Rappahannock River ahead of the Confederate army.

death at the head of his brave regiments. Colonel Krzyzanowski, while showing his men how to face the enemy, had his horse shot under him, and the ground was soon covered with our dead and wounded. When it had become evident that we on that spot were fighting alone and unsupported against immensely superior numbers, you ordered me to withdraw my division, and to take a position facing toward the left and front, on the next range of hills behind the stone house, which was the natural second position on this battlefield.

I gave the necessary orders at once. The regiments of Koltes' and Krzyzanowski's brigades came out of the fire in a very shattered condition. Their losses had been enormous....Captain Dilger's battery remained in position to check the pursuit of the enemy, whose infantry rushed upon him with great rapidity. He received them in two different positions, at short range, with a shower of grape-shot, obliged them twice to fall back, and then followed our column unmolested. His conduct cannot be praised too highly. When ascending the hill you had indicated to me as a rallying point we found that the troops who after the first repulse had rallied immediately behind us had disappeared; that the whole left wing of our army had given way, and that the enemy was rolling heavy masses of infantry after the retreating columns toward our second position. The enemy's artillery was commanding almost the whole battlefield. Behind the ridge where I was to form again, and which was the natural position of the general reserve, I expected to find an intact reserve of several brigades ready to pounce upon the enemy as he was attempting to ascend the slopes of the range of hills we were then occupying, but nothing of the kind seemed to be there. I found Major-General McDowell with his staff, and around him troops of several different corps and of all arms, in full retreat. I succeeded in inducing the captain of a battery, the name of which I do not know, to place his pieces upon the crest of the hill, and to resume the contest with the enemy's batteries immediately opposite us. My attempts to form compact bodies out of straggling soldiers met with very small success....

We had been under a continual shower of shot and shell until it grew dark, when the infantry fire on our left, as well as the artillery fire of the enemy, suddenly ceased, only now and then a projectile dropping among us. The fight on our left had evidently come to a stand. It is probable that the forces of the enemy, when arriving at the foot of the heights we were occupying, were so exhausted that a vigorous offensive on our part would have had an excellent chance of success. You remember, general, that this matter was earnestly discussed among us on the battlefield. But [your] order to retreat, and the fact that the main body of our army was already on its way to Centreville, put an end to this question.

In this letter home to his mother, an anonymous Confederate lieutenant described the action at Second Bull Run by recounting two particularly memorable aspects: first, the rapidity of Jackson's movement to engage Pope; and, second, the seizure and looting of the Federal supply depot at Manassas. The sutlers to which he refers were civilian provisioners.

MY DEAR MOTHER: I AM brimful of matter as an egg of meat. Let me try to outline our progress since my last letter....

On Monday morning the enemy appeared in heavy force, and the batteries of Hill's division were put in position and shelled their infantry. They retired the infantry, and bringing up a large number of batteries, threw a storm of shot and shell at us—we not replying. They must have exploded several thousand rounds, and in all, so well sheltered were we, our killed did not reach twenty. That evening Jackson's whole force moved up to Jefferson, in Culpeper County, Longstreet close to him. The enemy was completely deceived, and concluded we had given the thing up.

One of many Union supply depots established in Virginia, this one served the Fifth Corps.

Now comes the great wonder. Starting on the bank of the river on Monday, the twenty-fifth, we marched... between forty-five and fifty miles within the forty-eight hours....Upon reaching Manassas Junction, we met a brigade—the First New Jersey—which had been sent from Alexandria on the same supposition. They were fools enough to send a flag demanding our surrender at once. Of course we scattered the brigade, killing and wounding many, and among them the Brigadier General, who has since died. At the Junction there was a large depot of stores, five or six pieces of artillery, two trains containing probably two hundred large cars loaded down with many millions of quartermaster and com-

missary stores. Beside these, there were very large sutlers' depots, full of every thing; in short, there was collected there, in the space of a square mile, an amount and variety of property such as I had never conceived of (I speak soberly). 'Twas a curious sight to see our ragged and famished men helping themselves to every imaginable article of luxury or necessity, whether of clothing, food, or what not. For my part, I got a tooth-brush, a box of candles, and other things which I forget. But I must hurry on, for I have not the time to tell the hundredth part, and the scene utterly beggars description.

A part of us hunted that New Jersey brigade like scattered partridges over the hills just to the right of the battlefield of the eighteenth of July, 1861 [Blackburn's Ford], while the rest were partly plundering, partly fighting the forces coming on us from Warrenton. Our men had been living on roasted corn since crossing the Rappahannock, and we had brought no wagons, so we could carry little away of the riches before us. But the men could eat for one meal at least. So they were marched up, and as much of every thing eatable served out as they could carry. To see a starving man eating lobster-salad and drinking Rhine wine, bare-footed and in tatters, was curious; the whole thing was incredible.

SUN 31 AUG. ANGEL OF THE BATTLEFIELD

After the war began, Patent Office clerk Clara Barton, like many other Northern women, began collecting supplies for Union soldiers. Then, in July 1861, following the first battle of Bull Run, she began comforting injured soldiers directly as a nurse at one of the hospitals set up around the capital. Finally, a year later, she received permission to travel to the front lines as a battlefield nurse. In this excerpt from her memoirs, Barton recounts her experiences during the Second Bull Run Campaign. The battle of Cedar Mountain to which she refers was fought on August 9, when Stonewall Jackson's Confederate corps engaged a Union corps under Maj. Gen. Nathaniel P. Banks. The men she later treated at Fairfax Station were also casualties of the Second Bull Run Campaign.

I WAS STRONG AND THOUGHT I might go to the rescue of the men who fell....

But I struggled long and hard with my sense of propriety—with the appalling fact that I was only a woman whispering in one ear, and thundering in the other the groans of suffering men dying like dogs—unfed and unsheltered, for the life of every institution which had protected and educated me!

I said that I struggled with my sense of propriety and I say it with humiliation and shame. I am ashamed that I thought of such a thing.

When our armies fought on Cedar Mountain, I broke the shackles and went to the field....

At 10 o'clock Sunday [August 31] our train drew up at Fairfax Station. The ground, for acres, was a thinly wooded slope—and among the trees, on the leaves and grass, were laid the wounded who were pouring in by scores of wagon loads, as picked up on the field under the flag of truce. All day they came and the whole hillside was red. Bales of hay were broken open and scattered over the ground littering of cattle, and the sore, famishing men were laid upon it.

And when the night shut in, in the mist and darkness about us, we knew that standing apart from the world of anxious hearts, throbbing over the whole country, we were a little band of almost empty-handed workers literally by ourselves in the wild woods of Virginia, with 3,000 suffering men crowded upon the few acres within our reach.

After gathering up every available implement or convenience for our work, our domestic inventory stood at 2 water

Clara Barton

buckets, 5 tin cups, 1 camp kettle, 1 stew pan, 2 lanterns, 4 bread knives, 3 plates, and a 2-quart tin dish, and 3,000 guests to serve.

You will perceive by this, that I had not yet learned to equip myself, for I was no Pallas, ready armed, but grew into my work by hard thinking and sad experience. It may serve to relieve your apprehension for the future of my labors if I assure you that I was never caught so again.

But the most fearful scene was reserved for the night. I have said that the ground was littered with dry hay and that we had only two lanterns, but there were plenty of candles. The wounded were laid so close that it was impossible to move about in the dark. The slightest misstep brought a torrent of groans from some poor mangled fellow in your path.

Consequently here were seen persons of all grades from the careful man of God who walked with a prayer upon his lips to the careless driver hunting for his lost whip—each wandering about among this hay with an open flaming candle in his hands.

The slightest accident, the mere dropping of a light could have enveloped in flames this whole mass of helpless men.

How we watched and pleaded and cautioned as we worked and wept that night! How we put socks and slippers upon their cold feet, wrapped your blankets and quilts about them, and when we no longer had these to give, how we covered them in the hay and left them to their rest!

★ ★ ★ ★

SEPTEMBER
1862

TUE 2 SEP. McCLELLAN RESTORED TO COMMAND

With John Pope's damaged Army of Virginia now pulling back into Washington-area entrenchments, President Lincoln restored George McClellan to full command of all the Union forces in Virginia as well as those defending the capital—a move strongly opposed by both Secretary of War Edwin M. Stanton and Treasury Secretary Salmon P. Chase. Lincoln, too, had reservations—as noted in this September 1 diary entry made by the president's personal secretary, John Hay—but he suppressed them, at least for the time being. (As Hay wrote this, officials in Washington did not yet know of Pope's defeat at Second Bull Run.)

Edwin M. Stanton

WE TALKED ABOUT THE STATE of things by Bull Run and Pope's prospect. The President was very outspoken in regard to McClellan's present conduct. He said it really seemed to him that McC. wanted Pope defeated. He mentioned to me a despatch of McC. in which he proposed, as one plan of action, to "leave Pope to get out of his own scrape, and devote ourselves to securing Washington." He spoke also of McC.'s dreadful cowardice....

Later in the day we were in Halleck's room. H. was at dinner & Stanton came in while we were waiting for him and carried us off to dinner. A pleasant little dinner and a pretty wife as white and cold and motionless as marble, whose rare smiles seemed to pain her. Stanton was loud about the McC. business. He was unqualifiedly severe upon McClellan. He said that after these battles there should be one Court-Martial, if never any more. He said that nothing but foul play could lose us this battle & that it rested with McC. and his friends.

Pope's defeat at Second Bull Run sparked wild rumors in Washington that Lee's army would soon be assaulting the capital. Ironically, Washington at this time was one of the most heavily fortified cities on earth, protected by McClellan's 120,000 men as well as the remains of Pope's army and a network of more than thirty earthen forts guarding every possible approach. In this postwar recollection, Lt. Col. Richard B. Irwin described the confusion as General McClellan arrived in the city to take command. The battle

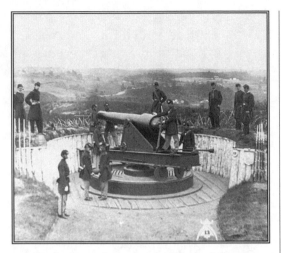

A hundred-pound Parrott gun defends the capital.

of Chantilly to which Irwin refers was the last in the Second Bull Run Campaign, fought September 1, after which Pope finally retreated within the capital's defensive perimeter.

As General McClellan's staff rode in on the morning of the 2nd of September, from their heartrending exile on the Seminary heights, condemned there to hear in helpless idleness the awful thunder of Manassas and Chantilly, we made our way through the innumerable herd of stragglers—mingled with an endless stream of wagons and ambulances, urged on by uncontrollable teamsters—which presently poured into Washington, overflowed it, took possession of its streets and public places, and held high orgie. Disorder reigned unchecked and confusion was everywhere. The clerks in the departments, many of whom had been hurried toward the front to do service as nurses, were now hastily formed into companies and battalions for defense; the Government ordered the arms and ammunition at the arsenal and the money in the Treasury to be shipped to New York, and the banks followed the example; a gun-boat, with steam up, lay in the river off the White House, as if to announce to the army and the inhabitants the impending flight of the Administration. It was at this juncture that the President, on his own responsibility, once more charged General McClellan with the defense of the capital....

Everything was at once put into motion to carry out General McClellan's orders, of which the first point was to restore order....

The improvised staff-officers were at once sent out to establish the picket lines, so broken and disconnected that virtually there were none. The troops were rapidly inspected, and their numbers, positions and wants ascertained....

The stragglers were promptly gathered in, the hotels and bar-rooms were swept of officers of all grades "absent without leave," while heavy details of cavalry reduced to obedience even the unruly teamsters whose unbroken trains blocked the streets, and checked the reckless and senseless galloping of orderlies and other horsemen, who kept the foot-passengers in terror. Thus in two days order was restored, and it was afterward maintained.

FRI 5 SEP. *One unexpected benefit of the Civil War was an increase in literacy, as Meta Morris Grimball of South Carolina noted in her diary entry for this day.*

Dr. Smith thinks the war will be a great benefit to the country, [an] enlargement of mind to very ignorant, contracted, country people. The families of soldiers now take newspapers, and if they can't read themselves they get people to read to them, and some of them have learned to read themselves. One woman in this neighborhood whose husband, a hard-working man and gone off to the wars, had learnt to write & read writing since her husband left her, and he had, too, learned to read & write that he might write to her, she could read his letters, but no other writing.

TUE 9 SEP. THE LOST ORDER

Special Order No. 191 contained Robert E. Lee's secret instructions regarding the disposition of his forces in preparation for their crossing of the Potomac River. Lee's plan was to take the war into the North by invading Maryland. However, on September 13, a misplaced copy of this September 9 order was found by two Union soldiers, who rushed it to McClellan. The Union commander was thus able to move his own troops with a foreknowledge of Lee's intentions. This precipitated a chain of events that resulted four days later in the battle of Antietam, the single bloodiest fight of the entire Civil War.

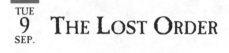 Headquarters, Army of Northern Virginia

The army will resume its march tomorrow, taking the Hagerstown road. General Jackson's command will form the advance, and, after passing Middletown, with such portion as he may select, take the route toward Sharpsburg, cross the Potomac at the most convenient point, and, by Friday night, take possession of the Baltimore and Ohio Railroad, capture such of the enemy as may be at Martinsburg, and intercept such as may attempt to escape from Harper's Ferry.

General Longstreet's command will pursue the same road as far as Boonsborough, where it will halt with the reserve, supply, and baggage trains of the army.

General McLaws, with his own division and that of General R. H. Anderson, will follow General Longstreet. On reaching Middletown he will take the route to Harper's Ferry, and by Friday morning possess himself of the Maryland Heights, and endeavor to capture the enemy at Harper's Ferry and vicinity.

General Walker, with his division, after accomplishing the object in which he is now engaged, will cross the Potomac at Cheek's Ford, ascend its right bank to Lovettsville, take possession of Loudoun Heights, if practicable, by Friday morning, Keys' Ford on his left, and the road between the end of the mountain and the Potomac on his right. He will, as far as practicable, co-operate with General McLaws and General Jackson in intercepting the retreat of the enemy.

General D. H. Hill's division will form the rear guard of the army, pursuing the road taken by the main body. The reserve artillery, ordnance, supply trains, &c., will precede General Hill.

General Stuart will detach a squadron of cavalry to accompany the commands of Generals Longstreet, Jackson, and McLaws, and with the main body of the cavalry will cover the route of the army

Harpers Ferry in 1862, with the destroyed Baltimore & Ohio Railroad bridge in the foreground.

and bring up all stragglers that may have been left behind.

The commands of Generals Jackson, McLaws, and Walker, after accomplishing the objects for which they have been detached, will join the main body of the army at Boonsborough or Hagerstown.

Each regiment on the march will habitually carry its axes in the regimental ordnance wagons, for use of the men at their encampments to procure wood, &c.

By command of General R. E. Lee:
R. H. Chilton,
Assistant Adjutant-General

SAT 13 SEP. *Abraham Lincoln's personal religious views remain a matter of controversy among historians. Because he never belonged to an orga-*

nized church, most of the president's contemporaries considered him an agnostic, or perhaps even a nonbeliever. Later observers have pointed to the religious imagery coursing through his letters and speeches as evidence that he was a closeted Christian. Whatever the case may be, Lincoln often became impatient with clergymen who presumed to know the will of God on matters relating to the war. Note the caustic tone of this reply to a religious group in Chicago that had been pressing him on the matter of emancipation.

THE SUBJECT PRESENTED IN THE memorial is one upon which I have thought much for weeks past, and I may even say for months. I am approached with the most opposite opinions and advice, and that by religious men who are equally certain that they represent the divine will. I am sure that either the one or the other class is mistaken in that belief, and perhaps in some respects both. I hope it will not be irreverent for me to say that if it is probable that God would reveal his will to others on a point so connected with my duty, it might be supposed he would reveal it directly to me; for, unless I am more deceived in myself than I often am, it is my earnest desire to know the will of Providence in this matter. And if I can learn what it is, I will do it. These are not, however, the days of miracles, and I suppose it will be granted that I am not to expect a direct revelation. I must study the plain physical facts of the case, ascertain what is possible, and learn what appears to be wise and right.

SUN 14 SEP. CRAMPTON'S GAP AND SOUTH MOUNTAIN

The first battles of the Antietam Campaign were fought on this day at Crampton's Gap and South Mountain. The left wing of McClellan's army, commanded by Maj. Gen. William B. Franklin, was sent to relieve the thin Union garrison at Harpers Ferry, which McClellan knew (from the Lost Order) was a target chosen by Lee. Franklin easily brushed aside the Confederates under Lafayette McLaws, who had advanced to meet him. But, fearing that he was outnumbered, Franklin dug in rather than continue his march to Harpers Ferry. As a result, Lee took the

town easily. At South Mountain, however, Union cavalry led by Alfred Pleasonton successfully defeated the Army of Northern Virginia's rear guard under D. H. Hill, capturing both Fox's Gap and Turner's Gap. Union Brig. Gen. Abner Doubleday, commanding the First Division of the First Corps, filed this report on the action.

I RELIEVED THEM JUST AT DUSK with my brigade, reduced by former engagements to about 1,000 men, who took position beyond the fence referred to, the enemy being in heavy force some 30 or 40 paces in our front. They pressed heavily upon us, attempting to charge at the least cessation of our fire. At last I ordered the troops to cease firing, lie down behind the fence, and allowed the enemy to charge to within about 15 paces, apparently under the impression that we had given way. Then, at the word, my men sprang to their feet and poured in a deadly volley, from which the enemy fled in disorder, leaving their dead within 30 feet of our line.

Brig. Gen. Abner Doubleday

I learned from a wounded prisoner that we were engaged with 4,000 to 5,000, under the immediate command of General Pickett, with heavy masses in their vicinity. He stated also that Longstreet in vain tried to rally the men, calling them his pets, and using every effort to induce them to renew the attack. The firing on both sides still continued, my men aiming at the flashes of the enemy's muskets, as it was too dark to see objects distinctly, until our cartridges were reduced to two or three rounds.

The crossroads village of Sharpsburg, Maryland.

General Ricketts now came from the right and voluntarily relieved my men at the fence, who fell back some 10 paces and lay down on their arms. A few volleys from Ricketts ended the contest in about thirty minutes, and the enemy withdrew from the field—not, however, until an attempt to flank us on our left, which was gallantly met by a partial change of front of the Seventy-sixth New York Volunteers, under Colonel Wainwright, and the Seventh Indiana, under Major Grover. In this attempt the enemy lost heavily, and were compelled to retreat in disorder.

Opposing Doubleday's division was a Confederate brigade commanded by Brig. Gen. Richard B. Garnett, who filed this report on the same action.

AFTER A SHORT REST, I PROceeded up the mountain, and, having gained the summit on the main road, I was sent, by a narrow lane bearing to the left, to a higher position. A portion of this route was commanded by several pieces of the enemy's artillery, which opened upon my column (marching by the flank) as soon as it came in sight, which they were enabled to do with considerable accuracy, as they had previously been practicing on other troops which had preceded mine. Several casualties occurred from this cause while I was approaching and forming my line of battle, which I did by filing my command to the right through an open field. My right rested in a thick woods, which descended quite abruptly in front, and my left in a field of standing corn. As soon as my troops were formed, I sent forward a line of skirmishers to ascertain the position of the enemy. When these dispositions had been completed (which was only a short time before sunset), I received an order from General Jones to detach my left regiment to Kemper's right (he being on my left), and to withdraw the rest of the brigade to a wooded ridge a little to the left and rear. The first part of this order had scarcely been executed when the Federal skirmishers made their appearance, immediately followed by their main body, so that the action at once became general.

The brigade sustained for some time a fierce attack by doubtless many times their number. It has subsequently been ascertained that General McClellan's army, consisting of at least 80,000 men, assailed our position, only defended by General D. H. Hill's division and a part of General Longstreet's corps. The left was the first to fall back, and finally the right was forced to retreat, being without support. Many renewed the contest a little farther to the rear, and stoutly disputed the approach of the enemy, but it had now become so dark it was impossible to distinguish objects, except at a short distance. About this time two regiments of Jenkins' brigade came up, and, the probable position of the enemy being pointed out, they advanced to the attack with great gallantry. Just as these troops moved forward, I was ordered to bring off my brigade, which I did.

MON 15 SEP. *The absence of men from the Confederate home front caused much anxiety in the women left behind. Isolated and vulnerable on farms and plantations, these ladies were particularly fearful of slave revolts. The following letter, written by Lettie Kennedy (yet representing the views of many ladies in Jasper County, Mississippi), entreated the Confederate War Office to render some assistance in the matter.*

SIR: ON THE TWELFTH OF THIS month I sent to you a petition signed by the Ladies of the northeast seat of Jasper County, Miss.—subject of said petition being a detail of six men to Guard the neighborhood from the insurrection of the negro population in said Seat. Being troubled, and in haste, I neglected to sign said petition, or date it. The object of this, is to inform you that if the said petition meet with your approbation that you inform the P[rovost] M[arshall] at Twistwood.

If you cannot grant the detail of men we do sincerely ask of you arms & ammunition that we [may] defend our desolate homes and firesides from their demoniac invasion. That we die with honor & innocence unstained—You will very much oblige us if you answer this appeal as soon as practicable.

WED 17 SEP. ANTIETAM (SHARPSBURG)

The collision of Lee's Army of Northern Virginia and McClellan's Army of the Potomac at Antietam Creek near

Confederate dead along the Hagerstown Road.

Sharpsburg, Maryland, made for the deadliest single day of fighting during the war. Although McClellan's seventy-five-thousand-man force outnumbered Lee's nearly two to one, the Union general first delayed his assault and then attacked only in a piecemeal fashion, refusing to bring up his strong reserve. Some of the day's fiercest fighting took place along a sunken road in the center, thereafter known as Bloody Lane. Another remarkably deadly ground was a cornfield in the northern sector of the battlefield. At nightfall, despite 12,469 Union and 13,724 Confederate casualties, both armies remained in place. In this report, Union Maj. Gen. Joseph Hooker described the files of dead soldiers.

WE HAD NOT PROCEEDED FAR before I discovered that a heavy force of the enemy had taken possession of a cornfield (I have since learned about a thirty-acre field) in my immediate front, and from the sun's rays falling on their bayonets projecting above the corn I could see that the field was filled with the enemy, with arms in their hands, standing apparently at "support arms." Instructions were immediately given for the assemblage of all of my spare batteries near at hand, of which I think there were five or six, to spring into battery on the right of this field and to open with canister at once. In the time I am writing every stalk of corn in the northern and greater part of the field was cut as closely as could have been done with a knife, and the slain lay in rows precisely as they had stood in their ranks a few moments before. It was never my fortune to witness a more bloody, dismal battlefield.

In this report, Brig. Gen. Robert Toombs detailed the action at Antietam from a Confederate point of view.

ON TUESDAY NIGHT THE ENEMY advanced his artillery and infantry much nearer my position, and on Wednesday morning threw forward his skirmishers and light infantry in greatly increased numbers, and before 8 o'clock drove in my pickets and advanced with heavy columns to the attack of my position on the bridge. This position was not strong. The ground descended gently to the margin of the river, covered with a narrow strip of woods, affording slight protection to the troops. Its chief strength lay in the fact that, from the nature of the ground on the other side, the enemy were compelled to approach mainly by the road which led up the river for near 300 paces, parallel with my line of battle, and distant therefrom from 50 to 150 feet, thus exposing his flank to a destructive fire the most of that distance.

At between 9 and 10 o'clock the enemy made his first attempt to carry the bridge by a rapid assault, and was repulsed with great slaughter, and at irregular intervals, up to about 1 o'clock, made four other attempts of the same kind, all of which were gallantly met and successfully repulsed by the Twentieth and Second Georgia. The Fiftieth Georgia and the half company from General Jenkins' brigade, before referred to, were on the right of the Second Georgia, rather below the main point of attack, and rendered little or no service in this fierce and bloody struggle. After these repeated disastrous repulses, the enemy, despairing of wresting the bridge from the grasp of its heroic

Lincoln meets with McClellan inside the general's field tent on October 1.

defenders, and thus forcing his passage across the river at this point, turned his attention to the fords before referred to, and commenced moving fresh troops in that direction by his left flank.

FRI 19 SEP. IUKA

The small town of Iuka, Mississippi, on the Chattanooga-to-Memphis railroad line, lay between the Union army of Ulysses S. Grant (leaving Corinth) and that of Don Carlos Buell, which was then defending Kentucky against the invading army of Braxton Bragg. Grant wanted to reinforce Buell, and Sterling Price, now commanding the Confederate District of the Tennessee, wanted to stop him at Iuka. Union Brig. Gen. William S. Rosecrans led the main attack, while Grant sent another column around Iuka to envelop Price. Realizing Grant's plan, Price disengaged from Rosecrans and retreated during the night, unable to assist Bragg any further. In his official report, Col. J. W. Whitfield described how his dismounted Texas cavalrymen successfully charged a Federal artillery emplacement. As in many of the battles it would fight against Grant, the Confederate army performed bravely, inflicted many casualties, took even more, and lost.

ON THE AFTERNOON OF FRIDAY, September 19, we formed in line of battle about 1 mile south of the town, on the Bay Springs road, the enemy approaching in large force. Soon after getting in position I was ordered to move my command in the direction of the enemy, which was then about 300 yards off. After having advanced about 100 paces the enemy opened a very heavy fire upon me with grape and canister from their artillery, besides a shower of balls from their small-arms. Under this galling fire my command moved on, and when within about 150 yards of the enemy I discovered that unless the battery was immediately silenced the result might be most disastrous, and gave the command to charge, which was responded to by loud cheers from my command and the gallant Third Texas Cavalry, being then dismounted, and at a double-quick they moved up and captured the six-gun battery, which, I am informed by one of the lieutenants, had been charged eight times before in different fights unsuccessfully, killing and wounding the greater portion of the men and nearly all the horses, and capturing several men and officers, among whom was a colonel, and driving back their entire line in great confusion. During this charge Captain Whitfield, of Company D, acting as major, discovered that the enemy had thrown out a regiment to flank us on our right; ordered Companies D, K, and M to charge them, which they did in gallant style, putting them to flight and driving them 200 or 300 yards. It was in this move that First Lieut. William W. Townsend killed the colonel of the enemy's regiment with a dragoon pistol. When I ordered the charge the gallant Lieut. Col. John Griffith, of the Seventeenth Arkansas Regiment, and the officers in command of the Fourteenth Arkansas Regiment, hearing and recognizing my voice, moved up with their commands in beautiful order on a three-gun battery on my left.

About an hour after the charge, it being then dark, we were ordered to the rear. In this short but hotly-contested charge I sustained a loss in killed and wounded of 106 officers and men, most of whom fell at or immediately about the battery.

By the fall of 1862, the institution of slavery was fast disintegrating in those parts of the Confederacy now under Union control. The following letter from New Orleans sugar planter John Wenderstrandt to military governor (and Union brigadier general) George Shepley reveals the newly assertive behavior of some of the slaves on his plantation. Wenderstrandt also refers to Gen. Neal Dow, an abolitionist officer, posted to the south of New Orleans, who had been encouraging this type of "insurrection" by issuing free papers to slaves expelled from their plantations (for defying their owners' will as well as for other forms of insubordination). Free papers were documents that certified a black person was indeed free and not a runaway slave.

ON MONDAY LAST, WHILE ON A visit to my plantation, I was startled at the dawn of day by the announcement of my brother in law Mr Smith the manager of the place, that the Negroes were in a state of insurrection, some of them refusing to work—Proceeding immediately to the Cabin Yard, I found them gathered in different groups & on enquiry learned, that some of them would not work at all, & others wanted wages, I informed them, I should not pay them wages, & being excited by their ingratitude & not wishing to feed and clothe those who would not work, & to avoid any difficulty, as my sister and her four small children were on the place, I said that it was better to part in peace & go off quietly & that I did not wish to lay eyes on them again, & they went away—I never drove any of them off the plantation, or told them according to the expression of Gen. Dow to shift for themselves—So far from it, I sent a written notice to the rice planters below, forbidding them to employ them under the pains & risks of the law, in regard to employment of runaway slaves   about twenty five of them left the plantation, some few of them remained & went to work the next day—

Under this anamolous state of affairs, I pray that the Governor & Provost Marshall, will…see into the condition of things on the plantation, that a suitable protection be afforded my sister and her children, that the Negroes may be informed how far the emancipation of Gen Dow may be valid, & the future conduct of the place & themselves, may be put upon such a footing & will restore peace & good order—

MON
22
SEP.

Less than a week after the battle of Antietam, Abraham Lincoln issued his preliminary Emancipation Proclamation—previously withheld on Seward's advice that he wait for a Union military victory. Antietam was hardly the triumph the secretary of state had in mind, but Lincoln was determined to move ahead, and Antietam seemed the best opportunity he might have for a while. The

Hannibal Hamlin

proclamation specifically announced his intention to free the slaves in Rebel-controlled territory as of January 1, 1863, if the South had not surrendered by that date. It was a tense time for Lincoln, who wondered how his new policy would be received in the North, especially among the ranks of the Union army. The president voiced many of these concerns in a letter to Vice President Hannibal Hamlin written on September 28.

MY DEAR SIR: YOUR KIND letter of the 25th is just received. It is known to some that while I hope something from the proclamation, my expectations are not as sanguine as are those of some friends. The time for its effect southward has not come; but northward the effect should be instantaneous.

It is six days old, and while commendation in newspapers and by distinguished individuals is all that a vain man could wish, the stocks have declined, and troops came forward more slowly than ever. This, looked soberly in the face, is not very satisfactory. We have fewer troops in the field at the end of six days than we had at the beginning—the attrition among the old outnumbering the addition of the new. The North responds to the proclamation sufficiently in breath; but breath alone kills no rebels.

Camp life had a tendency to bring out both the best and the worst in soldiers. Once in uniform, for example, many men forgot their domestic responsibilities. The following account, from the journal of Union officer John William DeForest, details the case of one particularly irresponsible man under DeForest's command.

YESTERDAY'S MAIL BROUGHT ME a letter from the wife of one of my private soldiers. She had not heard from her husband for a month, and she wanted to know if he was in trouble or was dead. She had received nothing from him since he enlisted but one remittance of nine dollars. A mortgage on her house had been foreclosed; and…she and her children are likely to be homeless as well as penniless.

I fear that she will get little aid from her husband. He is a mild, weak young fellow, easily led away by comrades, low-spirited under the slightest illness, given to cosseting himself with sutler's trash, and given also to seeking courage in whiskey. Thirteen dollars a month can easily be spent in these follies.

The letter is nicely written and correctly spelled; moreover, it is well phrased and loving and touching. It is full of her husband; full of adoration for the poor creature and of prayers for his unimportant safety; pious terrors lest he may have

Winslow Homer's 1863 lithograph The Coffee Call.

been drawn into evil ways; prayers to me that I will not conceal from her the possible worst; then declarations that the feeble lout is the best of husbands; it is no fault of his—no fault of Henry's—that his family suffers.

In short, here are four pages of pathos which make me want to call in Henry and kick him for not deserving them. Apparently a fairly educated and quite worthy girl has married a good-looking youth of inferior nature and breeding who has not the energy to toil effectively for her, nor the affection to endure privations for her sake. I shall give the letter to him with a few words of earnest, epauletted counsel. It may stop him from drinking himself into the gutter twice after every payday, and from sickening himself with bushels of abominable gingerbread and shameless pie.

WED 24 SEP. *On the same day, July 17, that Lincoln signed the Second Confiscation Act, he also approved a militia draft, calling up men between the ages of eighteen and forty-five for nine months' service. When the calls didn't go as well as expected, Lincoln tightened the net. Early on, he had suspended the writ of habeas corpus— meaning in Latin "to have the body"— when Union military authorities wanted to arrest and hold suspected spies and saboteurs in the border states. Now the president employed this same tactic against the draft evaders.*

A PROCLAMATION
Whereas it has become necessary to call into service not only volunteers but also portions of the militia of the States by draft in order to suppress the insurrection existing in the United States, and disloyal persons are not adequately restrained by the ordinary processes of law from hindering this measure and from giving aid and comfort in various ways to the insurrection;

Now, therefore, be it ordered, first, that during the existing insurrection and as a necessary measure for suppressing the same, all Rebels and Insurgents, their aiders and abettors within the United States, and all persons discouraging volunteer enlistments, resisting militia drafts, or guilty of any disloyal practice, affording aid and comfort to Rebels against the authority of the United States, shall be subject to martial law and liable to trial and punishment by Courts Martial or Military Commission:

Second. That the Writ of Habeas Corpus is suspended in respect to all persons arrested, or who are now, or hereafter during the rebellion shall be, imprisoned in any fort, camp, arsenal, military prison, or other place of confinement by any military authority or by the sentence of any Court Martial or Military Commission.

In witness whereof, I have hereunto set my hand, and caused the seal of the United States to be affixed.

Done at the City of Washington this twenty-fourth day of September, in the year of our Lord one thousand eight hundred and sixty-two, and of the Independence of the United States the 87th.

By the President: Abraham Lincoln

★ ★ ★ ★

OCTOBER
1862

CORINTH

Even after the Union victory at Iuka on September 19, the Confederate armies of Sterling C. Price and Earl Van Dorn still had considerable striking power. Targeting the well-fortified Union garrison at Corinth, Mississippi—and hoping once again to hold Grant's troops in Tennessee—the Rebels attacked on October 3. The battle was costly for both sides, with 2,500 Union casualties out of 23,000 engaged and nearly 4,300 Confederate losses out of 22,000 engaged. After two days of fighting, the Confederates withdrew, causing Union Brig. Gen. William Rosecrans, the field commander at Corinth, to receive a great deal of praise. More importantly, Van Dorn and Price failed to prevent Grant from reinforcing Don Carlos Buell in Kentucky. This, in turn, allowed Buell to mass his forces for the battle of Perryville on October 8. In his memoirs, however, Grant argued that Rosecrans actually performed poorly at Corinth, missing the opportunity for a truly decisive victory.

 ON THE NIGHT OF THE 3D, accordingly, I ordered General McPherson, who was at Jackson, to join Rosecrans at Corinth with reinforcements picked up along the line of the railroad equal to a brigade. Hurlbut had been ordered from Bolivar to march for the same destination; and as Van Dorn was coming upon Corinth from the north-west some of his men fell in with the advance of Hurlbut's and some skirmishing ensued

Maj. Gen. Earl Van Dorn

on the evening of the 3d. On the 4th Van Dorn made a dashing attack, hoping, no doubt, to capture Rosecrans before his reinforcements could come up. In that case the enemy himself could have occupied the defenses of Corinth and held at bay all the Union troops that arrived. In fact he could have taken the offensive against the reinforcements with three or four times their number and still left a sufficient garrison in the works about Corinth to hold them. He came near success, some of his troops penetrating the National lines at least once, but the works that were built after Halleck's departure enabled Rosecrans to hold his position until the troops of both McPherson and Hurlbut approached toward the rebel front and rear. The enemy was finally driven back with great slaughter: all their charges, made with great gallantry, were repulsed. The loss on our side was heavy, but nothing compared to Van Dorn's.

McPherson came up with the train of cars bearing his command as close to the enemy as was prudent, debarked on the rebel flank and got in to the support of Rosecrans just after the repulse. His approach, as well as that of Hurlbut, was known to the enemy and had a moral effect. General Rosecrans, however, failed to follow up the victory, although I had given specific orders in advance of the battle to pursue the moment the enemy was repelled. He did not do so, and I repeated the order after the battle....

Rosecrans did not start pursuit till the morning of the 5th and then took the wrong road....I now regarded the time to accomplish anything by pursuit as past and, after Rosecrans reached Jonesboro, I ordered him to return....The battle was recognized by me as being a decided victory, though not so complete as I had hoped for, nor nearly so complete as I now think within the easy grasp of the commanding officer at Corinth. Since the war it is known that the result, as it was, was a crushing blow to the enemy, and felt by him much more than it was appreciated at the North.

WED 8 OCT. PERRYVILLE

In Braxton Bragg's bold campaign to bring Kentucky into the Confederacy, the battle of Perryville was the turning point. Although both sides fought to a bloody standstill, and the Union suffered the worse casualties (forty-two hundred to thirty-four hundred for the South), the battle was a significant setback for the Rebels, who had no choice but to retire from Kentucky while they recouped their losses. The following account of the battle—from the memoirs of Pvt. Sam Watkins, First Tennessee Infantry—is unusual in that it reports hand-to-hand combat, something of a rarity during the Civil War. The Napoleon guns to which Watkins refers were twelve-pound field guns used extensively by both sides during the war. They were based on a French design and named in honor of Napoleon III, who ruled France during the 1850s when the guns were introduced. Workhorses of the Civil War artillery, they were highly effective at close range when loaded with either canister, grape, or solid shot.

WE DID NOT RECOIL, BUT OUR line was fairly hurled back by the leaden hail that was poured into our very faces. Eight color-bearers were killed at one discharge of their cannon. We were right up among the very wheels of their Napoleon guns. It was death to retreat now to either side. Our Lieutenant Colonel Patterson halloed to charge and take their guns, and we were soon in a hand-to-hand fight—every man for himself—using the butts of our guns and bayonets. One side would waver and fall back a few yards, and would rally, when the other side would fall back, leaving the four Napoleon guns; and yet the battle raged. Such obstinate fighting I had never seen before or since. The guns were discharged so rapidly that it seemed the earth itself was in a volcanic uproar. The iron storm passed through our ranks, mangling and tearing men to pieces. The very air seemed full of stifling smoke and fire which seemed the very pit of hell, peopled by contended demons.

Maj. Gen. Don Carlos Buell

MON 13 OCT. *Between October 9 and October 12, Confederate Maj. Gen. J. E. B. Stuart and eighteen hundred of his famous horsemen completed Stuart's Second Ride Around McClellan (the first having come outside Richmond in mid-June). Meanwhile, McClellan's massive but unbudging Army of the Potomac again ignored Lincoln's urgings that it press its advantage against Lee. The president was certainly leaning toward stripping McClellan of command, but he held off and instead wrote McClellan the following letter, which combined occasional browbeating with outright pleading.*

MY DEAR SIR: YOU REMEMBER my speaking to you of what I called your over-cautiousness. Are you not over-cautious when you assume that you cannot do what the enemy is constantly doing? Should you not claim to be at least his equal in prowess, and act upon the claim?

As I understand, you telegraph Gen. Halleck that you cannot subsist your army at Winchester unless the railroad from Harper's Ferry to that point be put in working order. But the enemy does now subsist his army at Winchester at a distance nearly twice as great from the railroad transportation as you would have to do without the railroad last named. He now wagons from Culpeper C.H. which is just about twice as far as you would have to do from Harper's Ferry. He is certainly not more than half as well provided with wagons as you are. I certainly should be pleased for you to have the advantage of the railroad from Harper's Ferry to Winchester, but it wastes all the remainder of autumn to give it to you; and, in fact ignores the question of *time*, which cannot, and must not be ignored.

Again, one of the standard maxims of war, as you know, is "to operate upon the enemy's communications as much as possible without exposing your own." You

A Union cemetery near City Point, Virginia.

seem to act as if this applies *against* you, but cannot apply in your *favor*. Change positions with the enemy, and think you not he would break your communication with Richmond within the next twenty-four hours? You dread his going into Pennsylvania. But if he does so in full force, he gives up his communications to you absolutely, and you have nothing to do but to follow, and ruin him; if he does so with less than full force, fall upon, and beat what is left behind all the easier.

Exclusive of the water line, you are now nearer Richmond than the enemy is by the route that you *can* and he *must* take. Why can you not reach there before him, unless you admit that he is more than your equal on a march. His route is the arc of a circle, while yours is the chord. The roads are as good on yours as on his.

You know I desired, but did not order, you to cross the Potomac below, instead of above the Shenandoah and Blue Ridge. My idea was that this would at once menace the enemy's communications, which I would seize if he would permit. If he should move northward I would follow him closely, holding his communications. If he should prevent our seizing his communications, and move toward Richmond, I would press closely to him, fight him if a favorable opportunity should present, and, at least, try to beat him to Richmond on the inside track. I say "try"; if we never try, we shall never succeed....It is all easy if our troops march as well as the enemy; and it is unmanly to say they cannot do it.

This letter is in no sense an order.
Yours truly,
A. Lincoln

SAT 25 OCT. *With McClellan continuing to keep his Army of the Potomac at a standstill, Lincoln became incensed and sent the general this acid-tongued note in response to a request for more horses. Two weeks later, on November 7, Lincoln went even further, relieving McClellan of command and replacing him with Maj. Gen. Ambrose Burnside.*

MAJR. GENL. MCCLELLAN:
I have just read your despatch about sore-tongued and fatigued horses. Will you pardon me for asking what the horses of your army have done since the Battle of Antietam that fatigues them anything?
A. Lincoln

★ ★ ★ ★

NOVEMBER
1862

SAT
1
NOV.

Just as advances in military technology played an important role in determining how the Civil War was fought, advances in agricultural technology determined how the North and South were fed. According to this article from the Cincinnati Gazette, the increasing scarcity of farm labor made investment in new machinery an absolute necessity. The world's fair to which the newspaper refers is the 1851 Crystal Palace exhibition, held in London, at which the Virginia Reaper manufactured by Cyrus H. McCormick won a well-publicized competition.

A HUNDRED THOUSAND AGRIcultural laborers are gone; how are we to meet the deficiency? We have met it chiefly by labor-saving machinery. A few years since, McCormick came to Cincinnati to manufacture his reapers. The idea then was, that they were suitable only for the large prairie wheat-fields. It was the only agricultural machine we had, and it was met, as usual, by doubt and hesitation. Soon after, this machine and others appeared at the World's Fair, and it was pronounced a great success. Since then we have reapers, mowers, separators, sowers, drills &c., making a great aggregate of agricultural machinery, which does the work of more than three-fold the number of men, who (without machinery) would have been required to do it. Indeed, without this machinery, the wheat, oats, and hay of Ohio, in 1862, could not have been got in safely. Besides, this machinery, which was at first only intended for large farms, now operates on the smallest; and on the large tracts steam is successfully employed, multiplying ten-

A McCormick reaper in action.

fold the labor-saving power. At Dayton, Springfield, Lancaster, Canton and Cleveland, large factories are engaged in turning out agricultural machines; so that we have the benefit both of the making and the use of agricultural machinery. The mode in which the harvest of 1862 has been principally got in is this. One farmer in the neighborhood buys a machine, whether reaper or separator, and goes round doing the work of his neighbors at so many cents per bushel. It is thus that machinery has done the work of thousands of men, who have thus been spared for the war.

TUE
4
NOV.
Shortages are always a fact of life during wartime, and, as the following excerpt from the Philadelphia Public Ledger *illustrates, the lack of one item (such as cotton) will often produce shortages of related goods (such as paper).*

COTTON WASTE LARGELY ENTERS into the manufacture of paper, but the high price of cotton, and the cutting off of its production at the South, have diminished the manufacture of cotton fabrics, and as a consequence the amount of "waste" which the cotton mills furnished. In addition to this the wants of our military hospitals have encroached upon the other sources of supply—cotton rags, which are now converted into lint for the soldiers' wounds. These causes have lessened the usual sources of supply to the paper mills and the effect is seen in the increased, and increasing price of paper, which is operating very severely upon newspaper publishers, and raising the price of newspapers. It becomes a duty, under these circumstances, that every housekeeper should save every cotton rag about the house rather than destroy it as worthless, as so many do. They can be sold for a price which pays well for the small trouble of putting them into a bag each day and sending them to the paper dealers, or purchasers of rags for the paper mills.

The Union blockade of Confederate ports made the paper shortage an even more pressing problem in the South. Readers of the Charleston Mercury, *for example, were asked on January 13, 1863, to begin an unusual form of conservation.*

SAVE YOUR RAGS

This would perhaps, in ordinary times, be quite an unnecessary piece of advice, but at this moment it is of vital importance. As our readers know, the price of paper has advanced enormously, and as a consequence, publishers have been compelled to make a corresponding advance on their prices. One great reason of this increased tariff on paper is the scarcity of rags with which to manufacture it. The manufacturers inform us that rags are exceedingly difficult to obtain, even when, as is the case, the rates paid are higher, by at least 800 percent, than formerly.

We write this article solely with the view of calling public attention to the scarcity, that it may, as far as possible, be remedied, and that speedily. The press is one of the most potent auxiliaries of this Government in carrying forward its

objects, and subserving its interests. As a medium of communication, in times like these, when every day adds some memorable event to our history, the newspaper is as indispensable as our daily food. And it is essential to our individual intelligence, and as a record of current events. And as we sit down to read the pages of the favorite book or journal, let us not fail to remember that the materials for its manufacture must be obtained, or we shall have no book or newspaper. Until the blockade is removed—a desideratum altogether among the uncertainties— we must rely upon our own resources. Let then every family carefully save up all the rags—all the shreds—all the scraps— either linen, cotton, or woollen, and furnish them to the Paper Mills, and the proprietors of those mills will pay them handsomely therefor. Husbands, tell your wives to see to this—and not only the wives, but let every member of the family, white and black, commence the saving of rags to make paper. The possible contingency of a country like ours deprived of newspapers is shocking to contemplate. And we will not believe but what, as we have thus sounded the note of alarm, every one interested (and who is not?) will do all in his or her power to keep the mills supplied with rags, that the press may thereby continue to dispense intelligence to the people.

THU 20 NOV. *In November 1861, Union naval expeditions secured many of the Sea Islands off the coasts of South Carolina and Georgia, encouraging a mass exodus among cotton plantation owners, who generally abandoned their* *slaves as well as their land. When word of this reached the North, abolitionists flocked to the Sea Islands, where they began an "experiment" in how to educate these former slaves. About a year into the task, volunteer teacher Charlotte Forten, a young black woman from an elite Philadelphia family, wrote to* Liberator *editor William Lloyd Garrison with this news of the progress she had made on St. Helena's Island.*

AS FAR AS I HAVE BEEN ABLE TO observe, the negroes here rejoice in their new-found freedom. It does me good to see how *jubilant* they are over the downfall of their "secesh" masters. I do not believe that there is a man, woman, or even a child that would submit to be made a slave again. They are a truly religious people. They speak to God with a loving familiarity. Another trait that I have noticed is their natural courtesy of manner. There is nothing cringing about it, but it seems inborn, and one might almost say elegant. It marks their behavior towards each other as well as to the white people.

My school is about a mile from here, in the little Baptist church, which is in a grove of white oaks. These trees are beautiful—evergreen—and every branch heavily draped with long, bearded moss, which gives them a strange, mournful look. There are two ladies in the school besides myself—Miss T and Miss M both of whom are most enthusiastic teachers. At present, our school is small—many of the children being ill with whooping cough—but in general it averages eighty or ninety. It is a great happiness to teach them. I wish some of those persons at the North who say the race is hopelessly and naturally inferior, could see the readiness with which these children, so long oppressed and deprived of every privilege, learn and understand.

Slave cabins on Hilton Head, one of the Sea Islands off the coast of South Carolina.

MON 24 NOV. *The dividing line between each side's military and political leadership remained blurred throughout the war. (For example, many army officers on both sides owed their commissions as much to political connections as to their battlefield prowess.) In the North, however, politics played an even more interesting role, with party distinctions among Democrats and Republicans never quite forgotten despite the patriotic upsurge. Many Republicans privately (and some not so privately) suspected the motives of such prominent Democratic generals as McClellan and Don Carlos Buell, interpreting their various shortcomings and defeats as evidence of inadequate commitment at the least or perhaps even treasonous designs. Some Republican party leaders had repeatedly urged Lincoln to relieve these men of command, but the president had resisted. His irritation with the constant proddings of these Republicans is apparent in this testy letter to Brig. Gen. Carl Schurz, a liberal Republican (and later Rutherford Hayes's secretary of the interior) who detested McClellan in particular. Yet as Lincoln himself notes, he had already relieved both McClellan (on November 7) and Buell (on October 24, for allowing Braxton Bragg's army to escape).*

Brig. Gen. Carl Schurz

I HAVE JUST RECEIVED, AND read, your letter of the 20th. The purport of it is that we lost the late elections, and the administration is failing, because the war is unsuccessful; and that I must not flatter myself that I am not justly to blame for it. I certainly know that if the war fails, the administration fails, and that I *will* be blamed for it, whether I deserve it or not. And I ought to be blamed, if I could do better. You think I could do better; therefore you blame me already. I think I could not do better; therefore I blame you for blaming me. I understand you *now* to be willing to accept the help of men, who are not republicans, provided they have "heart in it." Agreed. I want no others. But who is to be the judge of hearts, or of "heart in it"? If I must discard my own judgment, and take yours, I must also take that of others; and by the time I should reject all I should be advised to reject, I should have none left, republicans, or others— not even yourself. For, be assured, my dear sir, there are men who have "heart in it" that think you are performing your part as poorly as you think I am performing mine. I certainly have been dissatisfied with the slowness of Buell and McClellan; but before I relieved them I had great fears I should not find successors to them, who would do better; and I am sorry to add, that I have seen little since to relieve those fears. I do not clearly see the prospect of any more rapid movements. I fear we shall at last find out that the difficulty is in our case, rather than in particular generals. I wish to disparage no one—certainly not those who sympathize with me; but I must say I need success more than I need sympathy, and that I have not seen the so much greater evidence of getting success from my sympathizers, than from those who are denounced as the contrary. It does seem to me that in the field the two classes have been very much alike, in what they have done, and what they have failed to do.

SAT 29 NOV. *Although the Civil War linked the eastern and western halves of the Union in a joint crusade against the wayward Confederacy, sectional tensions, especially economic ones, made this common cause seem at times superficial. Westerners, for example, often complained that easterners benefited disproportionately from the awarding of government military contracts and that they enjoyed unfair advantages when it came to the nation's tax and tariff regulations. The following notice in this day's* Chicago Times *promoted "a western meeting to deliberate upon western interests."*

A MASS MEETING HAS BEEN called at Dixon, Ill., to be held December 1, of the farmers, manufacturers, and mechanics of Lee and adjoining counties, for the purpose of "taking measures to promote and protect the industrial interests and to give expression to their views and wishes on the subject of our national finances and currency."

These are stated to be the objects of the meeting....There is not a word respecting the African in the call. But interests directly affecting the individuals who assemble are to be considered. It is a western meeting to deliberate upon western interests. If the farmers of Lee and adjoining counties have ascertained that in the new tax law a heavy burden is laid upon their shoulders while New England farmers are but slightly taxed, we apprehend that they will take measures to reduce the inequality. If western manufacturers find that the peculiar manufactures in which they are interested are carefully hunted up and oppressively taxed while the cotton lords of New England are protected in both the tax and tariff laws, we think they will be very likely to inquire the wherefore. The Dixon meeting is a movement in the right direction. Irrrespective of all party feeling, there should be an earnest looking after their own interests by western men.

★ ★ ★ ★

DECEMBER
1862

LINCOLN'S STATE OF THE UNION MESSAGE

By the time that Abraham Lincoln sent this State of the Union message to Congress, he had already decided to make emancipation his official policy. It awaited only the formal release of the Emancipation Proclamation on New Year's Day. In the meantime, he chose to inform Congress in no uncertain terms that freeing the slaves would henceforth be the centerpiece of his administration and of the Union's war effort.

THE DOGMAS OF THE QUIET past, are inadequate to the stormy present. The occasion is piled high with difficulty, and we must rise—with the occasion. As our case is new, so we must think anew, and act anew. We must dis-enthrall ourselves, and then we shall save our country. Fellow-citizens, we cannot escape history. We of this Congress and this administration, will be remembered in spite of ourselves. No personal significance, or insignificance, can spare one or another of us. The fiery trial through which we pass, will light us down, in honor or dishonor, to the latest generation. We say we are for the Union. The world will not forget that we say this. We know how to save the Union. The world knows we do know how to save it. We—even we here—hold the power, and bear the responsibility. In giving freedom to the slave, we assure freedom to the free—honorable alike in what we give, and what we preserve. We shall nobly save, or meanly lose, the last best hope of earth. Other means may succeed; this

The White House as it appeared in the middle of the nineteenth century.

could not fail. The way is plain, peaceful, generous, just—a way which, if followed, the world will forever applaud, and God must forever bless.

WED 3 DEC. *Although decidedly a Northern publication, Harper's Weekly featured this day a poem expressing sentiments equally familiar to both Northern and Southern families. Entitled "Thanksgiving" and narrated by a soldier, it conveyed the sense of loss and loneliness shared by nearly all Americans during this difficult holiday season.*

 **THANKSGIVING**

I think of you all, dear Mother,
 Ned and Emma and Moll,
Dark-eyed Harry, and little Lou,
 Jim, and Bessie, and all!
How often we've met together
 For many a bright year past,
Till it seemed to me as if every one
 Was merrier than the last.

I greet you all, though so far away
 That your faces I cannot see;
I remember each with a sacred joy—
 Do you also remember me?
Looking up to the dear old flag
 With loyal hearts and true,

Do you smile to think for freedom's sake
    I am absent today from you?

Yes, I know who name me every day
    When they kneel to God in prayer—
I know who search every paper through
    To see if my name be there.
And now in this good Thanksgiving time,
    When the old house rings with glee,
There will be one toast to "Our absent
      ones,"
    And then you will think of me!

You always called me "wild," you know,
    Wondered what would be my fate—
"So giddy and mischievous, what will he do
    When he reaches man's estate?"
Well, here I am, twenty-one last month,
    And my holiday life is through:
I face death calmly day by day—
    How strange it must seem to you!

As I sit in my tent by this moonlight
    I hear your voices fall,
Like distant music, upon my ear,
    And your names I softly call.
How long before we shall meet again
    In the homestead far away?
No matter, we yet live—and God is good,
    And this is Thanksgiving day!

FRI 5 DEC. *In antebellum America, women were traditionally the family members primarily responsible for health care. Not surprisingly, many became nurses during the war; yet the experience of nursing masses of wounded and dying strangers, virtually all of them men, in the public setting of a military hospital was, for most, a challenge both frightening and exhilarating.*

In this passage from a letter to her sister, Union army nurse Rebecca Usher of Hollis, Maine, described her impressions of the army hospital at Chester, Pennsylvania, where she was stationed.

MY HEAD IS RUNNING OVER WITH incidents of life here which I want so much to tell you....

I rose this morning at quarter before seven & went down to Mrs Tyler's kitchen. I usually go down through the courts in the morning, as the men in the wards are not always ready to receive visitors so early in the morning, & when they are, it is some what embarrassing, to march down alone through a quarter mile of men. But one soon becomes accustomed to it, so that it is rather pleasant than otherwise, & you soon find yourself talking with one & another as you pass along....Our rooms have hard pine floors, unpainted & uncarpeted, two unpainted tables, a seven by nine looking glass, one chair, & our trunks, but we care little for our rooms, our whole interest is with the soldiers.

SUN 7 DEC.

PRAIRIE GROVE

By this stage of the war, northern Arkansas and southern Missouri had become a no-man's-land filled with guerrilla bands, deserters, and scattered detachments of Union and Confederate soldiers, more the former than the latter. On this day at Prairie Grove, Arkansas, about twelve miles southwest of Fayetteville, a remarkably large number of those elements converged. Almost simultaneously, Confederate Maj.

Gen. Thomas C. Hindman ran into two separate Union divisions, attempted to attack each one separately, and was ultimately foiled when a hard night's march allowed the Federal wings to consolidate. Surely the most idiosyncratic of the Federal units fighting at Prairie Grove was the First Regiment, Indian Home Guards, formed entirely of Native Americans. Its commander, Lt. Col. Stephen Wattles, was respectful of his men's heritage, and his report on the battle interestingly notes the difficulty he had in quantifying his casualties, because it was unseemly for a warrior to complain of any wounds.

ON ARRIVING AT THE BATTLE-ground, we dismounted and entered the wood on the left of the center, with the Eleventh Kansas Volunteers on our right and an Iowa regiment on our left, and rapidly penetrated to the line of battle of the enemy, which gave way on our approach. At this time the Iowa regiment gave our left the partial effect of a volley. This fire in front and rear forced us to retrace our steps, but we rallied and formed again on the first little eminence in the edge of the wood, after a five-minute panic. On account of the retreat of the Iowa regiment from this place, we were ordered to the support of Captain Allen's battery, through the cornfield. All the companies in the command were engaged, except Company B, which was on detached service.

Major Eilithorpe and all the other white officers were particularly active and efficient during the whole day.

Of the Indian officers, Captain Jonneh, of the Uches, and Capt. Billy Bowlegs, of the Seminoles, and Captain Tus-te-nup-chup-ko, of Company A (Creek), are deserving of the highest praise.

Our loss was 2 killed and 4 wounded, as far as reported, but the Indians entertain a prejudice against speaking of dangerous occurrences in battle, and report no wounds but such as the necessities of the case demand.

WED 10 DEC. *Despite the demands of his position, Robert E. Lee kept in constant communication with his family throughout the war. In this letter, he grieves with his daughter-in-law Charlotte, wife of his son Fitzhugh, over the death of their second child, the first having also died in infancy.*

I HEARD YESTERDAY, MY DEAR daughter, with the deepest sorrow, of the death of your infant. I was so grateful at her birth. I felt that she would be such a comfort to you, such a pleasure to my dear Fitzhugh, and would fill so full the void still aching in your hearts. But you have now two sweet angels in heaven. What joy there is in the thought! I can say nothing to soften the anguish you must feel, and I know you are assured of my deep and affectionate sympathy. May God give you strength to bear the affliction He has imposed, and produce future joy out of your present misery, is my earnest prayer.

I saw Fitzhugh yesterday. He is well, and wants much to see you. When you are strong enough, cannot you come up to Hickory Hill, or your grandpa's, on a little visit, when he can come down and see you? My horse is waiting at my tent door, but I could not refrain from sending these few lines to recall to you the thought and love of

Your devoted father

R. E. Lee

A Union artillery position on the outskirts of Fredericksburg.

SAT
13
DEC.   FREDERICKSBURG

Although Maj. Gen. Ambrose E. Burnside (who had reluctantly replaced McClellan) now commanded the Army of the Potomac, that army's overall goal had not changed: It remained the capture of Richmond, the Confederate capital. And Gen. Robert E. Lee's Army of Northern Virginia still blocked its way. Lee's army was now positioned at Fredericksburg, Virginia, a crossing site on the Rappahannock River, which lay between Burnside and Richmond. After crossing the Rappahannock on a pontoon bridge, Burnside attacked the Confederates in an unusual December battle. The Southerners were outnumbered, 130,000 to 75,000, but they were well entrenched

on Marye's Heights. As a Union attack force under Brig. Gen. George Meade crossed the plain before the Rebel positions on the heights, Stonewall Jackson's men mowed them down. It was a bloodbath: 12,653 Union casualties, which more than doubled the Confederate total of 5,309. Burnside retreated, and in a little more than a month, Lincoln relieved him of the command he never wanted. For sheer violence and as an example of the wastefulness of war, few military maneuvers compare to the assault on Marye's Heights. In his memoirs, Maj. Frederick Hitchcock of the 132nd Pennsylvania Volunteer Infantry Regiment recalled the horror.

 REACHING THE PLACE IN THE rear of that railroad embankment, where I had left the brigade, I found it had just gone forward in line of battle, and a staff officer directed me to bring the rest of the regiment forward under fire, which I did, fortunately getting them into their proper position. The line was lying prone upon the ground in that open field and trying to maintain a fire against the rebel infantry not more than one hundred and fifty yards in our front behind that stone wall. We were now exposed to the fire of their three lines of infantry, having no shelter whatever. It was like standing upon a raised platform to be shot down by those sheltered behind it. Had we been ordered to fix bayonets and charge those heights we could have understood the movement, though that would have been an impossible undertaking, defended as they were. But to be sent close up to those lines to maintain a firing-line without any intrenchments or other shelter, if that

Maj. Gen. Ambrose E. Burnside outside his headquarters tent.

A typical street in Fredericksburg after the battle.

was the purpose, was simply to invite wholesale slaughter without the least compensation. It was to attempt the impossible, and invite certain destruction in the effort....[W]e were evidently in a fearful slaughter-pen. Our men were being swept away as by a terrific whirlwind. The ground was soft and spongy from recent rains, and our faces and clothes were bespattered with mud from bullets and fragments of shells striking the ground about us, whilst men were every moment being hit by the storm of projectiles that filled the air. In the midst of that frightful carnage a man rushing by grasped my hand and spoke. I turned and looked into the face of a friend from a distant city. There was a glance of recognition and he was swept away. What his fate was I do not know.

Confederate Brig. Gen. Joseph B. Kershaw was on the other side of the infamous stone wall at Marye's Heights. In his official report, he described the inviolable position of Lee's troops.

THE POSITION WAS EXCELLENT. Marye's Hill, covered with our batteries,...falls off abruptly toward Fredericksburg to a stone wall, which forms a terrace on the side of the hill and the outer margin of the Telegraph Road, which winds along the foot of the hill. The road is about some 25 feet wide, and is faced by a stone wall about 4 feet high on the city side. The road having been cut out of the side of the hill, in many places this last is not visible above the surface of the ground.

In his memoirs, Pvt. William Fletcher of the Fifth Texas Infantry (which was not engaged in the fighting) recalled walking the battlefield afterward and surveying the carnage on Marye's Heights.

WE WERE NOT KEPT IN THIS position long, and while moving around I saw some parts of the battle line other than our own front had been busy, for in front and near the city I saw more dead bodies of the right kind, covering broad acres, than it was ever my pleasure to see before or since. Those who have never battled often think such expressions as this are brutal. If they are correct, all courageous soldiers are brutes; for they enlist to battle, if so ordered, and as fighting is a dangerous thing, the more dead the less risk; and if one shudders at a dead enemy, he has but little place in the ranks, for it is a sure sign it is the other fellow's work.

TUE 16 DEC. *Nurses often provided information about the war to people back home—and at the same time appealed to them for aid. In another letter to her sister in Maine, nurse Rebecca Usher offered a window on the needs of her "boys" at the Pennsylvania hospital where she was stationed.*

OUR PEOPLE IN MAINE KNOW nothing about this war. We consider ourselves very comfortable here, & feel modest about asking for anything; because we feel there must be so much greater need elsewhere, but our men frequently are obliged to wear their flannel shirts a month without washing because they have none to change. Now we are bending all our efforts towards giving them a change of stockings once a fortnight. We do not like to have our men wear their shirts a month, & their stockings three weeks without washing, but we know that in other places there are many that have neither stockings nor shirts to wear, & so we make the best of it....There are eight in our mess & we have a very

good table [and] plenty to eat & drink....I am very much interested in my ward. I have several Irishmen in it. Pretty rough looking men some of them, but they are gentle as lambs to me.

WED 17 DEC. # THE JEW ORDER

The most ignominious order of Maj. Gen. Ulysses S. Grant's career was never issued on a battlefield. Rather, his remarkable General Order No. 11, reprinted below, decreed that all Jews be expelled from the Department of the Tennessee, an administrative district that included Kentucky, Tennessee, and Mississippi. Defenders of Grant have tried to explain the order, rescinded January 7 at President Lincoln's insistence, by referencing the general's testy relationship with his father. Jesse Grant was in camp at the time, importuning his son for assistance with a business deal that called for the elder Grant and his partners—who happened to be Jewish—to buy cotton cheaply in the ravaged South and sell it for a large profit in the cotton-starved North. Grant found this war profiteering repellent, and some have interpreted his order as a denunciation of Jesse Grant and his partners. Yet this theory hardly accounts for the streak of anti-Semitism found in Grant's correspondence.

GENERAL ORDERS, NO. 11.

The Jews, as a class violating every regulation of trade established by the Treasury Department and also department orders,

This Union volunteer, like Sarah Wakeman, came from rural upstate New York.

are hereby expelled from the department within twenty-four hours from the receipt of this order.

Post commanders will see to it that all of this class of people be furnished passes and required to leave, and any one returning after such notification will be arrested and held in confinement until an opportunity occurs of sending them out as prisoners, unless furnished with permit from headquarters. No passes will be given these people to visit headquarters for the purpose of making personal application of trade permits.

By order of Maj. Gen. U. S. Grant

TUE 23 DEC. *Like the majority of their male counterparts, the hundreds of women who enlisted (as men) in the armies of the Union and the Confederacy typically came from poor, rural*

areas and were not particularly well educated. Most chose to enlist, at least in part, because military service represented a rare paying job. In this excerpt from a letter to her father—written from Alexandria, Virginia—Sarah Rosetta Wakeman (alias Pvt. Lyons Wakeman, 153rd New York Volunteers) discussed money and soldiering.

I CAN TELL YOU WHAT I DONE with my money if you want to know. I got when I enlisted 100 and 52$ in money. I was agoing to send it home but finally lent it to the first lieutenant and sergeant. They promised to pay me when we get [a] month's pay. We have not got it yet. They gave me their note on interest. When I get it I will send it home to you and the family. If you are [of] a mind to send me a Box of apples and a Bottle of cider, you may. The rest of the Boys are getting Boxes of stuff from home....Mother, don't mourn for me, for if I never return I hope I shall meet you all in Heaven....The weather is cold and the ground is froze hard, but I sleep as warm in the tents as I would in a good bed. I don't know the difference when I get asleep. We have boards laid down for a floor and our dishes is tin. We all have a tin plate and a tin cup, and a knife and Fork, one spoon. We have to use the floor for a table. I like to be a soldier very well.

FRI 26 DEC. # HANGINGS END SIOUX UPRISING

The Santee Sioux uprising in Minnesota, begun in August, escalated into a brief but fierce war against Federal troops led by former Minnesota governor Henry Hastings Sibley. By October, the fighting was over, and more than a thousand Sioux had been taken into custody, charged with "murder and other outrages." Sibley himself presided over the military trials, which became infamous for their summary judgments. More than three hundred Sioux were sentenced to death. White Minnesotans overwhelmingly approved of the verdicts, but President Lincoln did not: On November 10, he asked for the trial records, and on December 6, he reduced the number of capital sentences from 303 to 39. Shortly thereafter, another man's sentence was commuted. Therefore, on the day after Christmas and amid enormous controversy—whites believing Lincoln far too lenient, the Sioux feeling exploited and persecuted— thirty-eight men were hanged in one of the largest mass executions in U.S. history. One of the condemned men, Hdainyanka, wrote this letter from prison to his father-in-law, the Santee Sioux chief Wabasha. Following the letter is an account of the executions that appeared in the St. Paul Pioneer Press.

YOU HAVE DECEIVED ME. YOU told me that if we followed the advice of General Sibley, and gave ourselves up to the whites, all would be well; no innocent man would be injured. I have not killed, wounded or injured a white man, or any white persons. I have not participated in the plunder of their property; and yet today I am set apart for execution, and must die in a few days, while men who are guilty will remain in prison. My wife is your daughter, my children are your grandchildren. I leave them all in your care and under your protection. Do not let them suffer; and when my children are grown up, let them know that their father died because he followed the advice of his chief, and without having the blood of a white man to answer for to the Great Spirit.

AT PRECISELY TEN O'CLOCK the condemned were marshaled in a procession and, headed by Captain Redfield, marched out into the street, and directly across through files of soldiers to the scaffold, which had been erected in front, and were delivered to the officer of the day, Captain Burt. They went eagerly and cheerfully, even crowding and jostling each other to be ahead, just like a lot of hungry boarders rushing to dinner in a hotel. The soldiers who were on guard in their quarters stacked arms and followed them, and they in turn, were followed by the clergy, reporters, etc.

As they commenced the ascent of the scaffold the death song was again started, and when they had all got up, the noise they made was truly hideous. It seemed as if Pandemonium had broken loose. It had a wonderful effect in keeping up their courage....

The scene at this juncture was one of awful interest. A painful and breathless suspense held the vast crowd, which had assembled from all quarters to witness the execution.

Three slow, measured, and distinct beats on the drum by Major Brown, who had been announced as signal officer, and the rope was cut by Mr. Duly (the same who killed Lean Bear, and whose family were attacked)—the scaffold fell, and thirty-seven lifeless bodies were left dangling between heaven and earth. One of the ropes was broken, and the body of Rattling Runner fell to the ground. The neck had probably been broken, as but little signs of life were observed; but he was immediately hung up again. While the signal-beat was being given, numbers were seen to clasp the hands of their neighbors, which in several instances continued to be clasped till the bodies were cut down.

As the platform fell, there was one, not loud, but prolonged cheer from the soldiery and citizens who were spectators, and then all were quiet and earnest witnesses of the scene.

Jefferson and Varina Davis

JEFFERSON DAVIS'S "TOUR OF OBSERVATION"

In the fall of 1862, Jefferson Davis began what his wife, Varina, called a "tour of observation" through the war's Western Theater. In the wake of devastating Confederate defeats at Fort Donelson in February and Shiloh in April, Davis wanted to review the troops stationed there and shore up their morale. He delivered this speech before the legislature in his home state of Mississippi on the day after Christmas.

AFTER AN ABSENCE OF NEARLY two years I again find myself among those who, from the days of my childhood, have ever been the trusted objects of my affections, those for whose good I have ever striven, and whose interest I have sometimes hoped I may have contributed to subserve....

The issue before us is one of no ordinary character. We are not engaged in a conflict for conquest, or for aggrandizement, or for the settlement of a point of international law. The question for you to decide is, "Will you be slaves or will you be independent?" Will you transmit to your children the freedom and equality which your fathers transmitted to you or will you bow down in adoration before an idol baser than ever was worshipped by Eastern idolators? Nothing more is necessary than the mere statements of this issue....

The great end and aim of the government is to make our struggle successful. The men who stand highest in this contest would fall the first sacrifice to the vengeance of the enemy in case we should be unsuccessful. You may rest assured then for that reason if for no other that whatever capacity they possess will be devoted to securing the independence of the country. Our government is not like the monarchies of the Old World, resting for support upon armies and navies. It sprang from the people, and the confidence of the people is necessary for its success....

The issue then being: Will you be slaves; will you consent to be robbed of your property; to be reduced to provincial dependence; will you renounce the exercise of those rights with which you were born and which were transmitted to you by your fathers? I feel that in addressing Mississippians the answer will be that their interests, even life itself, should be willingly laid down on the altar of their country.

SUN 28 DEC. FREDERICK DOUGLASS ON EMANCIPATION

According to President Lincoln's preliminary Emancipation Proclamation, issued three months earlier, slaves held in states that remained in rebellion as of January 1, 1863, would be freed. As 1862 drew to a close and New Year's Day approached, abolitionists began preparing to celebrate what they called "The Day of Jubilee." In this address delivered at Rochester, New York, Frederick Douglass reflected on the demise of slavery.

 THIS IS SCARCELY A DAY FOR prose. It is a day for poetry and song, a new song. These cloudless skies, this balmy air, this brilliant sunshine, (making December as pleasant as May), are in harmony with the glorious morning of liberty about to dawn upon us. Out of a full heart and with sacred emotion, I congratulate you my friends, and fellow citizens, on the high and hopeful condition, of the cause of human freedom and the cause of our common country, for these two causes are now one and inseparable and must stand or fall together. We stand today in the presence of a glorious prospect. This sacred Sunday in all the likelihoods of the case, is the last which will witness the existence of legal slavery in all the Rebel slaveholding States of America. Henceforth and forever, slavery in those States is to be recognized, by all the departments [of] the American Government, under its appropriate character, as an unmitigated robber and pirate, branded as the sum of all villainy, an outlaw having no rights which any man white or colored is bound to respect. It is difficult for us who have toiled so long and hard to believe that this event, so stupendous, so far reaching and glorious is even at the door. It surpasses our most enthusiastic hopes that we live at such a time and are likely to witness the downfall, at least the legal downfall of slavery in America. It is a moment for joy, thanksgiving and Praise.

MON 29 DEC. CHICKASAW BAYOU

On December 21, Jefferson Davis, visiting Vicksburg, wrote a letter in which he stated that "the enemy has two principal objects in view, one to get control of the Missi. River, and the other to capture the capi.·¹ of the Confederate States." The recent Union loss at Fredericksburg, Davis correctly concluded, had made another Federal offensive against Richmond highly unlikely, at least until the following spring, but the Mississippi River was another matter. As Davis knew, Ulysses S. Grant was already marching on Vicksburg, the heavily fortified linchpin of the Rebels' river defenses. If Vicksburg fell to Grant, the Union would then control all of the Mississippi and thus be able to split the Confederacy in half. With this in mind, Grant had ordered Maj. Gen. William T. Sherman to lead a corps of thirty-two thousand men by riverboat from Memphis to a landing site north of Vicksburg, where Sherman's corps would rendezvous with Grant's army moving overland. However, raids by Rebel cavalry under Nathan Bedford Forrest blocked Grant's advance, leading him to withdraw back into Tennessee. Sherman struck anyway, assaulting the Confederates entrenched at the foot of some bluffs near Chickasaw Bayou. But the combination of dense swampland, effective obstacles (such as abatis, or felled trees that blocked strategic approaches), and a strong force of well-supplied Confederates foiled the attack. The difference in casualties—1,776 for the Union, compared to only 204 for the Rebels—suggests this battle's close resemblance to the futile assault on Marye's Heights made at Fredericksburg two weeks earlier. Unlike the Federal commanders at Fredericksburg, however, Sherman knew when to disengage from a hopeless fight, and he made this plain in the following description of the battle, taken from his memoirs.

THE SIXTH MISSOURI INFANTRY, at heavy loss, had also crossed by bayou at the narrow passage lower down, but could not ascend the steep bank; right over their heads was a rebel battery, whose fire was in a measure kept down by our sharp-shooters posted behind logs, stumps, and trees, on our side of the bayou.

The men of the Sixth Missouri actually scooped out with their hands caves in the bank, which sheltered them against the fire of the enemy, who, right over their heads, held their muskets outside the parapet vertically, and fired down. So critical was the position, that we could not recall the men till after dark, and then one at a time. Our loss had been pretty heavy, and we had accomplished nothing, and had inflicted little loss on our enemy. At first I intended to renew the assault, but soon became satisfied that…it would prove too costly, and accordingly resolved to look elsewhere for a point below Haines's Bluff or Blake's plantation. That night I conferred with Admiral Porter, who undertook the landing; and the next day the boats were all selected, but so alarmed were the captains and pilots, that we had to place sentinels with loaded muskets to insure their remaining at their posts. Under cover of night, Steele's division, and one brigade of Stuart's, were drawn out of line, and quietly embarked on steamboats in the Yazoo River. The night of December 30th was appointed for this force, under the com-

This 1863 lithograph depicts the action along Stones River on January 2.

mand of General Fred Steele, to proceed up the Yazoo just below Haines's Bluff, there to disembark about daylight, and make a dash for the hills.

WED 31 DEC. MURFREESBORO (STONES RIVER)

The final battle of 1862, like many of the previous year, was a bloody, vicious fight that had little clear impact on the war. Maj. Gen. William S. Rosecrans, advancing from Nashville with nearly forty-seven thousand men, desired to capture Murfreesboro, Tennessee, for use as a supply base. Disputing the advance of Rosecrans was Braxton Bragg's thirty-eight-thousand-man Army of Tennessee. Bragg attacked first, at dawn, forcing a Federal retreat to the Nashville Turnpike. Here, they formed their lines into a V and held off repeated Confederate assaults. Two days later, Bragg, still hoping for a victory,

decided on one last assault, but Union cannon chased the Rebel army. Exhausted, the Federals did not pursue. Rosecrans declared the battle a victory, but the casualties—about twelve thousand killed or wounded on each side— proved a heavy price for the capture of thirty miles of railroad. This account of the battle is taken from the diary of John Beatty, a Union colonel who had two horses shot out from underneath him at Murfreesboro and was later promoted to brigadier general for his performance there. After the war, he became, as did many Union war heroes, a U.S. congressman (from Ohio).

AT SIX O'CLOCK IN THE MORN-ing my brigade marches to the front and forms in line of battle. The roar of musketry and artillery is incessant. At nine o'clock we move into the cedar woods on the right to support McCook, who is reported to be giving way. General Rosseau points me to the place he desires me to defend, and enjoins me to "hold it until hell freezes over," at the same time telling me that he may be found immediately on the left of my brigade with Loomis' battery. I take position. An open wood is in my front; but where the line is formed, and to the right and left, the cedar thicket is so dense as to render it impossible to see the length of a regiment. The enemy comes up directly, and the fight begins. The roar of the guns to the right, left, and front of my brigade sounds like the continuous pounding on a thousand anvils. My men are favorably situated, being concealed by the cedars, while the enemy, advancing through the open woods, is fully exposed....I find a Michigan regiment and attach it to my command, and send a staff officer to General Rosseau to report progress; but before he has time to return, the enemy makes another and more furious assault upon my line. After a fierce struggle, lasting forty to sixty minutes, we succeed in repelling this also. I send again to General Rosseau, and am soon informed that neither he nor Loomis' battery can be found. Troops are reported to be falling back hastily, and in disorder, on my left. I send a staff officer to the right and ascertain that Scribner's and Shepperd's brigades are gone. I conclude that the contingency has arisen to which General Rosseau referred—that is to say, that hell has frozen over—and about-face my brigade and march to the rear, where the guns appear to be hammering away with redoubled fury. In the edge of the woods, and not far from the Murfreesboro pike, I find the new line of battle, and take position. Five minutes after, the enemy strike us. For a time—I can not even guess how long—the line stands bravely to the work; but the regiments on our left get into disorder, and finally become panic-stricken. The fright spreads, and my brigade sweeps by me to the open field in our rear. I hasten to the colors, stop them, and endeavor to rally the men. The field by this time is covered with flying troops, and the enemy's fire is most deadly. My brigade, however, begins to steady itself on the colors, when my horse is shot out from under me, and I fall heavily to the ground. Before I have time to recover my feet, my troops, with thousands of others, sweep in disorder to the rear and I am left standing alone. Going back to the railroad, I find my men, General Rosseau, Loomis, and, in fact, the larger part of the army. The artillery has been concentrated at this point, and now opens upon the advancing columns of the enemy with fearful effect, and continues its thunder until nightfall. The artillery saved the army. The battle during the whole day was terrific.

The retreat of the Confederate army after the battle badly depressed Rebel morale. Kate Cumming, who had become a Confederate nurse after Shiloh and was now stationed at a hospital in Chattanooga, first heard that the battle had been a terrific victory. But her joy, as expressed in these journal entries, turned to sorrow when she learned of the renewed fighting on January 2 and saw the resulting casualties.

A BATTLE WAS FOUGHT AT Murfreesboro on the 31st ultimo. We have come out of it victorious. Thousands of the enemy have been slain and wounded. We have taken upward of four thousand prisoners, and spoils of all kinds; but I can scarcely rejoice, for our wounded are coming in by the hundreds, and we have to witness the same sad spectacle as ever on such occasions. The weather is very cold, and I shudder to think what our men have had to suffer on the battlefield....Our hospital is filled with wounded.

Kate Cumming

...The wounded kept coming in last night, till 12 o'clock. Every corner of the hospital is filled with patients, and the attendants had to give up their beds for them. None but the slightly wounded are brought here, but they are bad enough. Many have had to be carried from the ambulances, as they are unable to walk. We have sent off a great many today, to make room for others who will be in tonight....

...We have had another battle—fought on Friday, the 2d. I believe we made the attack, and were repulsed with heavy loss. It is reported that our army is falling back. I hope this is not true, although we can scarcely expect to cope successfully with the enemy, as, comparatively speaking, our army is small, and we have the very flower of the northern army and one of their best generals to contend with. From what I have heard judges say, we ought to be satisfied if we can only hold our own.

STATEHOOD FOR WEST VIRGINIA

Populated largely by yeoman farmers (who owned small farms with few or no slaves), western Virginia felt little common cause with the state's Tidewater region and the wealthy, cotton-minded landowners who had led Virgina out of the Union. When delegates met in convention at Wheeling to establish a rival pro-Union government for the purpose of seceding from Virginia, their action touched off a furious political and constitutional debate. Although the North very much wanted western Virginia back in the Union, the Constitution stipulated clearly that no new state could be created within the territory of an existing state without the approval of that state's legislature. This was, of course, impossible as long as Virginia remained within the Confederacy. Confederate Virginians predictably denounced the pro-Union government, but Lincoln and others nevertheless found a way to grant the body just enough legitimacy to pass the constitutional test. On this day, the president signed the act of Congress approving statehood for West Virginia and issued the following rationale. On June 20, 1863, West Virginia formally became the nation's thirty-fifth state.

THE CONSENT OF THE LEGISLAture of Virginia is constitutionally necessary to the bill for the admission of West-Virginia becoming a law. A body claiming to be such Legislature has given its consent. We can not well deny that it is such, unless we do so upon the outside knowledge that the body was chosen at elections, in which a majority of the qualified voters of Virginia did not participate....It is not the qualified voters, but the qualified voters, *who choose to vote,* that constitute the political power of the state. Much less than to non-voters, should any consideration be given to those who did not vote, *in this case:* because it is also a matter of outside knowledge, that they were not merely neglectful of their rights under, and duty to, this government, but were also engaged in open rebellion against it. Doubtless among these non-voters were some Union men whose voices were smothered by the more numerous secessionists; but we know too little of their number to assign them any appreciable value. Can this government stand, if it indulges constitutional constructions by which men in open rebellion against it, are to be accounted, man for man, the equals of those who maintain their loyalty to it? Are they to be accounted even better citizens, and more worthy of consideration, than those who merely neglect to vote? If so, their treason against the constitution, enhances their constitutional value!...

But is the admission into the Union, of West-Virginia, expedient? This, in my general view, is more a question for Congress than for the Executive. Still I do not evade it. More than on anything else, it depends on whether the admission or rejection of the new state would under all the circumstances tend the more strongly to the restoration of the national authority throughout the Union. That which helps most in this direction is the most expedient at this time. Doutless those in

remaining Virginia would return to the Union, so to speak, less reluctantly without the division of the old state than with it; but I think we could not save as much in this quarter by rejecting the new state, as we should lose by it in West-Virginia. We can scarcely dispense with the aid of West-Virginia in this struggle; much less can we afford to have her against us, in congress and in the field. Her brave and good men regard her admission into the Union as a matter of life and death. They have been true to the Union under very severe trials. We have so acted as to justify their hopes; and we can not fully retain their confidence, and co-operation, if we seem to break faith with them. In fact, they could not do so much for us, if they would.

Again, the admission of the new state, turns that much slave soil to free; and thus, is a certain, and irrevocable encroachment upon the cause of the rebellion.

★ ★ ★ ★

A Union soldier poses with the tattered remains of his regimental colors.

JANUARY 1863

THU 1 JAN. THE EMANCIPATION PROCLAMATION

At first glance, this momentous document seems unimpressively dry and business-like. One is struck, for example, by the amount of text devoted to the people whom it does not *affect. Lincoln took obvious pains to make it clear that he was granting freedom only to slaves living in areas of the Confederacy not controlled by his armies (and therefore, ironically, beyond the reach of his proclamation). By carefully listing every county in every state where slavery would remain unaffected, Lincoln hoped to mollify the opposition of loyal slaveholders in the border states. He also pointed out that he was granting emancipation not in his political role as president but in his military role as commander-in-chief, thereby assuring the proclamation's legality on the relatively narrow grounds of war powers. He left it to Congress to make emancipation permanent and universal (which it did with the Thirteenth Amendment). Always an astute politician, Lincoln knew that emancipation was still an explosive issue in the North, where racism was no stranger. He therefore avoided the rhetorical flourishes for which he was justly famous and purposefully made the Emancipation Proclamation as bureaucratic and even boring as possible.*

A PROCLAMATION.
Whereas, on the twenty-second day of September, in the year of our Lord one thousand eight hundred and sixty-two, a proclamation was issued by

Mathew Brady took this view of Washington, D.C., sometime during 1863.

the President of the United States, containing among other things, the following, to wit:

"That on the first day of January, in the year of our Lord one thousand eight hundred and sixty-three, all persons held as slaves within any State or designated part of a State, the people whereof shall then be in rebellion against the United States, shall be then, thenceforward, and forever free; and the Executive Government of the United States, including the military and naval authorities thereof, will recognize and maintain the freedom of such persons, and will do no act or acts to repress such persons, or any of them,

in any efforts they may make for their actual freedom.

"That the Executive will, on the first day of January aforesaid, by proclamation, designate the States and parts of States, if any, in which the people thereof, respectively, shall then be in rebellion against the United States; and the fact that any State, or the people thereof, shall on that day be, in good faith, represented in the Congress of the United States by members chosen thereto at elections wherein a majority of the qualified voters of such State shall have participated, shall, in the absence of strong countervailing testimony, be deemed conclusive evidence that such States and the people thereof, are not then in rebellion against the United States."

Now, therefore I, Abraham Lincoln, President of the United States, by virtue of the power in me vested as Commander-in-Chief, of the Army and Navy of the United States in time of actual armed rebellion against authority and government of the United States, and as a fit and necessary war measure for suppressing said rebellion, do, on this first day of January, in the year of our Lord one thousand eight hundred and sixty-three, and in accordance with my purpose so to do publicly proclaimed for the full period of one hundred days, from the day first above mentioned, order and designate as the States and parts of States wherein the people thereof respectively, are this day in rebellion against the United States, the following, to wit:

Arkansas, Texas, Louisiana (except the Parishes of St. Bernard, Plaquemines, Jefferson, St. Johns, St. Charles, St. James, Ascension, Assumption, Terrebonne, Lafourche, St. Mary, St. Martin, and Orleans, including the City of New-Orleans), Mississippi, Alabama, Florida, Georgia, South-Carolina, North-Carolina, and Virginia (except the forty-eight counties designated as West Virginia, and also the counties of Berkley, Accomac, Northampton, Elizabeth-City, York, Princess Ann, and Norfolk, including the cities of Norfolk & Portsmouth); and which excepted parts are, for the present, left precisely as if this proclamation were not issued.

And by virtue of the power, and for the purpose aforesaid, I do order and declare that all persons held as slaves within said designated States, and parts of States, are, and henceforward shall be free, and that the Executive Government of the United States, including the military and naval authorities thereof, will recognize and maintain the freedom of said persons.

And I hereby enjoin upon the people so declared to be free to abstain from all violence, unless in necessary self-defence, and I recommend to them that, in all cases when allowed, they labor faithfully for reasonable wages.

And I further declare and make known, that such persons of suitable condition, will be received into the armed service of the United States to garrison forts, positions, stations, and other places and to man vessels of all sorts in said service.

And upon this act, sincerely believed to be an act of justice, warranted by the Constitution, upon military necessity, I invoke the considerate judgment of mankind, and the gracious favor of Almighty God.

In witness whereof, I have hereunto set my hand and caused the seal of the United States to be affixed.

Done at the City of Washington, this first day of January, in the year of our Lord one thousand eight hundred and sixty-three, and of the Independence of the United States of America the eighty-seventh.

By the President: Abraham Lincoln

One of the many performances celebrating this Day of Jubilee was a poetry reading staged at the Boston Music Hall. The event's featured work, entitled

"Boston Hymn," was written for the occasion by Ralph Waldo Emerson. It is excerpted here.

TODAY UNBIND THE CAPTIVE
So only are ye unbound;
Lift up a people from the dust,
Trump of their rescue, sound!

Pay ransom to the owner,
And fill the bag to the brim.
Who is the owner? The slave is owner,
And ever was. Pay him.

Oh North! give him beauty for rags,
And honor, O South! for his shame;
Nevada! coin thy golden crags
With Freedom's image and name.

Up! And the dusky race
That sat in darkness long—
Be swift their feet as antelopes,
And as behemoth strong.

Come, East and West and North,
By races, as snowflakes,
And carry my purpose forth,
Which neither halts nor shakes.

My will fulfilled shall be,
For, in daylight or in dark,
My thunderbolt has eyes to see
His way home to the mark.

Meanwhile, on the Union-occupied Sea Islands off South Carolina, Thomas Wentworth Higginson, a white officer commanding the black troops stationed there, took part in another kind of celebration. He recorded the experience in his journal.

THE SERVICES BEGAN AT HALF-past eleven o'clock, with prayer by our chaplain, Mr. Fowler, who is always, on such occasions, simple, reverential, and impressive. Then the President's Proclamation was read by Dr. W. H. Brisbane, a thing infinitely appropriate, a South-Carolinian addressing South-Carolinians; for he was reared among these very islands, and here long since emancipated his own slaves. Then the colors were presented to us by the Rev. Mr. French, a chaplain who brought them from the donors in New York. All this was according to the programme. Then followed an incident so simple, so touching, so utterly unexpected and startling, that I can scarcely believe it on recalling, though it gave the keynote to the whole day. The very moment the speaker had ceased, and just as I took and waved the flag, which now for the first time meant anything to these poor people, there suddenly arose, close beside the platform, a strong male voice (but rather cracked and elderly), into which two women's voices instantly blended, singing, as if by an impulse that could no more be repressed than the morning note of the song-sparrow—

My Country 'tis of thee,
Sweet land of liberty,
Of thee I sing!

People looked at each other, and then at us on the platform, to see whence came this interruption, not set down in the bills. Firmly and irrepressibly the quavering voices sang on, verse after verse; others of the colored people joined in; some whites on the platform began, but I motioned them to silence. I never saw anything so electric; it made all other words cheap; it seemed the choked voice of a race at last unloosed. Nothing could be more wonderfully unconscious; art could not have dreamed of a tribute to the day of jubilee that should be so affecting; history will not believe it; and when I came to speak of it, after it was ended, tears were everywhere. If you could have heard how quaint and inno-cent it was!

Elsewhere in South Carolina—and throughout the Confederacy—the Emancipation Proclamation went largely unmentioned. In her journal entry this day, for example, Meta Morris Grimball ignored Lincoln's decree and instead focused on events in her own household.

THIS IS NEW YEAR'S DAY. I FEEL most thankful for all the unmer-ited mercies, we have had troubles, & losses, but how much worse they might have been. Through all this dreadful war we have as yet been spared, how long that may be, O! Lord thou knowest.

We have had a most plentiful day, for breakfast, buttered eggs, hot rolls, butter, & sausages, tea, white sugar. For dinner a Turkey, ham, soup, stewed Beef, rice, a Batter pudding, and sauce, for Tea short cake.

We visited the Wilkinses, found them as usual, I sent her a present of some Beef, & 4 quarts of Peas this morning, & Mrs Irwin a cup of sugar Loaf, some tea, a quarter of a lb, & some spices. She sent me a piece of butter.

Southerners had long maintained that, for Abraham Lincoln and the Republi-can party, emancipation was the secret goal of the war. The Emancipation Proclamation, therefore, afforded Jefferson Davis and his countrymen a certain grim satisfaction. In his January 12 message to the Confederate Congress, Davis offered this unusual interpretation of the proclamation. Two years later, of course, Davis himself sug-gested emancipation as a last-ditch measure to stave off defeat.

THE PUBLIC JOURNALS OF THE North have been received, con-taining a proclamation, dated on the 1st day of the present month, signed by the President of the United States, in which he orders and declares all slaves within ten of the States of the Confed-eracy to be free, except such as are found within certain districts now occupied in part by the armed forces of the enemy. We may well leave it to the instincts of that common humanity which a beneficent Creator has implanted in the breasts of our fellowmen of all countries to pass judgment on a measure by which several millions of human beings of an inferior race, peaceful and contented laborers in their sphere, are doomed to extermination, while at the same time they are encouraged to a general assassi-nation of their masters by the insidious recommendation "to abstain from vio-lence unless in necessary self-defence." Our own detestation of those who have attempted the most execrable measure recorded in the history of guilty man is tempered by profound contempt for the impotent rage which it discloses....

This proclamation is also an authentic statement by the Government of the United States of its inability to subjugate the South by force of arms, and as such must be accepted by neutral nations, which can no longer find any justification in withholding our just claims to formal recognition. It is also in effect an intimation to the people of the North that they must prepare to submit to a separation, now become inevitable, for that people are too acute not to understand a restoration of the Union has been rendered forever impossible by the adoption of a measure which from its very nature neither admits of retraction nor can coexist with union.

Louisa May Alcott

SUN 4 JAN. *During the Civil War, Louisa May Alcott, later the author of* Little Women *(1868), served as a nurse in a Washington, D.C., hospital. Her journal entry for this date recounted the activities of a typical day in her ward.*

I SHALL RECORD THE EVENTS of a day as a sample of the days I spend—

Up at six, dress by gas light, run through my ward & fling up the windows though the men grumble & shiver; but the air is bad enough to breed a pestilence & as no notice is taken of our frequent appeals for better ventilation I must do what I can. Poke up the fire, add blankets, joke, coax, & command, but continue to open doors & windows as if life depended on it; mine does, & doubtless many another, for a more perfect pestilence-box than this house I never saw—cold, damp, dirty, full of vile odors from wounds, kitchens, wash rooms, & stables. No competent head, male or female, to right matters, & a jumble of good, bad, & indifferent nurses, surgeons & attendants to complicate the Chaos still more.

After this unwelcome progress through my stifling ward I go to breakfast with what appetite I may; find the inevitable fried beef, salt butter, husky bread & washy coffee....Till noon I trot, trot, giving out rations, cutting up food for helpless "boys," washing faces, teaching my attendants how beds are made or floors swept, dressing wounds, taking Dr. FitzPatrick's orders (privately wishing all the time that he would be more gentle with my big babies), dusting tables, sewing bandages, keeping my tray tidy, rushing up & down after pillows, bed linen, sponges, book & directions, till it seems as if I would joyfully pay down all I possess for fifteen minutes rest.

At twelve the big bell rings & up comes dinner for the boys who are always

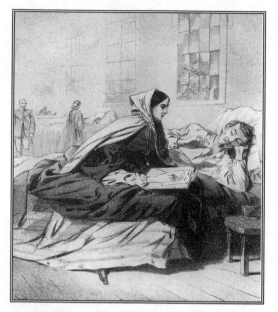

Winslow Homer's 1863 lithograph
The Letter for Home.

them the final doses for the night. At nine the bell rings, gas is turned down & day nurses go to bed.

Night nurses go on duty & sleep & death have the house to themselves.

THU 8 JAN. *With New Orleans already in Union hands and U. S. Grant moving his army closer and closer to Vicksburg, the people of Louisiana and Mississippi were becoming ever more fearful of a complete Federal takeover. In this letter, fifteen women of St. Helena's Parish, located not far north of New Orleans, implored Confederate generals John C. Pemberton (commanding Vicksburg) and Joseph E. Johnston (Pemberton's superior) to send soldiers to protect their families and lands. The "glorious national anniversary" to which the letter refers is presumably the forty-eighth anniversary of the battle of New Orleans, in which Andrew Jackson defeated the British.*

ready for it & never entirely satisfied. Soup, meat, potatoes, & bread is the bill of fare. Charley Thayer the attendant travels up & down the room serving out the rations, saving little for himself yet always thoughtful of his mates & patient as a woman with their helplessness. When dinner is over some sleep, many read, & others want letters written. This I like to do for they put in such odd things & express their ideas so comically I have great fun interiorly while as grave as possible exteriorly. A few of the men word their paragraphs well & make excellent letters....The answering of letters from friends after some one has died is the saddest & hardest duty a nurse has to do.

Supper at five sets every one to running that can run & when that flurry is over all settle down for the evening amusements which consist of newspapers, gossip, Drs. last round, & for such as need

HONORED SIRS: WE COME TO you—a band of helpless women— we, the mothers, daughters, and sisters of your soldiers...to appeal to you for aid, comfort, salvation upon this our glorious national anniversary....Our hearts are disquieted within us. Anxiety and apprehension crowd out every other emotion. Yesterday we sat beside our hearthstones in full security. The military force at Camp Moore, that had so long guaranteed protection and defense to this whole region, was our bulwark of strength; a gallant band that defied the foe and pledged safety to the friend. Today scarcely a soldier remains to shoulder a musket in our behalf. All gone—transported, 'tis true, to scenes of more active and stirring interest, but leaving us to the somber realities of our perilous position. What position? Generals, we beg for a brief moment to dwell upon it; we crave your ear—your eye for the picture.…[The Yankees'] fiendish designs upon the helpless and innocent are too fearfully revealed in the long, dark track of woe and crime that has marked their progress throughout our own fair State and land.…We appeal to you as Louisianians. Have we not a right to claim your sympathy and protection?…It has been our pride in the past, as it is our hope in the future, to escape the thral-

dom of our savage foe. We cannot afford to swell their list of conquered Louisianians and bow our souls to that hated oath which they have extorted from our crushed countrymen.

WED
14
JAN.

In the North, amid continuing public protestations of patriotism, there flowed nevertheless a steady undercurrent of antiwar politics. Its most notorious adherents were the Copperheads, Northern Democrats so named because they wore in their lapels Indian heads cut from copper pennies (and also because they were perceived

Clement L. Vallandigham (center), seated among fellow Copperheads.

by the Republican press as venomous). Their leader, Clement L. Vallandigham, was a U.S. representative from Ohio. His many tirades against the Lincoln administration, usually for gross usurpation of power, included the one delivered this day and excerpted here.

CONSTITUTIONAL LIMITATION was broken down; *habeas corpus* fell; liberty of the press, of speech, of the person, of the mails, of travel, of one's own house, and of religion; the right to bear arms, due process of law, judicial trial, trial by jury, trial at all; every badge and muniment of freedom in republican government or kingly government—all went down at a blow; and the chief law officer of the crown—I beg pardon, sir, but it is easy now to fall into this courtly language—the Attorney-General, first of all men, proclaimed in the United States the maxim of Roman servility: *Whatever pleases the President, that is law!* Prisoners of State were then first heard of here. Midnight and arbitrary arrests commenced; travel was interdicted; trade embargoed, passports demanded; bastiles were introduced; strange oaths invented; a secret police organized; "piping" began; informers multiplied; spies now first appeared in America. The right to declare war, to raise and support armies, and to provide and maintain a navy, was usurped by the Executive; and in a little more than two months a land and naval force of over three hundred thousand men was in the field or upon the sea. An army of public plunderers followed, and corruption struggled with power in friendly strife for the mastery at home.

FRI
16
JAN.

In early 1863, the U.S. and Confederate governments conducted an unusual prisoner exchange. In return for its captured soldiers, the Union sent to Richmond approximately six hundred women and children who had been detained in the North for a variety of reasons. In her journal entry for this day, Judith McGuire—now taking refuge in Ashland, Virginia, just north of Richmond—described the "most humiliating" treatment these Southerners endured at the hands of Northern officials. Evidently, given the contraband they were able to smuggle, the searches weren't thorough enough.

SEVERAL FRIENDS HAVE JUST arrived from Yankeedom in a vessel fitted out by the Northern Government to receive the exchanged prisoners. About six hundred women and children were allowed to come in it from Washington. They submitted to the most humiliating search, before they left the wharf, from men and women. The former searched their trunks, the latter their persons. Mrs. Hale, of California, and the wife of Senator Harlan, of Iowa, *presided* at the search. Dignified and lady-like! One young friend of mine was bringing five pairs of shoes to her sisters; they were taken as contraband. A friend brought me one pound of tea; this she was allowed to do; but woe betide the bundle of more than one pound! Some trunks were sadly pillaged if they happened to contain more clothes than the Northern Government thought proper for a rebel to possess. No material was allowed to come which was not made into garments. My friend brought me some pocket handkerchiefs and stockings, scattered in various parts of the trunk, so as not to seem to have too many. She brought her son, who is in our service, a suit of clothes made into a cloak which she wore. Many a gray cloth travelling-dress and petticoat which was on that boat is now in camp, decking the person of a Confederate soldier; having undergone a transformation into jackets and pants. The searchers found it a troublesome business; not the least assistance did they get from the searched. The ladies would take their seats, and put out first one foot and then the other to the Yankee woman, who would pull off the shoes and stockings—not a pin would they remove, not a string untie. The fare of the boat was miserable, served in tin plates and cups; but, as it was served gratis, the *"Rebs"* had no right to complain, and they reached Dixie in safety, bringing many a contraband article, notwithstanding the search.

TUE 20 JAN. *Not all the women attached to army units were masquerading as men. The overwhelming number,*

Southern women near Cedar Mountain, Virginia, sewing for the Confederate cause.

in fact, were legitimately employed as nurses, laundresses, sutlers, and cooks, among other support positions. Some of these women, however, occasionally found themselves thrust into combat situations. So war goes. As was the case with men, some quailed, yet others performed with great valor. The most famous of this latter group was Annie Etheridge, a nurse with the Fifth Michigan Infantry. The following article from the Whig and Courier *of Bangor, Maine, provides a thumbnail sketch of this Union army heroine, awarded the Kearney Cross for bravery in May 1863.*

A sutler's shack near Petersburg, Virginia, with a sign over the door reading "Fruit and Oyster House."

WE LEARN THROUGH A Washington correspondent... of the exploits of a heroine, Miss Anna Etheridge....She was born in Detroit and was about 23 years of age....On the breaking out of the rebellion, she was visiting her friends in the city.

Colonel [Israel B.] Richardson was engaged in raising the 2nd Michigan volunteers, and she and nineteen other females volunteered to accompany the regiment as nurses....[S]he has accompanied the regiment through all its fortunes, and declares her determination to remain with it during its entire term of service. She has for her use a horse furnished with side saddle, saddle-bags, etc. At the commencement of the battle she fills her saddle-bags with lint and bandages, mounts her horse, and gallops to the front, passes under fire, and regardless of shot and shell, engages in the work of staunching and binding up the wounds of our soldiers. In this manner she has passed through every battle in which the regiment has been engaged, commencing

with the battle of Blackburn's Ford, preceding the first battle of Bull Run, including the battles of the Peninsula and terminating with the battle of Fredericksburg.

General Berry [her brigade commander] declares that she has been under as hot fire of the enemy as himself....[O]n many occasions her dress has been pierced by bullets and fragments of shell, yet she has never flinched and never been wounded....When not actively engaged on the battlefield or in the hospital, she superintends the cooking at the headquarters of the brigade. When the brigade moves, she mounts her horse and marches with the ambulances and surgeons, administering to the wants of the sick and wounded, and at the bivouac she wraps herself in her blanket and sleeps upon the ground with all the hardihood of a true soldier.

Anna is of Dutch descent, about five feet three inches in height, fair complexion (now somewhat browned by exposure), brown hair, vigorous constitution, and decidedly good looking.…[S]he is held in the highest veneration and esteem by the soldiers as an Angel of Mercy. She is indeed the idol of the brigade, every man of which would submit to almost any sacrifice on her behalf.

FRI
23
JAN.
It quickly became obvious that the Emancipation Proclamation, urged on Lincoln by abolitionists since the outset of the war, was a shrewd political move as well as a courageous moral one. Writing from London, Henry Brooks Adams gleefully reported to his brother, Charles Francis Adams Jr., the British reaction to President Lincoln's proclamation.

THE EMANCIPATION PROCLAMATION has done more for us here than all our former victories and all our diplomacy. It is creating an almost convulsive reaction in our favor all over this country. The London *Times* is furious and scolds like a drunken drab. Certain it is, however, that public opinion is very deeply stirred here and finds expression in meetings; addresses to Pres. Lincoln; deputations to us; standing committees to agitate the subject and to affect opinion; and all the other symptons of a great popular movement peculiarly unpleasant to the upper classes here because it rests altogether on the spontaneous action of the laboring classes and has a pestilent squint at sympathy with republicanism. But the *Times* is on its last legs and has lost its temper. They say it always does lose its temper when it finds such a feeling too strong for it, and its next step will be to come round and try to guide it. We are much encouraged and in high spirits. If only you at home don't have disasters, we will give such a check-mate to the foreign hopes of the rebels as they never yet have had.

★ ★ ★ ★

FEBRUARY
1863

FRI 13 FEB. *Mounting losses, particularly the carnage at Fredericksburg, depressed Union morale during the winter of 1862–63. In New York City, however, Gotham's social elite (many war profiteers among them) managed to distract themselves with grand masquerade balls, opulent weddings, and other lavish entertainments. In the following journal entry, Maria Lydig Daly, a judge's wife and Democratic sympathizer, expresses her regret over the apathetic state of affairs. She also provides an interesting account of the popular reception given former major general Fitz John Porter, who was cashiered from the army January 10 for disobedience at Second Bull Run— specifically for allegedly refusing John Pope's order to attack.*

IT IS STRANGE TO SEE HOW apathetic our people are about the war. This last fortnight has been almost like a Saturnalia, and the celebrations will finish on Tuesday with a masquerade ball at Mr. Belmont's. I do not think I shall go, not at such a time. For the Judge to appear at such an entertainment would look, I think, somewhat undignified. Last evening we went to Judge Bell's; the day before to a musical matinee at Mrs. James Brooks'; Tuesday to a grand entertainment at Mr. Francis Cutting's on the occasion of his son's marriage. The beautiful bride and her eight pretty bridesmaids were very imposing with their long white veils.

It is a sign of the popular feeling to see Fitz John Porter, although dismissed from the service, going everywhere. He seems to feel it no disgrace, and the people seem disposed to make a lion of

The busy New York City waterfront during the Civil War.

anyone reprimanded or disgraced by the Administration. I am told that several regiments in the Army of the Potomac declare that they will never fire another shot, that the government can draft men but cannot make them fight, that they will no longer be butchered for political generals, etc. Two regiments at Baton Rouge have likewise laid down their arms on account of having Negro regiments raised. I'm sure that I cannot imagine how all this is to end. It is dreadful. Yet no one seems to think or care. The women dress as extravagantly as ever, and the supper and dinner parties are far more numerous than they have been for several winters.

WED 25 FEB. THE NATIONAL CURRENCY ACT

The United States entered the Civil War with an antiquated banking system, the legacy of Andrew Jackson's famous crusade against the Second Bank of the United States. (The governing "Sub-Treasury law" to which this document refers was originally put in place by Martin Van Buren during the depression that followed the Panic of 1837.) Far from a single entity coordinated by the federal government, the U.S. banking system prior to 1861 was a complicated mass of poorly regulated state and local banks that distributed myriad unrelated local currencies. The war, of course, quickly exposed the defects of this system, prompting Congress to draft the National Currency Act, which President Lincoln signed this day. The act not only established a uniform national banking system but also created a comptroller of the currency within the Treasury Department. In this speech, delivered as part of the debate on the measure, a congressman responds to long-standing complaints that such a law would unwisely subordinate the country's financial system to its political one.

SIR, THE UNITED STATES Government has thus far established no permanent system of national currency except that of gold and silver. Ever since the adoption of the Constitution there has been a conflict of opinion among the ablest statesmen of the country upon the question of a national currency. Jefferson opposed the creation of all banks, both State and national. Alexander Hamilton proposed a national bank during the struggle for American independence in 1780, but his suggestions were not then adopted....

No settled policy has as yet been established by which the Government has assumed permanent control over the national currency. State banks still go on issuing circulating notes, selling exchange, discounting promissory notes and bills, and receiving deposits, and the Sub-Treasury law is still unrepealed. A national currency, adequate to the operations of the Government in *peace* and *war,* has yet to be established. It seems that the present is a propitious time to enact this great measure as a permanent system, and that the duty of the Government in providing a national currency shall no longer be neglected....

Debt and taxation are the inevitable necessities of war. Hence the importance of a reunion of all parties in a vigorous prosecution of the war, in order to crush the rebellion in the shortest time and with the least possible expenditure of blood and treasure. This is the only way to stop the burdens and calamities of the present war. Fight vigorously and in earnest while the war lasts. Every consideration of duty and patriotism requires all the loyal people to come at their country's call, to fight the rebels forthwith, by all the means within the range of civilized warfare, to save us from a protracted war, save the further effusion of blood, and stop the vast expenditures which must, unless speedily terminated, burden present and future generations.

We need more economy in the management of the war. It is manifest there is not that close supervision and scrutiny over the expenditures that are necessary. Every man in the service should be required to perform with fidelity the duties devolved upon him. All supernumerary officers and men should be dispensed with. All disbursing officers should be held to a rigid economy and strict accountability. As we approach the termination of this war the expenses must be greatly reduced, and preparation made for a resumption of specie payments. Our public debt will then appear in all its vast proportions, for it must all be paid ultimately in gold and silver. This makes it necessary for us to cut off all unnecessary expenses of every kind.

THU
26
FEB.
To raise sagging morale among the populace, Union cheerleaders staged grand patriotic rallies in cities throughout the North. Pamphlets such as this one, which described one of

These women organized an event in New York City that raised over one million dollars.

these rallies in Indianapolis, were then circulated among soldiers in the hope that the enthusiasm contained within would be contagious.

NEVER BEFORE IN THIS STATE, or any other, have we witnessed a demonstration of popular feeling so magnificent in its proportions, and so impressive in its enthusiasm, as the great Union meeting yesterday. Nothing in any party campaign will compare with it. There was more than party at stake, and more than party devotion responded. The country is in peril and the people came out to encourage and hold up the hands of those whose courage must save it. It was the voice of the people crying to the army, "Be of good cheer, your friends have not forsaken you." There was no element of party in it. It was a broad, bold, noble assertion of the right of the nation to save itself. The spirit that animated it was as glorious as its own strength was invincible. It looked as if…a deluge of indignant feeling had risen to sweep from the earth all treason and disaffection.

MARCH
1863

In this letter to an English friend, Nathaniel Hawthorne expressed his "infinite weariness" with the war—a feeling shared by many of his countrymen in the North and South. Hawthorne may have been particularly weary, as he himself suggests, because of his well-known association with the Democratic party. A friend of Franklin Pierce from their days together at Bowdoin, Hawthorne wrote Pierce's 1852 campaign biography, and when Pierce won, he became the well-paid U.S. consul to Liverpool.

I OUGHT TO BE HEARTILY ashamed of my long silence, but in these revolutionary times, it is impossible to be ashamed of anything. When society is about to be overturned from its foundations, the courtesies of life must needs be a little damaged in advance of the general ruin; nor is it easy to write gossiping epistles when an earthquake is shaking one's writing table. So pardon me; and I will be

Nathaniel Hawthorne

as merciful to you when England is in a similar predicament.

You must not suppose, however, that I make myself very miserable about the war. The play (be it tragedy or comedy) is too long drawn out, and my chief feeling about it now is a sense of infinite weariness. I want the end to come, and the curtain to drop, and then go to sleep. I never did really approve of the war, though you may have supposed so from the violence and animosity with which I controverted your notions about it, when I wrote last. But you are an Englishman, you know, and of course cannot have any correct ideas about our country, and even if you had, a true American is bound not to admit them. The war-party here do not look upon me as a reliably loyal man, and, in fact, I have been publicly accused of treasonable sympathies;—whereas I sympathize with nobody and approve of nothing; and if I have any wishes on the subject, it is that New England might be a nation by itself. But, so far as I can judge of the temper of the people, they mean to have a re-union; and if they really mean it, it will be accomplished. The North has never yet put out half its means, and there is a great deal of fight left in us yet.

THU 12 MAR. *During the Civil War, relations between the U.S. government and Great Britain were, to put it politely, strained. Northerners were rightly apprehensive that the British might intervene at any time on the Confederacy's behalf—in much the same way that France had aided the*

At a British shipyard, the Confederate steamship Old Dominion *is refitted for service as a blockade runner.*

American colonists during the Revolutionary War. Of course, Great Britain never did commit its might and treasure to the Confederacy, yet the British did provide significant assistance in other ways, chiefly by permitting the construction in English shipyards of Confederate warships and blockade runners. In this letter to an English acquaintance, Massachusetts senator Charles Sumner, a frequent visitor to Britain, detailed Northern anxieties on this point.

I AM ANXIOUS, VERY ANXIOUS, on account of the ships building in England to cruise against our commerce. Cannot something be done to stop them? Our people are becoming more and more excited, and there are many who insist upon war. A very important person said to me yesterday, "We are now at war with England, but the hostilities are all on her side." I know the difficulties of your laws, and how subtle and pertinacious is the temptation to money-making; but it would seem as if there should be a way to prevent the unparalleled outrage of a whole fleet built expressly to be employed against us. Of course in this statement I presume what is reported and is credited by those who ought to be well informed. A committee from New York waited on the President yesterday and undertook to enumerate ships now building in English yards professedly for the Emperor of China, but really for our rebels. The case is aggravated by the fact that their armaments are supplied also by England; and their crews also, but it is not supposed there will be a rebel sailor on board.... I have seen the President twice upon this question, which I regard as grave.

SAT 14 MAR. THE PASSAGE OF PORT HUDSON

In order to travel north from New Orleans to Vicksburg, now the main Union target on the Mississippi River, Rear Adm. David G. Farragut had to run his squadron of gunboats past the Confederate battery at Port Hudson, Louisiana, near Baton Rouge. The battery was heavily fortified, and the Confederate forces there rained a furious bombardment on the Union flotilla. Two of Farragut's ships, his own USS Hartford and the USS Albatross, made it past the battery, but others, including the USS Monongahela and the USS Richmond, were too badly damaged to proceed upriver. Here are two accounts of the fight: The first—taken from the official report of James Alden, commander of the Richmond—described for Navy Secretary Gideon Welles the damage suffered by Alden's ship. The second, from the official report of Confederate Maj. Gen. Frank Gardner, slightly exaggerated the damage done to the Union vessels.

SIR: I HAVE RESPECTFULLY TO report that our attempt to pass the batteries at Port Hudson last night, in company with the admiral and the other ships of the squadron, was frustrated by a shot striking the steam pipe in the vicinity of the safety valves, upsetting them both and letting off the steam. At the time this accident occurred we were in position, second in the line which the admiral was leading, and were well up with the flagship, and with her, engaging the last battery. The turning point was gained, but I soon found, even with the aid of the *Genesee,* which vessel was lashed alongside, that we could make no headway against the strong current of the river, and suffering much from a galling crossfire of the enemy's batteries, I was compelled, though most reluctantly, to turn back, and by the aid of the *Genesee* soon anchored out of the range of the guns. My noble and gallant friend, Lieutenant-Commander Cummings, the executive officer of the ship, was shot down at my side just before this accident occurred, his left leg being taken off below the knee by a cannon shot while he was in the bravest manner cheering the men at the guns.

Enclosed I send you a list of casualties, and also reports of injuries done to the ship by the enemy's shot. To say in the most emphatic manner that all did their duty nobly and well under the most trying circumstances that men could be placed in is but a feeble tribute to their devotion and gallantry; for more than two hours they stood to their guns and replied in the steadiest manner to the most galling fire that I have ever witnessed....

Our difficulties in this action were heightened by the abrupt turn in the river, where the strongest of the enemy's batteries were placed, by the obscurity of the night, and by the humidity of the atmosphere, this last causing the smoke to settle around us so that we were frequently compelled to cease firing to find our way. Just before the accident to our steam pipe, a torpedo was exploded close under our stern, throwing the water up 30 feet, bursting in the cabin windows and doing other unimportant injury.

THE ENEMY'S FLEET CAME UP within range at 11 o'clock on the night of the 14th, and being discovered made a terrific fight with my batteries from 11 until 2, attempting to pass seven vessels by. The result was that the *Hartford* passed with the gunboat *Monongahela* lashed on the far side. The *Hartford* was very much damaged. The frigate *Mississippi* was burned immediately opposite, and the frigate *Richmond* was badly crippled and had to fall back.

The fleet consisted of fourteen vessels, steam frigates, sloops of war, gunboats, and mortar boats, and all except the mortar boats came within range. The firing was terrific for three hours. The enemy was very much damaged in all his vessels within range, and prisoners state that the loss must have been as much as 200. Our loss was 1 killed and 8 wounded.

Rear Adm. David G. Farragut

MON 23 MAR. Although the Emancipation Proclamation inspired many African Americans to volunteer for service with the Union military, some community leaders remained wary of the treatment blacks would receive in the armed forces of the United States. In the following letter, addressed to black businessman George T. Downing, Massachusetts governor John A. Andrew addressed specific concerns voiced by Downing, a distinguished abolitionist and opinion shaper. Andrew's assurances of equal treatment notwithstanding, black soldiers indeed received decidedly unequal treatment throughout the war.

A rare daguerreotype of an African-American corporal.

Dear Sir: In reply to your inquiries made as to the position of colored men who may be enlisted and mustered into the volunteer service of the United States, I would say, that their position, in respect to pay, equipments, bounty, or aid and protection, when so mustered, will be precisely the same, in every particular, as that of any and all other volunteers.

I desire further to state to you, that when I was in Washington, on one occasion, in an interview with Mr. Stanton, the Secretary of War, he stated in the most emphatic manner, that he would never consent that free colored men should be accepted into the service to serve as soldiers in the South until he should be assured that the Government of the United States was prepared to guarantee and defend, to the last dollar and the last man, to these men, all the rights, privileges and immunities that are given, by the laws of civilized warfare, to other soldiers. Their present acceptance and muster-in, as soldiers, pledges the honor of the Nation in the same degree and to the same rights with all other troops. They will be soldiers of the Union—nothing less and nothing different. I believe they will earn for themselves an honorable fame, vindicating their race and redeeming their future from disaspersions of the past.

THU 26 MAR. THE CONFEDERATE IMPRESSMENT ACT

By the spring of 1863, Confederate quartermasters had a rather large problem:

Southerners were becoming increasingly unwilling to sell food, livestock, and other provisional necessities to the army. Instead, civilians were either hoarding supplies for their own future use or selling them on the black market for prices far higher than the rates the military paid. In an attempt to correct this imbalance, the Confederate Congress approved on this day legislation allowing the government to seize, or "impress," civilian property for military use. As one might expect, Southerners were hardly eager to comply, as this army correspondence of November 1863 indicates.

Maj. Gen. Samuel Jones, Commanding, &c:
General: A telegram from Major Galt, of the 9th instant, states that Major King, chief commissary of your command, has called on him for flour. The chief commissary of that district has been addressed on the subject.

I now write to say that it is quite impossible for purchases to be made by officers of this bureau, and that impressments by them are constantly met by declarations of having no surplus over that needed for the consumption of their families, or for companies, railroads, corporations, &c. In fact, the people are individually and collectively arrayed against the army, the former being considered by the War Department as at liberty to collect and hold a year's supply, or up to the next crop. They have no restriction in prices and are anxious to convert their money into substantials, while we are limited to schedule prices.

Yours is now precisely the case provided for, when the exigencies of troops in the field require impressments under orders of the general commanding. Against this class there are no exemptions in the law. I recommend, therefore, as you are straitened, that you direct Major King to gather subsistence under the first class of impressments, which override all other demands.

Very respectfully, your obedient servant,

L. B. Northrop

Commissary-General of Subsistence

Union soldiers prepare supper in this 1863 lithograph.

SUN 29 MAR. *Among the women who secretly served in the U.S. military, Sarah Rosetta (alias Lyons) Wakeman, who enlisted in 153rd New York Infantry in November 1862, was particularly remarkable. Her secret remained undetected throughout her nearly two years of service, and evidence indicates that when she died—of chronic diarrhea in a Union army hospital in July 1864—she went to the grave with her masquerade intact. In this letter to her father, written from Alexandria, Wakeman even referred to herself as a "fellow."*

 [Y]OU MUSTN'T TROUBLE YOU Self about me. I am contented.... I believe that God will spare my life to come home once more. Then I will help you to pay you debts. I will send you more or less money while I am a soldier. When I get out of the service I will make money enough to pay all the debts that you owe....

Our regiment don't expect to stay here long. I don't know where we shall go to. Some think that we shall go into a Fort into heavy artillery. For my part I don't care where we go to. I don't fear the rebel bullets nor I don't fear the cannon. I have heard the heavy roar of the cannon. I have to go on guard every other day and drill the day that I am not on guard. I like to drill first rate. We have battalion drill every afternoon at 2 o'clock and drill till 4 o'clock. We load and fire our guns on drill. We fire blank cartridges....

It would make your hair stand out to be where I have been. How would you like to be in the front rank and have the rear rank load and fire their guns over you shoulder? I have been there my Self.

I am geting fat as a hog. The climate agrees with me first rate. I am the fattest fellow you ever see.

★ ★ ★ ★

APRIL
1863

THU 2 APR. THE RICHMOND BREAD RIOT

With the South's military effort consuming an ever larger part of its domestic resources and the Federal blockade growing tighter and tighter, most civilians in the Confederacy were forced to go without. Discontent soon followed. Some on the home front began to wonder midway through the war whether ordinary people should properly bear so much of the burden of a war fought most clearly to benefit the slaveholding elite. In this letter, a Richmond gentlewoman describes the riot that began in the Confederate capital when hungry people descended on stores whose shelves were loaded with bread.

SOMETHING VERY SAD HAS JUST happened in Richmond—something that makes me ashamed of all my jeremiads over the loss of the petty comforts and conveniences of life—hats, bonnets, gowns, stationery, books, magazines, dainty food. Since the weather has been so pleasant, I have been in the habit of walking in the Capitol Square before breakfast every morning....Yesterday, upon arriving, I found within the gates a crowd of women and boys—several hundreds of them, standing quietly together. I sat on a bench near, and one of the number left the rest and took the seat beside me. She was a pale, emaciated girl, not more than eighteen....As she raised her hand to remove her sunbonnet and use it for a fan, her loose calico sleeve slipped up and revealed the mere skeleton of an arm. She perceived my expression as

This engraving of the bread riot appeared in Frank Leslie's Illustrated Newspaper *on May 23, 1863.*

I looked at it, and hastily pulled down her sleeve with a short laugh. "This is all that's left of me!" she said. "It seems real funny, don't it?…We are starving. As soon as enough of us get together, we are going to the bakeries and each of us will take a loaf of bread. That is little enough for the government to give us after it has taken all our men."

…The crowd now rapidly increased, and numbered, I am sure, more than a thousand women and children. It grew and grew until it reached the dignity of a mob—a bread riot. They impressed all the light carts they met, and marched along silently and in order. They marched through Cary Street and Main, visiting the stores of the speculators and emptying them of their contents. Governor Letcher sent the mayor to read the Riot Act, and as

this had no effect he threatened to fire on the crowd. The city battalion came up. The women fell back with frightened eyes, but did not obey the order to disperse. The President [Jefferson Davis] then appeared, ascended a dray, and addressed them. It is said he was received at first with hisses from the boys, but after he had spoken some little time with great kindness and sympathy, the women moved quietly on, taking their food with them. General Elzey and General Winder wished to call troops from the camps to "suppress the women," but [Secretary of War James] Seddon, a wise man, declined to issue the order. While I write women and children are still standing in the streets, demanding food, and the government is issuing to them rations of rice.

FRI 17 APR. GRIERSON'S RAID

As Grant prepared to move once more against Vicksburg, he loosed today seventeen hundred cavalrymen on the territory east of that vital Mississippi River port. Operating independently under the command of Col. Benjamin Grierson, this cavalry brigade plunged deep into enemy territory, covering six hundred miles in sixteen days. Continually eluding his would-be captors, Grierson wreaked havoc on Rebel supply lines before returning once again to the safety of the Union lines. This report, from Col. R. V. Richardson of the First Tennessee Partisan Rangers, typifies the frustration experienced by the Confederate commanders attempting to catch Grierson.

On the night of April 16, Rear Adm. David Dixon Porter successfully led his Mississippi Squadron past the destructive Confederate guns of Vicksburg to join forces with Grant's army farther downstream.

WE MAY EXPECT A REPETITION OF this raid on a smaller and similar scale. We had forces enough to have captured and destroyed him, but his movements were so rapid and uncertain of aim that we could not concentrate our scattered forces or put them in concert of action. You had assigned to me men enough to have whipped him, but they were so scattered that I could not find half of them until the enemy had entered his own lines. While I had to pursue him, I could not do more than send out couriers to find the commands ordered to report to me. I followed him two days and nights with only 170 men, one day and two nights with 270 men, and one day and night with 470 men.

FRI 24 APR. *Faced with mounting war debt, the Confederate Congress enacted a new levy designed to tax the output of the Southern population directly (rather than rely solely on the support*

of the member states). It's difficult to imagine today how outrageous this unprecedented measure seemed to citizens of a nation explicitly created to defend states' rights. Farmers particularly resented this "tax in kind," which required them to tithe (that is, give one-tenth of) their crop to the federal treasury. Protest meetings were organized all over the South, and the resolution below typifies the sentiments expressed.

WE CONSIDER THE TITHING law...unconstitutional, antirepublican and oppressive for the simple fact, that if the Confederacy will furnish the people with a sound currency, the government will at all times be able to purchase such supplies as the army may need, provided the people have them to spare. In view of the above facts, and the probability that nine-tenths of the people in this section of the country will have nothing to spare, we are opposed to the payment of the same.

MAY
1863

FRI
1
MAY

CHANCELLORSVILLE

On April 12, nearly three months after Abraham Lincoln gave him command of the Army of the Potomac, Maj. Gen. Joseph Hooker wrote to the president proposing that his troops outflank Lee, then encamped at Fredericksburg on the south bank of the Rappahannock River. In fact, Hooker hoped to bypass Lee's army entirely and head straight for Richmond. In accordance with this plan, on April 28, he began leading seventy thousand Union troops across the Rappahannock into a densely forested area upstream from Fredericksburg known locally as the Wilderness. On April 30, still unknown to Lee, he set up camp around Chancellorsville. On May 1, Lee learned of the threat and hurried forty-seven thousand men from Fredericksburg to block Hooker's exit from the Wilderness. (Lee couldn't spare any more because forty thousand Union soldiers under Maj. Gen. John Sedgwick still threatened Fredericksburg, their presence having concealed Hooker's movement.) Were it not for the boldness of Stonewall Jackson, who executed one of the classic maneuvers in military history, Hooker's plan might have worked. Instead, things began to go wrong for Hooker on May 1 when he decided, after skirmishing only briefly with Lee's advance guard, to surrender the initiative and take up a defensive position around Chancellorsville. Then, early on the morning of May 2, taking advantage of the thick Wilderness vegetation, Jackson carefully led his force around

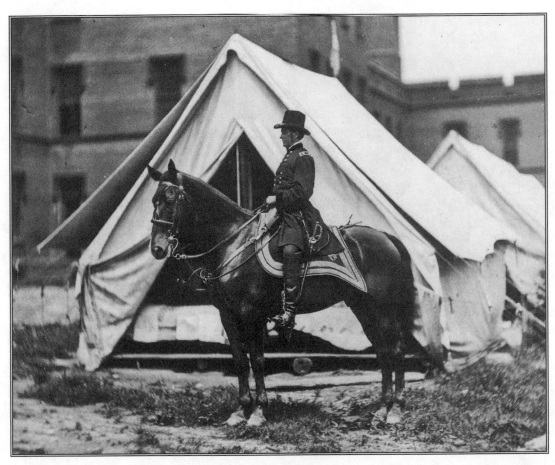

Maj. Gen. Joseph Hooker

the Army of the Potomac's right flank before crashing into its unprepared Eleventh Corps about 6:00 P.M. On May 3, additional Confederate attacks constricted the Federal lines, while Sedgwick (acting on Hooker's May 2 orders) unsuccessfully assaulted Fredericksburg. On the night of May 4, a bloodied Hooker decided to withdraw his forces back across the Rappahannock. In this letter to an aunt, dated May 9, Union Capt. Francis Donaldson offered a particularly vivid account of the battle.

ABOUT 10 P.M. [ON MAY 2], the cannonade having gradually slackened, I started out towards the front to find the pickets and was soon utterly lost in the bush....As I could go no further, and not knowing exactly what to do, but believing my chances good for a retreat in case I made a mistake, I called out, "Where is the picket line?" and instantly received a reply from a dear familiar voice which seemed close to me, "Which picket line?" I cautiously answered, "Is that you Crocker?" and received the welcome reply that it was,

Maj. Gen. John Sedgwick's corps entrenched along the Rappahannock River across from Fredericksburg.

as he pushed through the jungle and joined me....I was very tired, mentally tired. My brain had been on the strain all day, trying to fathom our mysterious maneuvers and to learn whether our army had been checked. I was otherwise greatly distressed and annoyed by our flounderings amidst the tangled thickets and woods, now forward, then back again, now here and now there, not knowing just where to locate the enemy or to expect his attack. If this was the case with me, a captain, what must have been the anxiety of our division General, for I do not think that he knew any more than I did of what was expected of us....

The battle [on May 3] was raging just ahead and the atmosphere was hazy from the smoke which enveloped us and which, drifting aloft, hung above our heads like a canopy. Running forward to the front of the Burns house, I gazed upon a battle scene, the like of which I think has been given to very few witnesses. The open ground of which I have spoken was about 150 yards in extent, and dipped somewhat towards the centre, then gradually rising terminated in a sparsely wooded elevation. The battle was plainly in view, and I could see our men with their lines nicely formed, who, with their backs towards us, were firing and loading as they slowly retired through the timber. Then came the waving battle flag, the gleaming muskets, and the butter nut and gray uniforms of the Confederates as their line of battle came in view in a fierce determined onset. On they swept, the men loading and firing as they came, the peculiar flash of their ram-rods being particularly noticed. Our line stood fast and their muskets spoke the notes of defiance, warning and death. There was a crash, a mingling of gray and blue and then cheers and cries, shouts, shrieks and shrill voices of command rent the air. My heart stood still, my blood fairly curdled, my breath came quick and fast, and the cold perspiration broke out all over me. God! Did ever mortal see such a sight? I could see the bayonet freely used and I could note the ever advancing flag of the enemy as it pushed down the slope, now sprinkled with blood.

SAT 2 MAY STONEWALL JACKSON IS SHOT

The Rebel victory at Chancellorsville, though substantial, was tempered by the death of Stonewall Jackson, who was fatally wounded in the arm on May 2 while riding forward with a small reconnaisance party. The soldiers who fired on Jackson were, in fact, his own men, who were regretfully unable to tell friend from foe in the forest's evening darkness. Jackson's arm was amputated that night, but he never recovered, dying finally on May 10. The following account of Jackson's death was penned by a member of his staff.

[GENERAL JACKSON] HAD RIDDEN but a short distance down the pike, when a volley was fired at the party by the Federals in front and to the right of the road. To escape this fire, the party wheeled out of the road to the left, and galloped to the rear, when our own men, mistaking them for Federal cavalry making a charge, and supposing the firing in front to have been directed at the skirmish line, opened a galling fire, killing several men and horses, and causing the horses that were not struck to dash, panic-stricken, toward the Federal lines, which were but a short distance in front. The General was struck in three places, and dragged from his horse by the bough of a tree. Captain Boswell was killed instantly—Lieutenant Morrison leaping from his horse, that was dashing into the enemy's lines, ran to an interval in our line and exclaimed: "Cease firing! You are firing into our own men." A colonel commanding a North-Carolina regiment in Lane's brigade, cried out: "Who gave that order! It's a lie! Pour it into them, boys." Morrison then ran to the colonel, told him what he had done, and assisted him to arrest the firing as soon as possible. He then went to the front, in search of the General, and found him lying upon the ground with Captain Wilbourn and Mr. Wynn of the Signal Corps, bending over him, examining his wounds....On examining his wounds, they found his left arm broken, near the shoulder, and bleeding profusely.

LINCOLN'S CABINET

The Lincoln cabinet was an extraordinary collection of able, ambitious, sometimes cantankerous men whom the president himself fashioned into an effective administrative team. On this day, at the height of the war, news-paperman (and Lincoln ally) Noah Brooks offered his readers the following vignettes of Secretary of State William H. Seward, Secretary of War Edwin M. Stanton, Secretary of the Treasury Salmon P. Chase, Secretary of the Navy Gideon Welles, and the other cabinet members.

THE CABINET SKETCHED.

Seward is small in stature, big as to nose, light as to hair and eyes, averse to all attempts upon his portrait, and very republican in dress and manner of living. He is affable and pleasant, accessible—from a newspaper point of view—smoking cigars always, ruffled or excited never, astute, keen to perceive a joke, apprecia-tive of a good thing, and fond of "good victuals," if not of luxurious furniture. He has a desire for the Presidency, and all of the protests to the contrary cannot shake my humble belief in that fact, and Seward's consummate tact and ability.

He is an advocate of conservatism and McClellan, not generally popular here, and sits on the small of his back, twirl-ing his watch guard and telling pleasant stories of the past and present. He is unpopular with Mrs. Lincoln, who would like to see Sumner in his place.

Stanton is what is popularly known as a "bull-head;" that is to say, he is opin-ionated, implacable, intent, and not easily turned from any purpose. He is stout, spectacled, black as to hair and eyes, and Hebraic as to nose and complexion. He has a little aristocratic wife, lives in hand-some style, consuming much of his large fortune, probably, in his ample and some-what gorgeous way of living. Stanton is exceedingly industrious, mindful of the interests of his Bureau, never off from his post, works like a trooper and spends day and night at his office when under a strong pressure. He does not appear to have the maggot of the next Presidency in his brain, but plugs right on, unmindful of what anybody says or thinks concern-ing him....

Secretary Chase...is dignified, able, and ambitious....Mr. Chase is large, fine

Gideon Welles

John P. Usher

looking, and his well flattered picture may be found on the left-hand end of any one dollar greenback, looking ten years handsomer than the light haired Secretary. He is reserved, unappreciative as to jokes, and has a low opinion of Presidential humor and fun generally. He gained a transient reputation for fairness by refusing to give positions to Ohio people when he first took his seat in the Cabinet, but afterward revenged himself and his fellow-citizens by filling his immediate office and many subordinate ones with Ohioans. He has a long head. He lives in a moderate style, is a widower, has a beautiful and somewhat airy daughter as the head of his household, and is a regular church-goer. If he should be the next President of these United States, the Executive chair would be filled with more dignity than it has known since the days of Washington. As to his ability, it is only a trifle below the dignity, or the Secretary is greatly deceived.

Father Welles, as the populace term our venerable Secretary of the Navy, is not so old as he is painted, although his white beard and snowy hair—wig, I mean—give him an apostolic mien which, in these degenerate days, is novel and unusual. He is a kind-hearted, affable and accessible man. Unlike his compeer of the Treasury, he does not hedge his dignity about him as a king, but is very simple and unaffected in his manners. He is tall, shapely, precise, sensitive to ridicule, and accommodating to the members of the press, from which stand-point I am making all of these sketches....

The rest of the members of the Cabinet can be "run in" in a single paragraph: [John P.] Usher, of the Interior, is fair, fat, fifty and florid, well fed, unctuous, a good worker, as good a liver, an able lawyer, an accidental member of the Cabinet by the law of succession, and is socially dignified and reservedly get-atable. [Attorney General Edward] Bates is a nice old gentleman, short as to stature, gray headed, modest, quiet, conservative, and painfully reserved....[Postmaster General] Montgomery Blair is the best scholar in the Cabinet, but beyond that he is of but little account; awkward, shy, homely and repellent, he makes but few friends.

Edward Bates

Montgomery Blair

TUE
12
MAY

On this spring day, the North and South were occupied with very different concerns. Throughout the Confederacy, the May 10 death of Stonewall Jackson dominated the news. The following entry from Judith McGuire's journal demonstrates the degree to which patriotic Southerners of all persuasions mourned the passing of the beloved major general much as they would the death of a dear friend.

HOW CAN I RECORD THE SORROW which has befallen our country! General T. J. Jackson is no more. The good, the great, the glorious Stonewall Jackson is numbered with the dead! Humanly speaking, we cannot do without him; but the same God who raised him up, took him from us, and He who has so miraculously prospered our cause, can lead us on without him. Perhaps we have trusted too much to an arm of flesh; for he was the nation's idol. His soldiers almost worshipped him, and it may be that God has therefore removed him. We bow in meek submission to the great Ruler of events. May his blessed example be followed by officers and men, even to the gates of heaven! He died on Sunday the 10th, at a quarter past three, P.M. His body was carried by yesterday, in a car, to Richmond. Almost every lady in Ashland visited the car, with a wreath or a cross of the most beautiful flowers, as a tribute to the illustrious dead. An immense concourse had assembled in Richmond, as the solitary car containing the body of the great soldier, accompanied by a suitable escort, slowly and solemnly approached the depot. The body lies in state today at the Capitol, wrapped in the Confederate

Mourners at the grave of Stonewall Jackson.

flag, and literally covered with lilies of the valley and other beautiful Spring flowers. Tomorrow the sad *cortège* will wend its way to Lexington, where he will be buried, according to his dying request, in the "Valley of Virginia."

In New York, meanwhile, Elizabeth Cady Stanton distributed this circular exhorting women to attend a meeting at which would be discussed their proper contributions to the Union war effort.

AT THIS HOUR THE BEST WORD and work of every man and woman are imperatively demanded. To man, by common consent, is assigned the forum, camp and field. What is woman's legitimate work, and how she may best accomplish it, is worthy of our earnest counsel one with another.

We have heard many complaints of the lack of enthusiasm among Northern women; but, when a mother lays her son on the altar of her country, she asks an object equal to the sacrifice. In nursing the sick and wounded, knitting socks, scraping lint and making jellies, the bravest and best may weary if the thoughts mount not in faith to something beyond and above it all. Work is worship only when a noble purpose fills the soul.

Woman is equally interested and responsible with man in the final settlement of this problem of self-government. Therefore let none stand idle spectators now. When every hour is big with destiny, and each delay but complicates our difficulties, it is high time for the daughters of the Revolution, in solemn council, to unseal the last will and testament of the Fathers—lay hold of their birthright of freedom, and keep it a sacred trust for all coming generations.

SAT 16 MAY CHAMPION'S HILL

As he moved his army closer to Vicksburg, having already displaced Joseph E. Johnston at Jackson, Maj. Gen. Ulysses S. Grant engaged two Confederate forces at Champion's Hill, Mississippi, near Edwards Station. One was Johnston's retreating army; the other was led by Johnston's subordinate, Maj. Gen. John C. Pemberton, the Confederate commander at Vicksburg. Preventing their consolidation were the intervening Federals on Champion's Hill, which changed hands three times before Pemberton felt compelled to retreat toward Vicksburg. The battle of Champion's Hill—with 2,481 Union casualties to 3,851 for the South— included some of the fiercest fighting of Grant's western campaign. In his official report, Col. William T. Spicely of the Twenty-fourth Indiana Infantry encapsulated part of the action.

FROM THE EDGE OF THE TIMBER we drove the enemy, step by step, for nearly 800 yards, over deep ravines and abrupt hills. At this time the rebels were heavily re-enforced, and again the struggle commenced, the most desperate and destructive of the day....Again the enemy massed their forces and threw their whole weight upon the right and center of our line, and here my men fell by scores, but yet with determined bravery held the enemy in check, and again it became necessary for me to change my position, as the enemy's fire was converging upon my lines. I moved to the rear about 75 yards, and again opened fire upon the rebels, who were still pressing forward.

Here we stood before a destructive fire fifteen minutes, when I was compelled to change my position, and again for twenty minutes we fought ten times our number. At this time word came to me that the left of the division was giving way, and that our troops to the right were overwhelmed, or nearly so. I again fell back and formed a line, returning the enemy's fire, which was kept up for a considerable time. Here it was that our colors fell. The gallant Lieutenant-Colonel Barter, believing that the bearer was wounded, rushed forward, seized them, and waved them with cheers in the very face of the enemy. The flagstaff was shattered and Lieutenant-Colonel Barter severely wounded. Being entirely out of ammunition, and overwhelmed in front, my command fell back nearly 300 yards, and here the Eleventh and Twenty-fourth formed a new line, replenished their cartridge-boxes, and again advanced to the field. By this time we were sufficiently re-enforced, and in less than an hour the enemy gave way, leaving our gallant troops in full possession of Champion's Hill.

SUN 17 MAY BIG BLACK RIVER BRIDGE

After hammering Pemberton the day before at Champion's Hill, Grant pursued him toward Vicksburg. At the Big Black River Bridge, the Confederates waited, dug in, for a missing division that never arrived (instead it joined Johnston's force). Under increasing pressure from Grant, Pemberton finally withdrew across the Big Black and, to cover his retreat, burned all the river bridges in the area. Burning the bridges did slow Grant's army, but it also helped commit the Rebels to what would become a dead end for them: the upcoming siege of Vicksburg. In this account of the day's action, Pemberton's chief engineer, S. H. Lockett, described the burning of the bridges.

THE FEDERALS ENGAGED US early in the morning from a copse of woods on our left. I was standing on the railroad bridge at the time, and soon saw signs of unsteadiness in our men, and reporting the fact to General Pemberton, received orders to prepare to destroy the bridges. Fence rails and loose cotton saturated with turpentine were piled on the railroad bridge, and a barrel of spirits of turpentine placed on the steamer *Dot,* which was swung across the river and used as a bridge. About 9 o'clock our troops on the left (Vaughan's brigade) broke from their breastworks and came pell-mell toward the bridges. Bowen's men, seeing themselves unsupported, followed the example, and soon the whole force was crossing the river by the bridges and by swimming, hotly pursued by the Federals. I was on the *Dot* at the time. Waiting until all the Confederates in sight were across the river I touched a match to the barrel of turpentine, and with the aid of one of my lieutenants tipped it over. In a moment the boat was in a blaze. The railroad bridge was likewise fired, and all immediate danger of pursuit prevented.

In his memoirs, Maj. Gen. William T. Sherman, then one of Grant's corps commanders, described the Federals' subsequent crossing of the river. The next day, Grant's army began to invest Vicksburg.

A PONTOON-BRIDGE WAS AT once begun, finished by night, and the troops began the passage. After dark, the whole scene was lit up with fires of pitch-pine. General Grant joined me there, and we sat on a log, looking at the passage of the troops by the light of those fires; the bridge swayed to and fro

under the passing feet, and made a fine war-picture. At daybreak we moved on, ascending the ridge, and by 10 A.M. the head of my column, long drawn out, reached the Benton road, and gave us command of the peninsula between the Yazoo and the Big Black.

TUE 19 MAY THE FIRST ASSAULT ON VICKSBURG

Many historians point to the fall of Vicksburg, Mississippi—rather than the battle of Gettysburg—as the true military turning point of the war. With the Union in control of New Orleans, Vicksburg represented the only practical link between the eastern and western

The pontoon bridge built by Sherman's engineers across the Big Black River.

*halves of the Confederacy, and it occu-
pied a commanding position along the
Mississippi River. As his troops encircled
the city, Grant pondered his options;
and before settling in for what would
become a six-week siege, he decided to
attempt an assault on Vicksburg's sturdy
defensive works. The first assault,
launched this day, although marginally
successful, could not ultimately be supported. A second assault on May 22
was also briefly successful, but strong
Confederate defenses again beat back
repeated Federal charges. After May 22,
Grant gave up charges altogether and
instead dug in and constructed artillery
positions. In the following excerpt from
their regimental history, two survivors
who served with the Forty-eighth Ohio
Volunteer Infantry describe the hellish
first assault on Vicksburg, during which
three thousand of their fellow Federals
were killed or wounded.*

THE ECHO OF THE SIGNAL-GUN
had scarcely died away, when our
brigade was ordered forward to take the
fort in our front, situated on a hill, in an
angle of their intrenchments, where their
guns commanded every approach. Down
the ravine we started at the double quick,
checking our speed for a moment in a
deep gully, to reform our line before facing
the fort, whose incessant fire shook the
ground at every discharge. Then on we
went, up the hill, through the brush and
undergrowth, but did not check our speed
until the right of the regiment, in conjunction with the left of the 77th Illinois,
reached the fort. Leaping into the ditch,
and climbing the parapet, the colors of the
48th Ohio and the 77th Illinois were

planted on the fort. The rebel gunners
surrendered and were hurried to the rear.
During this charge Major Moats was mortally wounded in the knee.

We were now exposed to an enfilading fire from the right and left, which
was thinning our ranks at a fearful rate.
We were left there to contend against
great odds, without any assistance whatever. At 4 P.M. the rebels massed their
troops, and attacked us with great fury,
and retook the fort, capturing the colors
and fifty men of the 77th Ills. Ike Carmin,
one of our color-guards, with a bayonet
wound in the leg, clung to our flag and
saved it from sharing the same fate. This
was the signal for a second attack on both
sides. Another charge was ordered all
along the line. It was a glorious sight to
see our troops advancing in plain view
over the hills, to our assistance. But as
soon as they got within range of the rebel
fire, they were mown down and almost
annihilated. So destructive was the concentrated fire of the enemy, that not a
single man of those sent to reinforce us
reached our line.

…[On May 22, the day of the second
assault,] the battlefield presented a ghastly
sight. The dead lay thick, in every con-
ceivable position on the hill-side beneath
the rebel intrenchments. Some of the
wounded were still alive, but in a terrible
condition, having lain between the contending armies for three days without
food, water, or medical attention.

*The first Union assault appeared equally
horrific from the Confederate side. This
account was written by a member of the
Twenty-seventh Louisiana Infantry.*

When the trajectory of their artillery pieces couldn't be lowered far enough to fire on the charging Federals, the Confederate defenders at Vicksburg began throwing their cannonballs down on the Union troops.

NOW THEY COME UNDER FIRE and the fight opens. The monster guns of the forts, aided by the field pieces, put in position, sweep the crests of the ridges as with brooms of fire, and men demoralized for the instant crowd into ravines for cover, only to find that there is no hiding place safe from shell and shot. Two or three times the blue mass pauses and wavers, and seems to circle round, but each time it gathers strength for a rush that carries it nearer the belching cannon and flaming muskets.

I could see over the smoke and see the ground blue with Federal dead, and I wondered if we would come to close fighting at all. Three or four times I felt sure that the columns were being recalled, but a fresh start brought them closer each time, and finally we saw that they were determined to make a rush at the fort.

Slowly, steadily, and with a determination which commanded the admiration of friend and foe alike, the advance finally gained the ditch in front of Fort Hill. Here the broken Twenty-seventh Illinois halted on the open ground, within half a pistol shot of five thousand hostile muskets, formed their lines anew, and with the first cheers of the assault dashed at the ditch and over it. The Eighty-third Indiana followed and the Thirteenth Regulars came up on the flank. The ditch was passed and the slope gained, but they could go no further. The slope was too steep to be surmounted, and to hold the position was to be fired down upon and exterminated, while the Federal bullets cleared the crest, and dropped to the ground far in the rear. Lighted shells were rolled down the slope and played terrible havoc, and the Federal flags planted in the earth were shot to shreds in less than ten minutes....

Until the recall came they could do nothing but take the steady fire poured down upon them. The wonder is that a single man was left alive. The Regulars lost one third of their total number, and the volunteers suffered such slaughter as few regiments were ever called upon to stand.

During the entire time the Federal troops were in that desperate position they kept banging away at the parapet, but I do not believe that we lost a man killed from their wild firing. The air above us was cut by bullets, and dirt and dust were showered upon us from those striking the parapet, but all the advantage was with us. It was a shameful thing to hold men there as they were held, and it seems a miracle that a single one escaped. The shells made horrible work among them, and after the fight was over and the smoke had blown away, the sight was such that I had never looked upon before or thought possible in war.

VALLANDIGHAM BANISHED

Historians have long debated the legality and wisdom of President Lincoln's policies concerning civil liberties and political dissent in the North. With regard to his administration's treatment of Confederate sympathizers, a considerable number have argued that he greatly exceeded his constitutional powers. The most widely publicized case of this sort involved Clement L. Vallandigham, a prominent Ohio Copperhead and once a U.S. congressman. In early

May, Vallandigham gave a speech in which he called the war "wicked and cruel" and claimed that the Republicans wanted to establish a dictatorship. For these and other remarks, he was arrested on May 5 in Dayton by Union military authorities and charged with treason. On this date, Lincoln personally ordered his banishment. Maj. Gen. Ambrose Burnside, then in command at Cincinnati, subsequently tendered his resignation (refused by Lincoln), while Democrats all over the country sponsored protest meetings—all to no avail. (Apparently, Jefferson Davis didn't want Vallandigham either and had him transferred to Canada.) With this letter of June 12, Lincoln responded to one of the many critical petitions he received.

GENTLEMEN: YOUR LETTER OF May 19th inclosing the resolutions of a public meeting held in Albany, N.Y. on the 16th of the same month, was received several days ago.

The resolutions, as I understand them, are resolvable into two propositions—first, the expression of a purpose to sustain the cause of the Union, to secure peace through victory, and to support the administration in every constitutional, and lawful measure to suppress the rebellion; and secondly, a declaration of censure upon the administration for supposed unconstitutional action such as the making of military arrests....Take the particular case mentioned by the meeting. They assert in substance that Mr. Vallandigham was by a military commander seized and tried "for no other reason than words addressed to a public meeting, in criticism of the course

of the administration, and in condemnation of the military orders of that general." Now, if there be no mistake about this... then I concede the arrest was wrong. But the arrest, as I understand, was made for a very different reason....[H]is arrest was made because he was laboring, with some effect, to prevent the raising of troops, to encourage desertions from the army, and to leave the rebellion without an adequate military force to suppress it....Long experience has shown that armies can not be maintained unless desertion shall be punished by the severe penalty of death.... Must I shoot a simple-minded soldier boy who deserts, while I must not touch a hair of a wily agitator who induces him to desert?...I think that in such a case, to silence the agitator, and save the boy, is not only constitutional, but, withal, a great mercy.

Abraham Lincoln in 1863

JUNE
1863

THU 4 JUN. *As soldiers of any era can attest, military service, even during wartime, can be expected to include long periods of unrelieved tedium. Although Nadine Turchin, wife of Nineteenth Illinois commander John Turchin, wasn't herself a soldier, she did travel with her husband's regiment from June 1861 until late 1864. During that time, she experienced much of what the Nineteenth Illinois experienced. In her diary entry for this date, for example, she expressed her continuing frustration with the dull routine of soldiering (and the restricted role reserved for women in nineteenth-century society). The "butter nuts" to which she refers are, of course, Confederates, whose uniforms were often light brown as well as gray.*

THE SAME DULL INACTION, THE same stagnation in spite of the most formidable situation, the same scattering of troops. All this brings about nothing but fatigue and exhaustion. The most insignificant movement of the enemy at the outposts—the operation of

Union officers of the First Brigade, Horse Artillery, pose with a lady at Brandy Station, Virginia.

some guerrillas coming to steal mules or cattle—puts everything in a flutter. The unfortunate cavalry has to run after them, and in the worst possible circumstances at that. Instead of sending immediately a company, a piece of light artillery, they send two divisions to attack, which is not easy to prepare; and the chief of cavalry considers it his duty to lead the expedition personally with his entire staff. The result? Failure, confusion, injured horses, and the "butter nuts" laughing their heads off, after retreating only to begin once again the next day. What is the reason for it all? Not necessarily ignorance, but the dominant passion of the American: a rage for notoriety at any price, a yearning to be talked about for whatever reason and as often as possible just to gain popularity.

No, in this great conflict I do not see any great man. Only the women are great, the majority because of their suffering, some for showing their great and high moral virtues. Poor ladies! Victims of all public catastrophes! Eternal slaves of fatal destiny! Shall we ever see the day when mankind is civilized enough to consider seriously our position in the society where they allow us to be everything but intelligent beings authorized to enjoy the rights guaranteed to All! by the American constitution: freedom, equality, and the pursuit of happiness?

SUN 7 JUN. VICKSBURG UNDER SIEGE

At Vicksburg during June, there was little action beyond the steady rain of artillery shells—although on this day, *below Vicksburg, Federals did sack and burn Brierfield, the plantation home of Confederate president Jefferson Davis. Meanwhile, residents of the city took refuge underground. This excerpt from an unusual memoir—*My Cave Life in Vicksburg, *written by Mary Ann Loughborough, a well-to-do wife and mother—describes the bizarre circumstance of life during the siege.*

SO CONSTANTLY DROPPED THE shells around the city, that the inhabitants all made preparations to live under the ground during the siege. M— sent over and had a cave made in a hill near by. We seized the opportunity one evening, when the gunners were probably at their supper, for we had a few moments of quiet, to go over and take possession. We were under the care of a friend of M—, who was paymaster on the staff of the same General with whom M— was Adjutant. We had neighbors on both sides of us; and it would have been an amusing

Baltimore dentist (and Southern sympathizer) Adelbert Johann Volck etched many provocative scenes during the Civil War, including this one of Vicksburg cave life.

On this commercial street in Vicksburg, the blurs are the passing carriages and pedestrians, moving too quickly for the slow shutter of the camera to capture them clearly.

sight to a spectator to witness the domestic scenes presented without by the number of servants preparing the meals under the high bank containing the caves.

Our dining, breakfasting, and supper hours were quite irregular. When the shells were falling fast, the servants came in for safety, and our meals waited for completion some little time; again they would fall slowly, with the lapse of many minutes between, and out would start the cooks to their work.

Some families had light bread made in large quantities, and subsisted on it with milk (provided their cows were not killed from one milking time to another), without any more cooking, until called on to replenish. Though most of us lived on corn bread and bacon, served three times a day, the only luxury of the meal consisting in its

warmth, I had some flour, and frequently had some hard, tough biscuit made from it, there being no soda or yeast to be procured....Our new habitation was an excavation made in the earth, and branching six feet from the entrance, forming a cave in the shape of a T. In one of the wings my bed fitted; the other I used as a kind of a dressing room; in this the earth had been cut down a foot or two below the floor of the main cave; I could stand erect here; and when tired of sitting in other portions of my residence, I bowed myself into it, and stood impassively resting at full height—one of the variations in the still shell-expectant life. M—'s servant cooked for us under protection of the hill. Our quarters were close, indeed; yet I was more comfortable than I expected I could have been made under the earth in that fashion.

The Rebel soldiers in the city fared no better, as Winchester Hall, an officer of the Twenty-seventh Louisiana Infantry, recalled in his memoirs.

 INDEED, AS TIME PASSED, FOOD and forage were at a premium; the law of supply and demand was entirely ignored, and various expedients were resorted to. The privates of the regiment successfully undertook a decrease in the rodent population. In my weakened condition camp fare was repulsive. I sent out a man to shoot a rat for me, imagining I could eat it boiled with relish, but the hunt failed to secure the game, and the fancy passed. The men cut up the young growth of the wild cane, boiled it and made a delectable dish.

TUE 9 JUN. BRANDY STATION

The Civil War saw the beginning of the end of cavalry warfare, because the range of many firearms was now too great for mounted charges to be effective. The romantic appeal of the cavalry, however, lingered, and the South took special pride in its mounted soldiers, particularly the famed cavalry corps of Maj. Gen. J. E. B. Stuart. On this day at Brandy Station, Virginia, Stuart's horsemen engaged the Union cavalry of Brig. Gen. Alfred Pleasonton in one of the last great cavalry battles in U.S. history. Lee had already decided to invade the North a second time, and Stuart's cavalry was his advance corps; meanwhile, Joseph Hooker, still commanding the Army of the Potomac, suspected that

Lee was preparing to move, so he sent Pleasanton across the Rappahannock to learn what he could of Lee's disposition. After ten hours of combat at extreme close range, the Rebels held the battlefield, but Pleasonton's cavalry had demonstrated, for the first time, that a Union mounted corps could hold its own against Stuart's men. These excerpts—from the regimental histories of the First New Jersey and the Ninth Virginia Cavalries—describe the battle from contrasting perspectives.

WITH A RINGING CHEER Broderick rode up the gentle ascent that led up to Stuart's headquarters, the men gripping hard their sabres, and the horses taking ravines and ditches in their stride. As the rebels poured in a random and ineffective volley, the troopers of the First Jersey were among them, riding over one gun, breaking to pieces the brigade in front of them, and forcing the enemy in confusion down the opposite slope of the hill. Stuart's headquarters were in our hands, and his favorite regiments in flight before us....

Not a man but had his own story of the fight to tell. [Lieutenant] Kitchen, left alone for a moment, was ridden at by two of the rebels. As one was disabled by his sabre, he spurred his horse against the other. As the animal bounded beneath the goad, a bullet penetrated his brain; and, throwing his rider twenty feet beyond him, the steed, all four feet in the air, plunged headlong to the earth. As the adjutant, trembling from the fall, slowly regained his senses, he saw another rebel riding at him. Creeping behind the body of his dead horse, he rested his revolver on the carcass to give steadiness to his aim; and frightening off his enemy, managed to escape to the neighborhood of the guns, and catch a riderless horse to carry him from the field.

TWO PIECES OF OUR artillery were advanced and posted upon a hill near a bend of the river, and four squadrons of the Ninth were posted in the rear for their support. Several attempts were made upon the position, but were repulsed by the dismounted men of the brigade, with severe losses to the enemy. By three o'clock the centre of our line was forced back to Miller's Hill, over half a mile in our rear. Our brigade was now ordered to fall back to Barbour's Hill. This change of position was critical, for, besides the enemy forces in our front, heavy masses of them were seen below Miller's Hill, and the line of our march crossed the road only about a half mile from them.

Bonus payments were often used to attract recruits.

THU 11 JUN. *On March 3, 1863, President Lincoln signed the United States' first national draft law (the Confederate Congress having already passed a similar act in April 1862). The U.S. act made eligible for military service all male citizens between the ages of twenty and forty-five. It granted exemptions to the physically and mentally unfit, to those with certain types of dependents, to convicted felons, and to high federal and state officials. (A drafted man, how-*ever, could buy a substitute or pay a commutation fee of three hundred dollars.) Overall, the draft had more of a political effect than a military one: During the entire war, it raised only 162,000 men, more than two-thirds of whom were hired substitutes (another 86,000 draftees paid commutation fees). Even so, in some parts of the North—particularly in the hilly backwoods of Pennsylvania, Ohio, and Indiana, where three hundred dollars was an unimaginable sum—draft calls sometimes produced armed opposition. Independent-minded farmers and miners, dissatisfied with the nation's war* *aims, usually refused to serve and resisted the draft. One method they favored was intimidation of the federal agents charged with registering those eligible for the draft. The following June 11 dispatch to the provost marshal general reported the circumstances surrounding a particularly violent case: the murder of two conscription officers in the Ohio River Valley.*

ON TUESDAY LAST ONE OF THE enrolling officers of Rush County was fired upon from the woods while in the performance of his duties, and returned to the headquarters of the district and reported the fact to the provost-marshal, who proposed to send one of his deputies and a squad of men with the enrolling officer to the same neighborhood where the firing took place. Mr. John F. Stephens, one of the deputy marshals for the district, advised, however, that it would be better not to send any force and proposed to go himself, taking with him only one or perhaps two detectives and the enrolling officer. He expressed the opinion that the shooting was done not with the intention of taking the life of the officer, but for the purpose of intimidating him and insisted on going without any other assistance than that before mentioned.

The provost-marshal agreed that the course advised by Mr. Stephens should be pursued, and accordingly on Tuesday morning he started with the enrolling officer, and I think two detectives. Mr. Stephens and one of the detectives traveled in a buggy and the enrolling officer and the other detective were on horseback.

Yesterday about noon, in the same neighborhood in which the previous shooting had taken place, the party came to a house situated a short distance from the road. The enrolling officer dismounted and went into the house and was making inquiries as to the persons residing there subject to enrollment, when some ten or twelve men rose from their place of concealment in a wheat field and fired upon the two men in the buggy, killing Mr. Stephens immediately and mortally wounding the other man, whose name was Craycraft.

SAT
13
JUN.

In the North, the war inspired a wide variety of philanthropic activity. One notable group of philanthropists was the American Missionary Association, originally formed by Christian abolitionists in 1846. This association, which played an important role in the education of freed slaves, received numerous requests from teachers eager to be employed in its service. In the following letter, one black applicant presents her desire to teach in terms of responsibility to her race.

I HAVE A GREAT DESIRE TO GO and labor among the Freedmen of the South. I think it is our duty as a people to spend our lives in trying to elevate our own race. Who can feel for us if we do not feel for ourselves? And who can feel the sympathy that we can who are identified with them? I would have gone upon my own responsibility but I am not able. I thought it would be safer for me to be employed by some Society. Then, I shall not be troubled about my livelihood, for it cramps one's energies to have to think about the means of living.

I suppose I must tell you something of myself. I teach the common English branches, viz. Reading, Writing, Arithmetic, Geography and Grammer. Should there be an opportunity for me to be employed will you please to inform me what the Salary will be and all the particulars. I shall be ready to leave Newport as soon as I can settle my present business. I have a Select School but I believe I can do more good among the Freedmen.

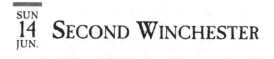

SUN 14 JUN. SECOND WINCHESTER

As Robert E. Lee moved north for another invasion of Union territory—one that he hoped would reverse the momentum of the war—a single, unfortunate Federal force stood in his way. Maj. Gen. Robert H. Milroy and his garrison of nearly seven thousand troops at Winchester had been warned of Lee's possible approach, but Milroy refused to believe that the Army of Northern Virginia could elude Hooker's force on the Rappahannock. Milroy was wrong. In fact, Lee had dodged the Army of the Potomac and was now bearing down on Winchester (at the northern end of the Shenandoah Valley), which stood directly in the path of his advance. On June 13, Rebel advance units drove in the Union pickets, and on this day the action became more general. Lt. Gen. Richard Ewell, who led the Confederate attack, split his corps into two divisions; one attacked Milroy's force from the west, forcing him to retreat

that night northeast toward Harpers Ferry. This line of march, however, was blocked by the other half of Ewell's corps. In fighting on June 15, a few of Milroy's men managed to escape, but nearly two-thirds were later reported missing or captured. Thus, the way was cleared for Lee's advance into Pennsylvania. In the midst of Ewell's June 14 attack, Union Maj. Gen. Robert C. Schenck sent this dispatch to his headquarters warning of Lee's intentions.

Maj. Gen. Robert H. Milroy

EWELL, WITH JACKSON'S OLD division, and in force, has been fighting us since last night at Winchester, and is pressing on to Martinsburg. I have not the means to check him at the Baltimore and Ohio Railroad or at the Potomac River. I shall concentrate all I can to hold the Maryland Heights.

With some glee, A. S. Pendleton, who was Lieutenant General Ewell's assistant adjutant general, summarized in his official report the Confederate rout of Milroy.

WITH WONDERFULLY SMALL loss—less than 300 killed, wounded, and missing—we have carried strong works, defended by an abundance of superior artillery, capturing over 3,000 prisoners and large quantities of military stores and supplies. Such a result should strengthen the reliance in the righteousness of our cause which has inspired every effort of our troops.

Lt. Gen. Richard Ewell

FRI 19 JUN. *Almost two years into her service as a Union army doctor, Mary Walker continued to be frustrated in her efforts to gain an official surgeon's commission. Among the many obstacles*

she faced, most related to her gender, was the negative reaction to her habit of wearing slacks. Even the author of this sympathetic and praiseful profile— which appeared in Walker's hometown paper, the Oswego Times—*could not help but chide her for crossing traditional gender lines. (The Esculapius to whom the aritcle refers is Asclepius, the Greek god of medicine.)*

AMONG THE UNMARSHALLED host of camp followers of the army, not the least noteworthy personage is Miss Mary E. Walker, or "Dr. Walker," as she is usually styled, a legitimate daughter of Esculapius and apparently a lady of commendable philanthropy. She is a native of New York, has received a regular medical education, and believes her sex ought not to disqualify her for the performance of deeds of mercy to the suffering heroes of the Republic. Dressed in male habiliments, with the exception of a girlish looking straw hat, decked off with an ostrich feather, with a petite figure and feminine features, the tout ensemble is quite engaging. Her reputation is unsullied and she carries herself amid the camp with a jaunty air of dignity well calculated to receive the sincere respect of the soldiers.

She has been with the army on several different occasions, was with it at Burnside's defeat and more recently at Sedgwick's crossing below Fredericksburg, where she was very active in her attention to our wounded. She can amputate a limb with the skill of an old surgeon and administer medicine equally as well. Strange to say, that although she has frequently applied for a permanent

Dr. Mary Edwards Walker was awarded the Medal of Honor in 1865.

WED
24
JUN.
In July 1862, John Turchin, commander of the Nineteenth Illinois Infantry, was called before a court-martial in part because he had allowed his wife onto the field of battle as an unofficial nurse. He was found guilty (although President Lincoln later overturned the verdict). In the meantime, Nadine Turchin was forced to remain in the rear of the regiment. In this excerpt from her diary dated almost a year after her husband's trial, Nadine Turchin rejoices at that news that she will finally be receiving an official change in her status.

REMARKABLE DAY! THE ARMY broke camp and set out not for Kentucky but towards the Tennessee River. Reluctant to remain behind with nothing to do when there may be fighting up front and much to do to help those engaged in battle, I had sent a request to the army chief of staff [and future U.S. president James A.] Garfield, to be permitted to follow my husband's division as a "nurse" and guardian of the sick…. Garfield has just sent me the permission that I requested, and although the division has left, I am free to follow it at the first opportunity. Thank you, General Garfield! You will not have lost anything by your favorable answer, because my request was not motivated by any selfish reasons, unless among an intricate pattern of human feelings you find one that may be called selfishness of sacrifice. I have never seen your face, but I promise to take care of you, like your own sister, if you should happen to come under my care when sick or wounded. As for the present, good-bye and thank you!

position in the medical corps, she has never been formally assigned to any particular duty.

In case red-tape etiquette or conventional rule should prevent her from obtaining a place in the medical department, she intends to renew the offer of her services to the proper authorities at Washington. She is at present temporarily attached to the Sanitary Commission, whose headquarters are at the Lacey House opposite Fredericksburg.

We will add that the lady referred to is exceedingly popular among the soldiers in the hospitals, and is undoubtedly doing much good.

SUN 28 JUN. MEADE TAKES COMMAND

McDowell, McClellan, Burnside, Hooker: In less than two years of war, President Lincoln had gone through four military commanders in the East. None proved capable of crushing the rebellion. Now, as Lee threatened Northern territory, Lincoln tried again. On this date, Maj. Gen. George Gordon Meade received orders from General-in-

Maj. Gen. George G. Meade

Chief Halleck placing him in command of the Army of the Potomac. Though not a talent of the same order as Lee, Jackson, or Grant, Meade would have luck when it counted—at Gettysburg, for example, now just three days away. After winning the most famous battle ever fought in the Western Hemisphere, Meade would continue in command

of the Army of the Potomac for the remainder of the war. Below is the order giving Meade command (as transmitted by Asst. Adj. Gen. E. D. Townsend), followed by an assessment of Meade from the memoirs of Confederate artillery chief Edward Porter Alexander.

BY DIRECTION OF THE PRESIdent, Maj. Gen. Joseph Hooker is relieved from command of the Army of the Potomac, and Maj. Gen. George G. Meade is appointed to the command of the army, and of the troops temporarily assigned to duty with it.

MEADE SUCCEEDED HOOKER. He was an excellent fighter, but too lacking in audacity for a good commanding general. He was also of cross and quarrelsome disposition, and unpopular with his leading officers.

★ ★ ★ ★

JULY
1863

WED 1 JUL. GETTYSBURG: DAY ONE

For many of those who would later chronicle the Civil War, the battle of Gettysburg came to seem the focal point around which four years of slaughter and strategy revolved. It is certainly the battle that has defined the war in the popular imagination, and it remains one of the defining moments in U.S. history. Robert E. Lee, convinced that the South's only hope lay in bringing the war to the North, ordered his Army of Northern Virginia across the Potomac River in mid-June. By June 28, his seventy-five thousand soldiers were spread across southern Pennsylvania—and then he learned that the Army of the Potomac under a new commander, Maj. Gen. George Meade, was marching against his dangerously scattered forces. Lee subsequently ordered his army to consolidate in the Gettysburg-Cashtown

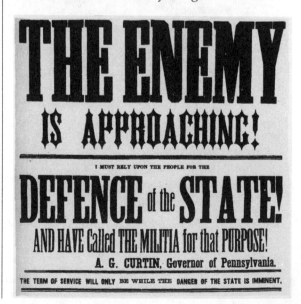

A view of quiet, prosperous Gettysburg taken before the battle.

area. Meanwhile, on July 1, a division of Confederate Lt. Gen. A. P. Hill's Third Corps under the direct command of Maj. Gen. Henry Heth probed the village of Gettysburg, where Hill and Heth expected to find only light resistance and perhaps useful supplies. Instead, when units of Heth's infantry tried to push aside what they thought were local militia, the Confederates received a heavy blow from the dismounted cavalry of Union Brig. Gen. John Buford, armed with powerful breech-loading rifles. Heth then made a crucial tactical mistake: He committed his entire division to the fight. As the day progressed, more units from both sides converged on the town and joined the action, deploying about various local landmarks that later became famous in Gettysburg lore: Cemetery Hill, Seminary Ridge, Little Round Top, and so on. By the end of the day, more

than 170,000 troops were committed, and Generals Lee and Meade had arrived in their respective camps to take direct charge of the battle—started almost accidentally by underlings but now of critical importance to both sides. The following account—from the memoirs of Col. Rufus R. Dawes, regimental commander of the Sixth Wisconsin Volunteers—describes some of the infantry fighting near the Cashtown Road at the start of the day. The Sixth Wisconsin was part of the legendary Iron Brigade, the first infantry to engage the Rebels. By the time the brigade (led by Maj. Gen. John F. Reynolds until he was killed in the action) retreated to Culp's Hill at the end of the day, it had paid a severe price for its staunchness. One regiment, for example, the Twenty-fourth Michigan, lost 316 of its 996 men. The Sixth Wisconsin itself lost no fewer than five color-bearers.

Mathew Brady examines the wheat field where Union Maj. Gen. John F. Reynolds was killed.

THE REGIMENT HALTED AT THE fence along the Cashtown Turnpike, and I gave the order to fire. In the field, beyond the turnpike, a long line of yelling Confederates could be seen running forward and firing, and our troops and Cutler's brigade were running back in disorder. The fire of our carefully aimed muskets, resting on the fence rails, striking their flank, soon checked the rebels in their headlong pursuit. The rebel line swayed and bent, and suddenly stopped firing and the men ran into the railroad cut, parallel to the Cashtown Turnpike. I ordered my men to climb over the turnpike fences and advance. I was not aware of the existence of the railroad cut, and at first mistook the maneuver of the enemy for retreat, but was undeceived by the heavy fire which they began at once to pour upon us from the cover of the cut.

Captain John Ticknor, always a dashing leader, fell dead while climbing the second fence, and many were struck on the fences, but the line pushed on. When over the fences and in the field, and subject to an infernal fire, I first saw the Ninety-Fifth New York regiment coming gallantly into line upon our left....

We were receiving a fairly destructive fire from the hidden enemy. Men who had been shot were leaving the ranks in crowds. With the colors at the advance point, the regiment firmly and hurriedly moved forward, while the whole field behind streamed with men who had been shot, and who were struggling to the rear or sinking in death upon the ground. The only commands I gave, as we advanced, were, "Align on the colors! Close up on the colors! Close up on the colors!" The regiment was being so broken up that this order alone could hold the body together. Meanwhile the colors fell upon the ground several times but were raised again by the heroes of the color guard. Four hundred and twenty men started in the regiment from the turnpike fence, of whom about two hundred and forty reached the railroad cut.

Later, when tales were told and memoirs written, it became obvious that the battle of Gettysburg had more than its share of strange and curious incidents. For example, the battlefield encounter this day between Confederate Brig. Gen. John B. Gordon and Union Maj. Gen. Francis Barlow (and its aftermath) surely ranks among the most bizarre of the war. The account here is from Gordon's memoirs.

Brig. Gen. John B. Gordon

IN THE MIDST OF THE WILD disorder in his ranks, and through a storm of bullets, a Union officer was seeking to rally his men for a final stand. He, too, went down, pierced by a Minié ball. Riding forward with my rapidly advancing lines, I discovered that brave officer lying upon his back, with the July sun pouring its rays into his pale face. He was surrounded by the Union dead, and his own life seemed to be rapidly ebbing out. Quickly dismounting and lifting his head, I gave him water from my canteen, asked his name and the character of his wounds. He was Major-General Francis C. Barlow, of New York, and of Howard's corps. The ball had entered his body in front and passed out near the spinal cord, paralyzing him in legs and arms. Neither of us had the remotest thought that he

could possibly survive many hours. I summoned several soldiers who were looking after the wounded, and directed them to place him upon a litter and carry him to the shade in the rear....He had but one request to make of me. That request was that if I should live to the end of the war and should ever meet Mrs. Barlow, I would tell her of our meeting on the field of Gettysburg and of his thoughts of her in his last moments....I learned that Mrs. Barlow was with the Union army, and near the battlefield....Passing through the day's battle unhurt, I despatched at its close, under flag of truce, the promised message to Mrs. Barlow. I assured her that if she wished to come through the lines she should have safe escort to her husband's side. In the desperate encounters of the two succeeding days, and the retreat of Lee's army, I thought no more of Barlow, except to number him with the noble dead of the two armies who had so

The Soldier's Return to His Home *was printed in 1866 as a premium for readers of the* Philadelphia Inquirer.

gloriously met their fate. The ball, however, had struck no vital point, and Barlow slowly recovered, though this fact was wholly unknown to me. The following summer, in battle near Richmond, my kinsman with the same initials, General J. B. Gordon of North Carolina, was killed. Barlow, who had recovered, saw the announcement of his death, and entertained no doubt that he was the Gordon whom he had met on the field of Gettysburg. To me, therefore, Barlow was dead; to Barlow, I was dead. Nearly fifteen years passed before either of us was undeceived. During my second term in the United States Senate, the Hon. Clarkson Potter, of New York, was a member of the House of Representatives. He invited me to dinner in Washington to meet a General Barlow who had served in the Union army. Potter knew nothing of the Gettysburg incident. I had heard that there was another Barlow in the Union army, and supposed, of course, that it was this Barlow with whom I was to dine. Barlow had a similar reflection as to the Gordon he was to meet. Seated at Clarkson Potter's table, I asked Barlow: "General, are you related to the Barlow who was killed at Gettysburg?" He replied: "Why, I am the man, sir. Are you related to the Gordon who killed me?" "I am the man, sir," I responded. No words of mine can convey any conception of the emotions awakened by those startling announcements. Nothing short of an actual resurrection from the dead could have amazed either of us more. Thenceforward, until his untimely death in 1896, the friendship between us which was born amidst the thunders of Gettysburg was greatly cherished by both.

THU 2 JUL. GETTYSBURG: DAY TWO

Fighting a major battle at Gettysburg was not part of Lee's plan. The proof, if any be needed, can be found in the simple fact that his cavalry commander, the flamboyant J. E. B. Stuart, was not even at Gettysburg, having been caught on the far side of the Army of the Potomac when the battle began. Stuart finally reached Gettysburg on July 2 but too late to take much part in that day's fighting, which grew ever more intense. During the night and early morning, Meade had secured his troops in a defensive line, shaped like a fishhook, that ran along the high ground from Culp's Hill on the Union right through Cemetery Hill and Cemetery Ridge south to the two hills known as the Round Tops. In the late afternoon of July 2, Confederate forces under Lt. Gen. James Longstreet attacked a weakness on the Union left near the Peach Orchard. Longstreet crushed the Union Third Corps under Maj. Gen. Daniel E. Sickles, but prompt deployment of reinforcements by Meade forced Longstreet to pull back to Seminary Ridge. Night fell grimly with neither side having gained much advantage. Meanwhile, some of the day's fiercest fighting occurred at Little Round Top (to the south of Sickles's position), when Maj. Gen. John Bell Hood led his division in a series of charges against the Union-held boulderstrewn mound. In his official report of the action, Confederate Lt. Col. K. Bryan of the Fifth Texas Infantry described Hood's unsuccessful assault.

The "slaughter pen" at the foot of Little Round Top.

ABOUT 4 P.M. ON THE 2D instant, General Hood's division was drawn up in line of battle, fronting the heights occupied by the enemy. The Fifth Texas Regiment occupied the right of the brigade, resting on General Law's left, whose brigade was the one of direction. At the word "Forward," the regiment moved forward in good order. The enemy had a line of sharpshooters at the foot of the first height, behind a stone fence, about three-fourths of a mile from our starting point, which distance was passed over by our line at a double-quick and a run.

At our approach, the enemy retired to the top of the first height, protected by a ledge of rocks. A short halt was made at the stone fence, to enable those who had fallen behind to regain their places. When the command "Forward" again fell from the lips of our gallant colonel, every man leaped the fence, and advanced rapidly up the hillside. The enemy again fled at our approach, sheltering himself behind his fortified position on the top of the second height, about 200 yards distant from the first.

From this position we failed to drive them. Our failure was owing to the rocky nature of the ground over which we had to pass, the huge rocks forming defiles through which not more than 3 or 4 men could pass abreast, thus breaking up our alignment and rendering its reformation impossible. Notwithstanding the difficulties to overcome, the men pressed on to the pass of the precipitous stronghold, forming and securing the enemy's second position, many of our officers and men

The view from Little Round Top toward the center of the Federal position.

A view of Little Round Top.

falling in passing the open space between the heights. Here we halted, there being small clusters of rocks far below the elevated position of the enemy, which gave us partial protection. From this position we were enabled to deliver our fire for the first time with accuracy.

Seeing that the men were in the best obtainable position, and deeming a farther advance without re-enforcements impracticable (a great many of the regiment having been already disabled), I looked

for Colonel Powell, to know his next order. Failing to see him, I concluded at once that he, like many of his gallant officers and men, had fallen a victim to the deadly missiles of the enemy, which were being showered like hail upon us. I moved toward the center, passing many officers and men who had fallen, having discharged their whole duty like true soldiers. I had not proceeded far when I discovered the prostrate form of our noble colonel, who had fallen at his post, his face to the foe. I hastened toward him, when I received a wound in my left arm. On reaching the colonel, I found that he was not dead; but seeing the rent in his coat where the ball had passed out, my fears were excited that his wound would prove mortal. The hemorrhage from my own wound forced me from the field, leaving the command upon Major Rogers.

One of the most courageous acts of the three-day battle was the late-afternoon charge of the First Minnesota Volun-

Maj. Gen. Winfield S. Hancock (seated) with his staff (left to right): Brig. Gen. Francis C. Barlow, Maj. Gen. David B. Birney, and Brig. Gen. John Gibbon.

teers. During Confederate Maj. Gen. Richard H. Anderson's offensive against the Union center, a huge gap opened in the Union lines. Needing to gain several minutes until reinforcements could fill the void, Union Maj. Gen. Winfield S. Hancock ordered into the breach the First Minnesota. Within ten minutes, 224 of the the regiment's 262 officers and men were killed or wounded—but the regiment's charge indeed held back the Rebels. Later, in his official report, Hancock praised the extreme bravery of these men.

THERE IS NO MORE GALLANT deed recorded in history. I ordered those men in there because I saw that I must gain five minutes' time. Reinforcements were coming on the run, but I knew that before they could reach the threatened point the Confederates, unless checked, would seize the position. I would have ordered that regiment in if I had known every man would be killed. It had to be done, and I was glad to find such a gallant body of men at hand, willing to make the terrible sacrifice that the occasion demanded.

FRI 3 JUL. GETTYSBURG: DAY THREE

Substantially outnumbered by the Union forces, and with their own men battered and exhausted after two days of fighting, Confederate generals began to question the wisdom of proceeding with their so far profitless attacks. But Lee, perhaps sensing how momentous a loss here would be, chose to make one final assault on Meade's center. Under the overall direction of Longstreet, division commanders George E. Pickett, Isaac Trimble, and Johnston Pettigrew led fifteen thousand infantrymen straight into the teeth of the entrenched Federal line. This decisive maneuver—often called Pickett's Charge, because Pickett's men received the brunt of the enemy fire— would become synonomous with both great courage and massive slaughter. At its end, after fifty thousand men on both sides had been killed or wounded, the great battle of Gettysburg was over,

and the beaten Confederates withdrew back to Southern soil. Surveying the disaster, Lee would be heard to mutter, "It is all my fault." This description of Pickett's Charge comes from the memoirs of Lt. Gen. James Longstreet, who had opposed the attack but nevertheless carried out Lee's orders in a faithful manner.

PICKETT SAID, "GENERAL, SHALL I advance?" The effort to speak the order failed, and I could only indicate it by an affirmative bow. He accepted the duty with seeming confidence of success, leaped on his horse, and rode gayly to his command....The officers saluted as they passed, their stern smiles expressing confidence. General Pickett, a graceful horseman, sat lightly in the saddle, his brown locks flowing quite over his shoulders. Pettigrew's division spread their steps and quickly rectified the alignment, and the grand march moved bravely on. As soon as the leading columns opened the way, the supports sprang to their alignments. General Trimble mounted,

Edwin Forbes made his initial sketches for this drawing of the action at Cemetery Ridge while under fire.

Harper's Weekly *artist Alfred R. Waud sketches at the Gettysburg battlefield.*

adjusting his seat and reins with an air and grace as if setting out on a pleasant afternoon ride. When aligned to their places solid march was made down the slope and past our batteries of position.

Confederate batteries put their fire over the heads of the men as they moved down the slope, and continued to draw the fire of the enemy until the smoke lifted and drifted to the rear, when every gun was turned upon the infantry columns. The batteries that had been drawn off were replaced by others that were fresh. Soldiers and officers began to fall, some to rise no more, others to find their way to the hospital tents. Single files were cut here and there, then the gaps increased, and an occasional shot tore wider openings, but, closing the gaps as quickly as made, the march moved on....

Pickett's lines being nearer, the impact was heaviest upon them. Most of the field officers were killed or wounded. Colonel Whittle, of Armistead's brigade, who had been shot through the right leg at Williamsburg and lost his left arm at Malvern Hill, was shot through the right arm, then brought down by a shot through his left leg.

General Armistead, of the second line, spread his steps to supply the places of fallen comrades. His colors cut down, with a volley against the bristling line of bayonets, he put his cap on his sword to guide the storm. The enemy's massing, enveloping numbers held the struggle until the noble Armistead fell beside the wheels of the enemy's battery. Pettigrew was wounded, but held his command.

General Pickett, finding the battle broken, while the enemy was still reinforcing, called the troops off. There was no indication of panic. The broken files marched back in steady step. The effort was nobly made, and failed from blows that could not be fended. Some of the files were cut off from retreat by fire that swept the field in their rear. Officers of my staff, sent forward with orders, came back with their saddles and bridles in their arms. Latrobe's horse was twice shot.

Looking confidently for advance of the enemy through our open field, I rode to the line of batteries, resolved to hold it until the last gun was lost. As I rode, the shells screaming over my head and ploughing the ground under my horse, an involuntary appeal went up that one of them might take me from scenes of such awful responsibility; but the storm to be met left no time to think of one's self.

In his official report, excerpted here, Union Col. Arthur Devereux of the Nineteenth Massachusetts Infantry, which was stationed at the center of the Union line, described the Confederate assault from a different perspective.

EVERYTHING REMAINED QUIET on our front until 1 P.M., when, at a signal of a gun fired to our left, a most terrific cannonade commenced on the batteries and the troops in the center of our line, a portion of which was held by our brigade. It was the most terrific cannonading of the war. I have been told that one hundred and ten pieces of the enemy were firing upon our center at once. The men lay quiet and steady, and I am sure none of my regiment left the position where I ordered them to lie down. The cannonade lasted two hours....

Just about 3 o'clock the enemy's cannonade slackened, and columns of attack appeared emerging from the woods across the open field in our front. They advanced gallantly upon our position, which was held firmly excepting immediately upon the right of our brigade line, at which point the left of the next brigade of our line seemed to give way in some confusion....

For an instant it seemed to hang in the balance whether we should drive the enemy out of our works, which they had entered, or they succeed in carrying the position; but I firmly believe that [because of] the extraordinary exertions of a few officers...the line was carried back to the rifle-pits, driving the enemy out.

Just at this moment the enemy, as if actuated by one instinct, threw down their arms in a body, burst into our lines by hundreds, delivering themselves up as prisoners and the battle was won, very few of the enemy attempting to retreat across the field to their own lines.

We must have killed, wounded, and captured the entire attacking column, with comparatively few exceptions.

The night of the charge, Pickett wrote this memorable note to his fiancée.

MY BRAVE BOYS WERE SO FULL of hope and confident of victory as I led them forth! Over on Cemetery Ridge the Federals beheld a scene which has never previously been enacted—an army forming in line of battle in full view, under their very eye—charging across a space nearly a mile in length, pride and glory soon to be crushed by an overwhelming heartbreak.

Well, it is all over now. The awful rain of shot and shell was a sob—a gasp.

I can still hear them cheering as I gave the order, "Forward!" the thrill of their joyous voices as they called out, "We'll follow you, Marse George, we'll follow you!" On, how faithfully they followed me on—on—to their death, and I led them on—on—on—Oh God!

I can't write you a love letter today, my Sally. But for you, my darling, I would rather, a million times rather, sleep in an unmarked grave.

Your sorrowing Soldier

SAT 4 JUL. *For the Union, this would be an Independence Day worth remembering. It began with a press release, issued by President Lincoln, informing the country of the fateful Union victory at Gettysburg.*

ANNOUNCEMENT OF NEWS FROM GETTYSBURG

Washington City, July 4, 10 A.M. 1863
The President announces to the country that news from the Army of the Potomac, up to 10 P.M. of the 3rd, is such as to

Maj. Gen. George E. Pickett

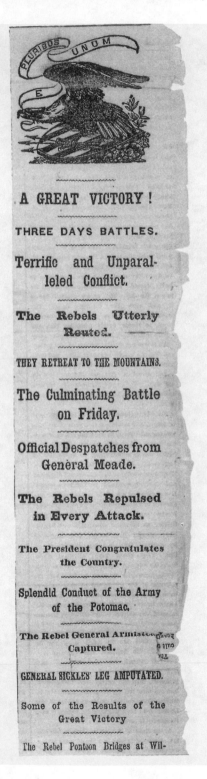

A GREAT VICTORY!

THREE DAYS BATTLES.

Terrific and Unparal-
leled Conflict.

The Rebels Utterly
Routed.

THEY RETREAT TO THE MOUNTAINS.

The Culminating Battle
on Friday.

Official Despatches from
General Meade.

The Rebels Repulsed
in Every Attack.

The President Congratulates
the Country.

Splendid Conduct of the Army
of the Potomac.

The Rebel General Armistead
Captured.

GENERAL SICKLES' LEG AMPUTATED.

Some of the Results of the
Great Victory

The Rebel Pontoon Bridges at Wil-

cover that Army with the highest honor, to promise great success to the cause of the Union, and to claim the condolence of all for the many gallant fallen. And that for this, he especially desires that on this day, He whose will, not ours, should ever be done, be everywhere remembered and reverenced with profoundest gratitude.

Abraham Lincoln

THE FALL OF VICKSBURG

As Lee pulled his battered army out of Gettysburg and began a retreat south, the Confederacy suffered an equally great blow in the war's Western Theater: the fall of Vicksburg, which surrendered to Maj. Gen. Ulysses S. Grant on July 4 after one of the longest sieges in American history. The effect was to cut the Confederacy in half and leave the Union in complete control of the entire Mississippi River. Before the end of the day, Grant stood in the center of the town and watched the Stars and Stripes ascend the flagpole of the Vicksburg courthouse. Two soldiers of the Forty-sixth Indiana Infantry recorded their impressions of the surrender in their regimental history.

ON JULY 3, ABOUT 10 O'CLOCK, white flags appeared on the rebel works to the left of our brigade line. Immediately all the works on both sides were covered with men, and great anxiety was manifested to discover what was going on. Shortly the flags were taken down and a squad of rebel officers went over to the [Federal] lines. Rumors came thick and fast, but nothing was known until night, when an order came saying that a grand national salute would be fired at daylight on the morrow; that if the rebels had surrendered, it would be blank cartridges; if they had not, it would be ball and shell. The salute in the morning told that the truce was not broken. At 10 o'clock a large white flag on the courthouse told the story of the great victory, and a shout from 40,000 throats welcomed it.

The dual Union victories at Gettysburg and Vicksburg were an enormous boost to sagging Northern morale and an equally huge blow to Confederate hopes. Here, two diarists record their emotions regarding the news of the day. In the first excerpt, Mrs. W. W. Lord, who had endured the siege of Vicksburg in a cave with her children, describes the capitulation of her city. In the second, Salome Myers of Gettysburg records how the townspeople were called upon to care for the many wounded on both sides.

ABOUT ½ PAST 8 O'CLOCK, before I was dressed, Mr. Lord came into the cave, pale as death and with such a look of agony on his face, as I would wish never to see again, said Maggie take the children home directly, the town is surrendered, and the Yankee army will enter at 10 o'clock....I was speechless with grief, no one spoke, even the poor children were silent....As I started up the hill with the children, the tears began to flow and all the weary way home, I wept incessantly....At last we reached the house, and such a scene of desolation you can hardly imagine. The dressing room was in ruins, the end where the fireplace had been was blown entirely out. The nursery uninhabitable, a hole deep almost as a cistern in the middle of the floor, every room in the house injured and scarcely a window left whole, *but this is a small matter....*You can imagine our feelings when the U.S. Army entered, their banners flying and their hateful tunes sounding in our ears. Every house was closed...filled with weeping inmates and mourning hearts. You may be sure none of us raised our eyes to see the flag of the enemy in the place where our own had so proudly and defiantly waved so long.

BROUGHT FROM THE HOSPITAL Mr. Andrew Crooks, a friend of Mr. Stewart who was wounded while helping Mr. S off the field. He has his right leg amputated. He is in the same company & from the same neighborhood as Mr. Stewart. The rebels have left and we are again in possession of the town. I never spent a happier Fourth. It seemed so bright when the surly rebels had gone. Evening. Brought Andrew Wintamute of Wyoming to our house. He is wounded in the arm and stomach. Mr. Stewart is worse. Capt. Leslie left. Our house is used as a sort of kitchen to cook for the wounded in the Hospital. The Catholic and United Presbyterian churches are used as hospitals. Kept pretty busy. Get little rest at night.

WED 8 JUL. *Five days after Pickett's Charge, the* Charleston Daily Courier *still did not have reliable news of the events at Gettysburg. This report was*

*apparently based on the author's inter-
pretation of a Northern newspaper's
account of the first day's fighting. Quite
obviously it strained to put a hopeful
spin on the meager information.*

THE BATTLE AT GETTYSBURG
disclosed the important fact that
the whole of General Lee's army is in
Pennsylvania. That event removed every
doubt touching the nature of that movement. It was seen that it is not a raid, but
a real campaign of vast proportions. The
consummate General who, under God,
holds in his hands the destinies of one
hundred thousand men, comprising his
command, had other and higher objects in
view than the replenishment of his stores
and the capture of fat cattle. He aimed
to accomplish results which will be felt
throughout the hostile land—results that
will strike terror and dismay into the mean
and boastful foe, and fill our own bosoms
with gladness....

The country watched the progress of
events beyond the Potomac with intense
interest, altogether free from doubt and
anxiety. No mind was clouded with apprehension or disquieted with solicitude.
It was felt that to harbor such feelings
would be unjust to the magnificent army
and its unsurpassed chiefs, for that army
had invariably come off victorious from
every battle it had fought....

The report of the first battle on
hostile soil increased that confidence
to assurance. The truth that was wrung
from the false pen of the most vile and
shameless of Yankee journalists warranted
the conclusion that our arms had been
crowned with a signal victory. For we were

*Pvt. Ira Fish of the 150th New York Infantry
was among those wounded at Gettysburg.*

certain that that unprincipled miscreant
would never have told the Yankee public
in the columns of his dirty sheet that the
Confederates remained in possession of
the battleground while the Federal army
was forced to fall back several miles, had
there not been some worse intelligence
for Yankee ears which must shortly cause
them distress and dark forebodings.

That news, though so meagre and
communicated through such a channel,
sent a thrill of joy through our hearts, and
we reckoned with perfect confidence on
hearing that the battle at Gettysburg had
resulted in a decisive victory for the
heroes under Gen. Lee....

The telegrams that inform us of that
splendid victory may have made misstate-
ments, but we are warranted in accepting
the result of that battle as the most decisive and brilliant victory the Almighty has
yet vouchsafed our arms.

We must receive further reports before we can venture to predict and conjecture the effect of that magnificent success upon the mind of the North. In the meantime it becomes us to acknowledge the good hand of God in that victory, and to laud and magnify His adorable name.

SAT 11 JUL. *Harriet Beecher Stowe, whose son fought at Gettysburg, had to withstand several days of anxiety before she finally learned that Frederick had been wounded, but not killed, in the battle. She immediately wrote him this letter expressing her relief and joy that he remained alive.*

YOU MAY IMAGINE THE ANXIETY with which we waited for news from you after the battle. The first we heard was on Monday morning from the paper, that you were wounded in the head. On hearing this your Father set off immediately to go to you & took the twelve o'clock train to Boston & the five o'clock New York cars to go right on to Baltimore.

Before he left Andover we got a telegraph from Robert saying that you were wounded, but not dangerously and would be sent home in a few days.

At Springfield that night a gang of pick pockets hustled your father among them as he was getting out of the cars & took from him his pocket book containing 130 dollars & all the letters which your sisters & I wrote to you—He went on to Baltimore & when he arrived there was so sick as to have to send for a doctor who told him that he was going to be very sick

& must go back immediately where he could be taken care of.

He however saw a Mr. Clark (uncle of our student Clark) who was going on to Gettysburg to attend to the wounded, & Gen. H. Wilson who both promised to look for you.

Several other friends also volunteered & Papa returned to Brooklyn where Jack Howard nursed him & this morning Saturday the 11th he is home & in bed—quite unwell but not so but what good news from you would revive him— Do get some one to write for you & tell us how to visit, & what we shall do for you—Do let us know when we may expect you—We have been looking for you every night, all your sisters waiting at the cars—We *must* see you & return thanks that your life is saved. God bless you. At last you have helped win a glorious victory. The cause is triumphant! God be thanked!—Your loving mother.

MON 13 JUL. THE NEW YORK CITY DRAFT RIOTS

On Saturday, July 11, the new federal draft law, signed by President Lincoln on March 3, took effect in New York City. The names of those selected appeared in the next day's newspapers, and the drawings were scheduled to resume on Monday morning. However, that morning, the city's festering resentment—of the war, of the draft, of the Republican administration—finally erupted. An angry mob stormed the headquarters of the draft, and others rioted throughout the city, overpowering the police and even the military authorities. Although local politicians, among them many Peace Democrats (Copperheads), helped stir the pot, the fiercest opposition to the draft came from laborers, who felt unfairly targeted (because the rich could buy their way out of service) and who believed their jobs would be threatened by an influx of former slaves into the workforce. The rioting was the worst the nation had ever seen: For three days, the city convulsed with violence as immigrant whites targeted the city's vulnerable black population. Many African Americans were savagely beaten and left for dead. Others were lynched from lampposts, their bodies desecrated. In the end, approximately 120 people were killed. The following account is taken from a July 13 diary entry written by New York City lawyer George Templeton Strong.

THE RABBLE WAS PERFECTLY homogeneous. Every brute in the drove was pure Celtic—hod-carrier or loafer. They were unarmed. A few carried pieces of fence-paling and the like. They turned off west into Forty-fifth Street and gradually collected in front of two three-story dwelling houses on Lexington Avenue, just below that street, that stand alone together on a nearly vacant block. Nobody could tell why these houses were singled out. Some said a drafting officer lived in one of them, others that a damaged policeman had taken refuge there. The mob was in no hurry; they had no need to be; there was no one to molest them or make them afraid. The beastly ruffians were masters of the situation and of the city. After a while sporadic paving-stones began to fly at the windows, ladies and children emerged from the rear and had a rather hard scramble over a high board fence, and then scudded off across the open, Heaven knows whither. Then men and small boys appeared at rear windows and began smashing the sashes and the blinds and shied out light articles, such as books and crockery, and dropped chairs and mirrors into the back yard; the rear fence was demolished and loafers were seen marching off with portable articles of furniture. And at last a light smoke began to float out of the windows and I came away. I could endure the disgraceful, sickening sight no longer, and what could I *do*?

Rioters burn the Colored Orphan Asylum on Fifth Avenue in New York City.

Unlike the helpless New York City police force, Union troops had the firepower to quell the rioting.

The fury of the low Irish women in that region was noteworthy. Stalwart young vixens and withered old hags were swarming everywhere, all cursing the "bloody draft" and egging on their men to mischief.

In the aftermath of the draft riots, a committee of merchants was formed to aid the city's African-American population. The committee eventually issued a report on the mayhem, which included this vivid account of Charles Jackson's experiences on July 15, the final day of the riots.

THE FOLLOWING CASE OF brutality is one of the worst, so far as beating is concerned, which has come under our observation: At a late hour on Wednesday night, a colored man, named Charles Jackson, was passing along West street, in the neighborhood of Pier No. 5, North river. He was a laboring man, and was dressed in a tarpaulin, a blue shirt, and heavy duck trousers. As he was passing a groggery in that vicinity, he was observed by a body of dock men, who instantly set after him. He ran with all the swiftness his fears could excite, but was overtaken before he had gone a block. His persecutors did not know him nor did they entertain any spite against him beyond the fact that he was a black man and a laborer about the docks, which they consider their own peculiar field of labor. Nevertheless they knocked him down, kicked him in the face and ribs, and finally by the hands of their leader, deliberately attempted to cut his throat. The body, dead they supposed it, was then thrown into the water and left to sink. Fortunately life was not extinct and the sudden plunge brought the poor fellow to his senses, and being a good swimmer he was enabled instinctively to seek for the network of the dock. This he soon found, but was so weak from the loss of blood and so faint with pain that he could do no more than hold on and wait for day. The day after, Messrs. Kelly and Curtis, of Whitehall, discovered him lying half dead in the water. They at once attended to his wants, gave him in charge of the Police-boat and had him sent to the hospital. The escape of the man from death by the successive abuses of beating, knifing, and drowning, is most wonderful. So determined and bitter is the feeling of the longshoremen against negroes that not one of the latter dared show themselves upon the docks or piers, even when a regular employee of the place.

The report of the Committee of Merchants for the Relief of Colored People Suffering for the Late Riots in the City of New York also documented the murder of a sixty-three-year-old Mohawk named Peter Heuston, demonstrating that the rioters targeted other racial minorities as well.

PETER HEUSTON, SIXTY-THREE years of age, a Mohawk Indian, with dark complexion and straight black hair, who has for several years been a resident of this city, at the corner of Roosevelt and Oak streets, and who has obtained a livelihood as a laborer, proved a victim to the late riots.

His wife died about three weeks before the riots, leaving with her husband an only child, a little girl named Lavinia, aged eight years, whom the Merchants' Committee have undertaken to adopt with a view of affording her a guardianship and an education. Heuston served with the New York Volunteers in the Mexican War, and has always been loyal to our government. He was brutally attacked on the 13th of July by a gang of ruffians who evidently thought him to be of the African race because of his dark complexion. He died within four days at Bellevue Hospital from his injuries.

News of the draft riots shocked the North. Walt Whitman, working at the time as a nurse in a Washington hospital, wrote this July 15 letter to his sister in which he reported the capital's immediate reaction to the riots.

SO THE MOB HAS RISEN AT LAST in New York—I have been expecting it, but as the day for the draft had arrived & every thing was so quiet, I supposed all might go on smoothly—but it seems the passions of the people were only sleeping, & have burst forth with terrible fury, & they have destroyed life & property, the enrollment buildings &c as we hear—the accounts we get are a good

Walt Whitman

deal in a muddle, but it seems bad enough—the feeling here is savage & hot as fire against New York, (the mob—*"copperhead mob"* the papers here call it), & I hear nothing in all directions but threats of ordering up the gunboats, cannonading the city, shooting down the mob, hanging them in a body, &c &c—meantime I remain silent, partly amused, partly scornful, or occasionally put a dry remark, which only adds fuel to the flame—I do not feel it in my heart to abuse the poor people, or call for rope or bullets for them, but that is all the talk here, even in the hospitals—

SAT 18 JUL. FORT WAGNER

Charleston, South Carolina, was a prize that the Union military leadership greatly desired. Capturing the port, however, required first the reduction of heavily defended Fort Wagner, situated on Morris Island, which guarded the approach to Charleston. This exceedingly difficult and deadly job was given to the Fifty-fourth Massachusetts Volunteer Infantry, one of the Union's first all-black regiments (excepting its white officers, of course). Nearly half of the six-hundred-man regiment died in the memorable though unsuccessful assault—including its white organizer and commander, Col. Robert Gould Shaw, who was subsequently immortalized in famous poems by fellow Bostonians Ralph Waldo Emerson and James Russell Lowell. In this contemporary account of the attack, George Stephens, a noncommissioned officer in the regiment (and perhaps the finest black correspondent of the war), detailed the valiant charge.

WE LEFT THE LOWER END OF Morris Island Saturday morning, and marched slowly and steadily to the front until in sight of Fort Wagner. We had heard of the previous attempt to take it by storm, and knew that nothing but hard fighting, with great sacrifice of life, could result in a successful storming of it. Gen. Strong, the hero of the attack of Saturday, when our regiment reached within range of the shells of the fort, rode out bravely a hundred yards in advance of us and reconnoitered the fort and its surroundings. Rode back to us and briefly addressed us, and asked, "Massachusetts men, are you ready to take that fort?" The universal answer was, "We will try." "They are nearly played out. They have but two effective guns," said he. About sundown we were ordered to advance at the double quick-step, cheering as if going on some mirthful errand. The rebs withheld their fire until we reached within fifty yards of the work, when jets of flame darted forth from every corner and embrasure, and even Fort Sumter poured solid shot and shell on our heads. The 54th, undaunted by the hellish storm, pushed up to the work, down into the moat, and like demons ascended the parapet, found the interior lined with rebel soldiers who were well sheltered and fought them one hour before we were re-enforced, and when the regiment reached us, the 3d New Hampshire, which was presumed to be our re-enforcements, they, to a man, emptied their rifles into us. Thus we lost nearly as many men by the bullets of our presumed friends as by those of our known enemies.

Some few entered the fort, and when they got in, it was so dark that friends could not be distinguished from foes, and

Currier & Ives's 1863 lithograph The Gallant Charge of the Fifty-fourth Massachusetts (Colored) Regiment.

there is no doubt but that many a Union soldier was killed by his comrades.

On the whole, this is considered to be a brilliant feat of the 54th. It is another evidence that cannot now be denied, that colored soldiers will dare go where any brave men will lead them. Col. Shaw, our noble and lamented commander, was the bravest of the brave. He did not take his thirty paces to the rear, but led the column up to the fort, and was the first man who stood on the parapet of the fort. When he reached it he said, "Come on, men! Follow me!" and he either received a mortal wound and fell over the wall or stumbled into the fort and was killed. If he still lives, it is miraculous, for he must have fell on glistening bayonets. One of the rebel prisoners says that he is wounded and still lives, but for my part I do not believe it.

Two days after the failed assault on Fort Wagner, Charlotte Forten, still teaching freed people on one of the South Carolina Sea Islands, learned the fate of what she and other African Americans considered "our regiment." In her July 20 diary entry, Forten wrote of her anguish at the loss of the men, not the least of whom was Colonel Shaw.

FOR NEARLY TWO WEEKS WE have waited, oh how anxiously, for news of our regt. which went, we know to Morris Is. to take part in the attack on Charleston. Tonight comes news, oh so sad, so heart-sickening. It is too terrible, too terrible to write. We can only hope it may not all be true. That our noble, beautiful young Colonel is killed, and the regt.

cut to pieces! I cannot, cannot believe it. And yet I know it may be so. But oh, I am stunned, sick at heart. I can scarcely write. There was an attack on Fort Wagner. The 54th put in advance; fought bravely, desperately, but was finally overpowered and driven back after getting into the Fort. Thank Heaven! they fought bravely! And oh, I still must hope that our colonel, *ours* especially he seems to me, is not killed. But I can write no more tonight.

Elsewhere, the draft remained a major topic of conversation throughout July. As a service to their readers, Northern newspapers printed notices explaining the legal grounds for various exemptions. This notice appeared in the July 18 issue of the Connecticut Post.

WIDOWS WITH TWO SONS.

We again call attention to the provision in the U.S. militia law by which a widow who has two sons upon whose labor she is dependent for support can elect which one she will have exempt from the draft. We have published the form which she must use in making her application.—It is our decided opinion that this election must be made before the draft takes place, and we therefore urge our readers to see to it. After one son has been drafted we do not see how the mother has power to make the other, who has not been drafted, serve in his place.

MON 20 JUL. *Following the grievous setbacks of early July, many Southerners became convinced that the time for desperate measures had indeed*

*Slaves preparing cotton for the gin on
Port Royal Island, South Carolina.*

*arrived. In the following letter to
President Jefferson Davis, Mississippi
planter O. G. Eiland argued that the
only hope for a Confederate victory
lay in permitting slaves to serve in
the Rebel army.*

VICKSBURG IS GONE AND AS A
consequence Mississippi is gone
and in the opinion of all most every one
here the Confederacy is gone. I can
myself see but one chance, but one
course to pursue to save it, and I fear it
is now too late for even that to check the
tide that is overwhelming us. It is simply
by your own authority, and without waiting for congress to give you authority,
to call out every able bodied *Negro* man
from the age of sixteen to fifty years old.
They will go readily and cheerfully. The
owners would gladly give them up and
afford every facility in getting them off.
On every road leading from the western
Country there is a constant stream of
negroes running into Ala & Georgia & the
Carolinas. They will destroy all the food
in those states like an army of locusts.
This if nothing else would starve us into
subjection in a few months. It is precisly
what our enemy want. Take our negro
men away and thereby relieve us of a
dangerous element. Force the young
white men, who are running off with
them, into the army and we, the old men,
will take care of the negro women and
children and make corn. Act promptly.
The negro men will all go to the enemy if
not taken to our own army. I believe fully
half of them had rather go into our ranks
than the Yankees. They want to be in the
frollick & they will be one way or the
other. Away with all squeamesness about
employing negroes in civilized warfare.
Our enemies are doing it as rapidly as
they can and we are left no other alternative.—If you knew with what pleasure I
would send off every negro man I have
tomorrow morning you would not dismiss
this hastily. I am only one of the masses
and what I say I believe nearly every slave
holder in the South would say and do.

**FRI
31
JUL.** *Of the many letters that President Lincoln received during
the war, this one—from an
African-American woman whose son
fought with the Fifty-fourth Massachusetts at Fort Wagner—may have been the
most powerful in its expression of both
the difficulties and the hopes of blacks
during the Civil War years.*

EXCELLENT SIR: MY GOOD friend says I must write to you and she will send it. My son went in the 54th regiment. I am a colored woman and my son was strong and able as any to fight for his country and the colored people have as much to fight for as any. My father was a Slave and escaped from Louisiana before I was born morn forty years agone. I have but poor edication but I never went to schol, but I know just as well as any what is right between man and man. Now I know it is right that a colored man should go and fight for his country, and so ought to a white man. I know that a colored man ought to run no greater risques than a white, his pay is no greater his obligation to fight is the same. So why should not our enemies be compelled to treat him the same, Made to do it.

My son fought at Fort Wagoner but thank God he was not taken prisoner, as many were. I thought of this thing before I let my boy go but then they said Mr. Lincoln will never let them sell our colored soldiers for slaves, if they do he will get them back quick, he will rettallyate and stop it. Now Mr. Lincoln dont you think you oght to stop this thing and make them do the same by the colored men. They have lived in idleness all their lives on stolen labor and made savages of the colored people, but they now are so furious because they are proving themselves to be men, such as have come away and got some edication. It must not be so. You must put the rebels to work in State prisons to making shoes and things, if they sell our colored soldiers, till they let them all go. And give their wounded the same treatment. It would seem cruel, but their is no other way, and a just man must do hard things sometimes, that shew him to be a great man. They tell me some do you will take back the Proclamation, don't do it. When you are dead and in Heaven, in a thousand years that action of yours will make the Angels sing your praises I know it. Ought one man to own another, law for or not, who made the law, surely the poor slave did not. So it is wicked, and a horrible Outrage, there is no sense in it, because a man has lived by robbing all his life and his father before him, should he complain because the stolen things found on him are taken. Robbing the colored people of their labor is but a small part of the robbery. Their souls are almost taken, they are made bruits of often. You know all about this

Will you see that the colored men fighting now, are fairly treated. You ought to do this, and do it at once, Not let the thing run along. Meet it quickly and manfully, and stop this mean cowardly cruelty. We poor oppressed ones, appeal to you, and ask fair play. Yours for Christ's sake,

Hannah Johnson.

★ ★ ★ ★

AUGUST
1863

SAT
1
AUG. *While the Union blockade continued to throttle the economy of the South, many sectors of the Northern economy thrived. This article in the August issue of the* Merchant's Magazine and Commercial Review *noted the many ways in which the war stimulated the Massachusetts economy.*

SELDOM, IF EVER, HAS THE business of Massachusetts been *more active* or *profitable* than during the past year. The war has brought into activity many mechanical employments for which there is little occasion in time of peace; for example, as the manufacture of arms and ordnance, camp and garrison equipage, saddlery and artillery harness, and military clothing and accoutrements. It has, also, greatly stimulated the manufacture of boots and shoes, and of woolen goods; while the subsistence of the army has furnished a constant and remunerative market for breadstuffs and provisions. There is hardly a branch of domestic

The wreck of a Confederate blockade runner.

industry which has not been actively employed. The cotton manufacture alone has been interrupted by the loss of the raw material, and has given less occupation to labor than usual; but there was never a time since this branch of industry established itself in New England, when the profits realized from it have been so considerable....The necessity of transporting great bodies of troops from point to point along our seaboard, and of furnishing them subsistence, has called into the service of the government a vast fleet of transports, for the hire of which owners have received rates of compensation greatly exceeding the ordinary profits of commerce. Every steam vessel, capable of navigating either the ocean or harbors and rivers, has been thus employed, and many more, previously regarded as worn out, and no longer seaworthy, having been flimsily repaired, and made to pass through a hasty or corrupt inspection, have gone out laden with valuable property, or invaluable lives, to be wrecked or rescued, as the chances of the weather, or as skillful seamanship might determine. The shipyards, both public and private, have been worked to their utmost capacity, in the construction of iron-clad gunboats and other vessels of war; while machine shops, rolling mills, and foundries have been equally busy in building their engines, rolling their armor plates, and casting their guns....The wants of the army have come in to make good the loss of the Southern market... and the government has been a liberal and sure, if not a ready paymaster. Labor has been in great demand, wages have risen, and the trade is again in a high state of prosperity. Wealth has flowed into the State in no stinted measure, despite of war and heavy taxes.

WED 5 AUG. *The process of Reconstruction began long before Lee surrendered at Appomattox. Already, large tracts of Confederate territory— in Arkansas, Tennessee, Louisiana, and elsewhere—had been returned to Union control, and the matter of their reintegration into the United States was being actively discussed. On this date, President Lincoln offered his thoughts in this letter to Nathaniel P. Banks, the ranking Union general in Louisiana.*

MY DEAR GENERAL BANKS: ...While I very well know what I would be glad for Louisiana to do, it is quite a different thing for me to assume direction of the matter. I would be glad for her to make a new Constitution recognizing the emancipation proclamation, and adopting emancipation in those parts of the state to which the proclamation does not apply. And while she is at it, I think it would not be objectionable for her to adopt some practical system by which the two races could gradually live themselves out of their old relation to each other, and both come out better prepared for the new. Education for young blacks should be included in the plan....

As an anti-slavery man I have a motive to desire emancipation, which pro-slavery men do not have; but even they have strong enough reason to thus place themselves again under the shield of the Union; and to thus perpetually hedge against the recurrence of the scenes through which we are now passing....

For my own part I think I shall not, in any event, retract the emancipation proclamation; nor, as executive, ever return to slavery any person who is free by the terms of that proclamation, or by any of the acts of Congress.

If Louisiana shall send members to Congress, their admission to seats will depend, as you know, upon the respective Houses, and not upon the President.

If these views can be of any advantage in giving shape, and impetus, to action there, I shall be glad for you to use them prudently for that object. Of course you will confer with intelligent and trusty citizens of the State, among whom I would suggest Messrs. Flanders, Hahn, and Durant; and to each of whom I now think I may send copies of this letter. Still it is perhaps better to not make the letter generally public. Yours very truly,

A. Lincoln

WED 12 AUG. *President Lincoln remained remarkably accessible throughout the Civil War, and many aspects of his daily routine were well known to residents of the capital. In this journal entry, Walt Whitman, who lived in Washington during the war, recorded his habit of watching the president and his retinue pass by on the street. The barouche in which Lincoln rode was a four-wheeled carriage with a driver's seat high in the front, two double seats inside facing each other, and a folding top over the backseat. The son Whitman mentions must have been Thomas Lincoln, known as Tad. (Whitman might possibly have confused Tad with his brother Willie, born three years*

earlier than Tad, but William Wallace Lincoln had died in February 1862 from "a bilious fever," probably typhoid. He was the only child of a president ever to die in the White House.)

I SEE THE PRESIDENT ALMOST every day, as I happen to live where he passes to or from his lodgings out of town. He never sleeps at the White House during the hot season, but has quarters at a healthy location, some three miles north of the city, the Soldiers' Home, a United States military establishment. I saw him this morning about 8 ½ coming in to business, riding on Vermont avenue, near L street. The sight is a significant one, (and different enough from how and where I first saw him). He always has a company of twenty-five or thirty cavalry, with sabres drawn, and held upright over their shoulders. The party makes no great show in uniforms or horses. Mr. Lincoln, on the saddle, generally rides a good-sized easy-going gray horse, is dress'd in plain black, somewhat rusty and dusty; wears a black stiff hat, and looks about as ordinary in attire, &c., as the commonest man. A Lieutenant, with yellow straps, rides at his left, and following behind, two by two, come the cavalry men in their yellow-striped jackets. They are generally going at a slow trot, as that is the pace set them by the One they wait upon. The sabres and accoutrements clank, and the entirely unornamental *cortege* as it trots towards Lafayette square, arouses no sensation, only some curious stranger stops and gazes. I see very plainly Abraham Lincoln's dark brown face, with the deep cut lines, the eyes, &c., always to me with a

President Lincoln with his son Thomas, known to the family as Tad.

deep latent sadness in the expression. We have got so that we always exchange bows, and very cordial ones.

Sometimes the President goes and comes in an open barouche. The cavalry always accompany him, with drawn sabres. Often I notice as he goes out evenings—and sometimes in the mottling, when he returns early—he turns off and halts at the large and handsome residence of the Secretary of War, on K street, and holds conference there. If in his barouche, I can see from my window he does not alight, but sits in the vehicle, and Mr. Stanton comes out to attend him. Sometimes one of his sons, a boy of ten or twelve, accompanies him, riding at his right on a pony.

Former slaves outside their home in Georgia.

TUE 18 AUG. *When Union forces gained control of Confederate territory, local plantation owners often fled to avoid capture. In their rush, they occasionally left behind slaves, who were thereafter compelled by circumstance to fend for themselves on the abandoned plantations. The following letter, written this day by an inspector of plantations working for the U.S. Treasury Department, described the existence of one such group of former slaves living on a plantation in southern Louisiana, their erstwhile master having lately fled to Texas.*

ON THE 14TH OF AUGUST, I visited the plantation Evacuated by the rebel, Dick Robinson; Some of the hovels are occupied by five or six negroes in a destitute condition— The dwelling house is abandoned and stripped of the little furniture it contained, one fine Piano is in the possession of Mrs. Baker in the town of Houmas— The old negroes appear to share the old house of their Master, it is open to the weather and is in a very filthy condition; the miserable hovels occupied by the Negroes are fast going to decay; the Sugarhouse also is in a very miserable Condition

The Negroes remaining on the plantation have cultivated Small parcels of ground, and made Sufficient Corn and vegetables to Supply them; they have Some Cane, I have given them written permission to grind it for their own use— These Negroes have succeeded beyond rebel Expectations in living without the assistance of white men—

Robinson took all his good or able Negroes to Texas, and left these old and crippled ones to starve— No White men in Louisiana could have done more or better than these Negroes & they well deserve the reward of their labor (the Crop) and the Encouragement of the Government— One old waggon, two Condemned Mules— two old ploughs and Six old hoes Comprise the inventory of this *joint Stock Company*— The condition of the Negro Cabins, no floors, no chimneys, built of pickets without regard to Comfort or Convenience, and their venerable appearance Confirms the Stories of cruelty related by the old Negroes of Dick Robinson the planter who made annualy 600 Hhds [hogsheads] Sugar—

FRI 21 AUG. QUANTRILL SACKS LAWRENCE

William C. Quantrill was the most notorious of the Confederate irregulars operating in Missouri and Kansas. Arguably more a criminal than a combatant, he had spent most of 1860 living in the abolitionist stronghold of Lawrence, Kansas, which he fled in December of that year after being charged with horse stealing. Once the war began, Quantrill fought with the Rebels at Lexington, Missouri, and subsequently formed a guerrilla band that plundered small towns along the Kansas-Missouri border—as much for profit as for any other reason. In 1862, he was mustered into the Confederate army and given the rank of captain. On this day, leading about 450 men (including Bloody Bill Anderson and George Todd), Quantrill revenged himself on the people of Lawrence, robbing and burning their town and killing

150 residents (including nearly every man he could find). The author of this account, H. D. Fisher, was one of the few who survived the raid.

FOR A LONG TIME RUMORS HAD been afloat that it was the intention of the Missouri guerrillas to sack Lawrence and slaughter her citizens. More than once guards had been placed on all the roads leading into town. The cry of "Wolf" had been raised too often. The people had served as pickets and had been frightened so many times, each time to learn that the alarm had been false, that they had come to look upon the danger of a raid upon their town as not even remotely possible, and had become accustomed and indifferent to alarms of this character. Thus it happened that when [Quantrill] came at last, with hellish and dire destruction, the guards had all been withdrawn and the town was asleep to danger.

The unnatural and barbarous state of affairs engendered by war was terribly emphasized on Kansas soil, where the anti-slavery people were exposed to the malignant hate of an enemy in the throes of defeat, whose schemes of revenge took form in arson, robbery, pillage and murder wherever defenceless border towns promised hope of success to these murderous marauders. How deadly their purpose, how sweeping in destruction were these guerrilla raids many a Kansas town was called upon to bear testimony to. But of them all none were made to suffer and mourn as Lawrence was made to suffer and mourn....

Entering the town from the Southeast they [Quantrill's band] marched in regular order until the center of the residence portion had been reached. Here they broke into a main body and squads of four, six and eight, the larger body galloping furiously down Massachusetts street to the business section, the smaller squads riding as fast as their horses could carry them to the various parts of the town assigned them for individual action. Some flew to the extreme Western limit, the residence of General Lane and other prominent citizens. Others galloped swiftly to the Southwest, skirting Mount Oread and the Southern edge of town. The river front needed but little guarding, yet here, too, pickets were quickly stationed. As the affrighted people flew for safety, no matter what the direction, they were confronted by squads of guerrillas so stationed as to cut off escape. A cordon of death had been thrown around us while we slept.

Fairly within the city the work of death and destruction was begun. With demoniac yells the scoundrels flew hither and yon, wherever a man was to be seen, shooting him down like a dog. Men were called from their beds and murdered before the eyes of wives and children on their doorsteps. Tears, entreaties, prayers availed nothing. The fiends of hell were among us and under the demands of their revengeful black leader they satiated their thirst for blood with fiendish delight....

Equally atrocious was the murder of Judge Carpenter. In delicate health he had not joined the army of the frontier, but he sympathized earnestly with the Union cause and served us nobly in many ways. His judicial utterances were always on the side of the right, and thus he became an object of hatred to the ruffian

element. Called from his home in early morn he saw the danger and attempted to escape by running around his house, hoping to get out by a side gate and away to some place of safety. They chased him, and when his wife saw he was certain to be caught she flew to his side and threw her arms around him, enfolding him in her skirts. The murderous guerrillas tried to wrest him away from her, failing in which they forcibly held her to one side and shot him down in her arms. She fell with him and again they tore her partially from him and finished their crime by repeatedly turning their revolvers upon him while still she clung to him and begged for mercy and his life.

THE SWAMP ANGEL

The failure of the July 18 Union assault on Fort Wagner caused Brig. Gen. Quincy A. Gillmore to reassess his plans for the taking of Charleston. Instead of continuing with infantry attacks against the powerful harbor fortifications, Gillmore decided to use his artillery pieces to reduce Charleston. The biggest of these was an enormous Parrott gun (a rifled cannon named for inventor Robert Parrott) that weighed twelve tons and fired two-hundred-pound shot. On August 10, Union engineers began building a platform for this gun, nicknamed the Swamp Angel, in a marsh between James and Morris Islands, just about five miles from the gun's main targets in Charleston. (Thirteen thousand sandbags, all carried by hand over a mile-long causeway, were used to stabilize the gun platform.) According to the

The Swamp Angel during its brief but effective lifetime.

existing rules of warfare, Charleston was a legitimate target—being an armed, fortified camp, with several munitions plants and wharves lined with a fleet of blockade runners. Nevertheless, Gillmore limited his initial bombardment to Forts Sumter, Wagner, and Gregg, against which six days of sustained pounding had little practical effect. On the fifth day of the bombardment, upon learning that the Swamp Angel had finally been made ready, Gillmore sent a letter to Confederate commander P. G. T. Beauregard demanding the immediate evacuation of Morris Island and Fort Sumter; otherwise, Charleston would be fired upon. The message reached Beauregard's headquarters (via Fort Wagner) about 10:45 P.M.; the general was gone, but the officer in charge, noting that Gillmore's message was unsigned, returned it for verification. Meanwhile, at 1:30 A.M. on August 22,

the Swamp Angel fired the first of sixteen rounds (most containing incendiaries) into the center of Charleston, starting fires and causing pandemonium. At 9:00 A.M., Gillmore's note, now signed, again reached Beauregard's headquarters. The enraged Confederate's reply accused Gillmore of barbarity. Gillmore's response appears below. After permitting the Confederates a day to evacuate noncombatants, Gillmore resumed firing on the evening of August 23. However, after launching its thirty-sixth round at Charleston, the breech of the Swamp Angel exploded, throwing the gun off its mount and injuring four crewmen. During its brief lifetime, the Swamp Angel accomplished two artillery firsts: Never before had an artillery piece been fired using only a compass reading (taken during the day), and never before had shells been thrown such a great distance.

Brig. Gen. Quincy A. Gillmore

Headquarters,
Department of the South,
In the Field, Morris Island, S.C.,
August 22, 1863—9 P.M.

Sir: The inadvertent omission of my signature doubtless affords ground for special pleading, but it is not the argument of a commander solicitous only for the safety of sleeping women and children and unarmed men....[I will] call your attention to the well-established principle, that the commander of a place attacked, but not invested..., has no right to expect any notice of an intended bombardment....The city of Charleston has had...forty days' notice of her danger. During that time my attack upon her defenses has steadily progressed.... If, under the circumstances, the life of a single noncombatant is exposed to peril by the bombardment of the city, the responsibility rests with those who have first failed to remove the noncombatants, or secure the safety of the city after having held control of all its approaches for a period of nearly two years and a half in the presence of a threatening force, and who afterward refused to accept the terms upon which the bombardment might have been postponed. From various sources, official and otherwise, I am led to believe that most of the women and children of Charleston were long since removed from the city, but, upon your assurance that the city is still "full of them," I shall suspend the bombardment until 11 P.M. tomorrow, thus giving you two days from the time you acknowledge to have received my communication of the 21st instant.

> Very respectfully,
> your obedient servant,
> Q. A. Gillmore,
> Brigadier-General, Commanding

WED 26 AUG. *Although eight months had passed since the issuance of the Emancipation Proclamation, emancipation remained a subject of often heated discussion in the North, where much opposition to Lincoln's action persisted. In the following letter to James C. Conkling of Springfield, Illinois, the president defended his proclamation on military grounds, arguing that the freeing of slaves in Rebel-held territory would deprive the Confederacy of an important element of its labor force and also give the slaves a motive—the promise of freedom—to sacrifice their lives for the Union.*

YOU DISLIKE THE EMANCIPATION proclamation; and perhaps would have it retracted. You say it is unconstitutional. I think differently. I think the

Constitution invests its Commander-in-Chief with the law of war in time of war. The most that can be said—if so much—is that slaves are property. Is there—has there ever been—any question that by the law of war, property, both of enemies and friends, may be taken when needed? And is it not needed whenever taking it, helps us, or hurts the enemy? Armies the world over, destroy enemies' property when they cannot use it; and even destroy their own to keep it from the enemy. Civilized belligerents do all in their power to help themselves, or hurt the enemy, except a few things regarded as barbarous or cruel. Among the exceptions are the massacre of vanquished foes, and noncombatants, male and female.

But the proclamation, as law, either is valid or is not valid. If it is not valid, it needs no retraction. If it is valid, it cannot be retracted, any more than the dead can be brought to life. Some of you profess to think its retraction would operate favorably for the Union. Why better *after* the retraction than *before* the issue? There was more than a year and a half of trial to suppress the rebellion before the proclamation [was] issued, the last one hundred days of which passed under an explicit notice that it was coming, unless averted by those in revolt, returning to their allegiance. The war has certainly progressed as favorably for us, since the issue of proclamation as before. I know, as fully as one can know the opinion of others, that some of the commanders of our armies in the field, who have given us our most important successes, believe the emancipation policy and the use of colored troops constitute the heaviest blow yet dealt to the rebellion, and that at least one of those important successes could not have been achieved when it was but for the aid of black soldiers. Among the commanders holding these views are some who have never had any affinity with what is called abolitionism, or with Republican party politics, but who hold them purely as military opinions. I submit these opinions as being entitled to some weight against the objections often urged that emancipation and arming the blacks are unwise as military measures, and were not adopted as such in good faith. You say you will not fight to free negros. Some of them seem willing to fight for you; but, no matter. Fight you, then, exclusively to save the Union. I issued the proclamation on purpose to aid you in saving the Union. Whenever you shall have conquered all resistance to the Union, if I shall urge you to continue fighting, it will be an apt time, then, for you to declare you will not fight to free negroes.

I thought that in your struggle for the Union, to whatever extent that negroes should cease helping the enemy, to that extent it weakened the enemy in his resistance to you. Do you think differently? I thought that whatever negroes can be got to do as soldiers, leaves just so much less for white soldiers to do in saving the Union. Does it appear otherwise to you? But negroes, like other people, act upon motives. Why should they do anything for us, if we will do nothing for them? If they stake their lives for us, they must be promoted by the strongest motive—even the promise of freedom. And the promise being made, must be kept.

SAT 29 AUG. *With military commanders pressing the government to find fresh troops, the Confederate Congress in Richmond began to close loopholes in the national draft law, while on the local level, militia agents scoured the countryside for more men. With all this in mind, the state legislature in Alabama passed a resolution this day advocating a number of policy revisions that might be undertaken on the national level, including the radical and potentially explosive step of arming impressed slaves for combat. Ultimately, the Confederate Congress would approve such a measure—but not until March 1865, when the war's end was already in sight.*

FIRST. *BE IT RESOLVED,* THAT in the opinion of this General Assembly public sentiment and the exigencies of the country require that all able-bodied men in the service of the Confederate States as clerks, or employed in any other capacity in any of the quartermaster or commissary departments of the Government, should be put in active military service without delay, and that their places be filled with soldiers or citizens who are unfit for active military service....

FIFTH. Be it further resolved, that in view of the fact that the Government of the United States has determined to put in the field negro soldiers, and are enlisting and drafting the slaves of the people of the South, this General Assembly submits for the consideration of Congress the propriety and policy of using in some effective way a certain percentage of the male slave population of the Confederate States, and to perform such services as Congress may by law direct.

SIXTH. Be it further resolved, that the Governor transmit a copy of these resolutions to the President of the Confederate States, the Secretary of War, and a copy to each of our Senators and Representatives from this State in the Confederate Congress.

MON 31 AUG. *The destitute former slaves who streamed into Washington as the war progressed strained the resources of the Northern capital. To help support these indigent refugees, black employees of the military working in the District of Columbia and Alexandria, Virginia, were taxed five dollars a month. The free blacks were understandably outraged that the burden should fall on their wages alone. The following letter of protest to Secretary of War Edwin M. Stanton was signed "Colord labours of Alexandria va Commissary Dept."*

DEAR SIR, WE A POTION OF THE free people of Alexandria Virginia, that has been employed in Lieut Co Bell Commissary in this place ever since the commencement of the war, and has laboured hard though all wheathers, night and day, sundies included, and we hope that you will pardon us for these liberties in writing to your honour for the porpose of asking you to add a little more to our wages as, L, Co, George Bell says it is with you to raise our wages or not, when we first went to the commissary to work, our pay was $30, per month, after one or

Former slaves employed as laborers by the U.S. Army Quartermaster in Alexandria, Virginia.

two months they was curtailed to $25 per month with which we made out to get along with, since the first of December 1862 we has been curtailed to $20 per month so said to be for the benefit of the contrabands, and the men that is in the employment is provided for by the government, houses to live in, provission for them selves and families, and even wood a coal to cook with; and has all the attention, and we the free men has to pay a tax of $5 per month for they benefit, and have to support our selves and families, and provide for them in every respect with the exceptions of our own rations, and we have tried to get along without saying any thing, but sir every thing is so high that you know your self sir that our $20 will not go any whare, it is true that the government, has a great expence, and

it is nomore then wright, that the contrabands employed in the government service should be curtailed in wages for the support of they fellow men, but we free people I dont think sir has any rite to pay a tax for the benefit of the contrabands any more then white labours of our class, which we have on our works, which they receive they 25 dollars and Co Bell has some favourite men whom he pays 25 dollars to and others has to get along the best they can, and undergo deprivation, so we embraced this opportunity of laying the case before you and if you thinks [it] right, sir, then we made our selves satisfied, but we believe that you will do all for us you can in the case, as we believe sir that you is a gentlemen that works on the squar.

★ ★ ★ ★

SEPTEMBER
1863

TUE 1 SEP. *As the third harvest season of the war approached, farmers' wives who had been left alone found their heavy workloads eased somewhat (at least in the North) by the labor-saving machines that had recently come on the market. According to an article in this month's issue of* Merchant's Magazine and Commercial Review, *the situation seemed almost idyllic.*

AT THE PRESENT TIME SO perfect is machinery that men seem to be of less necessity. Of all the labors of the field, mowing was formerly deemed to be the most arduous, and the strongest men were required for it. We have seen, within the past few weeks, a stout matron whose sons are in the army, with her team cutting hay at seventy-five cents per acre, and she cut seven acres with ease in a day, riding leisurely upon her cutter. This circumstance is indicative of the great revolution which machinery is making in production. War occupations, even on a most gigantic scale, do not seem to check the supply of food. That food is not produced, however, in much greater ratio per acre, while its value [is less] compared with what the farmer is required to purchase— necessary groceries and clothing require a far greater number of bushels of grain than formerly, and interchange is not readily effected.

SAT 5 SEP. *In the following letter to his friend Nathaniel Bloom, Walt Whitman described his work in a Washington hospital and the joy he found in being needed.*

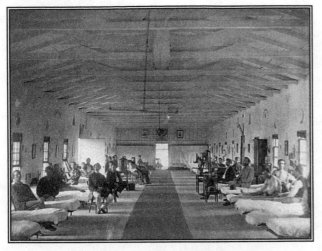

Ward K of Armory Square Hospital in Washington.

WHAT A DIFFERENCE IT IS WITH me here—I tell you, Nat, my evenings are frequently spent in scenes that make a terrible difference—for I am still a hospital visitor, there has not passed a day for months (or at least not more than two) that I have not been among the sick & wounded, either in hospitals or down in camp—occasionally here I spend the evenings in hospital—the experience is a profound one, beyond all else, & touches me personally, egotistically, in unprecedented ways—I mean the way often the amputated, sick, sometimes dying soldiers cling & cleave to me as it were as a man overboard to a plank, & the perfect content they have if I will remain with them, sit on the side of the cot awhile, some youngsters often, & caress them &c.—It is delicious to be the object of so much love & reliance, & to do them such good, soothe & pacify torments of wounds &c—You will doubtless see in what I have said the reason I continue so long in this kind of life—as I am entirely on my own hook too.

Life goes however quite well with me here—I work a few hours a day at copying &c, occasionally write a newspaper letter, & make enough money to pay my expenses—I have a little room, & live a sort of German or Parisian student life—always get my breakfast in my room (have a little spirit lamp) & rub on free & happy enough, untrammeled by business, for I make what little employment I have suit my moods—walk quite a good deal, & in this weather the rich & splendid environs of Washington are an unfailing fountain to me—go down the river, or off into Virginia once in a while—All around us here are forts, by the score—great ambulance & teamsters' camps &c—these I go to—some have little hospitals, I visit, &c &c—

THU 17 SEP. THE PRELUDE TO CHICKAMAUGA

Women traveling with Civil War regiments generally experienced the same conditions as the men with whom they served. In this excerpt from her diary, Nadine Turchin describes her regiment's grueling march through Tennessee in advance of the battle of Chickamauga. In mid-August, Maj. Gen. William S. Rosecrans had begun moving his Army of the Cumberland from Tullahoma (where, on July 1, he had displaced Braxton Bragg's Army of Tennessee) southeast toward Chattanooga, through which passed much vital Confederate rail traffic and to which Bragg had

Maj. Gen. William S. Rosecrans

retreated. While Rosecrans advanced ever so slowly, Bragg pleaded for reinforcements. With none forthcoming, he again pulled back, allowing the Federals to enter Chattanooga on September 9 unmolested. That same day, however, Jefferson Davis decided to detach James Longstreet's corps from the Army of Northern Virginia and send it by rail to Bragg's army, now in northwestern Georgia. Because Federal control of the Cumberland Gap blocked the most direct route, this movement (accomplished via North Carolina) took about ten days. Meanwhile, Rosecrans continued his deliberate probing and skirmishing.

AT DAWN I WAS AWAKENED IN our camp at the foot of Lookout [Mountain] by artillery fire. Immediately I called an orderly who was sleeping in a military wagon next to my tent, and I sent him to wake up my husband, whose tent was ten steps from mine. The General got

up, had his horse saddled, and left for the outposts. One hour later an order was issued to pack up tents and trunks and load them on the army wagons. My horse [was] saddled and tied to a tree, while I lay on a tree trunk, listening to the intermittent artillery fire mixed with musket fire and waiting for further developments. This went on almost until noon. About that time I noticed some sounds of shooting on the right and on a line much closer than our outposts. Then I grabbed on to several trees and hoisted myself as high as I could to try to get a glimpse of something over the bare plains on the right. As I was striving in vain to spy on the enemy, the order arrived to pass to the left as quickly as possible, for the enemy sharpshooters had infiltrated our lines between the wagon trains and the troops, evidently with the intention of seizing the trains and destroying them. So immediately all the trains of our brigade followed a crossroad on the left side and set up camp two miles away in an old unplowed field....

[The following day, a] strong, cold wind blew through the fields, bringing towards us a distant thunder of continuous cannonade....About six o'clock [in the evening], finally, our brigade started to move....I remained with the train, which moved at about eight o'clock, followed by several hundred army wagons belonging to many divisions. I shall never forget the march that night! It was an appropriate foretaste of the horrors of the two following days [September 19–20]. Just imagine a hilly country covered with thick forest, seemingly belonging to nobody, entirely sheltered from all damage except fire, nevertheless carefully enclosed by hedges, all six feet high, between which a narrow strip was left for the road. Now, on that night the hedges were on fire, seven to eight miles in length. And as if that was not enough…on both sides of the road the woods were on fire too, the strip of fire being twice as wide as the road. The smoke, churned and chased by the wind, spread in thick clouds all around; sparks were whirling in billows and falling on everything. And behind us was a munitions train of thirty or forty wagons. Our march lasted all night. One had to stop every so often and wait for half an hour before moving some hundred-odd steps and stop again. It must have been about eight o'clock in the morning, when exhausted by fatigue, eyes burning from smoke, I reached the troop camp and rejoined my husband. Worn out, we lay down each on his side on the clay in the backyard of a pitiful village shack perched on a hill at the foot of which our trains were stationed. Then the General was notified that he had to take his brigade to the left of the line, where strong cannon fire had just started. He left, and I did not see him during the two days of fighting.

Boxcars at a Union depot in Chattanooga.

SAT
19
SEP.
CHICKAMAUGA

Having already captured the strategically vital rail hub at Chattanooga, Union Maj. Gen. William S. Rosecrans cautiously moved his Army of the Cumberland forward in pursuit of Gen. Braxton Bragg's apparently retreating Army of Tennessee. However, with the first of Longstreet's troops arriving on the morning of September 18 and more expected soon, Bragg prepared instead to engage the enemy. The resulting battle took place about twelve miles from Chattanooga along a creek known as the Chickamauga, which in the native Cherokee language (as has been noted often) means "river of blood." The fighting began when Maj. Gen. George H. Thomas sent part of his corps forward to investigate the Confederate disposition, and the detachment encountered heavy opposition from the dismounted cavalry of Maj. Gen. Nathan Bedford Forrest. Other units then joined in until both armies were engaged along a ragged three-mile front. That night, Rosecrans tightened his line and built breastworks while Longstreet himself arrived from the East with more of his troops. On September 20, a powerful Confederate offensive gained little until Longstreet found a gap in the Federal center (caused by a mixup of orders). Hitting that gap, the Rebels cut the Union line and caused widespread flight. Only Thomas's corps held its ground, forming a new line on Snodgrass Hill. Despite the onslaught,

Thomas blocked Confederate pursuit of the disorganized Federals until nightfall, when he withdrew in an orderly fashion to Chattanooga. Overall, the two days of vicious fighting had produced some of the heaviest casualty totals of the war: losses of 16,170 for the Union, compared to 18,454 for the Confederacy. But the South had won an important victory, which might have been even more substantial were it not for the stoutness of Major General Thomas, thereafter known as the Rock of Chickamauga. After so many devastating losses, Chickamauga gave new hope to the Confederacy, as this October 6 editorial from the Richmond Enquirer *illustrates.*

Maj. Gen. George H. Thomas

SINCE THE DAY OF CHICKAMAUGA the face of the country grows brighter and its pulse beats more gaily. The State of Georgia, especially, as we see by her newspapers, is in high spirits, and in a good wholesome rage at the same time. Relieved and delighted as the Georgians are, that the Yankee hosts, as they came pouring through the Northern gateway of that noble State, were so fiercely met and driven back, they seem to feel that now is the moment for Georgia to rouse herself and help Bragg to finish his glorious work. They want to make the Yankees pay dear for their meditated ravage of the fair plains of the "Empire State," and are pouring in both men and supplies to make sure that Rosecrans shall be crushed in Chattanooga.

It is unnecessary, says the Savannah "Republican," to dwell on recent events in Northern Georgia. There is something so brilliant and grand in the recent achievement of our arms in that quarter that the most dispirited among us hold up their hands and shout for joy. The effect has been electric throughout the Confederacy. All eyes are bright, all hearts beat high, all arms seem nerved by the glorious result.

Gen. Braxton Bragg

An army and leader never before beaten, and in the very seventh heaven of their confidence, have been made to bite the dust or ingloriously fly for safety. One more blow, and they will both be prostrate at our feet. If appearances are not deceptive, that will be given at an early day, and then on for the Ohio! will be the word. If necessary for the complete demolition of the Yankee invaders, every man in Georgia capable of bearing arms should be summoned forthwith to the front.

In the midst of the general cheerfulness, we observe, also, that people are in better humor with the government. We hear no more complaints about the President clinging so obstinately to his Generals. Bragg was one of those pets, it was said, and now we are all much obliged to the President that he held on to Bragg until he presented us with a Chickamauga.

Lt. Ambrose Bierce

Noted literary misanthrope Ambrose Bierce enlisted on April 19, 1861, just a week after the war began, as a private in the Ninth Indiana Volunteers. He was only eighteen at the time, but he was often commended for his coolness under fire. Bierce fought at Shiloh and Murfreesboro before Chickamauga, and afterward served with Sherman in Georgia, where he was hit in the head at Kennesaw Mountain by a sharpshooter's bullet. Following a lengthy stay in the hospital and a convalescence at home, Bierce, now a first lieutenant, returned to his regiment and fought under Maj. Gen. John M. Schofield at Franklin and Nashville. What follows is Bierce's typically trenchant account of his experi-ences at Chickamauga. The Garfield to whom he refers is, of course, James A. Garfield, the twentieth president. The rebel yell was a prolonged, high-pitched holler uttered by Confederate soldiers during the war. Part hunting shout, part hog call, it was a well-known expression of both fear and bravado whose chill, veterans later said, could not be reproduced outside the battlefield.

I WAS AN OFFICER OF THE STAFF of a Federal brigade. Chickamauga was not my first battle by many, for although hardly more than a boy in years, I had served at the front from the beginning of the trouble, and had seen enough of war to give me a fair understanding of it. We knew well enough that there was to be a fight: the fact that we did not want one would have told us that, for Bragg always retired when we wanted to fight and fought when we most desired peace. We had maneuvered him out of Chatta-nooga, but had not maneuvered our entire

These Union soldiers from Kansas—in typical, if not regulation, dress—fought at Chickamauga.

army into it, and he fell back so sullenly that those of us who followed, keeping him actually in sight, were a good deal more concerned about effecting a junction with the rest of our army than to push the pursuit. By the time that Rosecrans had got his three scattered corps together we were a long way from Chattanooga, with our line of communication with it so exposed that Bragg turned to seize it. Chickamauga was a fight for possession of a road....

The day was not very far advanced when we were attacked furiously all along the line, beginning at the left. When repulsed, the enemy came again and again—his persistence was dispiriting. He seemed to be using against us the

law of probabilities: for so many efforts one would eventually succeed.

One did, and it was my luck to see it win. I had been sent by my chief, General Hazen, to order up some artillery ammunition and rode away to the right and rear in search of it. Finding an ordnance train I obtained from the officer in charge a few wagons loaded with what I wanted, but he seemed in doubt as to our occupancy of the region across which I proposed to guide them. Although assured that I had just traversed it, and that it lay immediately behind Wood's division, he insisted on riding to the top of the ridge behind which his train lay and overlooking the ground. We did so, when to my astonishment I saw the entire country in front swarming with Confederates; the very earth seemed to be moving toward us! They came on in thousands, and so rapidly that we had barely time to turn tail and gallop down the hill and away, leaving them in possession of the train, many of the wagons being upset by frantic efforts to put them about. By what miracle that officer had sensed the situation I did not learn, for we parted company then and there and I never again saw him.

By a misunderstanding Wood's division had been withdrawn from our line of battle just as the enemy was making an assault. Through the gap of a half a mile the Confederates charged without opposition, cutting our army clean in two. The right divisions were broken up and with General Rosecrans in their midst fled how they could across the country, eventually bringing up in Chattanooga, whence Rosecrans telegraphed to Washington the destruction of the rest of his army. The rest of his army was standing its ground.

A good deal of nonsense used to be talked about the heroism of General Garfield, who, caught in the rout of the right, nevertheless went back and joined the undefeated left under General Thomas. There was no great heroism in it; that is what every man should have done, including the commander of the army. We could hear Thomas's guns going— those of us who had ears for them—and all that was needful was to make a sufficiently wide detour and then move toward the sound. I did so myself, and have never felt that it ought to make me President....

Unable to find my brigade, I reported to General Thomas, who directed me to remain with him. He had assumed command of all the forces still intact and was pretty closely beset. The battle was fierce and continuous, the enemy extending his lines farther and farther around our right, toward our line of retreat. We could not meet the extension otherwise than by "refusing" our right flank and letting him enclose us; which but for gallant Gordon Granger he would inevitably have done.

This was the way of it. Looking across the fields in our rear (rather longingly) I had the happy distinction of a discoverer. What I saw was the shimmer of sunlight on metal; lines of troops were coming in behind us! The distance was too great, the atmosphere too hazy to distinguish the color of their uniform, even with a glass. Reporting my momentous "find" I was directed by the general to go and see who they were. Galloping toward them until near enough to see that they were of our kidney I hastened back with the glad tidings and was sent again, to guide them to the general's position.

It was General Granger with two strong brigades of the reserve, moving soldier-like toward the sound of heavy firing. Meeting him and his staff I directed him to Thomas, and unable to think of anything better to do decided to go visiting. I knew I had a brother in that gang—an officer of an Ohio battery. I soon found him near the head of a column, and as we moved forward we had a comfortable chat amongst such of the enemy's bullets as had inconsiderately been fired too high. The incident was a trifle marred by one of them unhorsing another officer of the battery, whom we propped against a tree and left. A few moments later Granger's force was put in on the right and the fighting was terrific!

By accident I now found Hazen's brigade—or what remained of it—which had made a half-mile march to add itself to the unrouted at the memorable Snodgrass Hill. Hazen's first remark to me was an inquiry about that artillery ammunition that he had sent me for.

It was needed badly enough, as were other kinds: for the last hour or two of that interminable day Granger's were the only men that had enough ammunition to make a five minutes' fight. Had the Confederates made one more general attack we should have had to meet them with the bayonet alone. I don't know why they did not; probably they were short of ammunition. I know, though, that while the sun was taking its own time to set we lived through the agony of at least one death each, waiting for them to come on.

At last it grew too dark to fight. Then away to our left and rear some of Bragg's people set up "the rebel yell." It was taken up successively and passed round to our front, along our right and in behind us again, until it seemed almost to have got to the point whence it started. It was the ugliest sound that any mortal ever heard— even a mortal exhausted and unnerved by two days of hard fighting, without sleep, without rest, without food and without hope. There was, however, a space somewhere at the back of us across which that horrible yell did not prolong itself; and through that we finally retired in profound silence and dejection, unmolested.

The rout cost Rosecrans his command. After his relief on October 17, however, there was speculation that, because his lack of favor in Washington was well known, he had been replaced for political, not military, reasons. This November 3 editorial from the New York Herald, *for example, made the case that the blame for Chickamauga lay more properly with Gen.-in-Chief Henry W. Halleck.*

One of the many Federal camps in Chattanooga during the subsequent siege.

GEN. ROSECRANS WAS REMOVED after the battle of Chickamauga, not because of the loss of that battle, but because the removal of a general immediately after the loss of a battle seems to put the government in the very popular attitude of requiring from all its generals the great requisite of success. His crime was committed before that battle was fought. Our readers must remember very well the weary and difficult march made by the Army of the Cumberland to the Tennessee river. Before that river was reached, and while the army toiled on in the mountain roads, Gen. Rosecrans was ordered by Gen. Halleck, in a telegram from Washington, to join his column to that of Gen. Burnside. Gen. Burnside's operations were on another line, and obedience to the order would have made it necessary for the Army of the Cumberland to retrace its steps for a hundred miles, lose all that it had gained by its advance, and at least three weeks time. Representations to that effect were made by Gen. Rosecrans, coupled with a proposition that the two columns should unite at a given point in front at some specified time. With that want of courtesy on General Halleck's part which characterizes all his intercourse with the men in our armies, no notice was taken of General Rosecrans' proposition and no reply made to it. Rosecrans, a general officer, deemed worthy to command eighty thousand men, had presumed to have an opinion on a purely military question, and as [such] had offended the power that presides over the management of our armies. After that there could be no response; but the determination was then made that he should be removed at the first good opportunity, and that came with the lost battle.

MON 28 SEP. *When the U.S. Congress first contemplated raising African-American troops, it was believed by most Northerners—including the troops themselves—that black soldiers would receive the same pay as whites in the army. The subsequent decision to pay black troops three dollars less per month precipitated a deluge of protests from black soldiers and their supporters. One such remonstrance was this eloquent letter written by James Henry Gooding of the Fifty-fourth Massachusetts Volunteer Infantry, then and now the most famous of the Union army's African-American regiments.*

YOUR EXCELLENCY, ABRAHAM Lincoln: Your Excellency will pardon the presumption of an humble individual like myself, in addressing you, but the earnest Solicitation of my Comrades in Arms beside the genuine interest felt by myself in the matter is my excuse, for placing before the Executive head of the Nation our Common Grievance....

Now the main question is, Are we *Soldiers*, or are we *Labourers?* We are fully armed, and equipped, have done all the various Duties pertaining to a Soldier's life, have conducted ourselves to the complete satisfaction of General Officers, who were, if any[thing], prejudiced *against* us, but who now accord us all the encouragement and honour due us; have shared the perils and Labour of Reducing the first stronghold that flaunted a Traitor Flag; and more, Mr. President. Today the

The Fourth U.S. Colored Infantry at Fort Lincoln in the District of Columbia.

Anglo-Saxon Mother, Wife, or Sister are not alone in tears for departed Sons, Husbands and Brothers. The patient, trusting Descendants of Afric's Clime have dyed the ground with blood, in defense of the Union, and Democracy....

Now your Excellency, we have done a Soldier's Duty. Why Can't we have a Soldier's pay? You caution the Rebel Chieftain, that the United States knows no distinction in her Soldiers. She insists on having all her Soldiers of whatever creed or Color, to be treated according to the usages of War. Now if the United States exacts uniformity of treatment of her Soldiers from the Insurgents, would it not be well and consistent to set the example herself by paying all her *Soldiers* alike?...

We appeal to you, Sir, as the Executive of the Nation, to have us justly Dealt with. The Regt. do pray that they be assured their service will be fairly appreciated by paying them as American *Soldiers,* not as menial hirelings. Black men, you may well know, are poor; three dollars per month for a year will supply their needy Wives and little ones with fuel. If you, as Chief Magistrate of the Nation, will assure us of our whole pay, we are content. Our Patriotism, our enthusiasm will have a new impetus, to exert our energy more and more to aid our Country. Not that our hearts have ever flagged in Devotion, spite the evident apathy displayed in our behalf, but We feel as though our Country spurned us, now that we are sworn to serve her. Please give this a moment's attention.

James Henry Gooding

WED 30 SEP. *As Election Day neared, political campaigns in the North began to heat up. In Pennsylvania, where Republicans were pushing to reelect Gov. Andrew Curtin, the following editorial appeared in the* Franklin Repository, *urging the women of Franklin County to persuade their men to vote for Curtin. Although the women themselves could not vote, they nevertheless wielded political power, as this excerpt points out.*

Andrew Curtin

The loyal women in every community have exerted a vast influence in sustaining the war and the government. Let them remember that in no way can they better uphold their country at this hour than by influencing votes for Curtin and against Woodward. They can influence fathers, husbands, and sons. To the young women we would say, that if after trying all their persuasive eloquence on their suitors they prove to be incorrigible Copperheads, give them the mitten all at once. Don't waste a smile on a fellow who refuses either by bullet or ballot to help put down the rebellion. Make these bucks face the Union music square, or go under! The sick and wounded soldiers everywhere bless our noble women. They will bestow upon them additional blessings if they aid in electing the soldier's truest friend, Andrew G. Curtin.

★ ★ ★ ★

OCTOBER 1863

Elsewhere in the North, more than two years of war meant belt tightening and some deprivation. However, in New York City, enriched by war profits, the elite of society sought pleasure and extravagance, as this New York Herald *correspondent lamented.*

ALL OUR THEATRES ARE OPEN except Mrs. John Wood's, which will open on Thursday, and they are all crowded nightly. The kind of entertainment given seems to be of little account. Provided the prices are high and the place fashionable nothing more is required. All the hotels are as crowded as the theatres; and it is noticeable that the most costly accommodations, in both hotels and theatres, are the first and most eagerly taken. Our merchants report the same phenomenon in their stores: the richest silks, laces and jewelry are the soonest sold. At least five hundred new turnouts may be seen any fine afternoon in the Park; and neither Rotten Row, London, nor the Bois de Boulogne, Paris, can show a more splendid sight. Before the golden days of the Indian summer are over these five hundred new equipages will be increased to a thousand. Not to keep a carriage, not to wear diamonds, not to be attired in a robe which cost a small fortune, is now equivalent to being a nobody. This war has entirely changed the American character. The lavish profusion in which the old Southern cotton aristocracy used to indulge is completely eclipsed by the dash, parade and magnificence of the new Northern shoddy aristocracy of this period. Ideas of cheapness and economy are thrown to the winds. The individual who makes the most money—no matter

A Currier & Ives lithograph of lower Broadway in New York City.

how—and spends the most money—no matter for what—is considered the greatest man. To be extravagant is to be fashionable. These facts sufficiently account for the immense and brilliant audiences at the opera and the theatres; and until the final crash comes such audiences will undoubtedly continue.

SAT 17 OCT. GRANT PROMOTED

After its rout at Chickamauga, Maj. Gen. William S. Rosecrans's Army of the Cumberland retreated to Chattanooga, where Confederate Gen. Braxton Bragg's Army of Tennessee laid siege to the town, establishing strategic positions atop Lookout Mountain and Missionary Ridge. Three weeks later, on October 16, President Lincoln assigned Maj.

Gen. Ulysses S. Grant to command the newly created Military Division of the Mississippi, which included the Armies of the Ohio and the Tennessee in addition to Rosecrans's Army of the Cumberland. When Grant met with Secretary of War Edwin M. Stanton this day at Indianapolis, he received two sets of orders: One left Rosecrans in command at Chattanooga; the other relieved him. Grant chose the latter set, replacing Rosecrans with Maj. Gen. George H. Thomas. Years later, in his memoirs, Grant recalled his actions that day.

I IMMEDIATELY WROTE AN order assuming command of the Military Division of the Mississippi, and telegraphed it to General Rosecrans. I then telegraphed to him the order from Washington assigning Thomas to the command of the Army of the Cumberland; and to Thomas that he must hold Chattanooga at all hazards, informing him at the same time that I would be at the front as soon as possible. A prompt reply was received from Thomas, saying, "We will hold the town till we starve." I appreciated the force of this dispatch later when I witnessed the condition of affairs which prompted it. It looked, indeed, as if but two courses were open: one to starve, the other to surrender or be captured.

FRI 23 OCT. THE SIEGE OF CHATTANOOGA

Despite bad roads and a recent injury (he had been on crutches since September 4, when his horse fell on him in New Orleans), Grant traveled immediately to Chattanooga, arriving this day and taking personal charge of the situation. His top priorities were the opening of a supply line into the besieged city (called the Cracker Line), which he achieved in less than a week, and the inauguration of regular artillery bombardments of the Rebel positions, which are recalled here by Confederate Capt. George Todd of the First Texas Infantry.

WE STAID THERE BESIEGING THE town two months. The federals erected a battery across the river on Moccasin Point, made by a bend in the Tennessee River, and every night, when they knew we had left the trenches and were asleep in our dog tents exposed to their fire, opened on some portion of our lines which formed a crescent around the city. In this way they killed and crippled some confederates before they could get under cover of the works. We became so accustomed to this nightly serenade that we only opened one ear to see what part of the line was selected, and if not near us went to sleep again.

★ ★ ★ ★

A view of Chattanooga during the siege with Lookout Mountain in the background.

NOVEMBER 1863

MON 9 NOV. *In some pockets of the North, such as Pennsylvania's Lehigh Valley, resistance to the war, and especially the draft, continued to be strong. In this letter to President Lincoln, a "Union man" complained about the inability of local authories to control the many disloyal activities of the region's coal miners.*

SINCE THE COMMENCEMENT OF the draft a large majority of the coal operatives have been law-defying, opposing the National Government in every possible way, and making unsafe the lives and property of the Union men.

They are so numerous that they have the whole community in terror of them. They dictate the prices for their work, and if their employers don't accede they destroy and burn coal breakers, houses, and prevent those disposed from working. They resist the draft, and are organized into societies for this purpose. The life of no Union man is secure among them, and the murder of such a citizen is almost a nightly occurrence.

The civil authorities make no effort to arrest this state of things. They say they are powerless and that to attempt the arrest and punishment of these traitors and miscreants, without having the ability to do it successfully and effectually, would only add fuel to the flames. Besides all this our "civil authorities" here seem to have too much sympathy for these very men, and they know it and are not slow to take advantage of it. They have closed up several large collieries and threaten that all must suspend work until the National Government suspends the operations of the draft against them.

These men are mostly Irish and call themselves "Buckshots."

SUN 15 NOV. *The U.S. Christian Commission offered comfort and care to the soldiers of the Union's armies— along with a healthy dose of religion, as this letter from a Christian Commission field-worker made plain.*

IT IS NOT LESS A DUTY THAN also proper to inform the public of the direction their contributions to the Christian Commission have taken. Being placed in a position from which he could see its operations on an extended scale, the undersigned can, with heartfelt confidence, assert that the intentions of the contributors have been fully carried out.

He has seen regiments and brigades, after a wearisome march, scarcely arrived at camp, when the delegate of the Christian Commission appeared, with greetings from his benevolent heart, and stores of good things in his haversack. Not a more busy man could stand beside him within the encircled camp-ground. From soldier to soldier, from tent to tent, he made his rounds, presenting to one a book, another a tract or pamphlet. Some boys needed writing materials; others wanted note-paper and envelopes. All were glad to receive reading-matter in the various forms at his command, and all were presented, according to their various wants, with what he had on hand. Comforts for the outer man were properly distributed, and due attention to the spiritual interests of the soldiers were promptly paid. The Holy Scriptures were read; a hymn once hallowed by the choral voices of parents, sisters, friends, was sung; a prayer was offered from the altar

Volunteers manning a U.S. Christian Commission field tent.

of the camp-ground to the Lord of Hosts on high; an exhortation given to be as faithful soldiers to the Captain of our salvation as they were sworn to be to their superiors in command. The emotions of many a sunburnt soldier, deep sunk, buried down in his heart, would ofttimes well forth, and its sluice-gates give way with copious tears of penitence, causing rejoicing among the marshalled hosts of heaven over one more sinner who had repented, and given his heart to God.

A priest gives mass to the Sixty-ninth New York, nicknamed the Fighting Irish.

MON 16 NOV. *During the fall of 1863, the widening gap between stagnant wages and rising prices produced labor unrest in many Northern cities, notably Philadelphia, Boston, and New York. On this day, the* Philadelphia Press, *a Democratic newspaper, published the following article, entitled "The Labor Movement," which linked the current demand for higher wages to the good times experienced by workers before the war (and to which they had become accustomed).*

 IN MANY PARTS OF THE COUNTRY, laboring men and mechanics are demanding higher wages....

The condition of the laboring man is better in America than in any other part of the world....The laboring man with us must have his morning newspaper, a weekly journal for the family, one of the magazines, and a few histories and volumes of reference for his children. He must have his holiday, his evenings for the prayer-meeting or the play. He sees a career in which the sons of other laboring men have become eminent, and so, instead of taking his boy with half-formed bones and sinews to earn his daily bread, he keeps him at school and undergoes privation that his tastes and habits may be gratified. This is the daily bread of the American laborer, and it is proper that he should earn money enough to gain it. Before the war all these things might have been obtained for less money than it is now necessary to pay. The war, which has stimulated business and trade, has reduced the value of money, as all wars invariably do. Taxation, the conscription, perhaps; the difference in values, the increase in the price of many necessary articles of life, consume that portion of the laboring man's income that formerly went towards giving him some of the luxuries of life. Many a laboring man is fortunate if he can live at all.

LINCOLN'S GETTYSBURG ADDRESS

THU
19
NOV.

President Lincoln left Washington on November 18 in a special train bound for Gettysburg, where a major battle-field cemetery was to be dedicated the following day. The main address was delivered by Edward Everett, a much-admired orator; but, out of politeness, the local dignitary in charge of the event also asked Lincoln to say a few words. Everett's speech lasted two hours; Lincoln's, scarcely more than two minutes. Yet over the years, Lincoln's three paragraphs have been recognized as among the great utterances of all time.

FOUR SCORE AND SEVEN YEARS ago our fathers brought forth on this continent a new nation, conceived in liberty and dedicated to the proposition that all men are created equal.

Now we are engaged in a great civil war, testing whether that nation, or any nation so conceived and so dedicated, can long endure. We are met on a great battlefield of that war. We have come to dedicate a portion of that field as a final resting-place for those who here gave their lives that that nation might live. It is altogether fitting and proper that we should do this.

But, in a larger sense, we can not dedicate—we can not consecrate—we can not hallow—this ground. The brave men, living and dead who struggled here, have consecrated it, far above our poor power to add or detract. The world will little note, nor long remember, what we say here, but it can never forget what they did here. It is for us the living, rather, to be dedicated here to the unfinished work

The crowd gathered at the Gettysburg cemetery to hear Edward Everett's address.

which they who fought here have thus far so nobly advanced. It is rather for us to be here dedicated to the great task remaining before us—that from these honored dead we take increased devotion to that cause for which they gave the last full measure of devotion—that we here highly resolve that these dead shall not have died in vain— that this nation, under God, shall have a new birth of freedom—and that government of the people, by the people, for the people shall not perish from the earth.

The immediate reaction to Lincoln's speech was mixed. Many of those present at the dedication, including Lincoln himself, thought the address had fallen somewhat flat. Yet within four days, as this account in the November 23 Ohio State Journal *demonstrates, that opinion had forever changed.*

THE PRESIDENT'S CALM BUT earnest utterances of this brief and beautiful address stirred the deepest fountains of feeling and emotion in the hearts of the vast throng before him, and when he had concluded, scarcely could an untearful eye be seen, while sobs of smothered emotion were heard on every head.

At our side stood a stout, stalwart officer, bearing the insignia of a captain's rank, the empty sleeve of his coat indicating that he had stood where death was reveling, and as the President, speaking of our Gettysburg soldiers, uttered that beautifully touching sentence, so sublime and so pregnant of meaning—"The world will little note nor long remember what we say here, but it can never forget what they did here"—the gallant soldier's feel-

ings burst over all restraint, and burying his face in his handkerchief, he sobbed aloud while his manly frame shook with no unmanly emotion.

In a few moments, with a stern struggle to master his emotions, he lifted his still streaming eyes to Heaven and in low solemn tones exclaimed, "God Almighty, bless Abraham Lincoln!" and to this spontaneous invocation a thousand hearts around him silently responded "Amen."

TUE 24 NOV. LOOKOUT MOUNTAIN

Having ordered Maj. Gen. William Tecumseh Sherman's Army of the Tennessee to join him at Chattanooga, Grant commenced—with an attack on November 23 at Orchard Knob—the offensive that would break the Confederate siege and send Bragg's Rebel troops fleeing into Georgia. On this day, three Union divisions under Joseph Hooker assaulted fog-enshrouded Lookout Mountain. They encountered some strong resistance at Cravens' Farm but by day's end had secured the mountain and forced its defenders back to the main Confederate position along Missionary Ridge. Meanwhile, Sherman, moving his army across the Tennessee River on a bridge of pontoon boats, stormed what he had thought was the north end of Missionary Ridge—only to find that his men had scaled an unimportant hill, separated from the Confederate lines by a wide ravine. Even worse, the mistake had alerted the Confederates to his force's position and intent. In this excerpt from his

After the battle, chewing his customary cigar, Grant inspects the new Union position on Lookout Mountain.

***memoirs, John Kountz, a drummer boy
with the Thirty-seventh Ohio Infantry,
recounted the initial (successful) stages
of Sherman's advance.***

THE NIGHT WAS DARK WITH A
drizzling rain. About midnight all
was ready and the signal given to cross,
Major Hipp's boat leading the fleet, John
Hess and the others of Company E, 37th,
being his companions. The major pushed
well into the river, and, after awhile,
headed straight for the south shore,
and on nearing the point where it was
proposed to land, a picket fire was discovered and our troops headed directly for it.
The men hurried out of the boats and up
the bank, surprising and capturing all of
the Confederate pickets but one. The surprise was so complete that the "Johnnies"
scarcely realized the situation. At this
time a Confederate vidette came up at
full speed, shouting "The Yankees are
coming!" He was promptly dismounted

and compelled to join his comrades just
captured.

Major Hipp recrossed the river followed by the flat boats. On getting back
the darkness made it difficult for him to
find our troops and he shouted for the
second division of the Fifteenth Corps,
when he was immediately answered in
suppressed voices to keep quiet or he
would be arrested. Having no time for
explanation and becoming impatient,
the Major cried out, "Where is General
Sherman?" The answer came promptly
through the darkness from the General
himself, who was not more than 50 feet
away, "What do you want?" The Major
answered, "I want a brigade, the boats
are in waiting." The General at once
asked, "Did you make a landing?" Major
Hipp answered, "Yes, and captured the
pickets." General Sherman, who was on
horseback surrounded by his staff, was
so pleased that he took off his hat and
cheered.

WED 25 NOV. MISSIONARY RIDGE

Grant's plan now called for Sherman's Army of the Tennessee to move against Tunnel Hill on the northern end of Missionary Ridge, while Hooker's three divisions atop Lookout Mountain attacked the southern end of the ridge. Then, once Sherman turned the Confederate right flank, the Army of the Cumberland under Maj. Gen. George H. Thomas would move against the Rebel center. Although seriously weakened by the November 4 transfer of Longstreet's sixteen thousand men to Knoxville, the two remaining Southern corps were dug in well enough to beat back Sherman's morning attack. By three o'clock in the afternoon, Grant, not wanting to delay further, ordered Thomas's corps to cross the open valley, where they would be exposed to concentrated enemy fire, and seize the Confederate breastworks at the foot of Missionary Ridge. With much bloodshed, these rifle pits were taken—at which point Thomas's men found themselves subject to a withering fire from the Rebels above, so they simply kept going. Given the option of retreating across the exposed valley floor or dodging bullets in the rifle pits, a rather disorganized charge up the steep, rocky slope seemed the safest option. Grant was initially incensed (after all, he had ordered the troops to seize but a limited objective), yet he continued to watch in amazement as this frenzied "backward retreat" produced flight among the Confederates. Soon enough, realizing

that a hole had indeed been punched in their center, other Rebel units began to panic and flee, and by evening, Grant had won a major victory that made him the obvious choice for still-higher command. In this account, Union Pvt. Benjamin Smith, attached to the staff of Maj. Gen. Philip H. Sheridan (whose division was part of Thomas's corps), describes the Federals' unconventional capture of Missionary Ridge.

THE TROOPS HAVING RESTED, started to climb the steep sides of the ridge. An aide having been sent to Genl. Granger for further orders, came back with a suggestion that the troops be recalled if it was judged expedient. By this time they were half way up the ridge. Every regiment had lost its organization, and were all massed in a sort of triangle with the point upwards. About every flag of our division was struggling to reach the top first, every man for himself. Now and then a flag would fall, its bearer being shot, but it appeared in an instant held by the next soldier. The General said, "Let them go, they will be over in five minutes," and so it proved. A dozen flags went over the works, the men following. Nothing could stop their rush. The rebels deserted their guns and fled, hundreds of them staying a moment too long were captured.

An old log hut standing just to the left to where our division went over was occupied by Genl. Bragg and his staff. They had barely time to mount and ride away. Some of the rebel guns were turned upon their retreating ranks and shots sent after them. More than fifty guns were captured.

DECEMBER
1863

TUE 8 DEC. LINCOLN'S PROCLAMATION OF AMNESTY AND RECONSTRUCTION

On this date, President Lincoln issued a Proclamation of Amnesty and Recon-struction, in which he outlined his plans for reintegrating the Southern states. Most importantly, he offered pardons to all those who "had participated in the existing rebellion" who would now take an oath of loyalty to the United States. (He made exceptions for high-ranking Confederate military officers, members of the Confederate government, officers who had resigned U.S. comissions to join the Confederate military, and oth-ers.) Furthermore, should one-tenth of the 1860 voters in any seceded state elect a new, loyal state government, Lincoln agreed to recognize that gov-ernment (and thereby readmit the state). At the time, Lincoln's plan was a mod-erate, if somewhat lenient, course between the radical demand that Southerners be excluded from the Reconstruction process and the con-servative desire to resurrect much that had characterized the antebellum period. (Some Democrats even wanted to rescind emancipation so that South-erners might be enticed to cooperate.) In his State of the Union message, read in Congress the following day, the presi-dent emphasized the pragmatic nature of his proposals.

LOOKING NOW TO THE PRESENT and future, and with reference to a resumption of the national authority within the States wherein that authority has been suspended, I have thought fit to issue a proclamation, a copy of which is herewith transmitted. On examination of this proclamation it will appear, as is believed, that nothing is attempted beyond what is amply justified by the Constitution. True, the form of an oath is given, but no man is coerced to take it. The man is only promised a pardon in case he voluntarily takes the oath. The Constitution authorizes the Executive to grant or withhold the pardon at his own absolute discretion; and this includes the power to grant on terms, as is fully established by judicial and other authorities.

It is also proffered that if, in any of the States named, a State government shall be, in the mode prescribed, set up, such government shall be recognized and guarantied by the United States, and that under it the State shall, on the constitutional conditions, be protected against invasion and domestic violence. The constitutional obligation of the United States to guaranty to every State in the Union a republican form of government, and to protect the State, in the cases stated, is explicit and full. But why tender the benefits of this provision only to a State government set up in this particular way? This section of the Constitution contemplates a case wherein the element within a State, favorable to republican government, in the Union, may be too feeble for an opposite and hostile element external to, or even within the State; and such are precisely the cases with which we are now dealing.

An attempt to guaranty and protect a revived State government, constructed in whole, or in preponderating part, from the very element against whose hostility and violence it is to be protected, is simply absurd. There must be a test by which to separate the opposing elements, so as to build only from the sound; and that test is a sufficiently liberal one, which accepts as sound whoever will make a sworn recantation of his former unsoundness.

But if it be proper to require, as a test of admission to the political body, an oath of allegiance to the Constitution of the United States, and to the Union under it, why also to the laws and proclamations in regard to slavery? Those laws and proclamations were enacted and put forth for the purpose of aiding in the suppression of the rebellion. To give them their fullest effect, there had to be a pledge for their maintenance. In my judgment they have aided, and will further aid, the cause for which they were intended. To now abandon them would be not only to relinquish a lever of power, but would also be a cruel and an astounding breach of faith. I may add at this point, that while I remain in my present position I shall not attempt to retract or modify the emancipation proclamation; nor shall I return to slavery any person who is free by the terms of that proclamation, or by any of the acts of Congress. For these and other reasons it is thought best that support of these measures shall be included in the oath, and it is believed the Executive may lawfully claim it in return for pardon and restoration of forfeited rights, which he has clear constitutional power to withhold altogether, or grant upon the terms which he shall deem wisest for the public interest.

**WED
30
DEC.**

Black men who escaped from slavery to join the Union army often left behind loved ones upon whom angry slaveholders were wont to visit some measure of retaliation. Martha Glover, an enslaved woman in Missouri, wrote the following letter to her soldier husband, in which she described some of the hardships she had experienced since his departure.

MY DEAR HUSBAND: I HAVE received your last kind letter a few days ago and was much pleased to hear from you once more. It seems like a long time since you left me. I have had nothing but trouble since you left. You recollect what I told you how they would do after you was gone. they abuse me because you went & say they will not take care of our children & do nothing but quarrel with me all the time and beat me scandalously the day before yesterday—Oh I never thought you would give me so much trouble as I have got to bear now. You ought not to [have] left me in the fix I am in & all these little helpless children to take care of. I was invited to a party tonight but I could not go. I am in too much trouble to want to go to parties. the children talk about you all the time. I wish you could get a furlough & come to see us once more. We want to see you worse than we ever did before. Remember all I told you about how they would do me after you left—for they do worse than they ever did & I do not know what will become of me & my poor little children. Oh I wish you had staid with me & not gone till I could go with you for I do nothing but grieve all the time I about you. Write & tell me when you are coming.

★ ★ ★ ★

Members of a slave family pose in front of their quarters.

JANUARY
1864

TUE 5 JAN. *A year later, a few Northerners were still arguing the merits of the Emancipation Proclamation (the legality of which remained less than certain). Most, however, had moved on to the question of what rights African Americans should have in the postwar society. For example, white Northerners were by no means in agreement as to whether emancipation should lead to political, legal, and social equality for blacks. Curiously, Louisiana, now almost entirely in Union hands, became a proving ground for Reconstruction policies. On this date, a group of more than one thousand free blacks in Louisiana wrote this petition, addressed to both the president and Congress, in which they appealed directly for the right to vote. Twenty-seven of those who signed the petition had actually fought with Andrew Jackson in the 1815 battle of New Orleans. Another two traveled to Washington in March to deliver the petition to Lincoln personally. (As the petition suggests, Nathaniel P. Banks had in December 1862 replaced Benjamin F. Butler as commander of the Federal Department of the Gulf.)*

 THE UNDERSIGNED RESPECTFULLY submit the following:

That they are natives of Louisiana, and citizens of the United States; that they are loyal citizens, sincerely attached to the Country and the Constitution, and ardently desire the maintenance of the national unity, for which they are ready to sacrifice their fortunes and their lives.

That a large portion of them are owners of real estate, and all of them are owners of personal property; that many of them are engaged in the pursuits of commerce and industry, while others are employed as artisans in various trades; that they are all fitted to enjoy the privileges and immunities belonging to the condition of citizens of the United States, and among them may be found many of the descendants of those men whom the illustrious Jackson styled "his fellow citizens" when he called upon them to take up arms to repel the enemies of the country....

Notwithstanding their forefathers served in the army of the United States, in 1814–15, and aided in repelling from the soil of Louisiana the haughty enemy, over-confident of success, yet they and their descendants have ever since, and until the era of the present rebellion, been estranged, and even repulsed— excluded from all franchises, even the smallest....During this period of forty-nine years, they have never ceased to be peaceable citizens, paying their taxes on an assessment of more than fifteen millions of dollars.

At the call of General Banks, they hastened to rally under the banner of Union and Liberty; they have spilled their blood, and are still pouring it out for the maintenance of the Constitution of the United States; in a word, they are soldiers of the Union, and they will defend it so long as their hands have strength to hold a musket....

Your petitioners aver that they have applied in respectful terms to Brig. Gen. George F. Shepley, Military Governor of Louisiana, and to Major Gen. N. P. Banks, commanding the Department of the Gulf, praying to be placed upon the registers as voters, to the end that they might participate in the reorganization of civil government in Louisiana, and that their petition has met with no response from those officers, and it is feared that none will be given; and they therefore appeal to the justice of the Representatives of the nation, and ask that all the citizens of Louisiana of African descent, born free before the rebellion, may be, by proper

Currier & Ives's rendering of the lower Mississippi Delta, now firmly under Union control.

orders, directed to be inscribed on the registers, and admitted to the rights and privileges of electors.

SAT 9 JAN. *Once Congress permitted black soldiers to enlist in the Union army, there arose a corresponding need for officers to command them; but white officers were not forthcoming. Among the reasons for their restraint were racial prejudice and the fear of Southern retaliation. Most knew what had happened to the body of Col. Robert Gould Shaw, the commander of the Fifty-fourth Massachusetts killed at Fort Wagner. (When a Union commander—following the practice of the day regarding senior officers—requested the return of Shaw's body, he learned that Shaw had been stripped and buried in a mass grave. "We have buried him with his niggers," a Confederate officer explained contemptuously.) Nevertheless, some whites did apply. The following advertisement, published in the New England Loyal Publication Society newsletter, even promised free military school to those whites who would agree to command colored troops.*

FREE MILITARY SCHOOL FOR APPLICANTS FOR COMMANDS OF COLORED TROOPS

The Supervisory Committee for Recruiting Colored Regiments, with a view of providing what the country so urgently needs—namely, applicants for the command of colored troops *competent* for that duty—has established a Military School at their Headquarters, in which Infantry Tactics and knowledge of Army Regulations are taught *gratuitously.*

Young Men having a fair common-school education, *and physically sound,* and especially *privates and noncommissioned officers* in the army, who desire to command colored troops, are invited to become students of this School.

Those who already have military knowledge may review it, and be prepared for immediate examination at Washington.

Those who are wholly unacquainted with tactics may remain until they are made proficient in them.

TUE 12 JAN. *In the Union-occupied South, freed blacks often remained as paid laborers on the very plantations that they had once served as slaves. Much appeared the same, yet as Fannie Bisland learned, freedom had somehow changed the way the workers on her husband's southern Louisiana plantation behaved. For example, when she tried to install a new overseer—a man named Grey—her former slaves ran him off the plantation, as this letter from Mrs. Bisland to her mother described.*

YOU WILL PROBABLY HEAR OF the *rebellion* on the place about Mr. Grey's (the overseer) coming there. On Sunday he sent his baggage down ahead of him and towards evening came himself in the buggy. He stopped here for a few moments and I told him I thought he would have a good deal of trouble before he could bring them straight, but never dreaming of the trouble he did have. He says, when he came in sight of the plantation, the bell commenced ringing

This poster was used to recruit white officers to serve with African-American regiments.

furiously, and by the time he crossed the bridge every man, woman and child on the plantation had collected around the overseer's house. Before he quite reached the house, one of the men seized the bridle and told him he should not set foot in that house, that the quarters belonged to them and no d— white man should live there. He tried to speak to them but they shut him up immediately and told him they did not want to hear a word from him. That he should not come on the place unless he could show a written order from Gen. Banks and if Gen. Banks himself said that he was to come there, he should not live down there but must live at the house

with *Mrs. Bisland.* Mrs. Bisland had no right to come there and give orders. &c. &c. They said too much for me to begin to tell you what they didn't say. He says every man woman and child were talking at the same time, one man told him if he went to live in that house they would burn powder and lead round it all night. When he started off, he told them his baggage would have to stay there all night as the mules would not pull it any further, they at first refused to let it stay there but at last consented to let it remain there till morning, under the cane shed.

★ ★ ★ ★

FEBRUARY
1864

MON
1
FEB.
As conditions across the Deep South deteriorated, more and more slaves felt the need (or seized the opportunity) to escape from their plantations. Some, such as Octave Johnson, found their way into the Union army. Johnson—who rose to the rank of corporal in the Fifteenth Regiment, U.S. Colored Troops—took refuge in Camp Parapet, Louisiana, during the fall of 1862, having escaped from slavery a year earlier. Subsequently, he told his story to the American Freedmen's Inquiry Commission in New Orleans.

I WAS BORN IN NEW ORLEANS; I am 23 years of age; I was raised by Arthur Thiboux of New Orleans; I am by trade a cooper; I was treated pretty well at home; in 1855 master sold my mother, and in 1861 he sold me to S. Contrell of St. James Parish for $2,400; here I worked by task at my trade; one morning the bell was rung for us to go to work so early that I could not see, and I lay still, because I was working by task; for this the overseer was going to have me whipped, and I ran away to the woods, where I remained for a year and a half; I had to steal my food; took turkeys, chickens and pigs; before I left our number had increased to thirty, of whom ten were women; we were four miles in the rear of the plantation house; sometimes we would rope beef cattle and drag them out to our hiding place; we obtained matches from our friends on the plantation; we slept on logs and burned cypress leaves to make a smoke and keep away mosquitoes; Eugene Jardeau, master of hounds, hunted us for three months; often those at work would betray those in the swamp, for fear of being implicated in their escape; we furnished meat to our fellow-servants in the field, who would return corn meal; one day twenty hounds came after me; I called the party to my assistance and we killed eight of the bloodhounds; then we all jumped into Bayou Faupron; the dogs followed us and the alligators caught six of them; "the alligators preferred dog flesh to personal flesh;" we escaped and came to Camp Parapet, where I was first employed in the Commissary's office, then as a servant to Col. Hanks; then I joined his regiment.

WED
17
FEB.
CSS HUNLEY

Among the technological innovations of the war was the CSS H. L. Hunley, an attack submarine sent into action for the first and last time this day off Charleston Harbor. Actually, the Hunley *looked more like an enormous metal cigar than a submarine. It consisted of an elongated steel tube with a torpedo (or mine) attached to a long spar on its prow. It operated just below the surface—but not very well: In harbor trials, it had killed no fewer than thirty-three crewmen. During its attack on the USS* Housatonic, *part of the blockading Union fleet, the* Hunley *successfully torpedoed the* Housatonic's *magazine, causing a massive explosion and sinking that ship immediately. But the* Hunley, *probably caught in that explosion, sank, too, killing its commander, Lt. George E. Dixon, and Dixon's six-man crew. This Union naval report, written by Lt. F. J. Higginson aboard the USS*

Canandaigua, *described the action, including the memorable first sighting of "something in the water...moving towards the ship."*

ABOUT 8:45 P.M. THE OFFICER of the deck, Acting Master J. K. Crosby, discovered something in the water about 100 yards from and moving towards the ship. It had the appearance of a plank moving in the water. It came directly towards the ship, the time from when it was first seen till it was close alongside being about two minutes.

During this time the chain was slipped, engine backed, and all hands called to quarters.

The torpedo struck the ship forward of the mizzenmast, on the starboard side, in a line with the magazine. Having the after pivot gun pivoted to port we were unable to bring a gun to bear upon her. About one minute after she was close alongside the explosion took place, the ship sinking stern first and heeling to port as she sank.

Most of the crew saved themselves by going into the rigging, while a boat was dispatched to the *Canandaigua*. This vessel came gallantly to our assistance and succeeded in rescuing all but the following-named officers and men, viz, Ensign E. C. Hazeltine, Captain's Clerk C. O. Muzzey, Quartermaster John Williams, Landsman Theodore Parker, Second-Class Fireman John Walsh.

The above named officers and men are missing and supposed to have been drowned.

Captain Pickering was seriously bruised by the explosion and is at present unable to make a report of the disaster.

Conrad Wise Chapman's painting of the CSS Hunley.

Confederate naval engineer J. H. Tomb offered this assessment of the Hunley *in notes found among his papers. Had the* Hunley *worked, of course, it would have threatened and perhaps defeated the Union blockades.*

THERE WAS A SUBMARINE TOR-pedo boat, not under orders of the Navy, and I was ordered to tow her down the harbor three or four times by Flag-Officer Tucker, who also gave me orders to report as to her efficiency as well as safety. In my report to him I stated, "The only way to use a torpedo was on the same plan as the 'David'—that is, a spar torpedo—and to strike with his boat on the surface, the torpedo being lowered to 8 feet. Should she attempt to use a torpedo as Lieutenant Dixon intended, by submerging the boat and striking from below, the level of the torpedo would be above his own boat, and as she had little buoyancy and no power, the chances were

the suction caused by the water passing into the sinking ship would prevent her rising to the surface, besides the possibility of his own boat being disabled." Lieutenant Dixon was a very brave and cool-headed man, and had every confidence of the boat, but had great trouble when under the water from lack of air and light. At the time she made the attempt to dive under the receiving ship in Charleston Harbor, Lieutenant Dixon, James A. Eason, and myself stood on the wharf as she passed out and saw her dive, but she did not rise again, and after a week's effort she was brought to the surface and the crew of seven men were found in a bunch near the manhole. Lieutenant Dixon said they had failed to close the after valve....

The power for driving this boat came from 7 or 8 men turning cranks attached to the propeller shaft, and when working at their best would make about 3 knots. She was very slow in turning, but would sink at a moment's notice and at times without it. The understanding was that from the time of her construction at Mobile up to the time when she struck *Housatonic* not less than 33 men had lost their lives in her. She was a veritable coffin to this brave officer and his men.

MON 22 FEB. OKOLONA (IVEY'S FARM)

After being frustrated in its attempt to join Maj. Gen. William T. Sherman's campaign against Meridian, Mississippi, Brig. Gen. William Sooy Smith's cavalry retreated back toward Memphis, pursued by the Confederate cavalry of Maj. Gen. Nathan Bedford Forrest. Early in the morning of February 22, Forrest charged the Federal lines at Okolona, Mississippi, where a Union regiment gave way, transforming the battle into a five-mile running fight. The Federals made another stand to cover their retreat, which then led to a prolonged period of hand-to-hand combat before a beaten Smith finally broke off the engagement and completed his retreat to Memphis. The victory was among Forrest's most substantial. Following are accounts of the action from Lt. Col. Thomas Browne of the Seventh Indiana Cavalry and Forrest himself. The contrabands to which Browne refers were parties of escaped slaves that had attached themselves to Smith's cavalry.

ON THE 22ND, THE REGIMENT was again placed at the rear of the brigade, and to the rear of the train of contrabands, captured mules and horses.

Upon arriving near Okolona, the enemy was discovered upon the right, moving in the same direction with ourselves in the open prairie, but keeping the embankment of the Mobile and Ohio Railroad between them and us. By the order of General Grierson the regiment left the train and moved to the right, deploying Company H as skirmishers, who soon became engaged with those of the enemy. Moving rapidly forward through the center of town and to the north side of it, the regiment formed in line of battle, the enemy forming in our front to the east, and still hugging closely the railroad embankment. The First Battalion engaged the enemy's skirmishers briskly for a few moments, and drove them rapidly back upon their line. Other regiments were soon brought to our rear and formed for our support, artillery put in position, and everything seemed to indicate that an engagement was at hand. Our regiment having been cut off from the brigade, left the rear of the train exposed and measurably unprotected; therefore, after occupying the above position for some time, we were, by General Grierson's order, relieved by another regiment and directed to resume our place in the column of march.

AFTER THE ENEMY SUCCEEDED in reaching the hills between Okolona and Pontotoc, the resistance of the enemy was obstinate, compelling me frequently to dismount my advance to drive them from favorable positions defended by the broken condition of the country. About 300 men of the Second Tennessee Cavalry, under Colonel Bateau, and the Seventh Tennessee Cavalry, Colonel Duckworth, received the repeated charges of seven regiments of the enemy in open ground, drove them back time after time, finally driving them from the field, capturing three stands of colors and another piece of their artillery. A great deal of the fighting was hand to hand, and the only way I can account for our small loss is the fact that we kept so close to them that the enemy overshot our men. Owing to the broken down and exhausted condition of men and horses, and being almost out of ammunition, I was compelled to stop pursuit.

WED 24 FEB. ANDERSONVILLE

With Union armies pushing deeper and deeper into the South, the Confederates found themselves with an ever-increasing number of prisoners to house. In December 1863, construction began on a new prisoner-of-war camp in southern Georgia, officially named Camp Sumter but better known as Andersonville (after the nearby hamlet). The camp was intended to house up to ten thousand inmates—but only temporarily, until they could be exchanged for Confederate captives. On this date, the first five hundred inmates were transferred to Andersonville from Belle Isle prison in Virginia's James River. Initially, conditions were good, but the cessation of prisoner exchanges ordered by Grant in April 1864 quickly caused the facility to become overwhelmed. By the time the prison population topped twenty-six thousand, the provision of such essentials

as food, housing, and medical care had long since become inadequate for human survival. (The Confederate commander overseeing the camp, Brig. Gen. John H. Winder, was known to brag that more Union soldiers were dying at Andersonville than being killed on the battlefield.) Sherman's destructive march through Georgia made the problem of securing rations and other supplies even worse. Meanwhile, left with only local militia to guard his prisoners, prison commander Henry Wirz established a "dead line" consisting of a rail of logs twenty-five feet inside the camp perimeter. It was Captain Wirz's standing order that any prisoner crossing the line be shot. Of the forty-five thousand men held at Andersonville during its fourteen months of operation, nearly thirteen thousand died. On November 10, 1865, Wirz was hanged after being convicted on charges of cruelty to Federal soldiers. Among those testifying at Wirz's trial was former prisoner of war Edward S. Kellogg.

 I WAS IN THE MILITARY SERVICE of the United States. I was in the 20th New York regiment. I was captured. I was taken to Belle Island. From thence I was taken to Andersonville. I arrived there the 1st of March, 1864....

I saw other men shot while I was there. I do not know their names. They were Federal prisoners. The first man I saw shot was shortly after the dead-line was established. I think it was in May. He was shot near the brook, on the east side of the stockade. At that time there was no railing; there was simply posts struck along where they were going to

The prison compound at Andersonville.

The hanging of Henry Wirz in November 1865.

MARCH
1864

put the dead-line, and this man, in crossing, simply stepped inside one of the
posts, and the sentry shot him. He failed
to kill him, but wounded him. I don't
know his name. I saw a man shot at the
brook; he had just come in. He belonged
to some regiment in Grant's army. I think
this was about the first part of July or the
latter part of June. He had just come in
and knew nothing about the dead-line.
There was no railing across the brook,
and nothing to show that there was any
such thing as a dead-line there. He came
into the stockade, and after he had been
shown his place where he was to sleep he
went along to the brook to get some water.
It was very dark, and a number of men
were there, and he went above the rest so
as to get better water. He went beyond the
dead-line, and two men fired at him and
both hit him. He was killed and fell right
into the brook. I do not know the man's
name. I saw other men shot. I do not
know exactly how many. I saw several.
It was a common occurrence.

★ ★ ★ ★

**THU
3
MAR.** *Many soldiers stationed (or on leave) in the North were highly suspicious of antiwar and anti-Lincoln sentiments, often perceiving them as treasonous. This attitude occasionally produced spasms of unrestrained hostility. For example, on this day in Dayton, Ohio, fifteen men belonging to the Forty-fourth Ohio wrecked the offices of the* Dayton Daily Empire, *an anti-Lincoln newspaper that had been running provocative editorials the past three days. Afterward, the regiment's captain gave the following speech, reported later (and sarcastically) in the* Cincinnati Enquirer.

FELLOW CITIZENS, BY THE GREAT God (hiccup) and Resurrector of everybody, I swear (hiccup) I am responsible for all this! and God damn you, I led this whole thing. These men (hiccup) are under my control and I am responsible. God damn you, two hundred veterans, such as we are, are worth one thousand citizens. There is no line of distinction (hiccup) between the Administration and the Government and I tell you, by God, if any action is taken against me and my men here, the city of Dayton shall suffer.

**MON
7
MAR.** *Did the Civil War change the racial attitudes of white Northerners? On the one hand, the North's discriminatory laws remained largely intact, and there were many instances of wartime racial violence. On the other, as this* New York Times *editorial suggested, there was some reason to believe, eight months after the* New York City draft riots, that a fundamental shift was taking place in the hearts and minds of whites in the North.

THERE HAS BEEN NO MORE striking manifestation of the marvelous times that are upon us than the scene in our streets at the departure of the first of our colored regiments. Had any man predicted it last year he would have been thought a fool, even by the wisest and most discerning. History abounds with strange contrasts. It always has been an ever-shifting melodrama. But never, in this land at least, has it presented a transition so extreme and yet so speedy as what our eyes have just beheld.

Eight months ago the African race in this City were literally hunted down like wild beasts. They fled for their lives. When caught, they were shot down in cold blood, or stoned to death, or hung to the trees or the lampposts. Their homes were pillaged; the asylum which Christian charity had provided for their orphaned children was burned; and there was no limit to the persecution but in the physical impossibility of finding further material on which the mob could wreak its ruthless hate....

How astonishingly has all this been changed. The same men who could not have shown themselves in the most obscure street in the City without peril of instant death, even though in the most suppliant attitude, now march in solid platoons, with shouldered muskets, slung knapsacks, and buckled cartridge boxes down through our gayest avenues and our busiest thoroughfares to the pealing strains of martial music and are everywhere saluted with waving handkerchiefs, with descending flowers, and with the acclamations and plaudits of countless beholders. They are halted at our most beautiful square, and amid an admiring crowd, in the presence of many of our most prominent citizens, are addressed in an eloquent and most complimentary speech by the President of our chief literary institution, and are presented with a gorgeous stand of colors in the names of a large number of the first ladies of the City, who attest on parchment, signed by their own fair hands, that they "will anxiously watch your career, glorifying in your heroism, ministering to you when wounded and ill, and honoring your martyrdom with benedictions and with tears."

It is only by such occasions that we can at all realize the prodigious revolution which the public mind everywhere is experiencing. Such developments are infallible tokens of a new epoch.

New York City, in particular, had become infamous for the racial viciousness of its July 1863 draft riots. Yet this same city could now be moved to great public pride by the sight of its first African-American regiment marching down Broadway and on to the front lines. Even otherwise virulent racists were impressed. Maria Lydig Daly, the wife of a local judge, recorded the scene in her diary.

IT WAS A VERY INTERESTING and a very touching sight to see the first colored regiment from this city march down the street for the front. They were a fine body of men and had

a look of satisfaction in their faces, as though they felt they had gained a right to be more respected. Many old, respectable darkies stood at the street corners, men and women with tears in their eyes as if they saw the redemption of their race afar off but still the beginning of a better state of affairs for them. Though I am very little Negrophilish and would always prefer the commonest white that lives to a Negro, still I could not but feel moved.

SAT 12 MAR. GRANT TAKES CHARGE OF ALL UNION ARMIES

Having searched thus far in vain, President Lincoln now believed that he had finally found a general who would fight and win. On March 9, in a White House ceremony, the president formally promoted Ulysses S. Grant to the rank of lieutenant general. Three days later, Grant assumed command of all Union armies, relieving Gen.-in-Chief Henry Halleck. (Meanwhile, Major General Sherman replaced Grant as head of the Military Division of the Mississippi— comprising the Departments of the Ohio, the Cumberland, and the Tennessee—and James B. McPherson took over Sherman's command of the Department of the Tennessee.) Lincoln later expressed his confidence in Grant in this April 30 letter to the general.

LIEUTENANT GENERAL GRANT: Not expecting to see you again before the spring campaign opens, I wish to express, in this way, my entire satisfaction with what you have done up to this time, so far as I understand it. The particulars of your plans I neither know, or seek to know. You are vigilant and self-reliant; and, pleased with this, I wish not to obtrude any constraints upon you. While I am very anxious that any great disaster, or the capture of our men in great numbers, shall be avoided, I know these points are less likely to escape your attention than they would be mine. If there is anything wanting which is within my power to give, do not fail to let me know it.

And now with a brave army, and a just cause, may God sustain you. Yours very truly,

A. Lincoln

WED 16 MAR. *The Confederacy never had the time to develop formal political parties, yet there were certainly active pro-Davis and anti-Davis factions. Confederate Vice Pres. Alexander H. Stephens, a Georgian, was the leading spokesman for the latter group, often excoriating his superior for pursuing what Stephens believed were unconstitutional policies regarding conscription and civil rights. Specifically, on February 17, the First Confederate Congress (on the final day of its fourth session) had suspended the right of the writ of habeas corpus until August 2 because of growing resistance to the conscription law. (The suspension was limited to arrests ordered by the president, the secretary of war, and the military commander of the Trans-Mississippi.) The unusual spectacle of a president being upbraided by his vice president reached its climax with this* *highly publicized speech that Stephens gave before the Georgia legislature.*

I COME, NOW, TO THE LAST OF these acts of Congress. The suspension of the writ of habeas corpus in certain cases. This is the most exciting, as it is by far the most important question before you. Upon this depends the question, whether the courts shall be permitted to decide upon the constitutionality of the late conscript act, should you submit that question to their decision; and upon it also depends other great essential rights enjoyed by us as freemen. This act, upon its face, confers upon the President, the Secretary of War, and the general commanding in the Trans-Mississippi Department...the power to arrest and imprison any person

Alexander H. Stephens

who may be simply charged with certain acts, not all of them even crimes under any law....

In my judgment this is not only unwise, impolitic, and unconstitutional, but exceedingly dangerous to public liberty....

You have been told that it affects none but the disloyal, none but traitors, or those who are no better than traitors, spies, bridge-burners, and the like; and you have been appealed to and asked if such are entitled to your sympathies. I affirm, and shall maintain before the world, that this act affects and may wrongfully oppress as loyal and as good citizens, and as true to our cause, as ever trod the soil or breathed the air of the South....Whether such was the real object and intention of its framers and advocates, I know not. Against their motives of patriotism I have nothing to say. I take the act as I find it....

[Tell me that the President] will never abuse the power attempted to be lodged in his hands! The abuses may not be by the President. He will not execute the military orders that will be given. This will necessarily devolve upon subordinates, scattered all over the country, from the Potomac to the Rio Grande. He would have to possess two superhuman attributes to prevent abuses—omniscience and omnipresence...!

Who is safe under such a law? Who knows when he goes forth, when or whether he shall ever return? The President, according to the act, is to have power to arrest and imprison whomever he pleases upon a bare charge made, perhaps by an enemy, of disloyalty—the party making the charge not being required to

swear it. Who, I repeat, is safe, or would be, under such a law?...

One other view only, that relates to the particularly dangerous tendency of this act in the present sate of the country, and the policy indicated by Congress—conscription has been extended to embrace all between seventeen and fifty years of age. It cannot be possible that the intention and object of that measure was really to call and keep in the field all between these ages. The folly and ruinous consequences of such a policy are too apparent. Details are to be made, and must be made, to a large extent. The effect and the object of this measure, therefore, was not to raise armies and procure soldiers, but to put all the population of the country between those ages under military law. Whatever the object was, the effect is to put much the larger portion of the labor of the country, both white and slave, under the complete control of the President. Under this system almost all the useful and necessary occupations of life will be completely under the control of one man. No one between the ages of seventeen and fifty can tan your leather, make your shoes, grind your grain, shoe your horse, lay your plow, make your wagon, repair your harness, superintend your farm, procure your salt, or perform any other of the necessary vocations of life (except teachers, preachers, and physicians, and a very few others) without permission from the President. This is certainly an extraordinary and a dangerous power....Could the whole country be more completely under the power and control of one man, except as to life and limb? Could dictatorial powers be more complete...?

Jefferson Davis

JEFFERSON DAVIS ON HABEAS CORPUS

Abraham Lincoln was considered by many, both during and after the war, too eager in his suspension of the writ of habeas corpus. How could one who truly believed in civil liberties, the argument went, so easily permit government officials to jail citizens indefinitely without showing cause for their imprisonment? Less often does one hear of Jefferson Davis's attitude on the subject of habeas corpus. Davis possessed simi-

lar powers to suspend the writ, and he used them often. From his point of view, excessive invocation of the writ by local judges hostile to the Confederate draft laws had done considerable damage to national recruiting efforts, as he made clear in his message to the Confederate Congress supporting the new legislation.

IN SOME OF THE STATES civil process has been brought to bear with disastrous efficiency upon the Army. Every judge has the power to issue the writ of *habeas corpus,* and if one manifests more facility in discharging petitioners than his associates, the application is made to him, however remote he may be. In one instance a general on the eve of an important movement, when every man was needed, was embarrassed by the command of a judge—more than two hundred miles distant—to bring...or send...before him, on *habeas corpus,* some deserters who had been arrested and returned to his command. In another, a commandant of a camp of conscripts, who had a conscript in camp, was commanded to bring him before a judge more than a hundred miles distant, although there was a judge competent to hear and determine the cause resident in the place where the writ was executed. He consulted eminent counsel, and was advised that, from the known opinions of the judge selected, the conscript would undoubtedly be released, and the officer

was therefore advised to discharge him
at once, and return the facts informally;
that such a return was not technically
sufficient, but would be accepted as
accomplishing the purpose of the writ.
He acted on the advice of his counsel, and
was immediately summoned by the judge
to show cause why he should not be
attached for a contempt in making an
insufficient return, and was compelled
to leave his command at a time when his
services were pressingly needed by the
Government and travel over a hundred
miles and a considerable distance away
from any railroad, to purge himself of the
technical contempt.

★ ★ ★ ★

APRIL
1864

**FRI
1
APR.** *Although Judith McGuire and her well-to-do family fared better in Richmond than most Confederates there or elsewhere, by the spring of 1864 even they were feeling the pinch of wartime scarcity and inflation. Here is McGuire's diary entry for the first of April, written as the war approached its third anniversary.*

OF COURSE PROVISIONS ARE scarce; but, thanks to our country friends and relatives, we have never been obliged to give up meat entirely. My brother-in-law, Mr. N., has lately sent us twelve hams, so that we are much better supplied than most persons. Groceries are extremely high. We were fortunate in buying ten pounds of tea, when it only sold for $22 per pound. Coffee now sells for $12, and brown sugar at $10 per pound. White sugar is not to be thought of by persons of moderate means. Milk is very scarce and high, so that we have only had it once for many months; and we, the Colonel, Mr. ——, and myself, are very glad to get a cup of tea, night and morning, sweetened with brown sugar, and without milk or cream. Before the war we would have scorned it, but now we enjoy it exceedingly, and feel ourselves very much blessed to have it. The girls have given up tea and coffee; I attempted to do it, and for several days drank only water, but such is the effect of habit upon old people, it made me perfectly miserable; I lost my elasticity of spirit; the accounts in the office went on heavily, everybody asked me if I had heard any bad news, and the family begged me not to look so unhappy. I struggled and strived against the feeling, but the girls pronounced me utterly subjugated, and insisted on my returning to my old beverage. I found myself much more easily persuaded than it is my wont to be, and was happy to resume my brown-sugar tea without cream.

**MON
4
APR.** *As the war dragged on and the Union continued its slow but steady seizure of Confederate territory, the northern flow of Southern refugees became something of a problem. In the following letter, Cincinnati resident George F. Davis complained to Ohio senator John Sherman about the large number of poor whites flooding his city.*

THE LARGE INFLUX OF POOR whites from "The Southern Border States," coming as they do from homes made desolate by the ravages of war, and in need of everything, has made it necessary to organize for their relief.…We find the work one of increasing magnitude, and presenting difficulties that we cannot surmount. The Refugees are mostly women, children, and old men. They are brought on Govt Transports and left on the Levee at Cairo and other points, dependent on the *charities* of the people whose sympathies are exercised by coming in contact with them. They are mostly the families of those who have relatives in the Union Army, and who are driven out because of their sympathy for the Federal Government. They have a right to the fostering care of the nation, and should not be thus humbled. We can only assist them temporarily, for they are already upon us by thousands.…It is not right for the Government to cast these people upon the Northern Border States, for while it will afford the Southern States the opportunity to get rid of their pauper population, they will all become such unless taken care of....The Contrabands are much more easily managed for they will work and can in a measure be made to do so if they refuse....The Southern people ought to look with shame upon these specimens of their white population....We cannot make a white woman work, and if today we should erect a "Refugees' Home" it would be permanently filled in a few days with as worthless a class of people as you can imagine.

Lt. Gen. Richard Taylor

FRI 8 APR. SABINE CROSSROADS (MANSFIELD)

In early March, Union Maj. Gen. Nathaniel P. Banks, at the head of an army of thirty-five thousand men, began a campaign up the Red River into the heart of the Confederacy's Department of the Trans-Mississippi. (Meanwhile, Maj. Gen. Frederick Steele, who had recently assumed command of the Federal Department of Arkansas, began moving his army south to meet Banks.) Determined to halt Banks's advance on Shreveport, Confederate Lt. Gen. Richard Taylor (son of President Zachary Taylor) placed his troops across the line of Banks's march at a junction called Sabine Crossroads, near Mansfield, Louisiana. The location was advantageous for Taylor because, at this point, the road swung far enough away from the Red River that Banks's flotilla of gunboats could not help him. (The gunboats were useless, in any case, because low water levels had trapped them at Grand Ecore.) The effectiveness of Taylor's attack was also aided by Banks's unwise decision to include wagons within his strung-out line of march (rather than collecting them at the rear, as was the usual practice); thus, when Taylor's men charged at Sabine Crossroads, Banks's advance units were pushed back directly into the slow-moving wagons. A Union division commanded by Brig. Gen. William H. Emory finally ended the panic with a stand at Pleasant Grove that allowed the rest of the army to withdraw in an orderly fashion to a new defensive position at Pleasant Hill. The following is an excerpt from the official report of George B. Drake, assistant adjutant general for Banks's Department of the Gulf.

ON THE MORNING OF LAST Friday our cavalry advance, after having skirmished for upward of 40 miles, was checked by a determined stand of the enemy's rear guard at a point about 4 miles from Mansfield, called sometimes Sabine Cross-Roads. The entire cavalry force at once deployed in line, and were in action as soon as so deployed. It soon became evident that our force in action was too small. Colonel Landram's division of the Thirteenth Army Corps went in on a hill in the center of the line of battle. The firing now became furious, and a general engagement began. General Cameron's division of the Thirteenth Corps was ordered up and soon became engaged. From the extreme right to the extreme left the most desperate efforts were made to dislodge our first line. After the most dreadful carnage for above three hours, and the most desperate resistance, the line gave way, retiring to a second position. This line was strengthened by new troops, but the enemy came on at a tremendous charge and drove our line in with much confusion and loss. We were now forced back by the impetuous enemy to our reserves. On they came, yelling like demons, firing tremendous volleys of musketry and salvos of artillery. The hopes of the army are concentrated in the reserve, which was General Emory's division of the Nineteenth Army Corps. They were on their knees, not firing a gun until the charge of the enemy reached about 50 yards, when a most furious fire was delivered and continued; not a man wavered. Like a wall of fire they held their position, inflicting the most terrible punishment until night, when the battle closed.

Low water on the Red River trapped the Union gunboats, which were freed by dams built to raise the water level.

SAT 9 APR. PLEASANT HILL

Having already captured the leading Federal supply wagons, Taylor's Confederates attacked Banks's army again at Pleasant Hill. This battle was marginally a Union victory—it ended with a successful Union counterattack—but both sides suffered, and afterward, Banks gave ground. Here, Confederate Lt. Gen. E. Kirby Smith, the Trans-Mississippi commander who arrived at the battlefield late that night, reports on the action that halted Banks's advance. The report is addresssed to Maj. Gen. Sterling Price, whose army was blocking the corresponding advance of Steele through southern Arkansas. (Stalled by Price at Prairie d'Ane, Steele decided the next day to give up his rendezvous with Banks and instead retreat back to Little Rock.)

 ON THE AFTERNOON OF THE 9TH, we had a severe fight, which was general. The enemy held their ground,

Lt. Gen. Edmund Kirby Smith

but retreated in great confusion during the night to Natchitoches. I have just returned from the front and regard Banks' grand expedition as certainly checked for some time, if not entirely broken up. I will soon be in position to give you assistance, and expect to dispose of Steele....We captured nineteen pieces of artillery, and prisoners are being still brought in. The Thirteenth, Nineteenth, and part of the Sixteenth Army Corps were engaged. Our loss has been heavy.

This April 11 telegram to his Southern counterpart bespeaks the suddenness of Banks's departure from Pleasant Hill.

SIR: WHEN THE TROOPS OF MY command evacuated Pleasant Hill there were left behind for want of ambulances quite a large number of wounded officers and men. At the moment it was impracticable to leave with them the proper supplies for men in their condition, but I request of you now the privilege of forwarding for them necessary supplies of food, medicines, clothing, &c.

Very respectfully, I am, sir, your obedient servant,

N. P. Banks,
Major-General, Commanding

TUE 12 APR. FORT PILLOW

Once the Union began putting blacks into uniform, some Confederate troops declared their intention to take no black prisoners; by mid-1864, numerous racially motivated killings had been reported. *The most notorious of these occurred during Nathan Bedford Forrest's assault on Fort Pillow, a large earthwork located on a bluff overlooking the Mississippi River in Tennessee. The Union garrison of 557 soldiers was about half black, and many were slaughtered—some say during the attack, some say after the surrender. Northerners were sufficiently outraged that Congress moved to open an official investigation into the matter. This editorial from a Boston newspaper typified the public response.*

WE DID NOT BELIEVE THAT THE rebels, brutal as they had proved themselves to be, were in earnest in their threats to give no quarter to our black soldiers, or that they would dare so to outrage the opinion of the world, as to murder colored captives in cold blood. The events—appalling, and almost surpassing all credence—at Fort Pillow, however, have proved, if proof before that were wanting, that they did mean what they said. They have been as bad as their word. Deliberately...they have butchered their prisoners by hundreds. Retaliation is now our reluctant duty.... The President has declared his purpose to retaliate....We trust he will call out two rebel prisoners to every negro...to immediate execution.

Published during the 1890s, Kurz & Allison's lithographs of the Civil War (including this one of the fighting at Fort Pillow) typically included casualty figures in the margins.

SUN 17 APR.
GRANT ENDS PRISONER EXCHANGES

On this date, Grant ordered a suspension of prisoner exchanges until the Confederates matched Federal releases. Specifically, Grant wanted no distinction "made in the exchange between white and colored prisoners." Although the general's action was criticized in both the North and South as inhumane, its impact on the military situation was even more significant: The Union army could easily fill the vacancies in its ranks, but the South, already desperately short of manpower, could not. This gave Grant a distinct advantage, even though it meant perhaps thousands of deaths in overcrowded, undersupplied prisoner-of-war camps. The notorious Southern camps, such as Andersonville, have received most of the attention, but Northern prisons during the bitter winter of 1864 could also be deadly. The author of this memoir, Alabama cavalryman John A. Wyeth, spent that winter at Indiana's Camp Morton.

TO MEN THE GREATER NUMBER of whom had never been in a cold climate the suffering was intense when with such surroundings, the mercury was near zero. A number were frozen to death, and many more perished from disease brought on by exposure, added to their condition of emaciation from lack of food. I counted eighteen bodies carried into the death house one morning after an intensely cold night.

During these very cold spells it was our habit to sleep in larger groups or "squads," so that by combining blankets and body heat the cold could be better combated. Another practice was, just at sundown, when we were forced to "go to bed," to dip the top blanket in water, wring it out fairly dry, so that, being thus made more impermeable, it would retain the warmth generated by the body. Lots were drawn for positions, and woe to the unfortunate end men, who, although captains of the squad for the night, paid dearly for their honors in having to shiver through the weary hours. And yet all this was not without a strong suggestion of the grotesque. The squad or file of men slept "spoon fashion." No one was allowed to rest flat on the back, for this took up too much room for the width of the blankets. The narrower the bulk to be covered, the thicker the blanket on top. At intervals through these intensely cold nights, above the shivering groans of the unhappy prisoners could be heard the order of the end men, "Boys, spoon!" and, as if on parade, they would flop over upon the other side, to the gratification of one end man and the disgust of the other, whose back by the change was once more turned on a cold world.

★ ★ ★ ★

MAY 1864

THU 5 MAY — THE WILDERNESS

After conferring with Maj. Gen. George Meade, who remained in direct command of the Army of the Potomac, Ulysses S. Grant made plans for a new drive against the Confederate capital. On May 3, he ordered Meade to cross the Rapidan River the next morning, march around the right flank of Lee's army (then located near Orange Court House), and head for Richmond. The Union forces, numbering 122,000, were double the size of Lee's 66,000-man army, but the densely forested region through which Grant and Meade first had to pass did much to equalize matters (as Joseph Hooker had found out at Chancellorsville the year before). The first major battle of 1864 began when two opposing corps met on the Orange Turnpike. After some desperate but inconclusive fighting, both sides spent the night entrenching. In the morning, as fighting resumed, Grant remained at his headquarters, smoking cigars and whittling, while Lee rode among his men on the front lines until protective subordinates insisted that he return to the rear. Once again, the Union's nose was bloodied—Federal casualties for the two days topped seventeen thousand, compared to perhaps seven thousand for the Rebels—but Grant had no intention of pulling back, as previous Union commanders had. Instead, he doggedly pushed forward, pursuing not so much the capture of the Confederate capital as the destruction of Lee's army. In pursuit of this

Burial of the Wilderness dead.

goal, Grant was brutally single-minded. "That man," Lt. Gen. James Longstreet (who was seriously wounded on May 6) warned, "will fight us every day and every hour till the end of the war." A victory for neither side, the battle of the Wilderness was but the beginning of a long confrontation between Grant and Lee. The following are recollections of the battle from a Union private and one of Grant's field commanders, who described the general's demeanor as he waited to hear news from the battlefield.

 NO ONE COULD SEE THE FIGHT fifty feet from him. The lines were very near each other, and from the dense underbrush and the tops of trees came puffs of smoke, the "ping" of the bullets and the yell of the enemy. It was a blind and bloody hunt to the death, in bewildering thickets, rather than a battle.

HE KEEPS HIS OWN COUNSEL, padlocks his mouth, while his countenance…indicates nothing—that is, gives no expression of his feelings and no evidence of his intentions. He smokes almost constantly, and…has a habit of whittling with a small knife. He cuts a small stick into small chips, making nothing.

THE REBEL RAM ALBEMARLE

The CSS Virginia *(alias the Merrimack) was not the only Southern ironclad to see action during the Civil War. Several others were built using different experimental designs, and Federal naval authorities continued to worry that one of these attempts might produce a new supership capable of breaking the Union blockade and changing the course of the war. The CSS* Albemarle *was one such ironclad, designed exclusively for operation within Albemarle Sound and similar shallow waters around the Outer Banks of North Carolina. The ship, which rode low in the water, had just two guns, mounted fore and aft; its primary weapon was, rather, a large iron ram attached to its bow. Its mission was to sail down the Roanoke River and challenge the Federal fleet blockading Albemarle Sound. In its only engagement, the* Albemarle *fought three Union ships. The following is an excerpt from the log of one of those ships, the USS* Sassacus. *The* Albemarle *survived the mission, but it was so badly damaged that repairs could not be completed before war's end.*

DURING THIS TIME THE RAM HAD kept up an intermittent fire on us and the other vessels, and had swung partly around, presenting her broadside to us, when, seeing that we had room to gather headway and a good opportunity to strike her, we rang four bells again and started for her full speed, working our battery as long as we could train and pouring into him solid and chilled-end shots. We struck him when going about 10 to 11 knots, square on his side, just where his casement roof joined the hull on his starboard quarter, giving him a tremendous shock, forcing his side under till the water flowed clear over his deck, and, keeping up our speed, tried to force his ports under water and hoping to hold him powerless until some of the squadron should attack his exposed sides. During this time we kept up a constant fire at her forward port, putting one or two shot square inside of it, and throwing hand grenades into her hatch from our top, at the same time trying to throw a cartridge down her smokestack.

As we first struck her she was unable to bring her guns to bear on us, but, gradually swinging on our starboard bow, she fired two shots—Brooke 100-pounder rifle—into our bow. The first was fired while the gun almost touched our bow, entering 10 feet abaft the stem and 3 feet above the copper on the starboard side, and, passing through the store room, crossed the berth deck and out the port side. The second shot was fired from the starboard forward port, entering the side abreast the foremast on the starboard side, and, cutting through planking and frames diagonally, kept on through the back of one knee and the throat of the next, smashing the dispensary, and from there passing through the forward coal bunker, entering the starboard boiler, going clean through it, and, keeping on through the engine room, passed between the cylinder and main condenser, cutting off a 3 inch iron stanchion, thence through steerage and wardroom bulkheads smashing doors and furniture, and, passing through the magazine screen, struck with spent force on an oak stanchion, and, glancing at right angles, lodged in one of the starboard staterooms.

FRI 6 MAY *As the war entered its fourth year, increasingly strained resources and growing disappointment contributed to a new bitterness among the Southern population, still angered by the "tax in kind" levied by the Confederate Congress in April 1863. With this petition, forty-six men from Randolph County, Alabama, asked Confederate Pres. Jefferson Davis to exempt their impoverished county from the particularly burdensome practice of impressing slaves into service as laborers in the Confederate army. If more black workers were taken away now, they argued, their county would not be able to produce enough food to feed itself.*

RANDOLPH IS A POOR & MOUN- tainous County with the largest population of any in the State. There are only 300 negroes (women and men) within the prescribed ages in the county & he [Colonel Blount, the local impressing agent] takes one Hundred. Seventy-five per cent of the White Males are now in the Service; leaving the great majority of their wives & children to be Supported by the remainder. There are numbers of widows & orphans of the Soldiers who have perished by the casualities of war to be also Supported by public funds—

The County does not in ordinary times produce more than a Sufficiency of food for its population; last year there was a deficit of over 40000 bushels of corn about one half of which has been provided from the tax in Kind; the ballance has to be purchased in the Canebrake; transported a distance of 125 miles on R.R., & hauled thence in waggons from 30 to 50 miles to reach the various points of distribution in the county—

There are now on the rolls of the Probate court, 1600 indigent families to be Supported; they average 5 to each family; making a grand total of 8000 persons. Deaths from Starvation have absolutely occurred; notwithstanding the utmost efforts that we have been able to make; & now many of the women & children are seeking & feeding upon the bran from the mills.

Women riots have taken place in Several parts of the County in which Govt wheat & corn has been seized to prevent Starvation of themselves & families; Where it will end unless relief is afforded we cannot tell.

We have entered into these details that your Excellency may See the deplorable condition of things in this County, & aid us if in your power & the exigencies of the Service permit—

To take the Negroes *now* from the fields when the crop is just planted & ready for cultivation would inevitably cause the loss of a portion of the crops So essential to feed the County. We have appealed to Col Blount asking that the impressment be delayed or abandoned; but without effect & we now appeal to your Excellency as our last resource under God to give us Such measure of assistance as you can.

SUN 8 MAY — SPOTSYLVANIA COURT HOUSE

The slugfest begun in the Wilderness entered its second phase as Grant moved around Lee toward the strategic crossroads at Spotsylvania Court House and Lee ordered a night march on May 7–8 to the same destination. (The dense terrain continued to suit Lee, who preferred to engage Grant's more numerous army in woodland rather than out in the open.) Beginning on May 8, the two armies struck repeatedly at one another in this same area. On May 10, the Confederates repulsed a major Federal attack, as they would do three times more before Grant's army shifted to the south and east on May 21. Federal casualties at Spotsylvania were again astronomical: 17,500 out of 110,000 men engaged. As was often the case in the latter stages of the war, there were no reliable figures for Southern casualties, yet these were certainly much lower. Nevertheless, the Union could quite easily replace its lost men; not so the Confederacy, especially with prisoner exchanges now suspended. In the following account, Union veteran E. M. Woodward describes some typical action during the Spotsylvania Campaign, notable for its high degree of trench warfare.

 EARLY IN THE DAY [MAY 9] WE were ordered to the right, where we took a position, and threw up breastworks. Hardly had they been completed before our line was slightly changed, which rendered it necessary to throw up new ones. Soon after we moved to the right, and crossing a deep ravine, advanced to a road through a growth of scrub oaks, in which we received a heavy fire, but so high that the minnies only tipped our bayonets. Crossing the road, we charged, driving the enemy before us, until within forty yards of a heavy woods, when we in turn were driven back by a new line that suddenly emerged from it. When we reached the road, the boys rallied and handsomely repulsed the enemy, who contented themselves with annoying us with desultory and long-ranged musket fire. Here we again threw up temporary entrenchments....

At one A.M., we moved into rifle pits, and at daybreak the enemy opened upon us a heavy fire of artillery, to which our guns promptly responded. Between us and the works occupied by the enemy,

One of the Confederate entrenchments at Spotsylvania.

there was a valley, covered by a heavy pine and scrub underbrush, the pits of each party crowning the opposite crests. Through the morning our guns having silenced the fire of the enemy's, we leaped over the pits, and charging through the valley, we went up to the breastworks, and planted our banners upon them, but such was the terrible fire of the enemy and the stubborn resistance that we were driven back to our own works. The boys were then laid down behind the pits and told to rest themselves and make coffee, after which we opened the fight again, charging twice over the valley and being driven back each time with heavy loss.…In the last charge we maintained our position for a long while, and did not retire until relieved by Colter's brigade.

SHERIDAN'S CAVALRY

On May 8, at the outset of the Spotsylvania Campaign, Grant sent Maj. Gen. Philip Sheridan on a raiding mission—to destroy Rebel supply lines and divert Lee's cavalry—that reminded many of Stuart's earlier Rides Around McClellan. (Sheridan had been transferred from the Western Theater on April 4 specifically to boost the performance of the Army of the Potomac's disappointing cavalry.) Afterward, Sheridan was to join Benjamin F. Butler's Army of the James for a joint attack on Richmond from the south. Meanwhile, a separate brigade of cavalry—led by Brig. Gen. George Armstrong Custer, the youngest general officer in the Union army—decimated Confederate rail lines and freed 378

prisoners taken during the fighting in the Wilderness. Notwithstanding the controversy surrounding his later Montana command, during the Civil War Custer proved himself a more-than-competent officer whose leadership qualities were much admired by the troops under him. This description of Custer comes from the memoirs of James H. Kidd, a cavalryman who served in Custer's Civil War brigade.

LOOKING AT HIM CLOSELY, THIS is what I saw: An officer superbly mounted who sat his charger as if to the manor born. Tall, lithe, active, muscular, straight as an Indian and as quick in his movements, he had the fair complexion of a school girl. He was clad in a suit of black velvet, elaborately trimmed in gold lace, which ran down the outer seams of his trousers, and almost covered the sleeves of his cavalry jacket. The wide collar of a blue navy shirt was turned down over the collar of his velvet jacket, and a necktie of brilliant crimson was tied in a graceful knot at the throat, the long ends falling carelessly in front. The double row of buttons were arranged in groups of twos, indicating the rank of brigadier general. A soft black hat with a wide brim adorned with gilt cord, and rosette encircling a silver star, was worn turned down on one side giving him a rakish air. His golden hair fell in graceful luxuriance nearly or quite to his shoulders, and his upper lip was garnished with a blonde mustache. A sword and belt, gilt spurs and top boots completed his unique outfit.…

That garb, fantastic as at first sight it appeared to be, was to be the distinguishing mark which, during all the remaining

Custer (right) poses with his Confederate prisoner (and former West Point classmate) James B. Washington.

Grant (leaning over a pew removed from Massaponax Church) confers with his staff on May 21.

years of that war, like the white plume of Henry of Navarre, was to show us where, in the thickest of the fight, we were to seek our leader—for, where danger was, where swords were to cross, where Greek met Greek, there he was, always.

MON 9 MAY *Throughout the war, Confederate diplomats labored to gain official recognition—along with military and economic aid—from several European nations. Their major efforts were directed at Britain and France, but Confederate agents—such as A. Dudley Mann, stationed in Brussels—pursued other avenues as well. On December 3, 1863, Mann was received sympathetically by Pope Pius IX, who gave him a letter for Jefferson Davis. With this note, dated May 9, Mann transmitted the pope's letter to his president.*

MR. PRESIDENT: HEREWITH I have the honor to transmit the Letter which His Holiness, Pope Pius IX, addressed to your Excellency on the 3rd of December last. Mr. W. Jefferson Buchanan has obligingly undertaken its conveyance and will deliver it in person.

This Letter will grace the archives of the Executive Office in all coming time. It will live too, forever, in Story, as the production of the first Potentate who formally recognized your official position and accorded to one of the diplomatic representatives of the Confederate States an audience in an established Court Palace, like that of St. James or the Tuileries.

I have the honor to be, with the most distinguished consideration,

Your Excellency's obedient servant, A. Dudley Mann

SAT 14 MAY RESACA

On May 7, Maj. Gen. William T. Sherman set in motion his one-hundred-thousand-man army. Its elements included the Army of the Cumberland under George Thomas, the Army of the Tennessee under James B. McPherson, and the Army of the Ohio under John M. Schofield. Leaving Chattanooga, he headed southeast into the Georgia interior, where he intended to engage and destroy the Confederate Army of Tennessee commanded by Joseph E. Johnston and also capture Atlanta. During the first week of the campaign, Sherman and Johnston probed one another, with Johnston cautiously drawing back from Dalton to Resaca, Georgia, on May 12. In the low hills around Resaca, Johnston's entrenched army waited for Sherman, who arrived on May 14, a day that saw only some preliminary fighting. On the following day, however, during the main attack, Sherman indicated that he would try to outflank Johnston to the south. Although the Confederate position in Resaca was itself strong enough to resist any direct attack, Johnston feared that, with his back to the Oostenaula River, he might become trapped. So on the night of May 15, the Confederates withdrew again. In his memoirs, Sherman described in a general way this opening act of the Atlanta Campaign.

These earthworks outside Resaca were used by Confederate soldiers of Polk's corps.

 THAT JOHNSTON HAD DELIBER-
ately designed in advance to give
up such strong positions as Dalton and
Resaca, for the purpose of driving us farther south, is simply absurd. Had he
remained in Dalton another hour it would
have been his total defeat, and he only
evacuated Resaca because his safety
demanded it....My army about doubled
his in size, but he had all the advantages
of natural positions, of artificial forts and
roads, and of concentrated action. We
were compelled to grope our way through
forests, across mountains, with a large
army, necessarily more or less dispersed.
Of course, I was disappointed not to have
crippled his army more at that particular
stage of the game; but as it resulted, these

rapid successes gave us the initiative, and
the usual impulse of a conquering army.

THU
19 CASSVILLE
MAY

*At Johnston's direction, Confederate
corps commanders John Bell Hood
and Leonidas Polk lay in wait near
Cassville, hoping to slam into the flank
of Sherman's army as it marched past.
As Hood was preparing to attack, however, he received word that a column of
Union soldiers had been spotted behind
Confederate lines. In fact, this small
detachment of Federal troops was not*

part of Sherman's strategy but merely lost. Nevertheless, Hood fell back, which forced Johnston to take up a defensive position as well (despite the bravado of the address he delivered to his troops before the battle, quoted here). This gave Sherman the chance to strike first, forcing the Confederates into yet another retreat.

Maj. Gen. James B. McPherson

 SOLDIERS OF THE ARMY OF Tennessee, you have displayed the highest quality of the soldier—firmness in combat, patience under toil. By your courage and skill you have repulsed every assault of the enemy. By marches by day and by marches by night you have defeated every attempt upon your communications. Your communications are secured. You will now turn and march to meet his advancing columns. Fully confiding in the conduct of the officers, the courage of the soldiers, I lead you to battle. We may confidently trust that the Almighty Father will still reward the patriot's toil and bless the patriot's banners. Cheered by the success of your brothers in Virginia and beyond the Mississippi, our efforts will equal theirs. Strengthened by His support those efforts will be crowned with the like glories.

WED 25 MAY · NEW HOPE CHURCH

After Cassville, the Confederate Army of Tennessee retreated through Cartersville to Dallas and New Hope Church, just twenty-five miles northeast of Atlanta, where, once again, the Rebels entrenched in anticipation of a Union

attack. Sherman advanced cautiously, then entrenched himself and began probing for weakness on the Confederate flanks. In advance of the two-week engagement that began on May 25, Union Maj. Gen. James B. McPherson outlined what he thought would occur in this May 24 communication to Maj. Gen. John Logan. The muddy fight that did take place on May 25 was marked by a raging thunderstorm. At battle's end, Sherman's advance was temporarily halted.

THE INDICATIONS ARE THAT WE shall have a heavy battle near Dallas tomorrow. The enemy has massed all his available force, consisting of Hood's, Hardee's, and Polk's commands. Hardee's corps is in our front. Thomas has been fighting Hood's and perhaps a part of Polk's this afternoon; result I have not heard, as I have not yet heard from

General Sherman. Have your command all brought up, except a sufficient guard for the train, which will be parked the west side of Pumpkin Vine Creek as compactly as possible, so that comparatively a small force can guard it. Have rations issued to your command and have them ready to move forward at an early hour in the morning in light fighting order. No wagons will follow except ammunition wagons and ambulances. We must be ready to perform our part.

THU
26
MAY

One might reasonably assume that Lincoln, the Great Emancipator, was universally admired by African Americans of his day, yet this was not the case. Among the dissenting voices was one belonging to the black correspondent who wrote this article for an African-American newspaper pointing out the moral weaknesses in Lincoln's approach to emancipation.

ONE OF THE MOST FATAL MIStakes of this war has been the false and indefinite policy of the Administration. The Emancipation proclamation should have been based as much on the righteousness of emancipation as on the great need of the measure, and then let the people see that the war for slavery and secession could be vigorously met only by war for the Union against slavery....

Did not President Lincoln offer the bait to the Southerners, "If you want to save your slaves, lay down your arms"? If this war is maintained by the North with a view to the restoration of the system, God, being just, will never prosper its stupendous villainy, and its criminality would make the North a byword and a disgrace; for it would then be a war for power and for conquest. Make it a war for the liberty of the human race, not liberty only for the slave, but liberty for the master and for every proscribed man; and for breaking every image of the slave-master's fetish.

SAT
28
MAY

Probably the most famous Northern counterpart to Belle Boyd and Rose O'Neal Greenhow was Union spy Pauline Cushman. This New York Times *article gives a reasonable account of Cushman's career.*

AMONG THE WOMEN OF AMERICA who have made themselves famous since the opening of the rebellion, few have suffered more or rendered more service to the Federal cause than Miss Maj. Pauline Cushman, the female scout and spy. At the commencement of hostilities she resided in Cleveland, Ohio, and was quite well known as a clever actress.

From Cleveland she went to Louisville, where she had an engagement in Wood's Theatre. Here, by her intimacy with certain rebel officers, she incurred the suspicion of being a rebel, and was arrested by the Federal authorities. She indignantly denied that she was a rebel, although born at the South, and having a brother in a rebel Mississippi regiment.

In order to test the love for the old flag, she was asked if she would enter the secret service of the Government. She readily consented, and was at once employed to carry letters between Louisville and Nashville. She was subsequently employed by Gen. Rosecrans, and was for many months with the Army of the Cum-

Pauline Cushman

berland. She visited the rebel lines time after time, and was thoroughly acquainted with all the country and roads in Tennessee, Northern Georgia, Alabama and Mississippi, in which sections she rendered our armies invaluable service. She was twice suspected of being a spy, and taken prisoner, but managed to escape.

At last, however, she was not so fortunate. After our forces had captured Nashville, Maj. Cushman made a scout toward Shelbyville to obtain information of the strength and position of the enemy, and while returning to Nashville was captured on the Hardin pike, eleven miles from the latter city. She was placed on a horse, and, in charge of two scouts, was being taken to Spring Hill, the headquar-

ters of Forrest....She was tried and condemned to be executed as a spy, but being sick her execution was postponed. She finally, after lying in prison three months, sent for Gen. Bragg, and asked him if he had no mercy. She received from him the comforting assurance that he should make an example of her, and that he should hang her as soon as she got well enough to be hung decently.

While in this state of suspense, the grand army of Rosecrans commenced its forward movement and one fine day the rebel town where she was imprisoned was surprised and captured, and the heroine of this tale was, to her great joy, released. She is now in this city visiting friends, having arrived at the Biddle House one day last week.

★ ★ ★ ★

JUNE
1864

WED 1 JUN. *In March 1864, Northern black Edmonia G. Highgate began teaching freed slaves in Norfolk, Virginia, as an American Missionary Association volunteer. In this letter to her AMA sponsor, the Rev. George Whipple, she described her first months on the job.*

THE MOST EARNEST MONTHS OF my existence were the two last which have just passed. I have been able to get so near to so many of my people who have spent most of manhood's and womanhood's freshness in slavery. There are peculiar crushing emotions which, at first, check even my utterance but go away and leave me with such deep compelling motive power to "do with my might whatsoever my hands find to do."

A case came under my notice of a woman and her three little girls who lived in the hollow of a tree several months to elude the vigilance of her rebel pursuers who aimed to send them to Richmond. She related many little incidents of her life in the tree amid audible smiles. It is predominating mirthfulness and appreciation of the ridiculous that enable these people to be so light hearted in spite of weighty sorrow.

FRI 3 JUN. ## THE CHARGE AT COLD HARBOR

After Spotsylvania Court House and a subsequent engagement along the North Anna River, Grant again tried to move around Lee, this time to Lee's right. After several days of marching, Lee blocked Grant's advance once more at Cold Harbor, near the battlefields of the 1862 Seven Days' Campaign. Fighting began on June 1, but the major Federal assault was delayed until June 3 because of bad weather, ammunition problems, and fatigue. Being so close to Richmond, Grant was determined to force a breach in the Confederate front. Yet, sadly for his men, neither Grant nor any of his senior officers had inspected the strongly fortified and thickly defended Rebel lines. (Union soldiers who had seen those lines fashioned crude dog tags, pinning to their clothing slips of paper bearing names and home addresses so that their bodies might be identified and buried properly.) Before dawn on June 3, three Union corps charged the Southern defenses, and in

less than ten minutes the main assault was over. In that brief time, instead of gaining a breakthrough that might have ended the war in Virginia, the Army of the Potomac lost seven thousand men (compared to fifteen hundred casualties for the Confederates). Lee had won a crucial victory (in fact, his last in battle), while Grant had only himself to blame. The following accounts appear in the memoirs of Confederate artillery chief E. P. Alexander and Union Maj. Gen. Martin McMahon. The Bloody Angle to which Alexander refers was the name given to a particularly deadly part of the fighting at Spotsylvania that took place on May 12. Enfilading fire, as McMahon uses the term, is gunfire directed from a flanking position along the length of an enemy's line.

Currier & Ives incorrectly titled this lithograph The Battle of Coal Harbor, Va.

THEN WE TURNED LOOSE ON them, everything, infantry & artillery, canister, shot, & shell. I think that at no point in the war, except at the Bloody Angle, were the woods so torn up by fire or the dead left so thickly strewn over the ground as in the center of that horseshoe.

PROMPTLY AT THE HOUR NAMED on the 3d of June the men moved from the slight cover of the rifle-pits, thrown up during the night, with steady, determined advance, and there rang out suddenly on the summer air such a crash of artillery and musketry as is seldom heard in war....The time of the actual advance was not over eight minutes. In that little period more men fell bleeding as they advanced than in any other like period of time throughout the war. A strange and terrible feature of this battle was that as the three gallant corps moved on, each was enfiladed while receiving the full force of the enemy's direct fire in front....No troops could stand against such a fire, and the order to lie down was given all along the line. At points where no shelter was afforded, the men were withdrawn to such cover as could be found, and the battle of Cold Harbor, as to its result at least, was over.

In his own memoirs, Grant discussed the charge at Cold Harbor ruefully.

I HAVE ALWAYS REGRETTED THAT the last assault at Cold Harbor was ever made. I might say the same thing of the assault of the 22nd of May, 1863, at Vicksburg. At Cold Harbor no advantage whatever was gained to compensate for the heavy loss we sustained. Indeed, the advantages, other than those of relative losses, were on the Confederate side. Before that, the Army of Northern Virginia seemed to have acquired a wholesome regard for the courage, endurance, and soldierly qualities generally of the Army of the Potomac. They no longer wanted to fight them "one Confederate to five Yanks." Indeed, they seemed to have given up any idea of gaining any advantage of their antagonist in the open field. They had come to much prefer breastworks in their front to the Army of the Potomac. This change seemed to revive their hopes temporarily; but it was of short duration.

WED 8 JUN. LINCOLN RENOMINATED

Convening in Baltimore on June 7 under the National Union party banner (in order to accommodate pro-Lincoln War Democrats), the Republicans on June 8 overwhelming renominated Abraham Lincoln. Next, at Lincoln's request, Vice President Hannibal Hamlin was dropped from the ticket in favor of War Democrat Andrew Johnson, currently the military governor of Tennessee. But not everyone was pleased: Some Republican party leaders, such as Salmon P. Chase and Horace Greeley, argued that, with the outcome of the war still in doubt, Lincoln could not win reelection in the fall. Others, such as this New York World *editorial writer, simply hated Lincoln, believing*

B-36

Mathew Brady's famous portrait of Grant at Cold Harbor.

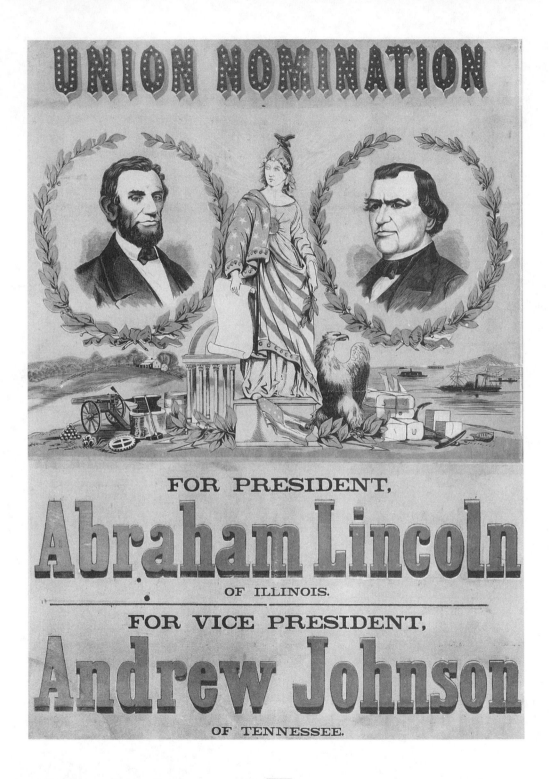

him to be an uncouth bumpkin, unfit for the office he held. (The World, *it should be noted, was a highly partisan Democratic newspaper.)*

 THE AMERICAN PEOPLE ARE IN no mood to re-elect a man to the highest office whose daily language is indecent, and who, riding over the field of Antietam, when thirty thousand of his fellow citizens were yet warm in their freshly made graves, could slap Marshal Lamon on the knee, and call for the negro song of "Picayune Butler." The war is a serious business to men whose sons have bitten the dust, whose brothers are under the Virginia hill-sides; it is a very serious business to women whose children have come home to them maimed for life, or whose husbands pine in the hospitals or have perished in the swamps of Virginia. They cannot be reminded of a smutty song; they cannot tread on fresh graves and grin and roar over a ribald nigger song.

FRI
10 BRICE'S CROSSROADS
JUN.

Though busy himself in Georgia, Major General Sherman (as commander of the Military Division of the Mississippi) ordered Brig. Gen. Samuel D. Sturgis, stationed in Memphis, to find and destroy the harassing cavalry of Confederate Maj. Gen. Nathan Bedford Forrest. Sturgis's combined force of eighty-five hundred cavalry and infantrymen should have been sufficient to stop Forrest's band of forty-three hundred, which had recently been raiding Sherman's long supply lines through

northern Mississippi—or so Sherman thought. The two armies met at Brice's Crossroads, south of Corinth, where Forrest gambled that Sturgis's cavalry would arrive well before his infantry and that, when the infantry did arrive, it would be fatigued from the heat of the Mississippi sun. Therefore, he attacked early, breaking the Union lines and sending the Northerners into full retreat. During the pursuit that followed, Forrest's men captured an additional 18 guns, 176 wagons, and 1,600 prisoners. John Hubbard, a Confederate private, penned this account of the battle.

WILL I EVER FORGET IT? THE enemy posted in a dense wood and behind a heavy fence poured a galling fire into our ranks. It looked like death to go to the fence, but many of the men reached it. Four of Company E were

Brig. Gen. Samuel D. Sturgis

killed in this charge. Men could not stay there and live. The Seventh Tennessee with Chalmer's Battalion on the left was driven back in confusion. With the steadiness of veterans, they re-formed for another onset. As I remember it, this time we went over the fence. Reinforcements were evidently at hand for the Federals, for they came on like a resistless tide. It was death not to give back. Another readjustment of the lines, and we were at them again. I cannot say how many times this was repeated, for men in the very presence of death take no note of time. The roar of artillery and the fusillade of small arms were deafening. Sheets of flames were along both lines while dense clouds of smoke arose above the heavily wooded field. No language is adequate to paint the verities of the moment.

Since the beginning of military operations in the South, it had become commonplace for slaves to attach themselves to Union forces as they moved through a region. (Most of these were later shipped to the North as refugees.) In her diary entry for this day, Judith McGuire reflected on this practice. Having been raised in the antebellum South, McGuire felt no animosity toward the contrabands but rather pity for these African Americans unwisely abandoning the beneficial paternalism of the plantation for the godforsaken commerciality of the North.

SAT
11
JUN.

SCARCELY A REPRESENTATIVE OF the sons and daughters of Africa remained in that whole section of country; they had all gone to Canaan, by way of

Black laborers collecting bones of the dead.

York River, Chesapeake Bay, and the Potomac—not dry-shod, for the waters were not rolled back at the presence of these modern Israelites, but in vessels crowded to suffocation in this excessively warm weather. They have gone to homeless poverty, an unfriendly climate, and hard work; many of them to die without sympathy, for the invalid, the decrepit, and the infant of days have left their houses, beds, and many comforts, the homes of their birth, the masters and mistresses who regarded them not so much as property as humble friends and members of their families. Poor, deluded creatures! I am grieved not so much on account of the loss of their services, though that is excessively inconvenient and annoying, but for their grievous disappointment. Those who have trades, or who are brought up as lady's maids or house servants, may do well, but woe to the masses who have gone with the blissful hope of idleness and free supplies! We have lost several who were great comforts to us, and others who were sources of care, responsibility, and great expense.

PETERSBURG

WED 15 JUN.

On June 12, nine days after the failed charge at Cold Harbor, Grant secretly began to move his enormous army toward the James River, which Union troops began to cross on June 14. Meanwhile, W. F. Smith's Eighteenth Corps, traveling by water up the peninsula, reported to Benjamin Butler at Bermuda Hundred, where Butler's Army of the James received orders to attack Petersburg on the fifteenth. Including W. S. Hancock's Second Corps, which had already crossed the river, the available Federal forces numbered sixteen thousand, compared to just a token three-thousand-man Confeder-

ate garrison under P. G. T. Beauregard. In all likelihood, Petersburg, which guarded the southern approach to Richmond, would have fallen that day had it not been for Smith's extreme caution and the fact that Hancock's corps didn't arrive until 7:00 P.M. Instead, Butler botched the attack, giving Beauregard time to bring up reinforcements; the Rebel lines held; and the Petersburg Campaign lengthened into a protracted siege. As the Army of the Potomac arrived, there were several renewed frontal assaults, but by June 18, the two sides settled into a routine that remained relatively stable until April 1865. In the letter of June 17 below, written from the Petersburg trenches, Union Brig. Gen. Robert McAllister described one of the early charges.

These log-and-dirt shelters at Petersburg, called "bombproofs," shielded occupants from artillery fire.

LAST EVENING WE ADVANCED and charged the enemy. I had command of all the New Jersey regiments and was in the front line of our Brigade. Genl. Mott commanded the last line. We had a hard fight. The Jersey troops suffered considerable loss. My regiment lost 36 killed and wounded. Captain Layton is killed. Several valuable men laid down their lives on that field. I was terribly exposed; but thank God, He protected me. I was unharmed. God be praised. Let us thank God for his protective care.

In this excerpt from his memoirs, Confederate Lt. William Nathaniel Wood recollects his unit's action elsewhere on the Petersburg perimeter.

UPON A HURRIED CONSULTATION, it was agreed to continue the advance until we met with some formidable obstacle. We expected the brigade was following us, but it turned out that at least a mile lay between us. We now moved cautiously and with less celerity, but continued to go forward. We soon emerged into a large opening, and immediately in front was a line of formidable-looking earthworks. Another hasty consultation. Must we advance upon the works? We had in all about forty muskets, but every musket was in the hands of a soldier. "Boys, yell like demons. Forward! double quick!" and away we went, making noise enough for a brigade, and fortunately, kicking up so much dust that the enemy doubtless thought it prudent to leave the works before our arrival, and thus we regained the earthworks on the Howlett line that had been vacated by Beauregard's troops when hurried to the defense of Petersburg.

THU 16 JUN. *On this day, President Lincoln attended the Great Central Sanitary Fair in Philadelphia, where he delivered a speech, excerpted here. Lincoln used the occasion to praise those benevolent organizations (such as the U.S. Sanitary Commission and the U.S. Christian Commission) tending to the needs and wants of the soldiers. Sanitary fairs, in general, were regional gatherings, organized by women to promote the Union cause. Their name refers to the U.S. Sanitary Commission, into which most of the money raised was channeled.*

I SUPPOSE THAT THIS TOAST WAS intended to open the way for me to say something. War, at best, is terrible, and this war of ours, in its magnitude and in its duration, is one of the most terrible. It has deranged business, totally in many localities, and partially in all localities. It has destroyed property, and ruined homes; it has produced a national debt and taxation unprecedented, at least in this country. It has carried mourning to almost every home, until it can almost be said that the "heavens are hung in black." Yet it continues, and several relieving coincidents have accompanied it from the very beginning, which have not been known, as I understood, or have any knowledge of, in any former wars in the history of the world. The Sanitary Commission, with all its benevolent labors, the Christian Commission, with all its Christian and benevolent labors, and the various places, arrangements, so to speak, and institutions, have contributed to the comfort and relief of the soldiers. You have two of these places in this city—the Cooper Shop and Union Volunteer Refreshment Saloons. And lastly, these fairs, which, I believe, began only in last August, if I mistake not, in Chicago; then at Boston, at Cincinnati, Brooklyn, New York, at Baltimore, and those at present held at St. Louis, Pittsburgh, and Philadelphia. The motive and object that lie at the bottom of all these are most worthy; for, say what you will, after all the most is due to the soldier, who takes his life in his hands and goes to fight the battles of his country. In what is contributed to his comfort when he passes to and fro, and in what is contributed to him when he is sick and wounded, in whatever shape it comes, whether from the fair and tender hand of woman, or from any other source, is much, very much; but, I think there is still that which has as much value to him [in the continual reminders he sees in the newspapers, that while he is absent he is yet remembered by the loved ones at home]—he is not forgotten. Another view of these various institutions is worthy of consideration, I think; they are voluntary contributions, given freely, zealously, and earnestly, on top of all the disturbances of business, the taxation and burdens that the war has imposed upon us, giving proof that the national resources are not at all exhausted, that the national spirit of patriotism is even stronger than at the commencement of the rebellion.

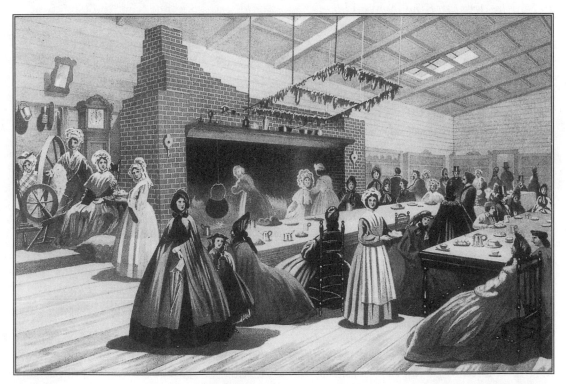

This lithograph was issued to honor the Brooklyn Sanitary Fair and its popular New England Kitchen exhibit.

SUN 19 JUN. THE KEARSARGE AND THE ALABAMA

Although the Union navy controlled most of the Confederate coastline, ships belonging to the titular Confederate States Navy nevertheless threatened Union shipping on the high seas. These raiders—most famously the CSS Georgia, the CSS Florida, and the CSS Alabama—were built in England specifically as government-run privateers, and they proved to be a major annoyance throughout the war. The Alabama, in particular, under the command of Capt. Raphael Semmes, became famous all over the world for astonishing forays that took the ship from the Caribbean to South Africa to Singapore and back. After capturing sixty-five Union merchant ships, Semmes put in to Cherbourg, France, on June 1 for a much-needed refit. There, on June 14, he was discovered by Capt. John Winslow of the USS Kearsarge. A chivalrous communication between the two officers produced an agreement that the Alabama would leave port on June 19 and face the Kearsarge in international waters. Thanks to the Alabama's international reputation, the impending naval duel became the talk of France, and many wealthy Parisians flocked to the coast to watch the engagement. For about an hour, the Kearsarge and the Alabama circled one another, exchanging broadsides as they moved closer and closer. Finally, the Kearsarge sent Semmes's ship to the bottom. Presented here are accounts written by the two commanders: first, Winslow's official report,
then the report filed by Semmes, in which the Confederate described his rescue by an English yacht viewing the battle.

I HAVE THE HONOR TO INFORM the Department that the day subsequent to the arrival of the *Kearsarge* off this port, on the 14th instant, I received a note from Captain Semmes, begging that the *Kearsarge* would not depart, as he intended to fight her and would not delay her but a day or two.

According to this notice, the *Alabama* left the port of Cherbourg this morning at about 9:30 o'clock. At 10:20 A.M. we discovered her steering towards us. Fearing the question of jurisdiction might arise, we steamed to sea until a distance of 6 or 7 miles was attained from the Cherbourg breakwater, when we rounded to and commenced steaming for the *Alabama*. As we approached her within about 1,200 yards she opened fire, we receiving two or three broadsides before a shot was returned. The action continued, the respective steamers making a circle round and round at a distance of about 900 yards from each other. At the expiration of an hour the *Alabama* struck [her colors], going down in about twenty minutes afterwards, and carrying a great many persons with her.

I STEAMED OUT OF THE HARBOR of Cherbourg between 9 and 10 o'clock on the morning of June 19 for the purpose of engaging the enemy's steamer *Kearsarge*, which had been lying off and on the port for several days previously. After clearing the harbor we descried the enemy, with his head offshore, at a distance of

Currier & Ives's The U.S. Sloop of War "Kearsarge" 7 Guns Sinking the Pirate "Alabama" 8 Guns.

about 9 miles. We were three-quarters of an hour in coming up with him. I had previously pivoted my guns to starboard, and made all my preparations for engaging the enemy on that side. When within about a mile and a quarter of the enemy he suddenly wheeled, and bringing his head inshore presented his starboard battery to me. By this time we were distant about 1 mile from each other, when I opened on him with solid shot, to which he replied in a few minutes, and the engagement became active on both sides. The enemy now pressed his ship under a full head of steam, and to prevent our passing each other too speedily, and to keep our respective broadsides bearing, it became

necessary to fight in a circle, the two ships steaming around a common center and preserving a distance from each other of from a quarter to half a mile. When we got within good shell range, we opened upon him with shell. Some ten or fifteen minutes after the commencement of the action our spanker gaff was shot away and our ensign came down by the run. This was immediately replaced by another at the mizzenmast head. The fire now became very hot, and the enemy's shot and shell began to tell upon our hull, knocking down, killing, and disabling a number of men in different parts of the ship. Perceiving that our shell, though apparently exploding against the enemy's

Capt. Raphael Semmes

my colors to prevent the further destruction of life, and dispatched a boat to inform the enemy of our condition. Although we were now but 400 yards from each other, the enemy fired upon me five times after my colors had been struck, dangerously wounding several of my men. It is charitable to suppose that a ship of war of a Christian nation could not have done this intentionally. We now turned all our attention toward the wounded and such of the boys as were unable to swim. These were dispatched in my quarter boats, the only boats remaining to me, the waist boats having been torn to pieces.

Some twenty minutes after my furnace fires had been extinguished, and the ship being on the point of settling, every man, in obedience to a previous order which had been given to the crew, jumped overboard and endeavored to save himself. There was no appearance of any boat coming to me from the enemy until after the ship went down. Fortunately, however, the steam yacht *Deerhound,* owned by a gentleman of Lancaster, England (Mr. John Lancaster), who was himself on board, steamed up in the midst of my drowning men and rescued a number of both officers and men from the water. I was fortunate enough myself thus to escape to the shelter of the neutral flag, together with about forty others, all told. About this time the *Kearsarge* sent one and then tardily, another boat....

The enemy was heavier than myself, both in ship, battery, and crew; but I did not know until the action was over that she was also ironclad. Our total loss in killed and wounded is 30, to wit, 9 killed and 21 wounded.

sides, were doing but little damage, I returned to solid shot firing, and from this time onward alternated with shot and shell. After the lapse of about one hour and ten minutes our ship was ascertained to be in a sinking condition, the enemy's shell having exploded in our sides and between decks, opening large apertures, through which the water rushed with great rapidity. For some few minutes I had hopes of reaching the French coast, for which purpose I gave the ship all steam and set such of the fore and aft sails as were available. The ship filled so rapidly, however, that before we had made much progress the fires were extinguished in the furnaces and we were evidently on the point of sinking. I now hauled down

Kurz & Allison used the battlefield topography to great effect in this lithograph of the engagement at Kennesaw Mountain.

MON 27 JUN. KENNESAW MOUNTAIN

During the Atlanta Campaign, Sherman repeatedly sought to dislodge the Confederate Army of Tennessee from strong entrenched positions by turning its flank. This had been the case at Dalton and at Resaca, but at Kennesaw Mountain, Sherman changed tactics, ordering a frontal assault against what he judged to be an overextended and thinly held Confederate position. As Sherman detailed in his memoirs, he was wrong.

ABOUT 9 A.M. OF THE DAY appointed, the troops moved to the assault, and all along our lines for ten miles a furious fire of artillery and mus-ketry was kept up. At all points the enemy met us with determined courage and in great force. McPherson's attacking column fought up the face of the lesser Kennesaw, but could not reach the summit. About a mile to the right (just below the Dallas road) Thomas's assaulting column reached the parapet, where Brigadier-General Daniel McCook (my old law partner) was desperately wounded, from the effects of which he afterward died. By 11:30 the assault was in fact over, and had failed. We had not broken the rebel line at either point, but our assaulting column held their ground within a few yards of the rebel trenches, and there covered themselves with parapet. McPherson lost about five hundred men and several valuable officers, and Thomas lost nearly two thousand men.

JULY 1864

SAT 2 JUL. *Black women who found employment with the Union army were usually given the title "laundress," even though they often performed the same duties as white "nurses" and "matrons." Susie King Taylor, for example, did much more for Union soldiers than simply wash their clothes, as this excerpt from her memoirs makes clear.*

ABOUT FOUR O'CLOCK, JULY 2, the charge was made. The firing could be plainly heard in camp. I hastened down to the landing and remained there until eight o'clock that morning. When the wounded arrived, or rather began to arrive, the first one brought in was Samuel Anderson of our company. He was badly wounded. Then others of our boys, some with their legs off, arm gone, foot off, and wounds of all kinds imaginable. They had to wade through creeks and marshes, as they were discovered by the enemy and shelled very badly. A number of the men were lost, some got fastened in the mud and had to cut off the legs of their pants, to free themselves. The 103d New York suffered the most, as their men were very badly wounded.

My work now began. I gave my assistance to try to alleviate their sufferings. I asked the doctor at the hospital what I could get for them to eat. They wanted soup, but that I could not get; but I had a few cans of condensed milk and some turtle eggs, so I thought I would try to make some custard. I had doubts as to my success, for cooking with turtle eggs was something new to me, but the adage has it, "Nothing ventured, nothing done," so I made a venture and the result was a very delicious custard. This I carried to the men, who enjoyed it very much. My services were given at all times for the comfort of these men. I was on hand to assist whenever needed. I was enrolled as company laundress, but I did very little of it, because I was always busy doing other things through camp, and was employed all the time doing something for the officers and comrades.

MON 4 JUL. LINCOLN VETOES THE WADE-DAVIS BILL

By this time, many of the radicals in Congress had aligned themselves behind what came to be known as the "state suicide" theory of Reconstruction—that is, that the states of the Confederacy had, in fact, dissolved their bonds with the Union and therefore needed to be readmitted (under whatever standards for readmission Congress chose to set). Lincoln, of course, had long since committed himself to the opposing theory— that the Southern states had never actually left the Union—so he naturally opposed the Wade-Davis Bill, which defenders of the state suicide theory introduced and passed during the spring of 1864. Named for sponsors Sen. Benjamin F. Wade of Ohio and Rep. Henry Winter Davis of Maryland, the bill placed Reconstruction under tight congressional control and made readmission quite difficult (requiring 50 percent of each state's voting population to swear an oath of allegiance to the Union, whereas Lincoln's more lenient plan required only 10 percent to swear a lesser oath). Convinced that he

Benjamin F. Wade

was right in principle as well as practice, President Lincoln withstood strong last-minute pressure to sign the bill, instead permitting Congress to adjourn without taking any action. This unusual pocket veto, however, had political consequences—a point evocatively made by this entry in the diary of Lincoln's private secretary, John Hay. (Charles Sumner, George Boutwell, and Zachariah Chandler were all influential Republican congressmen; Hay also makes reference to Secretary of State William H. Seward, Secretary of the Interior John P. Usher, and Chase's replacement at Treasury, William Fessenden.)

IN THE PRESIDENT'S ROOM WE were pretty busy signing & reporting bills. Sumner was in a state of intense

Charles Sumner

William Fessenden

anxiety about the Reconstruction Bill of Winter Davis. Boutwell also expressed his fear that it would be pocketed. Chandler came in and asked if it was signed "No." He said it would make a terrible record for us to fight if it were vetoed: the President talked to him a moment. He said "Mr. Chandler, this bill was placed before me a few minutes before Congress adjourns. It is a matter of too much importance to be swallowed in that way." "If it is vetoed it will damage us fearfully in the North West. It may not in Illinois, it will in Michigan and Ohio. The important point is that one prohibiting slavery in the reconstructed states."…

The President continued, "I do not see how any of us now can deny and contradict all we have always said, that congress has no constitutional power over slavery in the states." Mr. Fessenden, who had just come into the room, said "I agree with you there, sir. I even had my doubts

as to the constitutional efficacy of your own decree of emancipation, in such cases where it has not been carried into effect by the actual advance of the army."

Prest. "This bill and this position of these gentlemen seems to me to make the fatal admission (in asserting that the insurrectionary states are no longer states in the Union) that states whenever they please may of their own motion dissolve their connection with the Union. Now we cannot survive that admission I am convinced. If that be true I am not President, these gentlemen are not Congress. I have laboriously endeavored to avoid that question ever since it first began to be mooted & thus to avoid confusion and disturbance in our own counsels. It was to obviate this question that I earnestly favored the movement for an amendment to the Constitution abolishing slavery, which passed the Senate and failed in the House. I thought it much better, if it were possible, to restore the Union without the necessity of a violent quarrel among its friends, as to whether certain states have been in or out of the Union during the war: a merely metaphysical question and one unnecessary to be forced into discussion."

Seward, Usher and Fessenden seemed entirely in accord with this.

After we left the Capitol I said I did not think Chandler, man of the people and personally popular as he was, had any definite comprehension of popular currents and influence—that he was out of the way now especially—that I did not think people would bolt their ticket on a question of metaphysics.

The Prest. answered, "If they choose to make a point upon this I do not doubt that they can do harm. They have never been friendly to me & I don't know that this will make any special difference as to that. At all events, I must keep some consciousness of being somewhere near right: I must keep some standard of principle fixed within myself."

SAT 9 JUL. MONOCACY

Control of the Shenandoah Valley was important to both sides because the region's excellent roads provided quick and easy access to Pennsylvania, Maryland, and Washington, and because its farms, largely untouched since Stonewall Jackson's successful 1862 campaign, continued to produce bountiful crops for the Confederacy. When Ulysses S. Grant assumed overall command of the Union armies, he drew up

a master plan that included a renewed offensive in the valley so that Lee would be pressured to divert troops there from his lines around Richmond. On May 15, at New Market Heights, Union Maj. Gen. Franz Sigel attacked—and was defeated by—Confederates under Maj. Gen. John C. Breckinridge. On June 5, Sigel's replacement, Maj. Gen. David Hunter, beat a much smaller Confederate force at Piedmont, after which Lee dispatched a corps under Lt. Gen. Jubal A. Early to defend Lynchburg. Hunter subsequently withdrew into West Virginia, freeing Early to recapture Winchester and (on July 5–6) cross the Potomac River into Maryland, threatening both Baltimore and Washington. On July 9, Union Maj. Gen. Lew Wallace attempted to block Early's advance at the Monocacy River just east of Frederick. Many of Wallace's six thousand men (compared to fourteen thousand for Early) had been rushed north from Petersburg. They put up a stiff defense, but Confederate Maj. Gen. John B. Gordon was finally able to turn the Union's left flank and force a retreat. Nevertheless, Wallace's stubborn resistance accomplished his larger strategic goal, which was to delay Early long enough for Grant to reinforce the capital. Early arrived at Silver Spring on the outskirts of Washington on July 11, raising a panic that resulted in convalescents being ordered to man the capital's defenses. The arrival of two more corps from Petersburg, however, stabilized the situation, and Early, seeing that he was outnumbered, pulled back across the Potomac and retreated to the Strasburg area. Following are excerpts from the official reports of Wallace, written several weeks later in Baltimore, and Early, penned five days later at Leesburg.

THE SITUATION IN THE DEPART-ment of West Virginia, about the beginning of July, was very uncertain. Major-General Hunter had retreated westwardly from Lynchburg, leaving open the Shenandoah Valley, up which a column of rebels of unknown strength had marched and thrown General Sigel back from Martinsburg to Williamsport, thence down the left bank of the Potomac to Maryland Heights, where, with his command, he was supposed to be besieged.

The strength of the invading column, by whom it was commanded, what its objects were, the means provided to rebel it, everything in fact connected with it, were, on my part, purely conjectural. All that I was certain of was that my own department was seriously threatened....

...From 9 o'clock to 10.30 the action was little more than a warm skirmish and experimental cannonading, in which, however, the enemy's superiority in the number and caliber of his guns was fully shown. Against my six 3-inch rifles, he opposed not less than sixteen Napoleons. In this time, also, the fighting at the stone bridge assumed serious proportions; Colonel Brown held his position with great difficulty. About 10.30 o'clock the enemy's first line of battle made its appearance, and moved against Ricketts, who, mean time, had changed front to the left, so that his right rested upon the river-bank. This change unavoidably subjected his regiments to an unintermitted enfilading fire from the batteries across the stream. So

Lt. Gen. Jubal A. Early

great was the rebel front, also, that I was compelled to order the whole division into one line, thus leaving it without reserves. Still the enemy's front was greatest. Two more guns were sent to Ricketts. Finally, by burning the wooden bridge and the block-house at its further end, thus releasing the force left to defend them, I put into the engagement every available man except Tyler's reserves, which, from the messages arriving, I expected momentarily to have to dispatch to Colonel Brown's assistance. The enemy's first line was badly defeated. His second line then advanced, and was repulsed, but after a fierce and continuous struggle. In the time thus occupied I could probably have retired without much trouble, as the rebels were badly punished. The main objects of the battle, however, were unaccomplished, the rebel strength was not yet developed.

At 1 o'clock the three re-enforcing regiments of veterans would be on the ground, and then the splendid behavior of Ricketts and his men inspired me with confidence. One o'clock came, but not the re-enforcements; and it was impossible to get an order to them. My telegraph operator, and the railroad agent, with both his trains, had run away. An hour and a half later I saw the third line of rebels move out of the woods and down the hill, behind which they made their formation; right after it came the fourth. It was time to get away. Accordingly, I ordered General Ricketts to make preparations and retire to the Baltimore pike. About 4 o'clock he began the execution of the order. The stone bridge held by Colonel Brown now became all important; its loss was the loss of my line of retreat, and I had reason to believe that the enemy, successful on my left, would redouble his efforts against the right. General Tyler had already marched with his reserves to Brown's assistance; but on receipt of notice of my intention, without waiting for Gilpin and Landstreet, he galloped to the bridge and took the command in person. After the disengagement of Ricketts' line, when the head of the retreating column reached the pike, I rode to the bridge, and ordered it to be held at all hazards by the force then there, until the enemy should be found in its rear, at least until the last regiment had cleared the country road by which the retreat was being effected. This order General Tyler obeyed. A little after 5 o'clock, when my column was well on the march toward New Market, an attack on his rear convinced him of the impracticability of longer maintaining his post. Many of his men then took to the woods, but by

his direction the greater part kept their ranks, and manfully fought their way through. In this way Colonel Brown escaped. General Tyler, finding himself cut off, dashed into the woods, with the officers of his staff, and was happily saved. His gallantry and self-sacrificing devotion are above all commendation of words.

I FOUND WALLACE IN FORCE at Monocacy Junction, his force being stated in Northern accounts at 10,000, and consisting in part of the Third Division, of the Sixth Corps, under Ricketts, which had arrived the day before. This force we attacked on the afternoon of the same day, Ramseur demonstrating in front, while Gordon moved across the Monocacy on the enemy's flank by a route which had been opened by McCausland's brigade of cavalry in a very gallant manner. The enemy in a very short time was completely routed by Gordon, and left the field in great disorder and retreated in haste on Baltimore....

On the morning of the 10th I moved toward Washington, taking the route by Rockville, and then turning to the left to get on the Seventh-street pike. The day was very hot and the roads exceedingly dusty, but we marched thirty miles.

On the morning of the 11th we continued the march, but the day was so excessively hot, even at a very early hour in the morning, and the dust so dense, that many of the men fell by the way, and it became necessary to slacken our pace. Nevertheless, when we reached the right of the enemy's fortifications the men were almost completely exhausted and not in a condition to make an attack. Skirmishers were thrown out and moved up to the vicinity of the fortifications. These we found to be very strong and constructed very scientifically. They consist of a circle of inclosed forts, connected by breast-works, with ditches, palisades, and abatis in front, and every approach swept by a cross-fire of artillery, including some heavy guns. I determined at first to make an assault, but before it could be made it became apparent that the enemy had been strongly re-enforced, and we knew that the Sixth Corps had arrived from Grant's army, and after consultation with my division commanders I became satis-fied that the assault, even if successful, would be attended with such great sacri-fice as would insure the destruction of my whole force before the victory could have been made available, and, if unsuccessful, would necessarily have resulted in the loss of the whole force. I, therefore, reluc-tantly determined to retire, and as it was evident preparations were making to cut off my retreat, and while troops were gath-ering around me I would find it difficult to get supplies, I determined to retire across the Potomac to this county before it became too late.

THU
14 TUPELO
JUL.

An uneducated Lincoln-style back-woodsman who later amassed a fortune in the slave trade, Confederate Maj. Gen. Nathan Bedford Forrest was "the very devil," according to Union Maj. Gen. William T. Sherman. As comman-der of the Military Division of the

Maj. Gen. Nathan Bedford Forrest

Mississippi, where Forrest mainly operated, Sherman had the overall responsibility for subduing Forrest, whose bullet-quick and sharply exe-cuted cavalry raids kept much larger Union forces off balance. Moreover, Forrest's military skill combined with his personal magnetism and passionate proslavery ideology to make him seem almost superhuman to Northern sol-diers. In the letter excerpted below, Sherman memorably described Forrest for Secretary of War Edwin M. Stanton. Sherman wrote the letter after Brig. Gen. Samuel D. Sturgis failed to defeat Forrest at Brice's Crossroads on June 10 but before this day's engage-ment at Tupelo, Mississippi, between Forrest and Union Maj. Gen. A. J. Smith. Despite Sherman's assurance to Stanton that Smith (and Maj. Gen.

Joseph A. Mower) would certainly crush Forrest, the wily Confederate prevailed again. Fourteen thousand troops under Smith held their ground against Forrest's ten thousand, so the battle was tactically a Federal victory; however, the next day, Smith pulled back to Memphis, his strategic goal unaccomplished, leaving Forrest free once again to continue his maraudings.

I WILL HAVE THE MATTER OF Sturgis critically examined, and, if he be at fault, he shall have no mercy at my hands. I cannot but believe he had troops enough. I know I would have been willing to attempt the same task with that force; but Forrest is the very devil, and I think he has got some of our troops under cower. I have two officers at Memphis that will fight all the time—A. J. Smith and Mower. The latter is a young brigadier of fine promise, and I commend him to your notice. I will order them to make up a force and go out and follow Forrest to the death, if it cost 10,000 lives and breaks the Treasury. There will never be peace in Tennessee till Forrest is dead.

SAT 16 JUL. *In protest of the U.S. government's refusal to pay them at the same rate as white soldiers, the men of the Fifty-fourth and Fifty-fifth Massachusetts Volunteer Infantry Regiments decided, as of July 1863, to forgo all pay until the rates were equalized. More than a year later, with the government still holding fast to its position, disheartened members of the Fifty-fifth Massachusetts sent this petition to President Lincoln requesting*

their back pay and immediate discharge. (About this time, Congress finally gave in on the pay issue and increased the amount given black soldiers to thirteen dollars per month, the same that whites received.)

SIR: WE THE MEMBERS OF CO. D of the 55th Massachusetts vols Call the attention of your Excellency to our case

1st We wase enlisted under the act of Congress of July 1861 Placing the officers non Commissioned officers and Privates of the volunteer forces in all Respects as to Pay on the footing of Similar Corps of the Regular Army

2nd We Have Been in the Field now thirteen months & a Great many yet longer We Have Received no Pay & Have Been offered only seven Dollars Pr month Which the Paymaster Has said was all He Had ever Been authorized to Pay Colored Troops [T]his was not according to our enlistment Consequently We Refused the Money [T]he Commonwealth of Massachusetts then Passed an act to make up all Deficienceys which the general Government Refused To Pay But this We Could not Recieve as The Troops in the general service are not Paid Partly By Government & Partly By State

3rd that to us money is no object we came to fight For Liberty justice & Equality. These are gifts we Prise more Highly than Gold For these We Left our Homes our Familys Friends & Relatives most Dear to take as it ware our Lives in our Hands To Do Battle for God & Liberty

4th after the elaps of over thirteen months spent cheerfully & willingly Doing our Duty most faithfuly in the Trenches Fatiegue Duty in camp and conspicious valor & endurence in Battle as our Past History will Show

5th   therefore we Deem these sufficient Reasons for Demanding our Pay from the Date of our inlistment & our imediate Discharge Having Been enlisted under False Pretence as the Past History of the Company will Prove

6th   Be it further Resolved that if imediate steps are not takened to Relieve us we will Resort to more stringent mesures

We have the Honor to Remin your Obedint Servants

The members of Co D

SUN 17 JUL. *As the Confederacy's situation worsened, President Jefferson Davis found himself thinking more and more about emancipation as the last, best hope of the South. In an interview on this date given to Northern journalist James R. Gilmore, when questioned how peace might come about, Davis took the opportunity to distance himself from Alexander Stephens's fire-eating 1861 "corner-stone of slavery" speech and instead proclaim his primary goal to be Confederate independence.*

IN A VERY SIMPLE WAY. WITH-draw your armies from our territory, and peace will come of itself. We do not seek to subjugate you. We are not waging an offensive war, except so far as it is offensive-defensive—that is, so far as we are forced to invade you to prevent your invading us. Let us alone, and peace will come at once....

...I desire peace as much as you do. I deplore bloodshed as much as you do; but I feel that not one drop of the blood shed in this war is on *my* hands—I can look up to my God and say this. I tried all in my power to avert this war. I saw it coming, and for twelve years I worked night and day to prevent it, but I could not. The North was mad and blind; it would not let us govern ourselves, and so the war came, and now it must go on till the last man of this generation falls in his tracks, and his children seize his musket and fight our battle, *unless you acknowledge our right to self-government.* We are not fighting for slavery. We are fighting for Independence, and that, or extermination, we *will* have.

MON 18 JUL. *Many of the women who volunteered to teach in the schools newly established for freed people were often pressed to their limits. One such teacher was Emma V. Brown, an African American who described her difficulties in this letter to her friend Emily Howland. The Rebel threat to which she refers was that posed by Early's army during the second week of July.*

DEAR FRIEND: I HAVE NOT SEEN you since I have been teaching in Washington....We have had an average attendance of one hundred and thirty pupils. There is only one room for this multitude. Miss Perkins prefers to have the primary department. She teaches from the charts you gave. Her scholars recite in concert and I must have my classes at the same time. We have a regular Bedlam.

This is hard work—it has been too hard for me and Dr. Breed closed the school a week earlier than he intended because I was too sick to teach longer. I gave completely out.

Would you believe that I hate teaching now? I grow sick at the very thought of going back to teaching. I can scarcely realize that I who loved teaching so dearly should feel so. Dr. B. is kind and considerate, Miss P. I am devoted to, she is a faithful friend and an excellent teacher, the children have been good, yet the mere thought of going back to that school makes me sick.

I must work—there is no alternative, yet it is not right to teach with this feeling. What shall I do? How can I overcome this loathing, this hatred of teaching?

I have boarded in Washington but am at home [in Georgetown] now. The enemy made a daring attempt recently. Many of our citizens were alarmed. I did not believe they could get in. Is it not a shame that W. is so poorly defended? The rebels are far more solicitous about Richmond. The rebels are so daring, so courageous that were it not for the remembrance of Fort Pillow I fear I should be a sympathizer.

Yours ever,
E. V. Brown

WED 20 JUL. PEACHTREE CREEK

Displeased with Joseph E. Johnston's demoralizing strategy of withdrawal, Jefferson Davis replaced the cautious veteran on July 17 with Lt. Gen. John Bell Hood, a daring but brash thirty-

The Chattahoochee River bridge razed by Johnston and rebuilt by Federal engineers.

three-year-old. Hood, who had been severely wounded at both Gettysburg and Chickamauga, had a reputation for aggressiveness that Davis hoped would inspire the Army of Tennessee now that the fighting had reached the outskirts of Atlanta. On this day at Peachtree Creek, Hood attacked the Federal Army of the Cumberland under Maj. Gen. George Thomas. Although Hood's plan to engage seperately each of Sherman's three armies may have seemed reasonable, even Thomas's army alone proved too much for him. Two hours of frantic Confederate charges resulted in fewer than two thousand Union casualties, compared to nearly five thousand for Hood's army (both sides numbering about twenty thousand at the start). Three days later, Union Maj. James A.

Lt. Gen. John Bell Hood

Connelly offered this assessment of Hood, whom he considered more reckless than anything else. Meanwhile, Sherman's armies now had Atlanta half surrounded.

 HOOD FIRST MANIFESTED HIS dash and recklessness as a commander of the rebel army, when, on the 20th inst. He massed his whole army and hurled it against what he supposed was our right, but which, unfortunately for him, proved to be about our centre. The attack was a desperate one, but it failed, and the rebel loss was terrible; probably not less than 8000; I believe the Atlanta papers of the 21st admit a loss of about 6000; our loss was between two and three thousand. The attack struck the left of our Division, but we disposed of it in about ten minutes, and didn't have more than twenty men hurt, but we had worked all the night before building strong breastworks, and so were better prepared for the attack than many other Divisions, where the men had slept the night before, and were consequently, caught without fortifications, or but incomplete ones.

FRI 22 JUL. ATLANTA

Despite the disaster at Peachtree Creek, an undaunted Hood went to work on a bold plan to defeat Sherman at the very gates of Atlanta. First, the Confederates would pull back their forces within the inner defenses of the city so as to lure Sherman's armies closer; then, a reinforced Confederate corps under Lt. Gen. William J. Hardee would turn *the Union left flank as cooperating troops under Maj. Gen. Benjamin Cheatham held Sherman's front and cavalry units interrupted the Union supply lines. On July 21, Hardee's men made a fifteen-mile night march to position themselves at the rear of Union Maj. Gen. James B. McPherson's Army of the Tennessee. The next day's fighting was vicious, but it produced little more than a tactical standstill—and again, Confederate losses were staggering, perhaps ten thousand out of forty thousand troops engaged. (Union losses were fewer than four thousand, though Major General McPherson was among those killed in action.) In the following postwar recollection, Hood (who was not himself present on the battlefield) suggested, somewhat dubiously, that the attack was a qualified success because it had lifted the spirits of his men. The second sentence of the excerpt also indicates why the Federals were so cheered by his assumption of command: Johnston had kept evading them; now, against Hood, they could simply fight, win, and go home.*

Lt. Gen. William J. Hardee

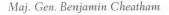 NOTWITHSTANDING THE NON-fulfillment of the brilliant result anticipated, the partial success of that day was productive of much benefit to the army. It greatly improved the *morale* of the troops, infused new life and fresh hopes, arrested desertions, which had hitherto been numerous, defeated the movement of McPherson and Schofield upon our communications in that direction, and demonstrated to the foe our determination to abandon no more territory without at least a manful effort to retain it.

Maj. Gen. Benjamin Cheatham

In his own postwar account of the battle, Union Maj. Gen. Oliver O. Howard described the specifics of McPherson's death.

McPHERSON MOUNTED, AND galloped off toward the firing. He first met Logan and Blair near the railway; then the three separated, each to hasten to his place on the battle line. McPherson went at once to Dodge; saw matters going well there; sent off aides and orderlies with dispatches, till he had but a couple of men left with him. He then rode forward to pass to Blair's left through the thick forest interval. Cheatham's division was just approaching. The call was made, "Surrender!" But McPherson, probably without a thought save to escape from such a trap, turned his horse toward his command. He was instantly slain, and fell from his horse. One of his orderlies was wounded and captured; the other escaped to tell the sad news.

Confederate soldiers stripped lumber from wood-frame houses to build these defenses outside Atlanta.

THE PETERSBURG CRATER

SAT 30 JUL.

For centuries, tunneling had been a staple of siege warfare. Medieval Europeans often dug large galleries under castle walls to reach and burn their supporting timbers. Later, with the advent of gunpowder, similar tunnels were dug, packed with powder, and exploded, destroying not only defenses but also many defenders. It should come as no surprise, therefore, that the Union army attempted such a feat beneath the siege lines at Petersburg. In fact, for more than a month, members of the Forty-eighth Pennsylvania (most of whom had been coal miners before the war) tunneled secretly beneath the four-hundred-foot gap separating Federal and Confederate lines east of the city. At 4:45 A.M. on July 30, the work was complete, and the mine was exploded. The enormous force of the blast easily breached the Confederate breastworks, leaving a gigantic crater where Elliott's Salient had been only moments before. The Federal Ninth Corps hurried through the breach, and by 8:30 A.M. there were fifteen thousand Union troops (many of them African Americans) fighting inside the thirty-foot-deep hole. And that was precisely the problem: Once the initial shock passed, the Rebels rallied quickly and began firing down into the crater from a commanding position on the upper rim. The massacre was extensive, and as at Fort Pillow, there were stories later of Confederates shooting down black soldiers even as they attempted to surrender. In the following excerpt from his memoirs, Confederate officer E. P. Alexander attempts to explain the animosity that fueled the Rebel fire.

IN FACT THERE WERE, COMPARA-tively, very few Negro prisoners taken that day. It was the first occasion on which any of the Army of Northern Virginia came in contact with Negro troops, & the general feeling of the men toward their employment was very bitter. The sympathy of the North for John Brown's memory was taken as proof of a desire that our slaves should rise in servile insurrection & massacre throughout the South, & the enlistment of Negro troops was regarded as advertisement of that desire & encouragement of the idea to the Negro....That made the fighting on this occasion exceedingly fierce & bitter on the part of our men, not only toward the Negroes themselves, but sometimes even to the whites with them....Some of the Negro prisoners, who were originally allowed to surrender by some soldiers, were afterward shot by others, & there was, without doubt, a great deal of unnecessary killing of them.

★ ★ ★ ★

AUGUST 1864

MOBILE BAY

At this point in the war, Mobile Bay was the most heavily defended Confederate waterway. Two forts, packed with heavy artillery, guarded the narrow channel that led into the bay from the Gulf of Mexico, and a flotilla of gunboats, led by the ironclad Tennessee, protected the bay's interior and the economically vital port of Mobile. At dawn on August 5, following much careful preparation, Rear Adm. David G. Farragut led a Union flotilla of eighteen ships into the channel. The guns of Forts Morgan and Gaines were manned, and the battle was engaged. Farragut directed the fight from the rigging of his flagship, the Hartford, and when a Rebel mine (then called a torpedo) crippled the USS Tecumseh, he uttered perhaps the most famous order in U.S. naval history: "Damn the torpedoes! Full speed ahead!" The Union ships complied, and by 10:00 A.M., the Tennessee, the only Confederate ship still operational, surrendered. Eight months would pass before the city of Mobile also capitulated, but the capture of the bay was nevertheless a huge strategic victory for the Union. Reprinted below is the August 8 telegram sent by Maj. Gen. Dabney H. Maury reporting the fall of Fort Gaines, followed by the congratulatory dispatch sent to Farragut by Navy Secretary Gideon Welles. The former Union naval officer to whom Welles refers is Confederate Rear Adm. Franklin Buchanan, who had earlier captained the CSS Virginia (though Buchanan was wounded and replaced the day before that ironclad's famous battle with the Monitor *off Hampton Roads, Virginia*).

IT IS PAINFULLY HUMILIATING to announce the shameful surrender of Fort Gaines at 9:30 this morning by Colonel Charles D. Anderson, of the Twenty-first Alabama Regiment. This powerful work was provisioned for six months and with a garrison of 600 men. He communicated with the enemy's fleet by flag of truce with[out] the sanction of General Page. General Page enquired by signal what his purpose was, but received no answer. His attention was attracted by signal guns. Page repeatedly telegraphed, "Hold on to your fort." The same night [Page] visited Fort Gaines and found Anderson on board the Yankee fleet arranging the terms of capitulation. He left peremptory orders for Anderson on his return not to surrender the fort, and relieved him of his command. Fort Morgan signaled this morning, but no answer was received except the hoisting of the Yankee flag off the ramparts of Fort Gaines. Anderson's conduct is officially pronounced inexplicable and shameful.

D. H. Maury,
Major-General

AGAIN IT IS MY PLEASURE AND my duty to congratulate you and your brave associates on an achievement

In this period watercolor, the CSS Tennessee *engages the* USS Richmond *on Mobile Bay.*

unequaled in our service by any other commander and only surpassed by that unparalleled naval triumph of the squadron under your command in the spring of 1862, when, proceeding up the Mississippi, you passed Forts Jackson and St. Philip, and, overcoming all obstructions, captured New Orleans and restored unobstructed navigation to the commercial emporium of the great central valley of the Union.

The bay of Mobile was not only fortified and guarded by forts and batteries on shore and by submerged obstructions, but the rebels had also collected there a formidable fleet, commanded by their highest naval officer, a former captain in the Union Navy, who, false to the Government and the Union, had deserted his country in the hour of peril and leveled his guns against the flag which it was his duty to have defended.

The possession of Mobile Bay, which you have acquired, will close the illicit traffic which has been carried on by running the blockade in that part of the Gulf, and gives point and value to the success you have achieved.

To you and the brave officers and sailors of your squadron who participated in this great achievement the Department tenders its thanks and those of the Government and country.

The bombed-out shell of Fort Morgan.

SUN 21 AUG. THE RAID ON MEMPHIS

At dawn, Maj. Gen. Nathan Bedford Forrest charged with two thousand Confederate cavalrymen into Union-held Memphis. The raiding party failed to capture Maj. Gen. C. C. Washburn (forced to flee in his underclothes) but still came away several hours later with fresh horses, prisoners, and surprisingly few losses. The raid embarassed and demoralized the Northern commanders, who recalled Maj. Gen. A. J. Smith from the field (to protect Memphis), thus leaving Forrest free once again to harass Sherman's supply lines. Even worse, all the time and resources spent chasing Forrest had been wasted. Here are accounts of the raid on Memphis from the official reports of both Washburn and Forrest. The "100-days' men" mentioned by Washburn were volunteers who had enlisted for that length of time.

MAJOR-GENERAL FORREST, WITH three brigades of cavalry, attacked this city at 4 A.M. today, making a sudden dash on our pickets and riding into the heart of the city. They were repulsed and driven out, with considerable loss. They obtained no plunder, but about 250 100-days' men were captured. They left General A. J. Smith's front at Oxford the evening of the 18th and made a forced march of nearly 100 miles. General Smith has all my cavalry but about 400 and I have taken measures to notify him and have him fall upon them and intercept their retreat. The whole thing has resulted very satisfactorily so far. What cavalry I have is harassing their rear.

I ATTACKED MEMPHIS 4 O'CLOCK this morning, driving enemy to his fortifications. We killed and captured 400, capturing their entire camp, with about 300 horses and mules. Washburn and staff escaped by darkness of the morning, leaving his clothes behind. My loss, 20 killed and wounded.

MON 22 AUG. *By this time, the Confederate currency was so devalued that everyday items required enormous sums of cash. In this diary entry, well-to-do refugee Judith McGuire enumerates some of the prices she had been required to pay during a shopping excursion in Richmond.*

JUST BEEN ON A SHOPPING EXPE-dition for my sister and niece, and spent $1,500 in about an hour. I gave $110 for ladies' morocco boots; $22 per yard for linen; $5 apiece for spools of cotton; $5 for a paper of pins, etc. It would be utterly absurd, except that it is melancholy, to see our currency depreciating so rapidly.

TUE 23 AUG. *Stalled after Gettysburg and facing the continuing threat posed by Early's army in the Shenandoah, the Union war effort seemed to have no end in sight. Lincoln was far from the only Northerner who thought that a war-weary public would likely vote him out of office in November. George McClellan,*

Currier & Ives's political cartoon The Chicago Platform and Candidate.

the presumptive Democratic nominee, was promising, if elected, to end the bloodshed through peaceful means— a policy that, Lincoln was convinced, would mean the end of the Union. At the low point of his despondency, the president wrote this brief memorandum, which he sealed and asked his cabinet members to sign without reading.

THIS MORNING AS FOR SOME days past, it seems exceedingly probable that this Administration will not be re-elected. Then it will be my duty to so co-operate with the President elect, as to save the Union between the election and the inauguration; as he will have secured his election on such ground that he can not possibly save it afterwards.

A. Lincoln

THE DEMOCRATIC PARTY PLATFORM

MON 29 AUG.

Things were not easy during the war for the Democratic party in the North. Stained by the taint of Southern Democratic treason, the party in the North had to tread carefully lest its own members be tarred as well. As the opposition to Lincoln, Northern Democrats certainly criticized the president and his policies, but they were careful (with the exception of some Copperheads) not to appear obstructionist. As a result, the Democratic party became a haven for all sorts of Americans disturbed by what they thought to be Lincoln's heavy-handedness with respect, particularly, to civil liberties. On this date, the Demo-

cratic national convention opened in Chicago, and delegates began drafting the platform on which General McClellan would run. As one can see, the document, excerpted below, keeps to the narrow middle ground between loyal opposition and Confederate sympathizing.

RESOLVED, THAT THIS Convention does explicitly declare, as the sense of the American people, that after four years of failure to restore the Union by the experiment of war, during which, under the pretence of a military necessity, or war power higher than the Constitution, the Constitution itself has been disregarded in every part, and public liberty and private right alike trodden down and the material prosperity of the country essentially impaired—justice, humanity, liberty, and the public welfare demand that immediate efforts be made for a cessation of hostilities, with a view to an ultimate Convention of the States, or other peaceable means, to the end that at the earliest practicable moment peace may be restored on the basis of the Federal Union of the States....

Resolved, That the aim and object of the Democratic Party is to preserve the Federal Union and the rights of the States unimpaired...and [its members] hereby declare that they consider that the administrative usurpation of extraordinary and dangerous powers not granted by the Constitution; the subversion of the civil by the military law in States not in insurrection; the arbitrary arrest, imprisonment, trial, and sentence of American citizens in States where civil law exists in full force; the suppression of freedom of speech and of the press; the denial of the right of asylum; the open and avowed disregard of State rights; the employment of unusual test-oaths, and the interference with and denial of the right of the people to bear arms in their defence, is calculated to prevent a restoration of the Union and the perpetuation of a Government deriving its just powers from the consent of the governed.

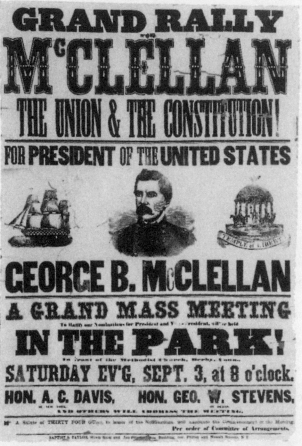

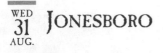

JONESBORO

WED
31
AUG.

Maj. Gen. Oliver O. Howard

Time and again during the
Atlanta Campaign, Sherman
had forced the Confederates
to pull back by threatening
their supply lines. After weeks
of partial siege and harassing
cavalry raids, the Union commander returned to this tactic,
ordering a large part of his forces
on a wide hook to the west and south
of the city. Initially—a triumph of wish-
ful thinking—the Rebels thought that
Sherman might be abandoning Atlanta
and retreating northward. Then reports
began to arrive of Union troops tearing

up rail lines south of the city.
On August 30, Sherman in
fact severed one of the last
two Confederate railroads
into Atlanta and threatened
to cut Hood off completely.
The next day, as McClellan
received the Democratic presidential nomination in
Chicago, two of Hood's corps
under Lt. Gen. William Hardee
mounted a fierce attack against the
entrenched positions of Maj. Gen. O. O.
Howard's Army of the Tennessee (inherited from the late McPherson) at
Jonesboro. The result was another
Confederate defeat with heavy losses:

In this magazine etching, Confederate prisoners taken at Jonesboro march north to Federal holding pens.

1,700 for the Rebels, compared to just 170 for the Federals. Finally accepting that he could not hold Atlanta, Hood made plans to evacuate the city. Meanwhile, the New York Herald *reported the death of a noncombatant who perished at Jonesboro.*

AMONG THE KILLED AT THE battle of Jonesboro was a Roman Catholic priest—Father Bliemel—chaplain of the Tenth Tennessee. He was killed while ministering to a dying soldier. I must say of the Catholic chaplains that I have ever found them in the front succoring the dying and wounded. Even in Atlanta the Catholic ministers have remained, while others have fled, to share the fate of their flocks. I would say to other chaplains, "Go and do likewise."

The Herald *also commented on the mood among the local residents as Sherman prepared finally to capture Atlanta.*

THE WARMEST SUPPORTERS of the Confederacy here confess that there is no hope for the rebel cause now, and the best thing the leaders could do would be to make peace on the best terms they could get…. Starvation threatens the people of Georgia. Refugees are crowding back on its stinted privations. The crops are much below an average. The conscription took away the old men and boys. The negroes were then called in to work on the trenches, and the corn and cotton were left uncared for, to run to weeds and ruin….

The military despotism of the South has made everything subservient to the army. It has swallowed up the blood and wealth of the land, and has now left its poor, deluded dupes stripped of everything that makes life valuable. Several houses here bear the inscriptions of slave auctions and marts; but the nigger is at such a discount that several owners are applying to the military authorities to take them off their hands.

★ ★ ★ ★

One of Atlanta's slave auction houses.

SEPTEMBER
1864

FRI 2 SEP. SHERMAN TAKES ATLANTA

Fearing a direct assault that would likely destroy his army, Lt. Gen. John Bell Hood ordered the Confederate evacuation of Atlanta, which began during the late afternoon of September 1. Lacking the time necessary to remove his extensive supplies, Hood ordered them burned, along with a great deal of railroad equipment. The following day, troops led by Union Maj. Gen. Henry W. Slocum, which had been holding the front lines during Sherman's encircling movement, entered the city. Sherman could scarcely believe the news, as he recalled in his memoirs.

WHILE BRINGING FORWARD troops and feeling the new position of our adversary, rumors came from the rear that the enemy had evacuated Atlanta, and that General Slocum was in the city. Later in the day I received a note in Slocum's own handwriting, stating that he had heard during the night the very sounds I have referred to; that he had moved rapidly up from the bridge about daylight, and had entered Atlanta unopposed. His letter was dated inside the city, so there was no doubt of the fact. General Thomas's bivouac was but a short distance from mine, and, before giving notice to the army in general orders, I sent one of my staff-officers to show him the note. In a few minutes the officer returned, soon followed by Thomas himself, who again examined the note, so as to be perfectly certain that it was genuine. The news seemed to him too good to be true. He

The site where Hood exploded twenty-eight boxcars of ordnance so that they wouldn't fall into Union hands.

snapped his fingers, whistled, and almost danced, and, as the news spread to the army, the shouts that arose from our men, the wild hallooing and glorious laughter, were to us a full recompense for the labor and toils and hardships through which we had passed in the previous three months.

SAT 3 SEP. *In the following letter to his family back home in Missouri, Spotswood Rice, a contraband serving in the Union army, expressed his affection for his children and his contempt for their owner.*

MY CHILDREN: I TAKE MY PEN in hand to rite you A few lines to let you know that I have not forgot you and that I want to see you as bad as ever now my Dear Children I want you to be contented with whatever may be your lots be assured that I will have you if it cost me my life   on the 28th of the mounth, 8 hundred White and 8 hundred blacke solders expects to start up the rivore to Glasgow and above there thats to be jeneraled by a jeneral that will give me both of you   when they Come I expect to be with, them and expect to get you both in return. Dont be uneasy my children   I expect to have you. If Diggs dont give you up this Government will and I feel confident that I will get you   Your Miss Kaitty said that I tried to steal you   But I'll let her know that god never intended for man to steal his own flesh and blood. If I had no confidence in God I could have confidence in her   But as it is If I ever had any Confidence in her I have none now and never expect to have   And I want her to remember if she meets me with ten thousand soldiers she [will] meet her enemy   I once [thought] that I had some respect for them but now my respects is worn out and I have no sympathy for Slaveholders. And as for her cristiananity I expect the Devil has Such in hell   You tell her from me that She is the first Christian that I ever hard say that a man could Steal his own child especially out of human bondage

WED 7 SEP. *Among African Americans, as among all Americans, perceptions of Abraham Lincoln varied widely: Before the Emancipation Proclamation was issued, some leaders, notably Frederick Douglass, criticized Lincoln for his reluctance to make emancipation a central war aim. Others were cautiously optimistic that the president would nevertheless abolish slavery. After the Emancipation Proclamation, the opinion of most Northern blacks was, of course, much more favorable, as demonstrated by this speech that the Rev. S. M. Chase delivered at a Baltimore ceremony honoring Lincoln's contribution to the African-American cause.*

MR. PRESIDENT: THE LOYAL colored people of Baltimore have entrusted us with authority to present this Bible as a testimonial of their appreciation of your humane conduct towards the people of our race….Since our incorporation into the American family we have been true and loyal, and we are now ready to aid in defending the country, to be armed and trained in military matters, in order to assist in protecting and defending the star-spangled banner.

The Second Massachusetts built this camp in front of Atlanta's City Hall.

Towards you, sir, our hearts will ever be warm with gratitude. We come to present to you this copy of the Holy Scriptures, as a token of respect for your active participation in furtherance of the cause of the emancipation of our race. This great event will be a matter of history. Hereafter when our children shall ask what mean these tokens, they will be told of your worthy deeds, and will rise up and call you blessed.

The loyal colored people of this country everywhere will remember you at the Throne of Divine Grace. May the King Eternal, and all wise Providence protect and keep you, and when you pass from this world to that of eternity, may you be borne to the bosom of your Savior and your God.

MON 12 SEP. *On September 7, now firmly in control of Atlanta, Major General Sherman ordered all its residents—*

446 families numbering about 1,600 people—to leave. The decision was based on his observation that "the use of Atlanta for warlike purposes is inconsistent with its character as a home for families." When the mayor and city council objected, citing the grief and pain such a large-scale displacement would cause, Sherman replied with the letter excerpted below.

GENTLEMEN: I HAVE YOUR letter of the 11th, in the nature of a petition to revoke my orders removing all the inhabitants from Atlanta. I have read it carefully, and give full credit to your statements of the distress that will be occasioned by it, and yet shall not revoke my order, simply because my orders are not designed to meet the humanities of the case, but to prepare for the future struggles, in which millions, yea hundreds of millions of good people

Sherman and his staff inspect one of Atlanta's captured forts.

outside of Atlanta have a deep interest. We must have *Peace*, not only at Atlanta, but in all America. To secure this, we must stop the war that now desolates our once happy and favored country. To stop war we must defeat the Rebel armies that are arrayed against the laws and Constitution which all must respect and obey. To defeat these armies we must prepare the way to reach them in their recesses, provided with the arms and instruments which enable us to accomplish our purpose....

War is cruelty, and you cannot refine it; and those who brought war on the country deserve all the curses and maledictions a people can pour out. I know I had no hand in making this war, and I know I will make more sacrifices today than any of you to secure peace. But you cannot have peace and a division of our country....

You might as well appeal against the thunderstorm as against these terrible hardships of war. They are inevitable, and the only way the people of Atlanta can hope once more to live in peace and quiet at home is to stop this war which can alone be done by admitting that it began in error and is perpetuated in pride. We don't want your negroes or your horses, or your houses or your land, or anything you have; but we do want and will have a just obedience to the laws of the United States. That we will have, and if it involves the destruction of your improvements, we cannot help it....

I want peace, and believe it can only be reached through Union and war, and I will ever conduct war purely with a view to perfect and early success.

★ ★ ★ ★

OCTOBER
1864

SAT
1
OCT. *In the ongoing debate concerning Reconstruction, some hard-liners pressed for policies that would reshape Southern society according to a Northern model. In this published essay, however, Orestes A. Brownson, a former Unitarian minister who had converted to Roman Catholicism, firmly rejected such a "New Englandizing" of the defeated South.*

WE HAVE SOME MADMEN amongst us who talk of exterminating the Southern leaders, and of New Englandizing the South. We wish to see the free-labor system substituted for the slave-labor system, but beyond that we have no wish to exchange or modify Southern society, and would rather approach Northern society to it, than it to Northern society. The New Englander has excellent points, but is restless in body and mind, always scheming, always in motion, never satisfied with what he has, and always seeking to make all the world like himself....

We insist that it were a gross perversion of the war to make it a war against Southern society or the Southern people. The war is just and defensible only when it is conducted as a war of the nation for its own existence and rights against an armed rebellion. In the war the nation seeks to reduce the rebels to their allegiance, not to destroy them, not to exile them, not to deprive them of their property or their franchises; it seeks to make them once more loyal citizens, and an integral portion of the American people, standing on a footing of perfect equality with the rest, not slaves or tributaries. Southern society must be respected, and any attempt to build up a new South out of the few Union men left there, Northern speculators, sharpers, adventurers, and freed negroes, is not only impolitic, but unconstitutional and wrong. Such a South would be a curse to itself and to the whole nation; we want it not....

We must suppress the Rebellion; but with the distinct understanding that the Southern States are to be restored, when they submit, to all the rights of self-government in the Union, and that no attempt in the meantime shall be made to revolutionize their society in favor of Northern or European ideas.

WED 5 OCT. ALLATOONA

In early October, Confederate Lt. Gen. John Bell Hood, having been forced out of Atlanta, began moving his Army of Tennessee south and then west of the Georgia capital to attack Union Maj. Gen. William T. Sherman's long supply lines from Chattanooga. The most significant of the resulting engagements took place on this day at Allatoona, where a Federal garrison of two thousand men under Brig. Gen. John M. Corse defended an important pass on the Chattanooga-to-Atlanta railroad against a similarly sized force of Confederates under Maj. Gen. Samuel G. French. The Rebels might have won the pass had French not received word during the battle that a major Union army was on its way to reinforce the Allatoona garrison. In fact, there was no such army on its way, but French could not afford to take the chance, so he pulled

back. This report of the fighting originally appeared in the Bulletin *of La Grange, Tennessee, and was later reprinted in the* Charleston Mercury.

 WHEN OUR ARMY CROSSED THE Chattahoochee river in front of Palmetto and Newnan, Stewart's corps was thrown across the Chattanooga railroad at Big Shanty—the camp and garrison at which place were captured without any resistance of consequence.

Everything worked prosperously until last Wednesday, when French's division of Stewart's corps was directed to take Allatoona. Dispositions were made around the town and the garrison and a formal demand for surrender sent in. This was refused, when an assault was ordered which succeeded in carrying the first and second lines. The Yankee commander then offered to capitulate but General French refused. Our men were led against the remaining works, but after a stubborn and bloody struggle they were repulsed. General French then drew off leaving his dead and wounded in the hands of the enemy.

Meanwhile, many Southerners comforted themselves with rumors of peace proposals and possible reconciliation with the North. Most of these rumors depended in some part on a McClellan victory in the upcoming Northern presidential election (although a few relied on the increasingly unlikely proposition that Great Britain or France would enter the war on the side of the Confederacy). After the fall of Atlanta, Jefferson Davis attempted to reverse this demoralizing

A blockhouse and permanent garrison defends this railroad bridge, a key link in Sherman's extended supply line, against the constant threat posed by Confederate cavalry.

trend with a speaking tour of the Southeast. In the following address— delivered in Augusta, Georgia—the Confederate president emphasized national pride and self-reliance as he endeavored to rally his beleaguered countrymen.

OURS IS NOT A REVOLUTION. WE are a free and independent people, in States that had the right to make a bet-ter government when they saw fit. They sought to infringe upon the rights we had; and we only instituted a new government on the basis of those rights. We are not engaged in a Quixotic fight for the rights of man; our struggle is for inherited rights; and who would surrender them? Let every paper guaranty possible be given, and who would submit? From the grave of many a fallen hero the blood of the slain would cry out against such a peace with the murderers. The women of the land driven from their homes; the children lacking food; old age hobbling from the scenes of its youth; the fugitives, forced to give way to the Yankee oppressor, and now hiding in your railroads, all proclaim a sea of blood that free men cannot afford to bridge. There is but one thing to which we can accede—separate State [national] independence. Some there are who speak of reconstruction with slavery maintained; but are there any who would thus measure rights by property? God forbid. Would you see that boy, with a peach-bloom on his cheek, grow up a serf—never to tread the path of honor unless he light the torch at the funeral pyre of his country? Would you see the fair daughters of the land given over to the brutality of the Yankees?

If any imagine this would not be so, let him look to the declaration of Mr. Lincoln, the terms he offers; let him read the declarations of the Northern press; let him note the tone of the Northern people; and he will see there is nothing left for us but separate independence.

MON 17 OCT. *Until Sherman captured Atlanta, the presidential campaign of 1864 was substantially more heated and competitive than the eventual results (and Abraham Lincoln's modern canonization) would suggest. The following letter to the editor of a local newspaper recounted a National Union party rally held at Princeton University. Although the author describes extensive pro-Lincoln sentiment, especially among the college's faculty members, three weeks later New Jersey would vote for McClellan.*

ON TUESDAY EVENING LAST A mass meeting was held here under the auspices of the Lincoln and Johnson Club. At this meeting we had the rare spectacle of three distinguished professors—men of studious, quiet habits, engaged in a work as remote as possible from mere politics—speaking to the people touching public questions, and urging them to support Republican candidates and measures. These professors were Alexander, McIlvaine and Guyot—the two former of whom spoke at some length with great power and earnestness as to the necessity of electing Mr. Lincoln, arguing that it is the duty of every right-minded citizen, no matter what his walk in life may be, to take the field and labor with all his strength for the sacred cause of Union and law. Professor McIlvaine has always been known as a democrat of the old school, and his course at this time will greatly affect the democracy here. Professor Guyot, who was called out by the audience, electrified the hearts of all in attendance by declaring that he had that very day been naturalized in order especially that he might vote for Mr. Lincoln—a declaration which amounted in itself to a better speech than one half of our orators are wont to make.

When you remember that Princeton was once the peculiar favorite of southerners, and that it has always held an extreme "conservative" position, you will agree with me that these present signs are most significant, and justify the prediction that other writers have made in your columns—that New Jersey means, this time, to be on the side of the country and the flag which her sons are daily honoring on the bloody field.

_{WED}
19
_{OCT.} SHERIDAN'S RIDE

Assuming that Lt. Gen. Jubal A. Early's mid-July withdrawal had ended the Second Valley Campaign, Union commanders returned the bulk of the forces deployed against him to their lines around Richmond and Petersburg. But on July 24, Early struck again in the Shenandoah, defeating the small force of Brig. Gen. George R. Crook at the second battle of Kernstown. Afterward, Early marched north to burn the Martinsburg, West Virginia, rail yards and the Pennsylvania town of Chambersburg. An enraged Grant sent the Sixth and Nineteenth Corps back to the valley, where he formed the Middle Military Division under the command of his trusted subordinate Maj. Gen. Philip H. Sheridan. Grant ordered Sheridan to destroy Early's army and everything else in the valley that couldn't be carried away. After a month of cautious maneuvering, Sheridan took advantage of an unwise dispersal of Early's forces to pound the Confederates with cavalry attacks at the third battle of Winchester on September 19 and at Fisher's Hill three days later. Then, after pursuing the defeated Early as far south as Staunton, Sheridan began burning the Shenandoah, destroying whatever supplies and structures might conceivably help the Southern war effort. In mid-October, Sheridan's army of thirty-two thousand men finally went into camp along Cedar Creek north of Strasburg. Meanwhile, moving with great stealth, Early's army of twenty-one thousand attacked the

Cedar Creek camp at dawn on October 19 while many Federals were still asleep in their tents (and Sheridan was away, leaving Maj. Gen. Horatio G. Wright in command). By the time the early morning fog (which had helped conceal the Rebel approach) had lifted, the divisions of Confederate major generals Joseph B. Kershaw and John B. Gordon had routed the Federal Eighth and Nineteenth Corps, capturing their earthworks and supplies. All that remained of Sheridan's army was the Sixth Corps, which Early now attacked. The Confederate advance was stalled, however, by the absence of celebrating soldiers, who had begun looting the Union camps. At the same time, Sheridan, who had stopped off in Winchester on his way back from a conference in Washington, learned of the attack and raced to Cedar Creek, arriving in time to rally his troops for a successful counterattack from which Early never recovered. In the end, the battle of Cedar Creek turned out to be the last major engagement of the Second Valley Campaign. Early continued to harass Federal units in the Shenandoah Valley until the end of the war, but his shattered army never again posed a significant offensive threat. On the other hand, Sheridan's furious ride became the stuff of legend, inspiring an epic poem by Thomas Buchanan Read, excerpted here.

UP FROM THE SOUTH AT BREAK
of day,
Bringing to Winchester fresh dismay,
The affrighted air with a shudder bore,
Like a herald in haste, to the chieftain's
door,

Maj. Gen. Philip H. Sheridan

The terrible grumble, and rumble, and
　　roar,
Telling the battle was on once more,
And Sheridan twenty miles away.

And wider still those billows of war
Thundered along the horizon's bar;
And louder yet into Winchester rolled
The roar of that red sea uncontrolled,
Making the blood of the listener cold,
As he thought of the stake in that fiery
　　fray,
With Sheridan twenty miles away.

But there is a road from Winchester town,
A good, broad highway leading down;
And there, through the flush in the
　　morning light,
A steed as black as the steeds of night
Was seen to pass, as with eagle flight;
As if he knew the terrible need,
He stretched away with his utmost
speed;
Hills rose and fell; but his heart was gay,
With Sheridan fifteen miles away.

Still sprang from those swift hoofs,
　　thundering south,
The dust like smoke from the cannon's
　　mouth,
Or the trail of a comet, sweeping faster
　　and faster,
Foreboding to traitors the doom of disaster.
The heart of the steed and the heart of
　　the master
Were beating like prisoners assaulting
　　their walls,
Impatient to be where the battlefield
calls;
Every nerve of the charger was strained to
　　full play,
With Sheridan only ten miles away.

Under his spurning feet, the road
Like an arrowy Alpine river flowed,
And the landscape sped away behind
Like an ocean flying before the wind;
And the steed, like a barque fed with
　　furnace ire,
Swept on, with his wild eye full of fire;
But, lo! he is nearing his heart's desire;
He is snuffing the smoke of the roaring
　　fray,
With Sheridan only five miles away.

The first that the general saw were the
　　groups
Of stragglers, and then the retreating
　　troops;
What was done? What to do? A glance
　　told him both,
Then striking his spurs, with a terrible
　　oath,
He dashed down the line 'mid a storm of
　　huzzas,
And the wave of retreat checked its
　　course there, because
The sight of the master compelled it to
　　pause.
With foam and with dust the black
　　charger was gray;
By the flash of his eye, and the red
　　nostril's play,
He seemed to the whole great army to
　　say,
"I have brought you Sheridan all the way
From Winchester down to save the day!"

Hurrah! Hurrah for Sheridan!
Hurrah! Hurrah for horse and man!
And when their statues are placed on
　　high,
Under the dome of the Union sky,
The American soldier's Temple of Fame;
There with the glorious general's name,

Be it said, in letters both bold and bright,
"Here us the steed that saved the day
By carrying Sheridan into the fight,
From Winchester, twenty miles away!"

*This somewhat less heroic account of
the battle appeared in Major General
Wright's official report.*

AT THE FIRST BLUSH OF DAWN
the camps were assaulted by a
considerable musketry fire upon our
extreme left and a fire of a much slighter
character upon our right. A moment's hesitation convinced me that the former was
the real attack, and I at once proceeded to
that point, the firing meanwhile growing
heavier....I felt every confidence that the
enemy would be promptly repulsed. In
this anticipation, however, I was sadly disappointed. Influenced by a panic which
often seizes the best troops, and some of
these I had seen behave admirably under
the hottest fire, the line broke before the
enemy fairly came in sight, and under a
slight scattering fire retreated in disorder
down the pike. Seeing that no part of the
original line could be held, as the enemy
was already on the left flank of the Nineteenth Corps, I at once sent orders to the
Sixth Corps to fall back to some tenable
position in rear; and to Gen. Emory, commanding the Nineteenth Corps, that as
his left was turned he should fall back
and take position on the right of the Sixth.
...About this time Maj. Gen. Sheridan came up and assumed command and
I returned to the command of the Sixth
Corps. Soon after the lines had been fully
formed the enemy made a sharp attack
upon the Sixth Corps, but was rudely

Maj. Gen. Horatio G. Wright

repulsed, falling back several hundred
yards to a stone wall behind which a part
of his line took shelter....But little further resistance was experienced in the
advance to Cedar Creek, where our
infantry was halted in its old camp, while
the pursuit was continued by the cavalry.
The enemy being entirely demoralized
and his ranks completely broken, he
retreated without regard to order. The
battle, which in its earlier stages looked
anything but favorable for our success
and occasioned a fear of defeat to many
a brave-hearted soldier, resulted through
the admirable courage of our troops, the
bravery and good conduct of their officers,
and the persistence of the commander of
the army, in a complete victory.

*After the battle, Early rebuked his men
for their laxity and misconduct in this
scathing address.*

SOLDIERS OF THE ARMY OF THE Valley: I had hoped to have congratulated you on the splendid victory won by you on the morning of the 19th at Belle Grove on Cedar Creek, when you surprised and routed two Corps of Sheridan's Army and drove back several miles the remaining Corps, capturing 18 pieces of Artillery, 1500 prisoners, a number of colours, a large quantity of small arms and many wagons and ambulances, with the entire camps of the two routed Corps; but I have the mortification of announcing to you that, by your subsequent misconduct, all the benefits of that victory were lost and a serious disaster incurred. Had you remained steadfast to your duty and your colours the victory would have been one of the most brilliant and decisive of the war, you would have gloriously retrieved the reverses at Winchester and Fisher's Hill and entitled yourselves to the admiration and gratitude of your country. But many of you including some commissioned officers yielded to a disgraceful propensity for plunder, deserted your colours to appropriate to yourselves the abandoned property of the enemy, and subsequently those who had previously remained at their posts, seeing their ranks thinned by the absence of the plunderers, when the enemy late in the afternoon, with his shattered columns made but a feeble effort to retrieve the fortunes of the day, yielded to a needless panic and fled the field in confusion, thereby converting a splendid victory into a disaster. Had any respectable number of you listened to the appeals made to you and made a stand even at the last moment, the disaster would have been averted and the substantial fruits of victory secured—but under the insane dread of being flanked and a panic-stricken terror of the enemy's cavalry, you would listen to no appeal, threat or order, and allowed a small body of cavalry to penetrate to our train and carry off a number of pieces of artillery and wagons which your disorder left unprotected. You have thus obscured that glorious fame won in conjunction with the gallant men of the Army of Northern Virginia who still remain proudly defiant in the trenches around Richmond and Petersburg. Before you can again claim these as comrades you will have to erase from your escutcheons the blemishes which now obscure them, and this you can do if you will but be true to your former reputation, your country and your homes.

THE RAID ON ST. ALBANS

This day also saw one of the war's most curious escapades when a raiding party of twenty-five Rebels led by Lt. Bennett H. Young swept down from Canada to sack the small town of St. Albans, Vermont, fifteen miles south of the Canadian border. The Confederates intended to burn and plunder a large swath of the northern Vermont countryside, but they managed only to rob the three St. Albans banks before residents chased them back across the border, where Young and twelve others were arrested. This article, written by the New York Herald *correspondent in Newport (which is practically on the Canadian border), suggests the excitement caused by the raid.*

THIS THRIVING VILLAGE, WHICH has extensive business connections with the eastern townships of Canada, and which, I am glad to say are of the most friendly character, has been the scene of stirring events within a few days past. On Friday morning, the 21st inst., the corps of Cadets of the Norwich University, under the command of Captain Kent, after a forced march, made their appearance here to resist an expected invasion of raiders, consequent upon that at St. Albans on the 19th, of which there was some apprehension....

You may imagine how all the good people felt here at the news from St. Albans. It would be but an easy undertaking, as we well understood, to have crossed from St. Albans to Magog, at the foot of the lake, taken possession of Captain Fogg's boat and captured Newport. Lots of plunder and money could have been obtained here, and by a short cut down the railway, through the rich villages along the line, the robbers could easily have laid under contribution or destroyed some of the finest villages in Northern Vermont.

The people of Newport, however, are determined not to yield without a fight. They heard that a gang was to come aboard the steamer on Friday, the 21st, on her return trip from Canada, and they made what preparation they could. About one hundred men were collected, with arms, ready to meet the foe, and were, at the supposed critical moment, much encouraged by the arrival of the cadets, a well instructed and gallant corps of young students, souls in arms and eager for the fray. The whole were drawn up on the line wharf in front of the hotel, and waited in silence the approach of the enemy. Presently, through the fast thickening darkness, the *Mountain Maid* was seen approaching, her steam pipe's whistle announcing her vicinity in the usual manner, and, as we supposed, most treacherous manner. Nothing less than a volley was now anticipated, and the cadet rifles were ready to respond. But, happily for us and all concerned, no raiders appeared, though it was resolved not to have a St. Albans's affair at Newport, if fighting would prevent it.

THU 27 OCT. THE RAID ON THE ALBEMARLE

Although the Confederate ironclad ram **Albemarle** *took part in only two engagements during the war, its existence (and the threat it posed to blockading Union ships off the Outer Banks) frightened the U.S. Navy. On this date, twenty-one-year-old Union Lt. William Cushing ended that threat with a daring raid on the ironclad as it sat docked in Plymouth, North Carolina. Cushing described his successful mission, which made use of a steam launch outfitted with a torpedo (mine), in his official report.*

SIR: I HAVE THE HONOR TO report that the rebel ironclad *Albemarle* is at the bottom of the Roanoke River. On the night of the 27th, having prepared my steam launch, I proceeded up toward Plymouth with 13 officers and men, partly volunteers from the squadron.

The distance from the mouth of the river to the ram was about 8 miles, the stream averaging in width some 200 yards, and lined with the enemy's pickets. A mile below the town was the wreck of the *Southfield,* surrounded by some schooners, and it was understood that a gun was mounted there to command the bend. I therefore took one of the *Shamrock's* cutters in tow, with orders to cast off and board at that point if we were hailed. Our boat succeeded in passing the pickets, and even the *Southfield,* within 20 yards, without discovery, and we cast off and ordered below, while we made for our enemy under a full head of steam.

The rebels sprung their rattle, rang the bell, and commenced firing, at the same time repeating their hail and seeming much confused.

The light of a fire ashore showed me the ironclad made fast to the wharf, with a pen of logs around her about 30 feet from her side.

Passing her closely, we made a complete circle so as to strike her fairly, and went into her bows on. By this time the enemy's fire was very severe, but a dose of canister at short range served to moderate their zeal and disturb their aim. Paymaster Swan, of the *Otsego,* was wounded near me, but how many more I know not. Three bullets struck my clothing, and the air seemed full of them.

In a moment we had struck the logs, just abreast of the quarter port, breasting them in some feet, and our bow resting on them. The torpedo boom was then lowered and by a vigorous pull I succeeded in diving the torpedo under the overhang and exploding it at the same time that the *Albemarle's* gun was fired. A shot seemed to go crashing through my boat, and a dense mass of water rushed in from the torpedo, filling the launch and completely disabling her.

The enemy then continued his fire at 15 feet range, and demanded our surrender, which I twice refused, ordering the men to save themselves, and removing my own coat and shoes. Springing into the river, I swam, with others, into the middle of the stream, the rebels failing to hit us.

The most of our party were captured, some were drowned, and only one escaped besides myself, and he in another direction. Acting Master's Mate Woodman, of the *Commodore Hull,* I met in the water half a mile below the town, and assisted him as best I could, but failed to get him ashore.

Completely exhausted, I managed to reach the shore, but was too weak to crawl out of the water until just at daylight, when I managed to creep into the swamp, close to the fort. While hiding a few feet from the path, two of the *Albemarle's* officers passed, and I judged from their conversation that the ship was destroyed.

Some hours traveling in the swamp served to bring me out well below the town, when I sent a negro in to gain information and found that the ram was truly sunk.

★ ★ ★ ★

NOVEMBER
1864

SUN
6
NOV.

On October 13, voters in Maryland narrowly adopted (by a margin of four hundred votes out of sixty thousand cast) a new state constitution outlawing slavery as of November 1. Nevertheless, many slaveholders refused to give up the institution and conspired to deprive former slaves of their new rights. Armed vigilantes intimidated blacks, and attacks were common. In the following letter, Sandy Point lighthouse keeper Thomas B. Davis informs emancipationist judge Hugh L. Bond of the situation in Davis's locality.

SINCE WE THE PEOPLE HAVE Proclaimed that Marland Should Be free the Most Bitter Hatred has bein Manifested againest the poor Devils that Have Just Escaped from beneath there Lash   there actions Since Tusday Last [November 1] Indicates to me that there is all Ready Orginized Bands Prowling apon Horse Back around the Country armed with Revolvers and Horse Whips threatning to Shoot every Negroe that gives Back the first word after they Lacerate his flesh with the Whip   i have bein told By Several Pearsons that a man By the name of Nick Phips...took in...a negroe Woman stript her and with a Cow Hyde Lasarated her flesh untill the Blood ozed from every cut and She with in a Month of giveing Burth to a child   She appeared Before Court with the Blood Still Streaming from her   To Cover his guilt he ivents a Charge   She is thrown in prson and he goes free   the Same parties caught a Man By the name of Foster Eight Miles from annapolis hand cuffed him and Drove him before them and they on Horse With Such Rapidity that when he got to Severen Ferry he fell apon the Beach Exausted Covered with foam and this Man was Born free   this mans offence was [to say] that he nor no wife of his Should be Treated in that maner without avenging it. What i have bein trying to get at is this   Sam Richardson has taken to annapolis four Childern of one of his Slaves   apon the face of the Mothers Objections in court he has had them Bound to him after She stating that all the cloth they had on were By her after Night there is a woman down heare By the name Yewel   She is allso Demanding of the wiman She has turned [out] without a stich of winters clothing all there childen to be bound to her When she cannot get Bread for her Self   On friday there was upwards of hundred young Neagroes on the ferry with there old Masters draged away forseble from there parents for the purpose of Haveing them Bound   a number of other cases i could cite that i Will Not Bother you with

In the Name of Humanity is there no Redress for those poor ignorant down troden Wreches. Is this or is it not Involuntarey Slavery[?]

Some former slaveholders sought to limit their losses by binding black children to them for long terms of service—a practice soon declared unconstititional. Yet the records of the Freedmen's Bureau contain many complaints from African-American parents whose children were thus "apprenticed."

MRS. MILL AND HER SON, holds my child in slavery, I went there and they ordered me out of the

Freed people at a refugee camp in Virginia.

house today, and they locked the door and took the key out of the door, and they tell her not to live with me. I want her to come home and go to school. I feel myself perfectly able to support her, she never was in a church in her life and don't know the Lord's prayer.

By her Mother,
Rebecca Sales

MON 7 NOV. *On this day, President Davis sent a surprisingly optimistic message to the Second Confederate Congress, which was gathering in Richmond for the start of its second session. (There would be no others.) Although Davis played down the capture of Atlanta, he did admit the severity of the manpower shortage by embracing the proposal that slaves be employed by the Confederate army—as laborers, to be sure, although Davis did leave open the possibility that sometime later they would be armed and used in battle. This use of slaves alone was quite a step for the Confederate president to be taking, yet Davis's message contained something even more amazing to the editors of the* Richmond Examiner: *his suggestion that the slaves thus enlisted be freed as a reward for their service. As the newspapermen reminded Davis quite pointedly in this editorial, it was the firm belief of nearly all white Southerners that emancipation was less a reward than a punishment, because slaves couldn't care for themselves without the paternalistic help of a white master. If this were not the case, they told Davis, then the institution of slavery would be as immoral as the abolitionists wrongly contended.*

As it is, Mr. Davis has chosen to open up questions both deep and dangerous which, if Congress do not close them up peremptorily, may gravely disquiet our people and compromise our cause. It is truly astonishing and almost incredible that now in the fourth year of our independence and of a terrible war waged to vindicate that independence— after breaking up the old Federal Union because we would not suffer the Washington Congress to interfere with our state institutions—the President of the Confederate States should "invite" the Richmond Congress to consider a project for emancipating slaves by the Confederate authorities; and should at the same time speak of this emancipation as "a reward for faithful services" as a boon and a blessing, as something which would place these Negroes in a better position than before. Mr. Davis thus intimates his opinion, first, that laws of Congress, or the action of the Confederate executive, can liberate slaves; and second, that slavery is so dire and hideous and evil as to make escape from its horrors a reward and a boon even to an old worn-out Negro at the end of a term of "faithful service."…

…According to his message it is a rich reward for faithful services to turn a Negro wild. Slavery, then, in the eyes of Mr. Davis, keeps the Negro out of something which he has the capacity to enjoy: it depresses him below the level to which nature has given him powers to attain; it hinders the development of his faculties for good; it forbids his pursuit of happiness. If the case be so, then slavery is originally, radically, incurably wrong and sinful, and the sum of barbarism.

TUE 8 NOV. THE 1864 PRESIDENTIAL ELECTION

As Lincoln had always known it would be, the 1864 presidential election was a national referendum on his conduct of the war—and, fortunately for Lincoln, that war was now going extremely well for him. With Sherman in Atlanta, Farragut controlling Mobile Bay, and Early's Army of the Valley crushed, the president no longer expected a McClellan victory, and the furloughs he had arranged for many Union soldiers (so that they could go home and vote) hardly seemed necessary. Southerners also monitored the election closely. As Georgian Dolly Sumner Lunt pointed out in this diary entry, the results were just as significant for the future of the Confederacy.

TODAY WILL PROBABLY DECIDE the fate of the Confederacy. If Lincoln is reelected I think our fate is a hard one, but we are in the hands of a merciful God, and if He sees that we are in the wrong, I trust that He will show it unto us. I have never felt that slavery was altogether right, for it is abused by men, and I have often heard Mr. Burge say that if he could see that it was sinful for him to own slaves, if he felt that it was wrong, he would take them where he could free them. He would not sin for his right hand. The purest and holiest men have owned them, and I can see nothing in the scriptures which forbids it. I have never bought or sold slaves and I have tried to make life easy and pleasant to those that have been bequeathed me by the dead.

UNION FOREVER

FOR PRESIDENT,
Abraham Lincoln.

VICE PRESIDENT,
Andrew Johnson.

PEACE COMMISSIONERS.
ULYSSES S. GRANT,
D. G. FARRAGUT,
WM. T. SHERMAN,
PHILIP H. SHERIDAN.

I have never ceased to work. Many a Northern housekeeper has a much easier time than a Southern matron with her hundred negroes.

When the votes were counted, Lincoln was reelected with a sizable popular majority that allowed him to carry all but three of the participating states. Another diarist, Lincoln private secretary John Hay, described in this entry how the president passed the evening.

THE HOUSE HAS BEEN STILL AND almost deserted today. Everybody in Washington not at home voting seems ashamed of it and stays away from the President....

The night was rainy steamy and dark. We splashed through the grounds to the side door of the War Department where a soaked and smoking sentinel was standing in his own vapor with his huddled-up frame covered with a rubber cloak. Inside a half-dozen idle orderlies: up stairs the clerks of the telegraph. As the President entered they handed him a despatch from Forney claiming ten thousand Union Majority in Philadelphia. "Forney is a little excitable." Another comes from Felton, Baltimore, giving us "15,000 in the city, 5000 in the State. All hail, Free Maryland." That is superb. A message from Rice to Fox followed instantly by one from Sumner to Lincoln claiming Boston by 5000 and Rice's & Hooper's elections by majorities of 4000 apiece., A magnificent advance on the chilly dozens of 1862.

Eckert came in shaking the rain from his cloak, with trowsers very disreputably muddy. We sternly demanded an explanation. He had slipped he said & tumbled prone, crossing the street. He had done it watching a fellow-being ahead and chuckling at his uncertain footing: Which reminded the Tycoon, of course. The President said "For such an awkward felow, I am pretty sure-footed. It used to take a pretty dextrous man to throw me. I remember, the evening of the day in 1858, that decided the contest for the Senate between Mr. Douglas and myself, was something like this, dark, rainy & gloomy. I had been reading the returns, and had ascertained that we had lost the legislature and started to go home. The path had been worn hog-backed & was slippery. My foot slipped from under me,

John Hay

knocking the other one out of the way, but I recovered myself & lit square: and I said to myself, *'It's a slip and not a fall.'"*

The President sent over the first fruits to Mrs. Lincoln. He said "She is more anxious than I."...

Despatches kept coming in all the evening showing a splendid triumph in Indiana [and] showing steady small gains all over Pennsylvania, enough to give a fair majority this time on the home vote. Guesses from New York and Albany which boiled down to about the estimated majority against us in the city 35,000 and left the result in the state still doubtful....

Towards midnight we had supper, provided by Eckert. The President went awkwardly and hospitably to work shovelling out the fried oysters. He was most agreeable and genial all the evening in fact....

Capt. Thomas came up with a band about half past two, and made some music and a small hifalute. The President answered from the window with rather unusual dignity and effect & we came home.

FRI
11
NOV.

At a cabinet meeting held this day, President Lincoln revealed to his close advisers how he had planned to handle the transfer of power should General McClellan have won the election. John Hay recorded the following exchange.

THE PRESIDENT SAID "I resolved, in case of the election of General McClellan being certain that he would be the Candidate, that I would see him and talk matters over with him.

I would say, 'General, the election has demonstrated that you are stronger, have more influence with the American people than I. Now let us together, you with your influence and I with all the executive power of the Government, try to save the country. You raise as many troops as you possibly can for this final trial, and I will devote all my energies to assisting and finishing the war.'"

Seward said, "And the General would answer you *'Yes, Yes'*; and the next day when you saw him again & pressed these views upon him he would say 'Yes—yes' & so on forever and would have done nothing at all."

"At least," added Lincoln, "I should have done my duty and have stood clear before my own conscience."

THE BURNING OF ATLANTA

TUE
15
NOV.

Suggesting what was soon to come, Sherman's army, following his orders, left the city of Atlanta in smoldering ruins. This account of the burning of Atlanta, which took place on the evening of November 15, was recorded in the diary of Union drummer boy William Bircher of Minnesota.

AT NIGHT WE DESTROYED THE city by fire. A grand and awful spectacle it presented to the beholder.... The heaven was one expanse of lurid fire; the air was filled with flying, burning cinders. Buildings, covering two hundred acres, were in ruins or in flames; every instant there was the sharp detonation of

the smothered, booming sound of exploding shells and powder concealed in the
buildings, and then the sparks and flames
would shoot up into the black and red
roof, scattering cinders far and wide.…
I heard the real fine band of the Thirty-
third Massachusetts playing, "John
Brown's soul goes marching on," by the
light of the burning buildings.

Atlanta during Sherman's occupation.

*The morning after the fire, as Sherman
rode out of town at the head of the Fourteenth Corps, an Atlanta boy named
Noble Williams hiked with two friends
to a rise above the city in order to survey
the wreckage. This is what he saw, as he
later recalled.*

THE COUNTRY FOR MILES
around presented a scene of
almost unequalled desolation. Many trees
had fallen…and those left standing were
but a shattered remnants of their former
selves.…The woods and fields were strewn
with carcasses of dead and decaying ani-

mals most of which,…becoming disabled,
were shot or left to die of starvation.

*With conditions in the South being
what they were, the concerns that moti-
vate this letter from Gen. Robert E. Lee
to his wife—mending things that are
badly worn, caring for the poor—seem
emblematic of the broader Confederate
situation.*

MY DEAR MARY: I SEND UP AN
old shirt which you thought might
be useful to some of our poor wounded
soldiers. I have another if you desire it. I
also send the pillow case you gave me last
year. You will see its forlorn condition. I
want another one badly, of any material
you have. You can guess at the size by the
one returned. Please mend my last pair of
drawers herewith sent & if no sick or
wounded soldier requires them, ask
daughter to put them in my trunk. I hope
you are all well. Love to everybody.
Very truly,
R. E. Lee

SHERMAN BEGINS HIS MARCH TO THE SEA

WED 16 NOV.

*Maj. Gen. William Tecumseh Sherman
left Atlanta on this day with four corps
of infantry and artillery numbering
sixty-five thousand men. His destination
was kept secret, but it soon became obvious that he was heading for the seaport
of Savannah, where he could rendezvous with Union supply ships (and thus
end his dependence on the vulnerable*

Maj. Gen. William Tecumseh Sherman

*Chattanooga-to-Atlanta railroad line).
Sherman's men traveled in two parallel
columns, cutting a wide swath of devastation that made him infamous in the
South. In this Special Field Order No.
119, he laid out for his troops, in general terms, the goals of their March to
the Sea.*

SPECIAL FIELD ORDERS, No. 119

The General commanding deems it proper at this time to inform the officers and men of the Fourteenth, Fifteenth, Seventeenth and Twentieth Corps, that he has organized them into an army for a special purpose, well known to the War Department and to General Grant. It is sufficient for you to know that it involves a departure from our present base, and a long and difficult march to a new one. All the chances of war have been considered and provided for as far as human sagacity can. All he asks of you is to maintain that discipline, patience and courage which have characterized you in the past, and he hopes, through you, to strike a blow at our enemy that will have a material effect in producing what we all so much desire—his complete overthrow. Of all things the most important is, that the men, during marches and in camp, keep their places and not scatter about as stragglers or foragers, to be picked up by hostile people in detail.

It is also of the utmost importance that our wagons should not be loaded with anything but provisions and ammunition. All surplus servants, non-combatants and refugees should now go to the rear, and none should be encouraged to encumber us on the march. At some future time we will be enabled to provide for the poor whites and blacks who seek to escape the bondage under which they are now suffering.

With these few simple cautions in your minds, he hopes to lead you to achievements equal in importance to those of the past.

By order of Major General W. T. Sherman

SAT 19 NOV. *In her diary, widowed Georgia plantation owner Dolly Sumner Lunt described the coming of Sherman's army and the subsequent ruination of her home and land by the invading Union forces. Her experience, while harrowing, was not atypical.*

I HASTENED BACK TO MY frightened servants and told them that they had better hide, and then went back to the gate to claim protection and a guard. But like demons they rush in! My yards are full. To my smoke-house, my dairy, pantry, kitchen, and cellar, like famished wolves they come, breaking locks and whatever is in their way. The thousand pounds of meat in my smoke-house is gone in a twinkling, my flour, my meat, my lard, butter, eggs, pickles of various kinds—both in vinegar and brine—wine, jars, and jugs are all gone. My eighteen fat turkeys, my hens, chickens, and fowls, my young pigs, are shot down in my yard and hunted as if they were rebels themselves. Utterly powerless I ran out and appealed to the guard....

As I stood there, from my lot I saw driven, first, old Dutch, my dear old buggy horse, who has carried my beloved husband so many miles, and who would so quietly wait at the block for him to mount and dismount, and who at last drew him to his grave; then came old Mary, my brood mare, who for years had been too old and stiff for work, with her three-year-old colt, my two-year-old mule, and her last little baby colt. There they go! There go my mules, my sheep, and, worse than all, my boys [slaves]!...

Sherman himself and a greater portion of his army passed my house that day. All day, as the sad moments rolled on, were they passing not only in front of my house, but from behind; they tore down my garden palings, made a road through my back-yard and lot field, driving their stock and riding through, tearing down my fences and desolating my home—wantonly doing it when there was no necessity for it....

As night drew its sable curtains around us, the heavens from every point were lit up with flames from burning buildings....My Heavenly Father alone saved me from the destructive fire.

WED 30 NOV. FRANKLIN

On November 21, Confederate Lt. Gen. John Bell Hood moved his Army of Tennessee north from Florence, Alabama, toward Columbia, Tennessee, his purpose being to separate and then defeat the two Federal garrisons at Pulaski and Nashville. In response, Union Maj. Gen John M. Schofield, commanding about twenty-five thousand troops in Pulaski, pulled out of that town and headed himself for Columbia, an important

river crossing on the main road to Nashville. Schofield won the race against Hood, arriving late on November 24 and entrenching in anticipation of a Confederate attack. On November 29, Hood sent two of his three corps across the Duck River above Schofield's position, threatening the Federals' rear and provoking Schofield into another retreat, this time to Franklin, where the two sides finally engaged on the following day. Knowing Nashville was at stake, Hood threw his thirty thousand infantrymen and eight thousand cavalrymen at the Federal lines with great ferocity; the Union forces gave initially but then held their interior lines before withdrawing into Nashville that night. The difference in casualties was marked: twenty-three hundred Union to sixty-two hundred Confederate. (Hood also lost six generals, including Maj. Gen. Patrick Cleburne.) The following report from the Charleston Mercury leaves the

Maj. Gen. John M. Schofield

erroneous impression that the Union army fled Franklin in defeat. However, the New York Herald's account of the battle, which lasted well into the night, gives a different impression.

THE FIRST LINE OF BREAST-works was swept clean. Our loss had been great. The noble Cleburne fell, shot through the head with four shells, and died on the ramparts. Gist, previously wounded in the leg, had refused to leave the field, and limping along on foot, cheering his men, finally received a ball through the breast, that took away his precious life; while Brown, Manigault, Johnson, Strahl, and scores of field and staff officers, who had exposed themselves at the head of their troops, were either killed or wounded. Still our men faltered not. Dashing on, they reached the second line. The Federals were stubborn. On the right they had charged Bates's division, and gained a momentary advantage; but, recovering, that gallant officer was again at the front, and with his brave Tennesseans, doing splendid service.

For a time, the Yankees held their breastworks, and the fighting was hand to hand between those in the ditch on the outside and those behind the entrench-ments. But the struggle was not long, and again the foe was flying across the field. It was night, however, and the difficulties of continuing the battle so great that, at 2 A.M. save the occasional spattering of musketry, the grand chorus of battle was at an end. The next morning, it was dis-covered that the Federals had evacuated the position, and were in full retreat to Nashville.

Maj. Gen. Patrick Cleburne

THE REPORTS OF THE BATTLE AT Franklin, Tennessee, which we publish this morning not only corroborate the accounts heretofore given, but greatly enhance the brilliancy and completeness of the victory. The capture of thirty stands of colors and a thousand prisoners by our troops, and the loss of six thousand in killed and wounded by the enemy, attest the desperate and sanguinary character of the combat. Among the rebel officers slain are General Ward Adams and General Patrick R. Cleburne, and it is reported that a rebel major general was borne off the field mortally wounded.... Reinforce-ments were rapidly arriving, while a fleet of wooden and iron-clad gunboats lay in the river ready to cooperate.

★ ★ ★ ★

DECEMBER
1864

FORT MCALLISTER

On December 10, Sherman's army reached Savannah, ending his destructive march from Atlanta. There he found Lt. Gen. William J. Hardee (recently transferred from the Army of Tennessee at Hood's request) strongly entrenched. Hardee had also flooded the rice fields around Savannah, thereby denying access to the city except by five narrow causeways. Understandably, Sherman decided to invest the Confederate stronghold rather than assault it directly, but this decision meant that his troops and cavalry horses would quickly run out of food and feed unless he established contact with the navy ships offshore. (Previously, his huge but moving army had been feeding itself off the land; camped in front of Savannah, however, the local crops and forage would soon run out.) To establish this new marine supply line, Sherman targeted Fort McAllister on the Ogeechee River south of Savannah. The fort's commanding position blocked access via the Ogeechee to Rear Adm. John Dahlgren's Union fleet; however, when it fell this evening, Sherman finally reached the sea. In the following letter, Union artillery officer Thomas Osborne described both the destruction caused by Sherman's army on its march and its assault on the fort.

SINCE I WROTE YOU FROM Marietta this army has marched about 300 miles, through the enemy's country, and that without serious difficulty. We have torn up and destroyed

A view of the port city of Savannah whose wharves were largely stilled by the Union blockade.

about 200 miles of railroad, burned all bridges and cleaned up the country generally of almost every thing upon which the people could live. The Army in this movement covered a strip of country about forty miles wide. We burned all cotton, took all provisions, forage, wagons, mules, horses, cattle, hogs and poultry and the many other things which a country furnishes and which may be made available for the support of an army. In fact, as we have left the country I do not see how the people can live for the next two years. Much of the country was very rich and a good deal of it very poor. There has been some fighting, but not much, except what the cavalry has done. We brought all our wounded with us in the ambulances and army train and what is surprising about this is we have never known men to do as well in hospital as they have done in the train on the road.

When we reached here we had driven 15,000 or 20,000 of the enemy into the city. The enemy had taken every possible precaution to prevent us from reaching the fleet. Troops, forts, torpedoes and all else their engineers could devise or furnish were employed. To get to the fleet, Fort McAllister on the Ogeechee River had to be taken. This is one of the oldest war forts and was considered safe from the possibility of capture. General Hazen with his division of 5,000 men took it in twenty minutes after he moved to the assault. It was desperately defended and besides being well garrisoned and mounted was protected by torpedoes buried in the sand outside the fort and also by strong and complete lines of abatis covering the entire front of the fort. The fort itself is a well built and strong work. General Hazen lost twenty-four men killed and 110 wounded. The most of this loss was from torpedoes which exploded as they were stepped on by the men just in front of the fort. The enemy's loss was forty-eight killed and wounded and in all about 280 prisoners. The taking of this fort was one of the most brilliant incidents of the war.

This is how the **Charleston Mercury** *reported the fall of Fort McAllister.*

FROM SAVANNAH—FALL OF FORT MCALLISTER.

We have no very full budget of intelligence from Savannah. Sherman seems, for the present, to have abandoned the direct attack on the city, and appears to be turning his attention to the reduction of the outworks. We regret to announce the fall of Fort McAllister. That post was carried early yesterday morning by assault, in which a heavy column of Sherman's best troops participated. It is believed that the enemy will next make a desperate effort to gain possession of Genesis Point. The news given above is perfectly authentic; but we have heard no details of the assault or of the casualties.

Along the line of the Charleston and Savannah Railroad all continues quiet.

THU 15 DEC. NASHVILLE

John M. Schofield's November 30 withdrawal into Nashville had sufficiently reinforced Maj. Gen. George Thomas's Army of the Cumberland that it was now strong enough to take on Hood's Army of Tennessee. A week later, however, Thomas had not yet moved against Hood, and Grant became impatient. On December 6, he gave Thomas a direct order: "Attack Hood at once and wait no longer for remount of your cavalry." The next day, Grant told Secretary of War Stanton that Thomas should be replaced unless he attacked immediately. Two days after that, Grant (who feared that Hood might bypass Nashville and reach the Ohio River) issued orders for Schofield to relieve Thomas, but he suspended those orders when he learned that ice storms and other bad weather were keeping Thomas in Nashville. Finally, on December 15, Thomas emerged and pushed back Hood's forces. The next day, he smashed them in what would be the last major battle in the war's Western Theater. As with Early's Army of the Valley after Cedar Creek, so Hood's Army of Tennessee continued to harass Federal operations, but after Thomas's skillful decimation of it outside Nashville, it never again posed a serious threat. In this report from within the Union ranks, **New York Herald** *correspondent D. P. Conygham described the final assault on December 16.*

THE ROAR OF THE REBEL

artillery was becoming fainter, while the sound of our guns rang nearer and nearer. The Fourth corps for a moment halted and lay down to have Smith connect. We could soon see the rebels breaking pell mell from their works. Infantry, cavalry and artillery were sweeping across the plain. What does it mean?

A wild cheer rang from our lines, and the batteries redoubled their iron storm.

Behind the Union lines at Nashville on December 16.

Soon a column was seen emerging from the woods on the rebel flanks. Who are they? The Stars and Stripes float proudly in their front. They are our right, which has swung around their flank. Louder grow the huzzas—hats are flung in the air—civilians rush forward, helping the gunners. The Fourth Corps jump to their feet and sweep right on the flying enemy. Alas! Darkness was setting in. Oh, for a Joshua to command the sun to stand still!—just two hours!

The battle was fought, the victory won; Nashville was saved and Hood was repulsed, shattered and broken.

TUE 20 DEC. HARDEE EVACUATES SAVANNAH

Leaving behind copious supplies but none of his ten thousand men, Hardee's garrison fled Savannah this day and headed north to rendezvous with Confederate units in South Carolina. Sherman was later criticized for not moving more swiftly to cut off Hardee's route of escape across the Savannah River (on a pontoon bridge made from rice flats), but the Union commander correctly pointed out that, had he threatened this route, Hardee would simply have fled sooner. The loss of Savannah overall dealt a major emotional blow to an already disappointed Confederate populace while inspiring the North. Two days later, Sherman sent this telegram to President Lincoln.

To His Excellency President Lincoln: I beg to present you as a Christmas gift the city of Savannah, with one hundred and fifty heavy guns and plenty of ammunition, also about twenty-five thousand bales of cotton.

W. T. Sherman
Major-General

SAT 24 DEC. *Georgians living in the wake of Sherman's march had a mournful Christmas, as Dolly Sumner Lunt described in her diary. The custom of setting off firecrackers to which she refers was a traditional Christmas ritual in the South.*

THIS HAS USUALLY BEEN A VERY busy day with me, preparing for Christmas not only for my own tables, but for gifts for my servants. Now how changed! No confectionery, cakes, or pies can I have. We are all sad; no loud, jovial laugh from our boys is heard. Christmas Eve, which has ever been gaily celebrated here, which has witnessed the popping of fire-crackers and the hanging up of stockings, is an occasion now of sadness and gloom. I have nothing even to put in Sadai's stocking, which hangs so invitingly for Santa Claus. How disappointed she will be in the morning, though I have explained to her why he cannot come.

Poor children! Why must the innocent suffer with the guilty?

Eliza Andrews, a Georgia teenager who had recently traveled with her family across the path of Sherman's army, described the blighted landscape in her journal this Christmas Eve.

WE STRUCK THE "BURNT COUNTRY" as it is well named by the natives, and then I could better understand the wrath and desperation of these poor people. I almost felt as if I should like to hang a Yankee myself. There was hardly a fence left standing from Sparta to Gordon. The fields were trampled down and the road was lined with carcasses of horses, hogs and cattle, that the invaders, unable either to consume or carry away with them, had wantonly shot down to starve out the people and prevent them from making their crops. The stench in some places was unbearable....The dwellings that were standing all showed signs of pillage and on every plantation we saw the charred remains of the gin-houses....Crowds of [Confederate] soldiers were tramping over the road in both direction[s]....They were mostly on foot, and I saw numbers seated on the roadside greedily eating raw turnips, meat skins, parched corn—anything they could find, even picking up the loose grain that Sherman's horses had left.

★ ★ ★ ★

JANUARY 1865

SAT 7 JAN. *This article, published in today's New York World, lamented an unforeseen side effect the war was having in New York City and elsewhere.*

THE GREAT INCREASE OF assaults with deadly weapons within the past year, as is shown by our police reports, is, of course, one of the penalties we are compelled to pay for being in a state of war. Men with military tastes get in the habit of carrying pistols and dirks, and, as a consequence, quarrels which would otherwise have no worse result than a game of fisticuffs become homicides because of the handiness of deadly weapons. Our police magistrates have very properly taken this matter in hand, and are determined hereafter to punish with the utmost rigor of the law all who disregard the statute against carrying concealed weapons. This law, by the way, should be perfected to meet the changed condition of things, and, in addition to the law, a healthy public opinion should be formed against the essentially cowardly practice of carrying deadly weapons in a peaceful city.

FRI 13 JAN. *As the Confederate army's ranks thinned and the debate regarding the enlistment of slaves thickened, the Arkansas Telegraph weighed in with this editorial demonstrating that not all Southerners agreed with Jefferson Davis that national independence should be their primary goal.*

WE FIGHT FOR INDEPENDENCE. But this independence is itself valuable only as a means to a higher end.

The institutions which we cherish, and which by means of independence we hope to secure and perpetuate for the advancement of civilization, and the elevation and consequent happiness and dignity of ourselves and posterity, are the true objects of the struggle. They are the only worthy ones. Independence, with social degradation, and hopeless national poverty, is not worth the cost. It is a curse. For ourselves we wish none of it. Independence with anarchy and continual fluctuation of governments is hardly more desirable....

The great conservative institution of slavery, so excellent in itself, and so necessary to civil liberty and the dignity of the white race, is one of the grand objects of our struggle. It should never be lost sight of, nor under any pressure should we ever take any step incompatible with the relation of master and slave. No entering wedge to emancipation should ever be allowed. It should not be held forth to the slave as a boon for his services. Our theory is, that he is better off as a slave; and even if he were not, we could not safely have an emancipated class of them amongst us. Much less can we put arms in his hands. That would ruin him forever. Slavery afterwards would become impossible.

Rear Adm. David Dixon Porter

SUN 15 JAN. THE CAPTURE OF FORT FISHER

By this point in the war, the military reputation of Maj. Gen. Benjamin F. Butler had been substantially sullied, particularly by his failure at Petersburg

in June 1864. In what would become his last major operation, the quarrelsome but politically connected general sailed with two army divisions on December 18, bound for Fort Fisher. The fort, located at the mouth of the Cape Fear River, guarded the port of Wilmington, North Carolina, the last remaining Confederate link to the outside world. Rear Adm. David Dixon Porter, now commanding the North Atlantic Blockading Squadron, acted as Butler's naval counterpart. Porter's sixty warships began bombarding Fort Fisher on December 24, and the next day, Christmas, his transports landed Butler's assault force two miles north of the fort. But the naval bombardment had little effect on the earth-and-sand structure, and when elements of Braxton Bragg's six-thousand-man Wilmington garrison approached from the north, Butler decided to recall his troops and return to Hampton Roads. The fiasco ended Butler's active military career, and he was replaced on January 7 as commander of the Department of Virginia and North Carolina by Maj. Gen. E. O. C. Ord. Meanwhile, on January 4, Porter had again sailed for Wilmington, this time accompanied by Maj. Gen. Alfred H. Terry in command of the army divisions. For three days beginning January 13, Porter's 627 guns fired 20,000 shells at Fort Fisher, which was finally stormed and captured on January 15 (with surprisingly little opposition from Bragg). Confederate Col. William Lamb, who commanded the fort's garrison (and was wounded in the thigh during the final hours of the fort's defense), later recalled the assault. The spiking of guns to which Lamb refers often occurred when artillery companies feared that their guns might be captured by the enemy. The most common method was to drive a nail or file into the touchhole of the gun, thereby making it impossible to light the powder charge until the hole was repaired.

An interior view of Fort Fisher.

THE ENEMY'S ADVANCE HAD ceased entirely; protected by the fleet, they held the parapet and gun-chambers, but their massed columns refused to move and appeared to be intrenching in the work. I believed a determined assault with the bayonet upon their front would drive them out....

I passed quickly in rear of the line and asked the officers and men if they would follow me; they all responded fearlessly that they would. I returned to my post, and, giving the order "Charge bayonets," sprang upon the breastwork, waved my sword, and, as I gave the command "Forward! double-quick, march!" fell on my knees, a rifle-ball having entered my left hip. We were met by a heavy volley, aimed too high to be effective; but our column wavered and fell back behind the breastworks. A soldier raised me up; I turned the command over to Captain Daniel Munn and told him to keep the enemy in check, and that I would bandage my wound and soon return. Before I could reach the hospital I was made to realize that I was incapacitated from joining my men again....

About 8 o'clock at night my aide came to me and said the ammunition was giving out; that he and Chaplain McKinnon had gathered all on the dead and wounded in a blanket and had distributed it; that the enemy had possession of nearly all of the land-face; that it was impossible to hold out much longer, and suggested that it would be wise to surrender, as a further struggle might be a useless sacrifice of life. I replied that so long as I lived would not surrender the fort; that Bragg must soon come to the rescue, and it would save us....

In less than an hour a fourth brigade (three were already in the fort under General Ames) entered the sally-port and swept the defenders from the remainder of the land-face. Major Reilly had General Whiting and myself hurriedly removed on stretchers to Battery Buchanan, where he purposed to make a stand. When we left the hospital the men were fighting over the adjoining traverse and the spent balls fell like hail stones around us. The garrison then fell back in an orderly retreat along the sea-face, the rear guard keeping the enemy engaged as they advanced slowly and cautiously in the darkness as far as the Mound Battery, where they halted. Some of the men, cut off from the main body, had to retreat as best they could over the river marsh, while some few unarmed artillerists barely eluded the enemy by following the seashore.

When we reached Battery Buchanan there was a mile of level beach between us and our pursuers, swept by two 11-inch guns and a 24-pounder, and in close proximity to the battery, a commodious wharf where transports could have come to carry the men off. We expected to cover with this battery the retreat of the remnant of the garrison, but we found the guns spiked, and every means of transportation, even the barge and crew of the colonel commanding, taken by Captain R. F. Chapman, of our navy, who, following the example of General Bragg, had abandoned us to our fate.

None of the guns of Fort Fisher were spiked, the men fighting them until they were destroyed or their defenders were killed, wounded, or driven out of the batteries by overwhelming numbers. The enemy threw out a heavy skirmish-line and sent their fourth brigade to Battery Buchanan, where it arrived about 10 P.M. and received the surrender of the garrison from Major James H. Hill and Lieutenant George D. Parker.

Dr. Mary Walker, the only female surgeon on either side of the fighting, was now in charge of a military prison for women in Louisville, Kentucky. With this letter to the ranking officer in Louisville, she complained about a "disturbance" at the prison that resulted, in large part, from what she viewed as the prisoners' refusal to accept her authority.

THE SUBSTANCE OF THE WHOLE cause of disturbance, can be summed up in the following—First, I would not allow rebel songs and disloyal talk. The Lieut. would say "O! they are women." Second, I would not allow familiarity between the Guards, male cooks and prisoners. Third, all four of the male cooks were relieved and females supplied in their places....Fourth, I exacted cleanliness. Fifth, I would not allow prisoners to abuse each other. Sixth, I would not allow them to neglect their small children, or abuse them. To explain—One woman when her babe was but 4 or 5 weeks old would put it in a crib nights, and leave it until morning without any attention and it would cry until it was hoarse, and I finally took the crib out of the room and compelled her to take it in bed with her and take care of it. Another who has two children under 4 years, would allow them to cry and scream in their filth and wish them dead, until I told her if she did not pay them sanitary attention, I would have them given to some one who would....

Seventh, I watched their rebel friends when they came here and would not allow them to pass letters without examining them, and would not allow talk I did not hear.

Eighth, I had one woman handcuffed about two hours for calling the Guard to his face "D. S. B." and threatening to "kill two other prisoners" and daring me to come up stairs. I also had several locked up in the outside store house for waving their handkerchiefs and yelling for Jeff Davis when rebel prisoners were passing....

...Col Fairleigh has learned my true motives for all that I have done, and appreciates the trying position I hold, and all my greatest superior officers have confidence in my having done *well* under all circumstances, and that confidence is *merited.*

TUE 31 JAN. CONGRESS PASSES THE THIRTEENTH AMENDMENT

The Senate first approved the Thirteenth Amendment abolishing slavery throughout the United States in April 1864. Two months later, a majority of the House voted for the amendment— but not the two-thirds necessary for passage. The amendment was reintroduced in January 1865, when Republicans put pressure on Democrats to switch their votes. (The newly elected Republican Congress was sure to approve the measure, but its first session was nearly a year away and Lincoln wanted passage of the amendment before the end of the war.) The ensuing debate dominated the House for weeks, but on this day the members, with the end of the war in sight and the postwar legal status of Lincoln's Emancipation Proclamation unclear, finally consented. Although the significance of their action was well understood at the time, its importance has since been often overlooked. Without this constitutional amendment, slavery would still have been permitted in areas under Union control when the Emancipation Proclamation was issued, and the proclamation itself might conceivably have been reversed by a future president. Congress therefore acted to make emancipation irreversible. The very next day, the Illinois legislature became the first state to ratify the Thirteenth Amendment, whose text appears below. The ratification process ended on December 18, 1865, when Secretary of State Seward declared its approval by twenty-seven states.

1. NEITHER SLAVERY NOR INVOLuntary servitude, except as a punishment for crime whereof the party shall have been duly convicted, shall exist within the United States, or any place subject to their jurisdiction.

2. Congress shall have power to enforce this article by appropriate legislation.

★ ★ ★ ★

FEBRUARY
1865

THE HAMPTON ROADS CONFERENCE

On January 28, in response to overtures from Maryland power broker Francis P. Blair Sr., Jefferson Davis named three comissioners to attend an informal peace conference. The Confederate delegation consisted of Vice President Alexander H. Stephens, Confederate Senate president pro tem R. M. T. Hunter, and former U.S. Supreme Court justice John A. Campbell. Joining these men aboard the River Queen, anchored in the Hampton Roads estuary off Fort Monroe, were Lincoln and Seward. After some small talk, Lincoln made his position clear: There would be no negotiation unless and until the rebellious states accepted the sovereignty of the U.S. government. The Confederates proposed an armistice and other options, but Lincoln simply repeated himself: No agreements could be reached, or even discussed, with an entity whose existence the United States did not recognize. Thus ended the first and only significant effort to make peace. Although the commissioners' official report to President Davis, dated February 5 and excerpted below, gives January 30 as the date of the Hampton Roads conference, that was actually the day on which Lincoln approved passes for the Confederate commissioners to travel across Union lines. The December message to which the report also refers was Lincoln's annual State of the Union message, in which he had declared, "the abandonment of armed resistance to the national authority on the part of the insurgents [is] the only indispensable condition to ending the war."

THE CONFERENCE WAS GRANTED and took place on the 30th ult., on board of a steamer anchored in Hampton Roads, where we met President Lincoln and the Hon. Mr. Seward, Secretary of State of the United States. It continued for several hours, and was both full and explicit. We learned from them that the message of President Lincoln to the Congress of the United States, in December last, explains clearly and distinctly his sentiments as to the terms, conditions, and method of proceeding by which peace can be secured to the people, and we were not informed that they would be modified or altered to obtain that end. We understood from him that no terms or proposals of any treaty, or agreement looking to an ultimate settlement, would be entertained or made by him with the authorities of the Confederate States, because that would be a recognition of their existence as a separate power, which under no circumstances would be done; and, for a like reason, that no such terms would be entertained by him for the States separately; that no extended truce or armistice (as at present advised) would be granted or allowed without a satisfactory assurance in advance of the complete restoration of the authority of the Constitution and laws of the United States over all places within the States of the Confederacy; that whatever consequences may follow from the re-establishment of that authority must be accepted; but that individuals subject to pains and penalties under the laws of the United States might

rely upon a very liberal use of the power confided to him to remit those pains and penalties if peace be restored.

During the conference, the proposed [Thirteenth] amendment to the Constitution of the United States adopted by Congress on the 31st ultimo was brought to our notice.

This amendment provides that neither slavery nor involuntary servitude, except for crime, should exist within the United States, or any place within their jurisdiction, and that Congress should have power to enforce this amendment by appropriate legislation.

MON 6 FEB. LEE NAMED GENERAL-IN-CHIEF

Following creation of the post by the Confederate Congress on January 23, President Davis named Robert E. Lee general-in-chief of all Confederate armies. Although Lee was certainly a capable commander, the move came too late to affect the outcome of the war. Despite the grim prospects facing him, Lee accepted the position with characteristically valiant language.

DEEPLY IMPRESSED WITH THE difficulties and responsibilities of the position, and humbly invoking the guidance of Almighty God, I rely for success upon the courage and fortitude of the army, sustained by the patriotism and firmness of the people, confident that their united efforts under the blessing of Heaven will secure peace and independence.

SAT 11 FEB. *In the border states and other hotly contested regions where guerrilla bands were active, women were sometimes among the Confederate irregulars. For instance, in this letter to Brig. Gen. R. W. Johnson, commander of the Union defenses along the Tennessee & Alabama Railroad, Lt. Col. A. Matzdorff of the Seventy-fifth Pennsylvania Volunteers described an incident in which a Tennessee woman helped one band ambush a party of Union soldiers. (The word* bushwhackers, *meaning "guerrillas," first came into use during the Civil War.)*

GENERAL: I HAVE THE HONOR to submit to you herewith the report of [the] scouting expeditions ordered by me to clear the neighborhood of the bushwhackers which infest it:

On the 16th of January I ordered Lieut. C. Haserodt, with a squad of my mounted infantry, to secure the arrest of John Burke, a notorious bushwhacker, who was reported to be with his gang on the Wilson pike, fifteen miles from Franklin. At the house of a Mrs. Cherry, Lieutenant Haserodt fell in with five mounted men, whom he ordered to surrender, three of whom did so at once, but the other two took refuge in the house. On asking Mrs. Cherry whether she had seen said Burke she replied she had not, "but you are welcome to search my house." Lieutenant Haserodt then ordered Sergeant Mahring and two men to search the upper part of the house, but before they reached the upper rooms they were fired upon....Burke and another man by the name of Birch were both wounded, but Burke made his escape through a window in the back part of the house. Another of the band was killed instantly. After the affair Lieutenant Haserodt ordered the inmates to leave the house and set fire to the house.

SUN 12 FEB. *In this letter to Major General Sherman, Union spy Nora Winder passed on the results of her recent assignment in Georgia, correctly reporting Lt. Gen. John Bell Hood's January 13 resignation and his subsequent replacement by Lt. Gen. Richard Taylor. She also took the opportunity to remind Sherman of the army's financial obligation to her.*

HONORABLE SIR: ...I WILL write you the most important news I know. I left Milledgeville the 25th of November...and came to Augusta. I arrived at that place the 28th of November. Augusta was in a great excitement at that time...[in preparation for being] evacuated and then surrendered. There were 3,000 men sent on Brier Creek at Ellison's Bridge, and all the rest of the forces [about 5,000 men] were sent through South Carolina to Savannah....

I remained in Augusta...for two weeks. Then I came to Warren County and remained there three days. During that time I saw about 200 wagons or more, all going to Gordon to haul supplies to Mayfield to be sent by railroad to North Carolina and Virginia....[O]n the 30th of January my son...and myself started out on foot for Savannah....I heard it rumored that Hood's army was near Augusta and coming on. I did not see a man from

Mathew Brady took this group portrait of Sherman and his general staff in 1865.

Hood's army. I saw and read a letter myself from one of Hood's men to his wife, an acquaintance of mine....He wrote that Hood's army was cut all to pieces. There was not a horse saved. They lost all their cannon, but saved the carriages which bore up the guns. He also said Hood have given up his command to Dick Taylor....

General: I am very sorry I could [not] come to you sooner. The young man who was to hand me the money the day I left Milledgeville forgot to do so, and consequently I had to work my way a part of the time. Weaving pays well in the Confederacy, and I am a splendid weaver; so I stopped in Warren County and Jefferson County and wove for families, and by that means I paid my son's and my own way to Savannah....I came to you soon as I could under those circumstances, having to

work my way back. I would like to go to New Orleans as soon as possible. I cannot go until the commander of the post at this place hears from you. I have no means to go on. I have only my child with me.

FRI
17
FEB. THE BURNING OF COLUMBIA

In early January, Sherman began moving his troops from Savannah into South Carolina, leaving himself for Beaufort on January 21. For the following week, as he reconnoitered, he tried to conceal his next move, making feints toward both Charleston and Augusta. Once his army began to advance in earnest, however, it headed directly for Columbia, the state capital. Hardee's army, evacuated from Savannah, harassed the Union advance, but it was powerless to stop Sherman. (Muddy roads, burned bridges, felled trees, and swamps caused at least as much delay as the Confederate cavalry.) Leaving even more devastation as it had in Georgia, Sherman's army arrived on the southern bank of the Congaree River across from Columbia on February 16. There was some skirmishing, and a few Union shells were fired into the city, but Sherman generally allowed Confederate commander P. G. T. Beauregard to evacuate before accepting the city's surrender the following day. (Meanwhile, Hardee was evacuating Charleston.) On the night of February 17, however, much of Columbia burned. Southerners have perhaps never stopped blaming Sherman for intentionally starting the blaze (or at least for permitting looters to do so), but its origins remain a mystery. In any case, strong winds carried burning wooden shingles far and wide, extending the damage. Here, Sherman describes the fire (in an excerpt from his memoirs), followed by contemporary accounts from Columbia resident Emma LeConte (her diary entry for the day) and novelist William Gilmore Simms (a newspaper article). Simms, a renowned writer, was a refugee in Columbia, having fled his plantation in advance of Sherman's march.

HAVING WALKED OVER MUCH OF the suburbs of Columbia in the afternoon, and being tired, I lay down on a bed…to rest. Soon after dark I became conscious that a bright light was shining on the walls; and, calling some one of my staff (Major Nicholls, I think) to inquire the cause, he said there seemed to be a house on fire down about the market-house.…He soon returned, and reported that the block of buildings directly opposite the burning cotton of that morning was on fire, and that it was spreading.… The fire continued to increase, and the whole heavens became lurid.…The whole air was full of sparks and of flying masses of cotton, shingles, etc., some of which were carried four or five blocks, and started new fires. The men seemed generally under good control, and certainly labored hard to girdle the fire, to prevent its spreading; so long as the high wind prevailed, it was simply beyond human possibility. Fortunately, about 3 or 4 A.M., the wind moderated, and gradually the fire was got under control; but it had burned out the very heart of the city.

AT ABOUT SEVEN O'CLOCK I WAS standing on the back piazza in the third story. Before me the whole southern horizon was lit up by camp fires which dotted the woods. On one side the sky was illuminated by the burning of Gen. Hampton's residence a few miles off in the country, on the other side by some blazing buildings near the river. I had scarcely gone downstairs again when Henry told me there was a fire on Main Street. Sumter Street was brightly lighted by a burning house so near our piazza that we could feel the heat. By the red glare we could watch the wretches walking— generally staggering—back and forth

The ruins of Columbia, as viewed from the grounds of the State House.

from the camp to the town—shouting—hurrahing—cursing South Carolina—swearing—blaspheming—singing ribald songs and using such obscene language that we were forced to go indoors.

AT 1 O'CLOCK, THE HOUR WAS struck by the clock of the Market Hall, which was even then illuminated from within. It was its own last hour which it sounded, and its tongue was silenced forevermore. In less than five minutes after, its spire went down with a crash, and, by this time, almost all the buildings within the precinct were a mass of ruins.

Very grand, and terrible, beyond description, was the awful spectacle.

It was a scene for the painter of the terrible. It was the blending of a range of burning mountains stretched in a continuous series of more than a mile. Here was Aetna, sending up its spouts of flaming lava; Vesuvius, emulous of like display, shooting up with loftier torrents, and Stromboli, struggling, with awful throes, to shame both by its superior volumes of fluid flame. The winds were tributary to these convulsive efforts, and tossed the volcanic torrents of sulphurous cloud—wreaths of sable, edged with sheeted lightnings, wrapped the skies, and, at short intervals, the falling tower and the tottering wall, avalanche-like, went down with thunderous sound, sending up at every crash great billowy showers of glowing fiery embers.

WED 22 FEB. THE FALL OF WILMINGTON

The capture of Fort Fisher had closed the port of Wilmington, North Carolina, to blockade runners and made its fall a certainty. However, the Union's uncontested occupation of the city on this day had another benefit: It freed the army of Maj. Gen. John M. Schofield to join Grant's forces in Virginia. During the two-pronged advance on Wilmington, Schofield, in overall command, had led the Union troops on the eastern bank of the Cape Fear River; those on the western bank were commanded by Maj. Gen. Jacob D. Cox. In his diary, Cox described his entry into Wilmington.

AS I EXPECTED, WE ENTER Wilmington this morning without opposition, and as it is Washington's birthday we hail the event as a good omen. The enemy has retreated up the line of the Goldsborough road. I complete the repair and relaying of the rebel pontoon bridge and by noon cross the Brunswick River and the island to the ferry across Cape Fear River (the channel on the west of the island is called Brunswick River), and so into Wilmington with my troops. General Terry, being on the same side of the river, marches through in pursuit of Hoke. My troops are put in camp around the town, and I assume command of the place.

TUE 28 FEB. As the Union army consolidated its authority over large swaths of Confederate territory, freed slaves began to reap some of the fruits of emancipation. One such plum was the opportunity to participate in a marriage ceremony recognized by civil law. (Slaves had, of course, previously wed one another, but these marriages were denied legal legitimacy because the spouses were both considered property rather than people.) In the following letter, the chaplain of a black regiment in Arkansas described the high demand for his services.

WEDDINGS, JUST NOW, ARE very popular and abundant among the Colored People. They have just learned of the Special Order No. 15 of Gen. Thomas by which they may not only be lawfully married, but have their Marriage Certificates *Recorded* in a *book furnished by the Government*. This is most desirable; and the order was very opportune; as these people were constantly losing their certificates. Those who were captured from the "Chepewa" at Ivy's Ford, on the 17th of January, by Col Brooks, had their Marriage Certificates taken from them; and destroyed; and then were roundly cursed, for having such papers in their possession. I have married, during the month, at this Post, Twenty five couples; mostly, those who have families & have been living together for years. I try to dissuade single men, who are soldiers, from marrying, till their time of enlistment is out as that course seems to me to be most judicious.

The Colored People here generally consider this war not only their *exodus* from bondage but the road to Responsibility; Competency; and an honorable Citizenship—God grant that their hopes and expectations may be fully realized.

MARCH
1865

FRI 3 MAR. THE FREEDMEN'S BUREAU

At the close of its last session (which didn't adjourn until 8:00 A.M. on the morning of Lincoln's second inauguration), the Thirty-eighth Congress passed a bill creating the Bureau for the Relief of Freedmen and Refugees. The Freedmen's Bureau (as it was more commonly known) was to act as the legal guardian of the four million newly freed slaves, protecting their interests against the assault expected to come from a defeated and vengeful white South. The bureau was specifically charged with meeting the everyday needs of African-American men and women who had little education and no apparent means of support, and its aid was expected to include food, clothing, education, and jobs. The following article, which appeared in Harper's Weekly *prior to the bill's passage, championed the bureau as a debt owed the freed people by white society. Yet, by most accounts, the Freedmen's Bureau could do nothing right. Often reviled by Northern radicals for doing far too little and by Southern conservatives for intruding unnecessarily into the lives of Southern residents, the always underfunded, always understaffed bureau was finally disbanded in July 1872.*

THERE ARE TWO BILLS BEFORE Congress of the utmost importance, the passage of which should not be delayed, but which have been put aside for matters of much less moment. They are the bill regulating the payment of colored troops and the bill establishing a Freedmen's Bureau. Both of them relate to the negro question, but considering that shirking the negro question has brought us into the war, it is tolerably clear that continued shirking will not get us out. The three most vital points to which public and legislative attention should be constantly directed are the financial question, the military question, and the negro question. They may be very disagreeable subjects, all of them, but they are unavoidable....There is no more pressing or practical issue than the payment of the colored troops....Nor is the other point of the Freedmen's Bureau less pressing or less practical. Statesmen and sensible men are to deal with facts, and the fact is that the overthrow of slavery, a natural and inevitable result of the war, has cast almost a race upon our hands. Under the circumstances we can not abandon them. We are bound to give them the same chance that all other people have, and to leave them alone is to deprive them of that chance. Our policy, therefore, should be universal and uniform. The freedmen are to be protected in their equal rights with other men and nothing more. They are not to be made serfs attached to the land; they are to be defended against the consequences of slavery as shown in their servile fear of the white race and against the contempt bred by slavery in the whites themselves, which holds that they have no rights to be respected. The effects of slavery and the condition of the emancipated are every where effectively the same, and there is consequently not to be one policy in Louisiana, and another in South Carolina, and another in Alabama. The late slave-

holders in all these regions are to be made to understand clearly that the colored people are free, and have exactly the same rights of respect and protection under this government that they have. They are to make fair bargains with them and keep them fairly, or suffer the consequences, as we are all suffering the direful consequences of departure from this simple and equitable rule hitherto.

SAT 4 MAR. LINCOLN'S SECOND INAUGURATION

On a cold, rainy day in Washington, President Lincoln stood before the Capitol and delivered his second inaugural address. Calling for reconciliation and healing, he spoke with an eloquence matched by few American presidents. John Wilkes Booth was among those listening in the audience.

FELLOW-COUNTRYMEN: AT THIS second appearing to take the oath of the Presidential office there is less occasion for an extended address than there was at the first. Then a statement somewhat in detail of a course to be pursued seemed fitting and proper. Now, at the expiration of four years, during which public declarations have been constantly called forth on every point and phase of the great contest which still absorbs the attention and engrosses the energies of the nation, little that is new could be presented. The progress of our arms, upon which all else chiefly depends, is as well known to the public as to myself, and it is, I trust, reasonably satisfactory and

Lincoln's second inauguration on the steps of the Capitol.

encouraging to all. With high hope for the future, no prediction in regard to it is ventured.

On the occasion corresponding to this four years ago all thoughts were anxiously directed to an impending civil war. All dreaded it, all sought to avert it. While the inaugural address was being delivered from this place, devoted altogether to saving the Union without war, urgent agents were in the city seeking to destroy it without war— seeking to dissolve the Union and divide effects by negotiation. Both parties deprecated war; but one of them would make war rather than let the nation survive; and the other would accept war rather than let it perish. And the war came.

One-eighth of the whole population were colored slaves, not distributed generally over the Union, but localized in the southern part of it. These slaves constituted a peculiar and powerful interest. All knew that this interest was somehow the cause of the war. To strengthen, perpetu-

ate, and extend this interest was the object for which the insurgents would rend the Union even by war, while the Government claimed no right to do more than to restrict the territorial enlargement of it. Neither party expected for the war the magnitude or the duration which it has already attained. Neither anticipated that the cause of the conflict might cease with or even before the conflict itself should cease. Each looked for an easier triumph, and a result less fundamental and astounding. Both read the same Bible and pray to the same God, and each invokes His aid against the other. It may seem strange that any men should dare to ask a just God's assistance in wringing their bread from the sweat of other men's faces, but let us judge not, that we be not judged. The prayers of both could not be answered. That of neither has been answered fully. The Almighty has His own purposes. "Woe unto the world because of offenses; for it must needs be that offenses come, but woe to that man by whom the offense cometh." If we shall suppose that American slavery is one of those offenses which, in the providence of God, must needs come, but which, having continued through His appointed time, He now wills to remove, and that He gives to both North and South this terrible war as the woe due to those by whom the offense came, shall we discern therein any departure from those divine attributes which the believers in a living God always ascribe to Him? Fondly do we hope, fervently do we pray, that this mighty scourge of war may speedily pass away. Yet, if God wills that it continue until all the wealth piled by the bondsman's two hundred and fifty years of unrequited toil shall be sunk, and until every drop of blood drawn with the lash shall be paid by another drawn with the sword, as was said three thousand years ago, so still it must be said "the judgments of the Lord are true and righteous altogether."

With malice toward none, with charity for all, with firmness in the right as God gives us to see the right, let us strive on to finish the work we are in, to bind up the nation's wounds, to care for him who shall have borne the battle and for his widow and his orphan, to do all which may achieve and cherish a just and lasting peace among ourselves and with all nations.

SUN
5
MAR.

In this letter to Willoughby Newton, a Confederate congressman from Virginia, Jefferson Davis—who, five weeks before Lee's surrender, must surely have known the war was lost—expressed his dogged

belief (or hope) that the Confederate national will would somehow prevail.

MY DEAR SIR: YOUR KIND LETTER written June 6th was after some lapse of time received by me, and I reply now to thank you for your generous confidence and friendly encouragement in an hour when so many believed brave have faltered and so many esteemed true have fallen away.

In such words and feelings as you extend to me, I find the most gratifying reward for my labours in the public service.

In spite of the timidity and faithlessness of many who should give tone to the popular feeling and hope to the popular heart, I am satisfied that it is in the power of the good man and true patriots of the country to reanimate the wearied spirit of our people. The incredible sacrifices made by them in the cause will be surpassed by what they are still willing to endure in preference to abject submission, if they are not deserted by their leaders. Relying upon the sublime fortitude and devotion of my countrymen, I expect the hour of deliverance.

I thank you from a heart wrung by domestic affliction....

Very respectfully and truly yours,
Jefferson Davis

MON
6
MAR.

Meta Morris Grimball's diary entry for this day eloquently depicts the deteriorating state of Confederate affairs.

I HAVE NO HEART TO WRITE A journal now. The war goes on but

so much distress and suffering. Charleston evacuated, Columbia sacked & burned…& other places visited by the Army of Sherman & sacked and burned. Our Army now under Johnston following Sherman and all things in gloom & trouble. Arthur & Berkley are with the troops from the Coast in Raleigh & Hillsborough. Lewis was with us for 10 days, looking quite well; he is now with the Army in North Carolina. Harry received an appointment from the Gov. for the Arsenal, & today left us for Greenville where they are to be located. This has been a great trial to me for he is the youngest and not yet sixteen. I fear all the fatigue & hardship he will not be able to stand; and my heart yearns over this child. He left a very good school for this appointment and they have no books to educate the Cadets. My only comfort is in prayer.

THU
9
MAR.
By the time the Northern government called its third draft, the view that the Civil War was being fought by the poor on behalf of the rich was commonplace. The article below was but one articulation of that argument. It appeared in the admittedly partisan New York World *accompanying a notice of the draft.*

A DRAFT ON THE 15TH INST.
It is officially announced that the draft will commence in this city on the 15th inst. (next Wednesday), which will be continued until the whole of the uncompleted quota, some thirteen thousand, is raised. This will be sad news in tens of thousands of homes. It will not affect the rich, for they can buy substitutes; nor the idle and thriftless, for they can leave the city; nor the large floating population, for they cannot be found; but the real sufferers will be men of small means with families and homes, who cannot go to the war without extreme hardship, and yet who have not money enough to pay for substitutes. It is a burning shame that the rich and influential among our citizens do not bestir themselves, and by effort and money hurry up the recruiting, and so save poor and worthy men the intolerable hardships of conscription. This is a matter that should be taken in hand by the Chamber of Commerce—the various organized political organizations, such as the Tammany and the Republican General Committee, and by the aldermen in their respective wards. This immensely rich city could easily raise the men if those who owned the wealth would but half try.

MON
13
MAR.
On this late date, the dispute over whether or not to impress slaves was resolved when the Confederate Congress finally empowered Jefferson Davis to call upon slaveholders to supply men for army service. There remained, of course, the significant task of persuading the Southern populace that this policy was sound, but Lee's surrender, now less than a month away, would soon render such debate meaningless. The following remarkably encouraging article appeared in the Richmond Daily Dispatch *on March 21. By this time, the first black troops had already been raised and their training begun. Later in March, a few black*

soldiers even appeared in Confederate uniform on the streets of Richmond.

IT WILL BE SEEN BY THE ORDER of the Secretary of War, published above, that the undersigned have been authorized to proceed at once with the organization of Companies composed of persons of Color, free and slave, who are willing to volunteer under the recent acts of Congress and the Legislature of Virginia. It is well known to the country that Gen. Lee has evinced the deepest interest on this subject, and that he regards prompt action in this matter, as vitally important to the country....

The governments, Confederate and State, having settled the policy of employing this element of strength, and this class of our population having given repeated evidence of their willingness to take up arms in the defence of their homes, it is believed that it is only necessary to put the matter before them in a proper light to cause them to rally with enthusiasm for the preservation of the homes in which they have been born and raised, and in which they have found contentment and happiness; and to save themselves and their race from the barbarous cruelty invariably practised upon them by a perfidious enemy claiming to be their friends.

Will not the people of Virginia, in this hour of peril and danger, promptly respond to the call of our loved General-in-Chief, and the demands of the Confederate and State governments?

Will those who have freely given their sons and brothers, their money and their property, to the achievement of the liberties of their country, now hold back from the cause their servants, who can

well be spared, and who will gladly aid in bringing this fearful war to a speedy and glorious termination!

Let every man in the State consider himself a recruiting officer, and enter at once upon the duty of aiding in the organization of this force, by sending forward recruits to this rendezvous.

THE SIEGE OF PETERSBURG CONTINUES

SUN 19 MAR.

The siege of Petersburg dragged on through the winter of 1864–65 with the armies hunkered down in damp, miserable trenches. As soon as the season permitted, Grant planned to launch an offensive designed to destroy Lee's army. The Confederates, however, clung to the hope that Lee could escape and join with the other Confederate armies to prolong the war indefinitely. These two letters, the first from Grant to his father (dated this day) and the second from Lt. L. R. Mills of the Twenty-sixth Virginia to his brother (dated March 2), provide an interesting colloquy on life in and around Petersburg as the end of the siege neared.

WE ARE NOW HAVING FINE weather and I think will be able to wind up matters around Richmond soon. I am anxious to have Lee hold on where he is a short time longer so that I can get him in a position where he must lose a great portion of his Army. The rebellion has lost its vitality and if I am not much mistaken there will be no rebel Army of

A dead Confederate soldier in one of the earthworks ringing Petersburg.

any great dimentions a few weeks hence. Any great catastrophy to any one of our Armies would of course revive the enemy for a short time. But I expect no such thing to happen.

I WOULD REGRET VERY MUCH TO have to give up the old place. The soiled and tattered Colors borne by our skeleton Regiment is sacred and dear to the heart of every man. No one would exchange it for a new flag. So it is with us. I go down the lines, I see the marks of shot and shell, I see where fell my comrades, the Crater, the grave of fifteen hundred Yankees; when I go to the rear I see little mounds of dirt, some with head-boards, some with none, some with shoes

protruding, some with small piles of bones on one side near the end showing where a hand was left uncovered; in fact every-thing near shows desperate fighting. And here I would rather "fight it out." If Petersburg and Richmond [are] evacu-ated—from what I have seen and heard in the army—our cause will be hopeless. It is useless to conceal the truth any longer.

BENTONVILLE

From Columbia, Sherman had quickly resumed his northward march, and by this time, his army was well into North Carolina. Meanwhile, on February 22, Joseph E. Johnston had been returned to command of the (few) Confederate forces opposing Sherman. The Southern general responded as best he could given limited resources, cautiously staging a series of indecisive battles. The most significant of these was the engagement fought this day at Bentonville, North Carolina. In what would be his final attempt to halt Sherman's advance, Johnston lay in wait for the unsuspecting Federal left wing commanded by Maj. Gen. Henry W. Slocum. Although the initial Confederate charge did breach some Union breastworks on the left side of the line, Slocum's men soon rallied behind Maj. Gen. Jefferson C. Davis (the other Jefferson Davis) and withstood two more assaults before darkness fell and the demoralized Rebels pulled back. Johnston's attack did slow Sherman's army, thus giving Lee a little more time to attempt an escape from Grant, but it accomplished little else. Here is Sherman's March 22 dispatch to Grant on the fighting, which lasted until late on March 21.

Maj. Gen. Jefferson C. Davis

GENERAL JOS. JOHNSTON HAD, the night before, marched his whole army (Bragg, Cheatham, S. D. Lee, Hardee, and all the troops he had drawn from every quarter), determined, as he told his men, to crush one of our corps, and then defeat us in detail. He attacked General Slocum in position from 3 P.M. on the 19th till dark; but was everywhere repulsed, and lost heavily. At the time, I was with the Fifteenth Corps, marching more to the right; but on hearing of General Slocum's danger, directed that corps over, and on the 20th marched rapidly on Johnston's flank and rear. We struck him about noon, forced him to assume the defensive, and to fortify. Yesterday we pushed him hard, and came very near to crushing him, the right division of the Seventeenth Corps (Mower's) having broken to within a hundred yards of where Johnston himself was, at the bridge across Mill Creek. Last night he retreated, leaving us in possession of the field, dead, and wounded.

SAT 25 MAR. FORT STEDMAN

Fort Stedman, located on the outskirts of Petersburg, was a base of operations for Union forces besieging the city. Early this morning, about 3:00 A.M., a group of Southern soldiers, pretending to be deserters, appeared at the fort. Actually, they were advance units of Maj. Gen. John B. Gordon's assault force bent on sabotage. An hour later, Gordon's full force staged a massive attack, storming the fort and temporarily overwhelming

An interior view of Fort Stedman.

its Federal defenders. The Confederates seized nearly a mile of Union line and threatened the central supply depot at City Point before their attack lost momentum. Meanwhile, the Federals regrouped, added reinforcements, and counterattacked. In the end, the Rebels were forced to give back Fort Stedman and take four thousand casualties to fifteen hundred for the Union. Below are two documentary records: The first is an account of the attack that Gordon prepared for his memoirs; the second is an excerpt from the official report of Capt. Samuel A. McClellan of the First New York Light Artillery.

SIMULTANEOUSLY WITH THE seizing and silencing of the Federal sentinels, my stalwart axemen leaped over our breastworks, closely followed by the selected 300 and the packed column of infantry. Although it required but a few minutes to reach the Union works, those minutes were to me like hours of sus-

pense and breathless anxiety; but soon was heard the thud of the heavy axes as my brave fellows slashed down the Federal obstructions. The next moment the infantry sprang upon the Union breastworks and into the fort, overpowering the gunners before their destructive charges could be emptied into the mass of Confederates. They turned this captured artillery upon the flanking lines and on each side of the fort, clearing the Union breastworks of their defenders for some distance in both directions. Up to this point, the success had exceeded my most sanguine expectations.

ABOUT DAYBREAK YESTERDAY morning, March 25, 1865, I was aroused by cheering and firing of musketry in the direction of Fort Stedman. I immediately rose and started out to ascertain the cause, and had not proceeded in that direction but a short distance when I met stragglers going to the rear, who reported that the enemy had captured Fort Stedman, and was advancing on Meade's Station. Without delay I caused my battery to be harnessed, and moved the section of guns remaining in park to take a position, for the purpose of assisting in checking the advance of the enemy. Soon after arriving on the crest of the heights in rear of Fort Stedman, Major Miller rode up and gave orders to take position and open on the enemy, which I did, with apparently very good effect, causing their advance skirmishers, who were near the base of the hill, to fall back in rear of our old line of rifle-pits, about 200 yards in rear of Fort Stedman. Believing that I could get a nearer and

A bombproof at Fort Stedman.

more effective position I rode down to the front to select one. On returning I met General Tidball, who gave me orders to take the new position which I had selected. While moving into this new position the enemy opened upon my column with two light 12-pounder guns, which he had taken with the fort, but his fire was so inaccurate that he did me no harm.

FRI 31 MAR. DINWIDDIE COURT HOUSE

In the first move of the Union army's final push to break the Confederate lines around Petersburg, Maj. Gen. Philip H. Sheridan led twelve thousand cavalrymen, closely followed by two corps of infantry, to Dinwiddie Court House on Lee's extreme right flank south of Petersburg. From this position, he threatened not only to turn Lee's flank but also to seize the strategic crossroads known as Five Forks, thus cutting Lee's most important supply line and cutting off his escape route. The following is Lee's regretful dispatch to Jefferson Davis explaining that, following this Union action, he now has no choice but to abandon the defense of Richmond and attempt to join Johnston in North Carolina.

THE MOVEMENT OF GEN GRANT to Dinwiddie C.H. seriously threatens our position, and diminishes our ability to maintain our present lines in front of Richmond and Petersburg. In the first place, it cuts us off from our depot at Stony Creek at which point, forage for the cavalry was delivered by the Weldon R.R., and upon which we relied to maintain it. It also renders it more difficult to withdraw from our position, cuts us off from the White Oak road, and gives the enemy an advantageous point on our right and rear. From this point, I fear he can readily cut both the South Side & the Danville Railroads, being far superior to us in cavalry. This in my opinion obliged us to prepare for the necessity of evacuating our position on the James River at once, and also to consider the best means of accomplishing it, and our future course.

★ ★ ★ ★

APRIL 1865

FIVE FORKS

Grant's strategy was now obvious: to weaken the Confederate lines by forcing them to stretch farther and farther westward. On this day, those lines snapped at Five Forks on the Rebel right. "Hold Five Forks at all hazards," Lee had told Maj. Gen. George E. Pickett that morning, knowing full well that giving up this crossroads meant the likely loss of his last supply line to the south. That afternoon, Sheridan's dismounted cavalry stormed Pickett's entrenched defenders, while Maj. Gen. Gouverneur K. Warren's Fifth Corps infantry attacked from the left. The defenses caved, Pickett's force was split off from the rest of the Confederate army, and the Federals seized nearly complete control of the Petersburg perimeter south of the Appomattox River. All that remained to Lee was the South Side Railroad, his last escape route. Below are accounts of the battle from the official report of Lee's son, Maj. Gen. Fitzhugh Lee, and the memoirs of Major General Sheridan.

EVERYTHING CONTINUED QUIET until about 3 P.M., when reports reached me of a large body of infantry marching around and menacing our left flank. I ordered Munford to go in person, ascertain the exact condition of affairs, hold his command in readiness, and if necessary order it up at once. He soon sent for it, and it reached its position just in time to receive the attack. A division of two small brigades of cavalry was not able long to withstand the attack of a Federal

Some of the twenty-four hundred Confederate prisoners captured by Sheridan at Five Forks.

corps of infantry, and that force soon crushed in Pickett's left flank, swept it away, and before Rosser could cross Hatcher's Run, the position at the Forks was seized and held and an advance toward the railroad made. It was repulsed by Rosser. Pickett was driven rapidly toward the prolongation of the right of his line of battle by the combined attack of this infantry corps and Sheridan's cavalry, making a total of over 26,000 men, to which he was opposed with 7,000 men of all arms. Our forces were driven back some miles, the retreat degenerating into a rout, being followed up principally by the cavalry, whilst the infantry corps held the position our troops were first driven from, threatening an advance upon the railroad, and paralyzing the force of reserve cavalry by necessitating its being stationary in an interposing position to check or retard such an advance.

OUR SUCCESS WAS UNQUALIFIED; we had overthrown Pickett, taken six guns, thirteen battle-flags, and nearly six thousand prisoners. When the battle was practically over, I turned to consider my position with reference to the main Confederate army. My troops, though victorious, were isolated from the Army of the Potomac, for on the 31st of March the extreme left of that army had been thrown back nearly to the Boydton plank-road, and hence there was nothing to prevent the enemy's issuing from his trenches at the intersection of the White Oak and Claiborne roads and marching directly on my rear. I surmised that he might do this that night or early the next morning. It was therefore necessary to protect myself in this critical situation, and General Warren having sorely disappointed me, both on the moving of his corps and in its management during the battle, I felt that he was not the man to rely upon under such circumstances, and deeming that it was to the best interest of the service as well as but just to myself, I relieved him, ordering him to report to General Grant.

In Richmond, newspapers scrambled for the latest news of the battle.

 THE WEATHER IS COOL AND pleasant. Excited couriers have arrived from off the line of the Southside Railroad and report the Yankees are fighting their way through our lines, and their numbers as so great that we cannot much longer hold Petersburg....News reaches us tonight that General Pickett has lost control of his troops at Five Forks, and that the Yankees are gradually moving towards Richmond. It seems that our troops have become discouraged and are easily confused. The Yankee assault on Pickett's Division has completely demoralized it, if reports are true.

Meanwhile, Jefferson Davis scrambled for men and matériel. The Tredegar Iron Works to which he refers in this message to Lee was the most important industrial firm in the South, producing the bulk of its ammunition and casting nearly all its heavy artillery.

[I] HAVE DIRECTED THAT ORDERS be given to the commanders of Reserves in the several States to employ their officers to recruit negroes. If there be an officer or soldier to whose command the masters would prefer to intrust, and the slaves would prefer to go, he can be appointed when the company or battalion reaches its destination. I have prepared a circular letter to the governors of the States invoking their aid, as well by appeals to the owners as by recommendations to the legislatures, to make the most liberal provisions for those who volunteer to fight for the safety and independence of the State.

...The desire to confer with you would have caused me to go to Petersburg before this date but for the pressure which recent events have put upon me, and the operations in your vicinity prevented me from inviting you to come here.

Today the Secretary of War presents propositions from the proprietors of the Tredegar Works which impress me very unfavorably. We will endeavor to keep them at work, though it must be on a reduced scale. There is also a difficulty in getting iron, even for shot and shell, but hope this may, for the present, be overcome by taking some from the navy, which, under the altered circumstances, may be spared. Last night we had rumors of a general engagement on your right. Your silence in regard to it leads to the conclusion that it was unwarranted....

The question is often asked of me "Will we hold Richmond?" to which my only answer is, "If we can; it is purely a question of military power." The distrust is increasing, and embarrasses in many ways.

SUN 2 APR. SELMA

On March 22, in conjunction with the new Federal offensive against Mobile, three cavalry divisions under Maj. Gen. James Harrison Wilson (about 13,500 men) left the Tennessee River for Selma, Alabama, whose factories had thus far been spared the ravages of war. Opposing Wilson in a weeklong series of running battles was Confederate Lt. Gen. Nathan Bedford Forrest. On this day, Wilson reached Selma and faced off against the heretofore invincible Forrest. But Forrest's current command was not the equal, in numbers or spirit, of the group that had humbled Union forces at Tupelo, Memphis, and elsewhere. The Rebel defenses crumbled in several places, and Forrest was forced to flee the city along with his senior staff. (Lt. Gen. Richard Taylor, the Confederate departmental commander, also took flight.) The account below—written by Confederate Lt. George Cowan, who was assigned to Forrest's personal escort—describes some of the action of the previous day, April 1, that led to Forrest's final withdrawal into Selma. It gives an excellent perspective on the desperate character of the day's fighting and how closely pressed the Confederates were during the entire Selma Campaign.

Maj. Gen. James H. Wilson

AS THE FEDERALS DASHED FORward in their charge upon our line, they evidently recognized General Forrest's headquarters flag, near which he himself was, with his escort gathered about him. He told us to draw our six-shooters and stand our ground, no matter how many rode into us. As they came on, we fired with our rifles one volley, and then drew both of our pistols and rode forward to meet them....Fortunately for the escort the Federals were using the sabre while we had our six-shooters, and this accounts for the difference in the losses on both sides. I saw General Forrest surrounded by six Federals at one time, and they were all slashing at him. One of them struck one of his pistols and knocked it from his hand. Private Phil Dodd was fortunately near and spurred his horse to the general's rescue, and shot the Federal soldier who was so close upon him, thus enabling General Forrest to draw his other pistol, with which he killed another of the group, who was still persistent in his attack upon our commander. General Forrest and Captain Boone, of the escort, were both wounded. Although Federals rode through us and over us, those that survived were beaten back, and we did not leave the field until we saw their main column advancing later.

In his official report, Union Brig. Gen. Eli Long described the capture of the strongly fortified but thinly defended Confederate lines at Selma. (Total casualties were 319 for the Federals, about 2,700 for the Confederates.)

I MOVED FORWARD AT 5 P.M., my entire line advancing promptly, and in less than twenty-five minutes after the command to advance had been given the works were ours. The works carried consisted of a heavy line of earth-works eight or twelve feet in height, and fifteen feet in thickness at the base, with a ditch in front partly filled by water, four feet in width and five feet deep, and in front of this a stockade or picket of heavy posts planted firmly in the ground, five feet high and sharpened at the top. Four heavy forts with artillery in position also covered the ground over which the men advanced. The ground was rough, and a deep ravine had to be passed before the works could be reached. The men fully understood the difficulties before them. There was no flinching; all seemed confident of their ability to overcome them. As soon as we uncovered on the hill about 600 yards from the earthworks, the enemy opened a rapid and destructive fire of musketry and artillery on the line, but we moved forward steadily until within short range, when a rapid fire was opened by our Spencers, and with a cheer the men started for the works on a run, sweeping forward in solid line over fences and ravine, scaling the stockade and the works with resistless force, the enemy fighting stubbornly, many of them clubbing [with] their guns, but forced to retreat in the greatest disorder, our men continuing in pursuit through the city, and taking many prisoners.

In his memoirs, Taylor recounted the excitement of his last few moments in Selma. The "deceit practiced" by two of Forrest's brigades probably referred to their running away, which was likely the fate of the missing third brigade.

FORREST FOUGHT AS IF THE world depended on his arm, and sent to advise me of the deceit practiced by two of his brigades, but hoped to stop the enemy if he could get up the third, the absence of which he could not account for. I directed such railway plant as we had to be moved out on the roads, retaining a small yard engine to take me off at the last moment. There was nothing more to be done. Forrest appeared, horse and man covered with blood, and announced the enemy at his heels, and that I must move at once to escape capture. I felt anxious for him, but he said he was unhurt and would cut his way through, as most of his men had done, whom he had ordered to meet him west of the Cahawba. My engine started toward Meridian and barely escaped.

THE ASSAULT ON PETERSBURG

Capitalizing on Sheridan's victory at Five Forks, Grant ordered an offensive this morning all along the Petersburg front. Beginning at 4:40 A.M., the assault was everywhere successful. Importantly, the Union Sixth Corps under Horatio G. Wright reached the South Side Railroad, while Confederate Lt. Gen. A. P. Hill was killed as he attempted to rally his men west of the Boydton Plank Road. The nine-month siege of Petersburg was over, and Lee made hurried plans to evacuate what remained of his army. Stiffened Confederate resistance at Forts Baldwin and Gregg gave him just enough time to pull out across the Appomattox River west of the city. "This is a sad business, colonel," Lee told a subordinate. "It has happened as I told them in Richmond it would happen. The line has been stretched until it is broken." Meanwhile, that evening, President Davis and most of his cabinet left on a special train for Danville. Many of those remaining in Richmond wept as they prepared for the imminent arrival of Federal troops. Here, Northern war correspondent Sylvanus Cadwallader, who had covered Grant's commands for several years, reports on the war's dramatic endgame.

SOMETIME DURING THE DAY of April 2d, headquarters were moved up to within four or five miles of the Petersburg public square. By night of that day, the entire outer line of the city's intrenchments, had [been] carried by our troops, and the Union army lay strongly posted from the Appomattox river below Petersburg, to the river above it. Sheridan had cut off large detachments of rebel troops, as he followed up his victory at Five Forks, which had been driven up the river towards Burkesville Junction, or across it to join Lee towards Richmond. Our troops went into camp at night, with orders to assault everywhere as soon after daylight next morning as they could be put into motion.

A segment of the Petersburg lines.

MON 3 APR.

THE FALL OF RICHMOND

Lee's withdrawal late on April 2, though the only way to keep his army fighting, nevertheless surrendered both Petersburg and Richmond to the Federals. In his memoirs, Union Second Corps commander A. A. Humphreys described the events of April 3's early morning hours. That afternoon, groups of jubilant African Americans crowded the streets of Richmond, even though much of the city was still burning from the fires of the night before.

ORDERS WERE GIVEN BY General Grant for the assault of the Petersburg and Richmond lines early on the morning of the 3d, but at three o'clock in the morning it was discovered that General Lee had abandoned all his intrenchments. Petersburg was taken pos-

A view looking north from Petersburg across the James River to the ruined city of Richmond.

session of by General Willcox with his division, his troops and those at City Point being placed under the command of General Warren.

The formal surrender of Richmond was made to General Weitzel at City Hall, at 8:15 A.M.

In his memoirs, Confederate artillery chief E. P. Alexander described what he saw as he gazed back toward the burning Confederate capital on the morning of April 3. The Manchester high grounds are on the south bank of the James River across from Richmond.

IT WAS AFTER SUNRISE OF A bright morning when from the Manchester high grounds we turned to take our last look at the old city for which

we had fought so long & so hard. It was a sad, a terrible & a solemn sight. I don't know that any moment in the whole war impressed me more deeply with all its stern realities than this. The whole river front seemed to be in flames, amid which occasional heavy explosions were heard, & the black smoke spreading and hanging over the city seemed to be full of dreadful portents. I rode on with a distinctly heavy heart & with a peculiar sort of feeling of orphanage.

TUE 4 APR. LINCOLN VISITS RICHMOND

While Grant pressed his pursuit of Lee's army, which was fleeing westward, President Lincoln visited the captured Con-

federate capital. He traveled up the James River aboard the River Queen, *transferred to the warship* Malvern, *and then was put ashore in a rowboat. He was met by Rear Adm. David Dixon Porter, three other officers, and a party of ten sailors armed with carbines, who escorted his walk from the river to the White House of the Confederacy, which President Davis had lately vacated. That afternoon, with a much more substantial bodyguard, Lincoln and Porter toured Richmond in a carriage. From the Union headquarters at City Point, Lincoln had sent this telegram to Secretary of War Stanton on the eve of his visit.*

YOURS RECEIVED. THANKS FOR your caution; but I have already been to Petersburg, staid with Gen. Grant an hour & a half and returned here. It is certain now that Richmond is in our hands, and I think I will go there tomorrow. I will take care of myself.

WED
5
APR.

The Confederate government's departure from Richmond on April 2 had been a pitiable affair: the entire national government reduced to a single rickety train with the names of each department—War, State, and so on—hastily painted onto the sides of each boxcar. And yet Jefferson Davis remained steadfast enough—or deluded enough—to issue this final proclamation as he set up an executive office in Danville. Much later, he wrote, with considerable understatement, that "viewed by the light of subsequent events, it may be fairly said [the proclamation] was oversanguine." Meanwhile,

Sheridan, pursuing Lee along a parallel route, arrived at Jetersville on the Danville Railroad, thus blocking Lee's further advance from Amelia Court House along that line.

THE GENERAL-IN-CHIEF FOUND it necessary to make such movements of his troops as to uncover the capital. It would be unwise to conceal the moral and material injury to our cause resulting from its occupation by the enemy. It is equally unwise and unworthy of us to allow our energies to falter and our efforts to become relaxed under reverses, however calamitous they may be. For many months the largest and finest army of the Confederacy, under a leader whose presence inspires equal confidence in the troops and the people, has been greatly trammeled by the necessity of keeping constant watch over the approaches to the capital, and has thus been forced to forego more than one opportunity for promising enterprise. It is for us, my countrymen, to show by our bearing under reverses, how wretched has been the self-deception of those who have believed us less able to endure misfortune than to encounter danger with courage.

We have now entered upon a new phase of the struggle. Relieved from the necessity of guarding particular points, our army will be free to move from point to point, to strike the enemy in detail far from his base. Let us but will it, and we are free.

Animated by that confidence in your spirit and fortitude which never yet failed me, I announce to you, fellow-countrymen, that it is my purpose to maintain your cause with my whole heart and soul; that I will never consent to abandon to the enemy one foot of the soil of any of the States of the Confederacy; that Virginia—noble State, whose ancient renown has been eclipsed by her still more glorious recent history; whose bosom has been bared to receive the main shock of this war; whose sons and daughters have exhibited heroism so sublime as to render her illustrious in all time to come—that Virginia, with the help of the people and by the blessing of Providence, shall be held and defended, and no peace ever be made with the infamous invaders of her territory.

If, by the stress of numbers, we should be compelled to a temporary withdrawal from her limits or those of any other border State, we will return until the baffled and exhausted enemy shall abandon in despair his endless and impossible task of making slaves of a people resolved to be free.

Let us, then, not despond, my countrymen, but, relying on God, meet the foe with fresh defiance and with unconquered and unconquerable hearts.

THU 6 APR. SAYLER'S CREEK

On April 5, Lee pulled out of Amelia Court House. He was bound for Danville but planned to stop on the way at Farmville, a town on the South Side Railroad where he hoped to receive supplies. (Lee's ultimate destination was, of course, North Carolina, where he hoped to combine his army with that of Joseph Johnston.) However, in the swampy bottomland along Sayler's Creek, Lee's column became dangerously strung out.

Sheridan's cavalry and Horatio Wright's Sixth Corps isolated Lt. Gen. Richard S. Ewell's reserve corps and forced its surrender, while father north, the Federal Second Corps under A. A. Humphreys engaged a smaller Confederate corps under John B. Gordon, cutting it to pieces. Altogether, the Rebels lost about eight thousand men, or a third of the number that Lee had the night before. The once-proud Army of Northern Virginia was thus rapidly melting away. The following is an excerpt from Ewell's report on the battle.

 MY LINE RAN ACROSS A LITTLE ravine which leads nearly at right angles toward Sailor's Creek. General G. W. C. Lee was on the left, with the Naval Battalion, under Commodore Tucker, behind his right. Kershaw's division was on the right. All of Lee's and part of Kershaw's division were posted behind a rising ground that afforded some shelter from artillery. The creek was perhaps 300 yards in their front, with brush pines between and a cleared field beyond it. In this the enemy's artillery took a commanding position, and finding we had none to reply, soon approached within 800 yards and opened a terrible fire. After nearly half an hour of this, their infantry advanced, crossing the creek above and below us at the same time. Just as it attacked, General Anderson made his assault, which was repulsed in five minutes. I had ridden up near his lines with him to see the result, when a staff officer, who had followed his troops in their charge, brought word of its failure. General Anderson rode rapidly toward his command. I returned to mine to see if it

were yet too late to try the other plan of escape. On riding past my left I came suddenly upon a strong line of the enemy's skirmishers advancing upon my left rear. This closed the only avenue of escape, as shells and even bullets were crossing each other from front and rear over my troops, and my right was completely enveloped. I surrendered myself and staff to a cavalry officer who came in by the same road General Anderson had gone out on. At my request he sent a messenger to General G. W. C. Lee, who was nearest, with a note from me telling him he was surrounded, General Anderson's attack had failed, I had surrendered, and he had better do so too, to prevent useless loss of life, though I gave no orders, being a prisoner. Before the message had reached him General Lee had been captured, as had General Kershaw, and the whole of my command.

The morning following Sheridan's victory at Sayler's Creek, Lincoln sent this telegram from City Point.

 LIEUT. GEN. GRANT: GEN. Sheridan says "If the thing is pressed I think that Lee will surrender." Let the *thing* be pressed.
　　A. Lincoln

FRI 7 APR. GRANT ASKS FOR LEE'S SURRENDER

This afternoon, Grant and Lee began exchanging the messages that would eventually produce Lee's surrender.

 5 P.M., April 7th, 1865

General R. E. Lee, Commanding C.S.A.: The results of the last week must convince you of the hopelessness of further resistance on the part of the Army of Northern Virginia in this struggle. I feel that it is so, and regard it as my duty to shift from myself the responsibility of any further effusion of blood by asking of you the surrender of that portion of the Confederate States army known as the Army of Northern Virginia.
　　U.S. Grant, Lieutenant-General

Grant's note was carried through the Confederate lines, and Lee's response was prompt.

 April 7th, 1865

General: I have received your note of this date. Though not entertaining the opinion you express of the hopelessness of further resistance on the part of the Army of Northern Virginia, I reciprocate your desire to avoid useless effusion of blood, and therefore, before considering your proposition, ask the terms you will offer on condition of its surrender.
　　R. E. Lee, General

SUN 9 APR. APPOMATTOX

On April 8, Grant and Lee continued to exchange notes regarding the terms of a possible surrender. At the same time, Federal troops converged on Lee's Army of Northern Virginia, now trapped along the Lynchburg Road near Appomattox Station. The Union Second and Sixth Corps brought up Lee's rear, while Sheridan's cavalry, the Union Fifth Corps, and some elements of E. O. C. Ord's Army of the James leapfrogged ahead of Lee and blocked the road out. At dawn on April 9, John B. Gordon's infantry and Fitzhugh Lee's cavalry tried to clear a passage through Sheridan's lines to Lynchburg, but the effort failed—the cavalry charge had been effective, but there were simply too many Union infantrymen on the road for the bedraggled Southerners to push aside. Later that morning, when Sheridan counterattacked and Meade hit the Confederate rear guard from the east, Lee had no choice but to surrender. Here are accounts of the fighting from the memoirs of Confederate Lt. Col W. W. Blackford and Union Maj. Gen. Philip H. Sheridan.

THE MORNING OF THE 9TH OF April was clear and bright and to our surprise we did not get marching orders as usual at daylight. We could hear cannon in front with some musketry occasionally. About nine or ten o'clock orders came from General Lee for us to move up to the support of a battery then in action on the edge of the little village of Appomattox, and the regiment marched on towards the place. When within half a mile we came in sight of the ridge on which the village was, and the smoke of the battery. We presented a splendid appearance, six or seven hundred men strong, marching in solid well-closed column, as we moved through the disorganized mass of stragglers crowding

The McLean House at which Lee surrendered.

the road. It struck me as something strange that there should be so many men in this condition, but I paid little attention to it, as we were evidently now going into action. The battery on the ridge was firing at an enemy beyond and out of sight.

AS THE CAVALRY MARCHED along parallel with the Confederate line, and in toward its left, a heavy fire of artillery opened on us, but this could not check us at such a time, and we soon reached some high ground about a mile from the Court House, and from here I could see in the low valley beyond the village the bivouac undoubtedly of Lee's army. The troops did not seem to be disposed in battle order, but on the other side of the bivouac was a line of battle— a heavy rear-guard—confronting, presumably, General Meade.

I decided to attack at once, and formations were ordered at a trot for a charge by Custer's and Devin's divisions down the slope leading to the camps. Custer was soon ready, but Devin's division being in rear its formation took longer, since he had to shift further to the right; Devin's preparations were, therefore, but partially completed when an aide-de-camp galloped up to me with the word from Custer, "Lee has surrendered; do not charge; the white flag is up."

LEE SURRENDERS

Just before noon, a messenger carrying a note from Lee found Grant at the crossroads of Appomattox Court House. After reading Lee's note, Grant, who had been suffering since dawn with a severe headache, dismounted, sat down on the road, and immediately composed a reply. The text of these messages appears below.

GENERAL: I RECEIVED YOUR note of this morning on the picketline, whither I had come to meet you and ascertain definitely what terms were embraced in your proposal of yesterday with reference to the surrender of this army. I now ask an interview, in accordance with the offer contained in your letter of yesterday, for that purpose.

R. E. Lee, General

GENERAL R. E. LEE, Commanding C.S. Army: Your note of this date is but this moment (11:50 A.M.) received, in consequence of my having passed from the Richmond and Lynchburg road to the Farmville and Lynchburg road. I am at this writing about four miles west of Walker's Church, and will push forward to the front for the purpose of meeting you. Notice sent to me on this road where you wish the interview to take place will meet me.

U. S. Grant, Lieutenant-General

The two commanders met in the early afternoon at the nearby home of Wilmer McLean. In his memoirs, Grant described the scene and explained the reason for his tattered appearance on such a momentous occasion.

WHEN I HAD LEFT CAMP THAT morning I had not expected so soon the result that was then taking place, and consequently was in rough garb. I was without a sword, as I usually was when on horseback in the field, and wore a soldier's blouse for a coat, with the shoulder straps of my rank to indicate to the army who I was. When I went into the house I found General Lee. We greeted each other, and after shaking hands took our seats. I had my staff with me, a good portion of whom were in the room during the whole of the interview.

What General Lee's feelings were I do not know. As he was a man of much dignity, with an impassable face, it was impossible to say whether he felt inwardly glad that the end had finally come, or felt sad over the result, and was too manly to show it. Whatever his feelings, they were entirely concealed from my observation; but my own feelings, which had been quite jubilant on the receipt of his letter, were sad and depressed. I felt like anything rather than rejoicing at the downfall of a foe who had fought so long and valiantly, and had suffered so much for a cause, though that cause was, I believe, one of

Lee was photographed by Mathew Brady soon after the surrender.

the worst for which a people ever fought, and one for which there was the least excuse. I do not question, however, the sincerity of the great mass of those who were opposed to us.

Here, John Esten Cooke, a novelist and former aide to Maj. Gen. J. E. B. Stuart, describes the moment of surrender from the perspective of a Confederate officer (and passionate cavalier). Much of Cooke's writing depicts the war as a happy romp, yet this description of the events at Appomattox Court House from Cooke's memoirs evokes nothing if not enormous pathos.

IT MAY BE ASKED WHY I HAVE omitted from my sketch the scene of surrender. There was no such scene, except afterwards when the troops stacked arms and marched off. The real surrender was an event which was felt, not seen. It was nothing apparently; the mere appearance of a Federal column waving a white flag, and halting on a distant hill. But the tragic event was read in the faces of all. No guns in position with that column so near; no line of battle; no preparations for action! A dreamy, memorial sadness seemed to descend through the April air and change the scene. Silence so deep that the rustle of the leaves could be heard—and Longstreet's veterans, who had steadily advanced to attack, moved back like mourners. There was nothing visible in front but that distant column, stationary behind its white flag. No band played, no cheer was heard; the feelings of the Southern troops were spared; but there were many who wanted to die then.

After accepting Grant's terms—which allowed officers to keep their side arms and private mounts and permitted all soldiers to return home after promising not to resume the fight once released— Lee left the McLean house and delivered to his former army this terse speech.

I HAVE DONE FOR YOU ALL THAT was in my power to do. You have all done your duty. Leave the result to God. Go to your homes and resume your occupations. Obey the laws and become as good citizens as you were soldiers.

MON **10** APR.

As news of Lee's surrender spread through Washington this day, crowds of revelers, accompanied by musical bands, gathered in front of the White House, where they chanted for the president. Finally, Abraham Lincoln appeared and delivered this impromptu speech, which exhibited once again his famous sense of humor, seemingly long absent.

I AM VERY GREATLY REJOICED TO find that an occasion has occurred so pleasurable that the people cannot restrain themselves. I suppose that arrangements are being made for some sort of a formal demonstration, this, or perhaps, tomorrow night. If there should be such a demonstration, I, of course, will be called upon to respond, and I shall have nothing to say if you dribble it all out of me before. I see you have a band of music with you. I propose closing up this interview by the band performing a particular tune which I will name. Before this is done, however, I wish to mention one or

This photograph of Abraham Lincoln was taken on April 10, 1865.

two little circumstances connected with it. I have always thought "Dixie" one of the best tunes I have ever heard. Our adversaries over the way attempted to appropriate it, but I insisted yesterday that we fairly captured it. I presented the question to the Attorney General, and he gave it as his legal opinion that it is our lawful prize. I now request the band to favor me with its performance.

At about the same time Lincoln was speaking, Rep. Thaddeus Stevens, leader of the Radical Republicans who would control the next Congress, addressed a public meeting in Lancaster, Pennsylvania. Using much darker language, Stevens outlined some of his views on reconstructing the South, including his demand that Confederate property be confiscated and redistributed among Union veterans and freed people.

I AM NOT WITHOUT ANXIETY FOR the future. Under the respectable plea of humanity and conservatism, I fear we shall forget justice to living rebels and to slaughtered dead, and shall overlook our future safety, and deal too mercifully with assassins and traitors. I can understand how forgiveness should be extended to the ignorant, the poor and deluded; but to permit the ringleaders to escape with impunity, is absolute cruelty. At least, take their property, if you allow them to live. To forgive the penitent is Christian; to suffer the proud murderer to escape, and thus endanger the government, is weakness. Take the riches of those nobles who would found an empire on slavery. Divide their broad manors, acquired by the

unpaid toil of others—sell enough of it to pay our national debt now weighing so heavily on our loyal tax-payers—give a portion of it to our war-worn veterans, who have conquered it, and to freedmen. Sell enough of it to set apart a perpetual fund, to enable us to double the pensions, (as we ought to do) of our maimed and wounded soldiers, and of bereaved parents and helpless children.

If you spare the lives of those who have plotted treason for thirty years, and who have caused all this misery, it is all, perhaps more, than they have a right to claim, or true Christian humanity demands.

TUE 11 APR. THE CONFEDERATES EVACUATE MOBILE

In mid-March, seven months after Farragut's capture of Mobile Bay, Maj. Gen. E. R. S. Canby began the final Union push to capture the port city of Mobile. On March 27, he completed his investment of the city, focusing first on Spanish Fort and later also on Fort Blakely. Canby's Army of the West Mississippi, numbering thirty-two thousand men, dwarfed the Confederate garrison of five thousand defending the city, so the success of the siege was merely a matter of time. Two weeks later, on the night of April 8, Spanish Fort was evacuated, and Fort Blakely fell to Union assault the following day, leaving only Forts Huger and Tracy in Rebel hands. These were also abandoned on April 11, when Confederate Maj. Gen. Dabney H. Maury began evacuating Mobile proper, an action he completed on the morning of April 12. Here, Maury recalls the Confederate leave-taking.

MY EFFECTIVE FORCE WAS NOW reduced to less than 5,000 men, and the supply of ammunition had been nearly exhausted in the siege of the two positions [Spanish Fort and Fort Blakely] which the enemy had taken from me. Mobile contained nearly forty thousand non-combatants. The city and its population were entirely exposed to the fire which would be directed against its defences. With the means now left me an obstinate or protracted defence would have been impossible, while the consequences of its being stormed by a combined force of Federal and negro troops would have been shocking—my orders were to save my troops, after having made as much time as possible—therefore I decided to evacuate Mobile at once....I completed the evacuation of Mobile on Wednesday morning, having dismantled the works, removed the stores best suited for troops in the field, transferred the commissary stores to the Mayor for the use of the people, and marched out with 4,500 infantry and artillery, twenty-seven light cannon, and brought off all the land and water transportation.

FRI 14 APR. LINCOLN ASSASSINATED

While attending an evening performance of Our American Cousin *at Ford's Theatre, President Abraham*

Lincoln was shot in his box by actor (and Confederate sympathizer) John Wilkes Booth. The president was carried across the street to the modest home of William Peterson, where he died at 7:22 A.M. the following day. Soon it became clear that Lincoln's assassination had been part of a larger plot to murder several important Union leaders. Secretary of State Seward was stabbed in his bed (he barely survived), while Grant and Vice President (now President) Andrew Johnson were stalked but unharmed. Walt Whitman captured the nation's despair in his ode to Lincoln, "O Captain, My Captain."

O CAPTAIN! MY CAPTAIN! OUR fearful trip is done,
The ship has weather'd every rack, the
    prize we sought is won,
The port is near, the bells I hear, the
    people all exulting,
While follow eyes the steady keel, the
    vessel grim and daring;
But O heart! heart! heart!
O the bleeding drops of red,
Where on the deck my Captain lies,
Fallen cold and dead.

O Captain! my Captain! rise up and hear
    the bells;
Rise up—for you the flag is flung—for
    you the bugle trills,
For you bouquets and ribbon'd wreaths—
    for you the shores a-crowding,
For you they call, the swaying mass, their
    eager faces turning;
Here Captain! dear father!
The arm beneath your head!
It is some dream that on the deck,
You've fallen cold and dead.

The assassination of President Lincoln as rendered by Currier & Ives.

My Captain does not answer, his lips are
    pale and still,
My father does not feel my arm, he has
    no pulse or will,
The ship is anchor'd safe and sound, its
    voyage closed and done,
From fearful trip the victor ship comes in
    with object won:
Exult O shores, and ring O bells!
But I with mournful tread,
Walk the deck my Captain lies,
Fallen cold and dead.

*Although Lincoln's murder certainly
shocked all Americans, not all of them
grieved, as the following entry from
Emma LeConte's diary (dated April 21)
suggests.*

HURRAH! OLD ABE LINCOLN
has been assassinated! It may be
abstractly wrong to be so jubilant, but I
just can't help it. After all the heaviness
and gloom of yesterday this blow to our
enemies comes like a gleam of light.
We have suffered till we feel savage.
There seems no reason to exult, for this
will make no change in our position—
will only infuriate them against us. Never
mind, our hated enemy has not the just
reward of his life. The whole story may
be a Yankee lie. The despatch purports
to be from Stanton to Sherman—It says
Lincoln was murdered in his private box
at the theatre on the night of the 14th....
The assassin brandished a dagger and
shouting, "Sic semper tyrannis—Virginia
is avenged," shot the president through
the head. He fell senseless and expired
next day a little after ten. The assassin
made his escape in the crowd. No doubt
it was regularly planned and he was surrounded by Southern sympathizers. "Sic
semper tyrannis." Could there have been
a fitter death for such a man? At the same

hour nearly, Seward's house was entered—he was badly wounded as also his son. Why could not the assassin have done his work more thoroughly? That vile Seward—he it is to whom we owe this war—it is a shame he should escape.

MON 17 APR. *It took weeks for word of Lee's surrender to reach all the towns and villages of the Confederacy. Nurse Kate Cumming, for example, received the news with disbelief at a hospital in Griffin, Georgia, eight days after the event.*

MR. MOORE CAME IN TODAY and told us very calmly that Lee and his whole army were captured. I was mute with astonishment, and looked at Mr. Moore, thinking I had seen our people take disasters coolly, but had never seen any thing to equal his coolness in telling of such a terrible one. After awhile he laughed, and said he had frightened us enough; that such news had come by a lady from Chattanooga; she had seen it in the northern papers. He said it was one of the tales invented by the enemy to dismay us, but we were not to be so easily frightened.

After Mr. Moore had left us, I commenced thinking over the news, and concluded that it probably might be true. I had just read an account of the last three days' fighting around Petersburg, and it had filled me with dismay. How our men ever withstood such a host is a perfect miracle. They were behind breastworks, but the enemy came on them eight deep, and as fast as one line was mowed down another took its place. It is said that in these three days at least sixty thousand of the enemy were killed; and that our loss was nothing in comparison, but God knows it was enough. General Lee did not have fifty thousand in his army, and the enemy at least two hundred and fifty thousand. It seems like downright murder attempting to oppose such a force. O, how terrible is this cruel, cruel war! When will it cease?

When I saw Mr. Moore again, I told him I had made up my mind to try and think that our late disaster might possibly be true. Perhaps General Lee had been overwhelmed by numbers, and compelled to surrender with his handful of men. We seem to have forgotten that he is mortal, and liable to failures like all others.

Mr. Moore would not listen to me, and said that such a thing was a moral impossibility. We can hear nothing reliable. It seems as if we are shut out from the whole world.

Meanwhile, the Philadelphia Inquirer *published this description of Northern reaction to more recent news: the assassination of President Lincoln. Like many other Northern newspapers, the* Inquirer *called specific attention to the irony that John Wilkes Booth had killed the single Union politician most sympathetic to the needs of the vanquished Confederacy.*

THE GREAT NATIONAL TRAGEDY The monstrous crime of Friday night shocked this city with an agony unutterable. Yesterday morning men walked the streets, and looked into each other's eyes, and found no words willing to leave their lips. Their hearts were surcharged with grief and a wrath inexpressible.

That any Rebel ever could be so base as to assassinate the man who within the past ten days has held out the olive branch of peace, and exhibited so great a desire to forgive, was a crime for which Washington, as well as the nation, was unprepared. But the deed was consummated, and Washington, lowering her flags of joy, clothed them in habiliments of mourning. The transition from jubilance to grief and woe was a shock more sudden than ever before befell a community or people. The glorious banner which went up in the morning in honor of its restoration to Fort Sumter, in the short space of twenty-four hours came down to half-mast.

The rejoicing of Friday was turned to mourning, and the light of joy which illumed all faces but a few hours previous, gave way to tears and gloom. When the news of President Lincoln's death was announced, universal silence and grief pervaded the city. Everybody was impressed with the solemn and awful event. Funeral weeds were hung from every window, and the sables of mourning were draped on fronts and about the marble columns of all the public buildings.

John Wilkes Booth

WED 26 APR. JOHN WILKES BOOTH IS KILLED

After shooting Lincoln, John Wilkes Booth escaped south into Virginia along with one of his accomplices, David E. Herold. Secretary of War Stanton directed the manhunt, which ended twelve days later with Federal troops trapping Booth inside a barn. (The structure was located on a tobacco farm south of the Rappahannock River near Port Conway belonging to Richard H. Garrett.) After Herold surrendered, the Federals set fire to the barn, intending to force out the still-defiant Booth. However, before Booth emerged, one of the soldiers (believed to be a religious fanatic) fired a shot that mortally wounded him. He was dragged from the burning barn and died on the Garrett porch about 7:00 A.M. This account was penned by Pvt. John Millington, one of the twenty-six soldiers who chased Booth down.

A YOUNG MAN RAN FROM THE direction of an outbuilding and asked, "What do you men want?" Our officer said, "We want the two men who are stopping here and at once." He said, "They're in the barn." Part of our company was detailed to surround the barn and part to surround the house. I was with the party sent to the barn. Our lieutenant, who heard some whispering in the barn, called, "Come out at once." One of the men inside the barn asked, "Who are you?" Our officer said, "It doesn't make any difference who we are, but we know who you are. You had better come out at once." The man in the barn who had done the talking was the man we were after— Booth. He refused to come out. He said, "If you will withdraw your men 30 rods, I will come out and we'll shoot it out." We could hear Booth accusing the man who was with him, David E. Harold [sic], of being a coward. Harold was willing to surrender and Booth said, "You're a coward to desert me." Finally, Booth called out and said, "Harold will surrender, but I will not."...Once more the officer summoned Booth to surrender. Booth responded, "I'll fight you single handed, but I'll never surrender." Detective Conger went to the opposite side of the barn and lit some loose straw under the sill. I heard a shot and a moment later saw the door was open. Booth had been shot through the neck. They brought him out, carried him to the Garrett house and put him on the porch. A soldier was sent to Port Royal for a doctor, who arrived about daylight. Meanwhile, the barn had burned down and some of the men were hunting in the ruins for relics. They found two revolvers and one of our boys got Booth's carbine.

The revolvers were spoiled by the fire. Booth lived about three hours. He was wrapped in a government blanket, his body was placed in an old wagon and a Negro drove the rig to Acquia Creek, which we reached at dusk.

JOHNSTON SURRENDERS

On the same day that Booth was shot in Virginia, Gen. Joseph E. Johnston surrendered the remaining Confederate Eastern Theater troops to Maj. Gen. William T. Sherman near Durham Station, North Carolina. This was the second time the two generals had met for such a purpose. On April 17, they had discussed not only the terms of Johnston's surrender but also terms for an armistice of all remaining Confederate forces. This discussion resulted in a highly controversial memorandum, signed April 18, calling for, among many things, recognition of existing state goverments, a general amnesty for Confederates, and even the retention of arms in the respective state arsenals. Those terms generated such uproar in the North, however, that President Johnson rejected them and on April 24 ordered Sherman to resume hostilities after forty-eight hours' notice unless Johnston surrendered under the same terms given Lee. Left with no choice, Johnston accepted those terms: Specifically, all arms and public property were to be turned over immediately to the Federals, the side arms and private mounts of officers could be retained, and soldiers were permitted to return home after pledging themselves not to take up arms again. Here, Sam Watkins, a soldier in Johnston's army, recalls the day.

WELL, ON THE 26TH DAY OF April, 1865, General Joe E. Johnston surrendered his army at Greensboro, North Carolina. The day that we surrendered our regiment it was a pitiful sight to behold. If I remember correctly, there were just sixty-five men in all, including officers, that were paroled on that day. Now what became of the original 3,200? A grand army you may say. Three thousand two hundred men! Only sixty-five left! Now, reader, you may draw your own conclusions....It was indeed a sad sight to look at the Old First Tennessee Regiment. A mere squad of noble and brave men, gathered around the tattered flag that they had followed in every battle through that long war. It was so bullet-riddled and torn that it was but a few blue and red shreds that hung drooping while it, too, was stacked with our guns forever.

THU 27 APR. THE SULTANA DISASTER

The boiler explosion that sank the Union steamboat Sultana *this evening stands as one of the most tragic incidents of a tragic war. The ship—overcrowded with paroled Union prisoners, many of whom had recently been freed from Andersonville—was traveling up the Mississippi River north of Memphis at the time. More than a thousand homeward-bound men were killed by the explosion or drowned later in the river trying to swim to shore. In this account, one sur-*

vivor described the scene aboard ship following the blast.

WE WAITED HOPING, BUT IN vain, to be rescued from the burning wreck. When at length the last shadow of hope had expired, and we were forced to leave the burning boat and try our luck in the seething, foaming, cold and turbulent waters of the mighty Mississippi, and this too at about two o'clock in the morning and almost total darkness prevailing, except the light from the burning wreck, we proceeded to perform carefully, but hurriedly, the most heart-rending task that human beings could be called upon to perform—that of throwing overboard into the jaws of certain death by drowning those comrades who were unable on account of broken bones and limbs to help themselves. Some were so badly scalded by the hot water and steam from the exploded boiler that the flesh was falling from their bones. Those comrades who were doubly endeared to us through mutual suffering and starvation while we were penned up in the rebel h—s, or so called Confederate prisons, and who instead of throwing them overboard, we were wanting to render every kindness to, dress their wounds and soothe their sufferings. But alas! this was impossible; the only alternative was to toss them overboard.

★ ★ ★ ★

MAY 1865

JEFFERSON DAVIS CAPTURED

On the same day that President Johnson declared armed resistance virtually at an end, Jefferson Davis was captured near Irwinsville, Georgia. Having fled farther and farther south—from Danville, Virginia, through the Carolinas and finally across the Savannah River— Davis reached Washington, Georgia, on May 4, the day that Lt. Gen. Richard Taylor surrendered the Confederate forces of the Department of Alabama, Mississippi, and East Louisiana. On May 9, Davis rejoined his wife, Varina, along the Oconee River near Dublin, as Federal cavalry closed in on his dwindling retinue. Early the next morning, Union soldiers surprised his camp and captured Davis, reportedly dressed in women's clothes to conceal his identity. He was taken first to Macon and then transferred to Fort Monroe, Virginia, where he was imprisoned (without a trial) until his release in May 1867. The following New York Herald *report described Northern reaction to this peculiar anticlimax.*

THE CAPTURE OF JEFF. DAVIS did not create in this city the degree of excitement which such an event might be expected to occasion. People took the matter quite coolly and calmly. Nobody, in fact, seemed much astonished or exercised in consequence, and things went on pretty much the same as usual to all outward appearances. The cause of this lack of excitement is doubtless the declining interest in everything concerning the rebellion. The community feel that the fighting is over and the Union restored, and therefore, care little for what may follow. Had the capture occurred a few months, or even weeks, sooner there would have been a very different condition of things to report; but occuring at this late day, and when people daily expected some such winding up of the arch-traitor's career, it only awakens the customary interest that any ordinary event might give rise to. It shows how very insignificant the rebel ex-President must have become, too, when people do not even think it worth their while to glory over his misfortune.

The probable disposition of Jeff. was much discussed yesterday. Some hoped he would be hanged without a moment's delay for his treason, while others…were in favor of leaving him to the sting of his own conscience. All, however, agreed that if he is implicated in the assassination scheme, hanging would be too good for him.

FRI 12 MAY BRAZOS SANTIAGO (PALMITO RANCH)

In the last significant military encounter of the Civil War, an African-American infantry regiment stationed at Brazos Santiago, Texas, attacked Confederate troops along the Rio Grande near Palmito Ranch. Union cavalry initially captured the Rebel position on the morning of April 12, but the arrival of superior Confederate reinforcements lead to a Federal retreat. The next morning, an augmented Federal force, commanded by Col. Theodore H.

Barrett, retook Palmito Ranch. That night, however, a large Confederate cavalry unit, commanded by Col. John S. Ford, hammered Barrett's men with artillery, forcing another Federal retreat. The result was thus, ironically, a Confederate victory. In his official report, Barrett described the initial Union movements.

ON THE EVENING OF MAY 11, 1865, an expedition consisting of 250 men of the Sixty-second U.S. Colored Infantry, properly officered, and fifty men and two officers of the Second Texas Cavalry (not yet mounted)…was sent by me, then commanding U.S. forces at Brazos Santiago, Tex., from the island onto the mainland. Crossing the Boca Chica, which owing to a severe storm was effected with difficulty, the force marched nearly all night, and after a short rest, early next morning attacked a strong outpost of the rebels at Palmetto [sic] Ranch, Tex., on the banks of the Rio Grande. The enemy was driven in confusion from his position, his camp, camp equipage, and stores falling into our hands. Some horses and cattle were also captured and a number of prisoners taken.

THU 18 MAY *News of Jefferson Davis's arrest dismayed those Southerners who were defiantly, if unreasonably, holding out hope that the Confederate struggle might continue. Even after she learned of Davis's capture, Emma LeConte of Columbia, South Carolina, wrote in her diary that the South should continue its resistance to Northern authority. Her refusal to accept defeat* foreshadowed much of the bitterness and acrimony that would consume the South and its people during the coming decade of Reconstruction.

THIS MORNING WE RECEIVED the last crowning piece of bad news. I did not think it possible anything worse could happen. We heard of the capture of President Davis! This is dreadful, not only because we love him, but because it gives the final blow to our cause. If he could have reached the West he might have rallied the army out there and continued the resistance. But now where can we look for a head? I was studying my German when father came in and told me. I laid my head on the table without a word. I did not cry—the days of weeping are past—but, ah! the heartache—the only thing left to hear now is the surrender of the army in the West and that must come pretty soon. I think I have given up hope at last—at least for the present. We will be conquered. Only in the future can we still hope, either for a foreign war in which we can join the enemies of the United States, or else that after years of recuperation we may be strong enough and wiser by experience to renew the struggle and throw off the hateful yoke. The only other chance is that by their oppression and insolence they may drive the people to Guerilla warfare and be wearied out at last.

FRI 26 MAY THE LAST REBEL ARMY SURRENDERS

On this day, E. Kirby Smith, Confederate commander of the Trans-Mississippi Department, surrendered to Maj. Gen. E. R. S. Canby under the same terms given Lee and Johnston. Two days later, when news of Smith's surrender reached the East Coast, the front page of the New York Times declared, "PEACE AT LAST." During the preceding four years, the integrity of the country had been sorely tested, competing visions of liberty and freedom had murderously clashed, and hundreds of thousands of Americans had perished for what each side believed to be the cause of right. Now the war was over.

PEACE AT LAST

SURRENDER OF GEN. KIRBY SMITH'S ENTIRE FORCE

FINAL OFFICIAL ACT OF INSURGENT AUTHORITY.

THE GREAT REBELLION HAS PASSED AWAY.

THEIR LAND AND NAVAL FORCES DECLARED DISBANDED.

THE STARS AND STRIPES AGAIN DOMINANT OVER ALL THE COUNTRY.

ALL MILITARY PRISONERS DURING THE WAR SET FREE.

RE-UNION, PEACE, FREEDOM AND PROSPERITY.

E PLURIBUS UNUM!

★ ★ ★ ★

ABOUT THE CONTRIBUTORS

MAJ. ROBERT L. BATEMAN, commissioned in 1989 as an infantry second lieutenant, is currently assigned to the U.S. Military Academy as an instructor of military history. In addition to holding a master's degree in military history from Ohio State University, he is a graduate of the Armor Officer Advanced Course as well as the Airborne, Ranger, and Air Assault courses. His assignments in light and mechanized infantry have included multinational peacekeeping operations, and he is the author of *Digital War: A View from the Front Lines* (Presidio, 1999).

MAJ. PHILLIP R. CUCCIA is an instructor in the department of military history at the U.S. Military Academy, his alma mater. A native of East Texas, Cuccia has spent many hours walking the battlefields of the Red River Campaign, on which he had written extensively.

BRIAN DIRCK, who holds a doctorate from the University of Kansas in the legal and constitutional history of the Civil War period, is an assistant professor of history at Anderson University. He is the 1995 recipient of the Arkansas Civil War Roundtable's Dale Bumpers Award for Best Article in Civil War History and is the author of the forthcoming *Imagining America: Abraham Lincoln, Jefferson Davis, and National Identity, 1809–1865* (University Press of Kansas).

CHRISTINA ERICSON, who holds a master's degree in the history of the Civil War from the University of Maryland, has chosen to focus her study of the Civil War era on its social and cultural aspects, particularly using gender as a tool of historical analysis. She is currently an adjunct instructor of history at Gettysburg College, where she is also a program assistant in the Office of Civil War Era Studies. Her article on female-authored eyewitness accounts of the battle of Gettysburg will appear in the forthcoming *Making and Remaking Pennsylvania's Civil War*, edited by Gary W. Gallagher, William Pencak, and William Blair (Penn State University Press).

ELIZABETH D. LEONARD is an associate professor of history and the director of women's studies at Colby College. She is the author of two books on women in the Civil War: *Yankee Women: Gender Battles in the Civil War* (Norton, 1994) and *All the Daring of the Soldier: Women of the Civil War Armies* (Norton, 1999). Leonard has also edited and annotated the Civil War memoir of Sarah Emma Edmonds (alias Franklin Thompson of the Second Michigan Infantry), which has been reissued as *Memoirs of a Soldier, Nurse, and Spy* (Northern Illinois University Press, 1999). She is currently at work on a new project dealing with Mary Surratt and the Lincoln assassination.

MAJ. ROBERT MACKEY, a career army officer and combat veteran of both Panama and Desert Storm, was until recently an assistant professor of military history at the U.S. Military Academy. He is currently attending the Command and General Staff College at Fort Leaven-worth, Kansas. A native of Arkansas, Mackey proudly claims ancestors who wore both blue and gray and fought one another in the Ozarks. He has written extensively on nineteenth-century military history and admits to a lifelong obsession with the Civil War.

MITCHELL MCNAYLOR's interest in the War of Northern Aggression predates his clear memories. As a child, he read all he could find on the war and was fortunate enough to have indulgent parents who took him to most of the Civil War battle-fields. He currently teaches history, the subject in which he holds a master's degree from Ohio State University, at Our Lady of the Lake College in Baton Rouge, Louisiana.

INDEX